PREPARATION FOR COUNSELING

WILLIAM C. COTTLE *is professor of education and director of counselor education and counseling psychology program at Boston College.*

N. M. DOWNIE *is professor of psychology at Purdue University.*

SECOND EDITION

Preparation
for
Counseling

WILLIAM C. COTTLE

N.M. DOWNIE

PRENTICE-HALL, INC.

Englewood Cliffs, New Jersey

Library of Congress Catalog Card Number: 70–105999
Printed in the United States of America
Current printing (last number):
10 9 8 7 6 5 4 3 2 1

PRENTICE-HALL INTERNATIONAL, INC., *London*
PRENTICE-HALL OF AUSTRALIA, PTY. LTD., *Sydney*
PRENTICE-HALL OF CANADA, LTD., *Toronto*
PRENTICE-HALL OF INDIA PRIVATE LIMITED, *New Delhi*
PRENTICE-HALL OF JAPAN, INC., *Tokyo*

Contents

v

Preface

Counseling is not synonymous with psychotherapy. By far the majority of clients coming to a counselor for help are seeking information about who they are, how they became what they are, and what they can become, in order to make more informed choices in the ordinary processes of living.

As a counselor initiates the counseling process he is in a sounder professional position when he has acquired some prior knowledge of the attributes and behavior of the client. He is thus in a better position to anticipate and to assist the client's attempts to make more effective life choices.

The material presented here is intended for use by individuals at three levels of preparation for counseling: the support person or the counselor beginning his training who wishes an *overview* of the processes by which a counselor gathers and prepares data about the client; the counselor who is beginning counseling practicum who wants to *review* the functions he performs as he prepares for practicum interviews; and the practicing counselor in any agency, who wants to *refresh* his knowledge and *rethink* his approach to counseling.

The theme expressed is that there are common elements in the dynamics of counseling with normal clients which transcend counseling orientations and their particular biases or emphases. Limited exposure during graduate work may cause a counselor to focus on a specific approach—such as nondirective counseling, behavioral counseling, T-grouping (group dynamics), or the use of computerized processes—which, though important, distract attention from the variety of tools and processes available to him. A broader knowledge of counseling tools and processes permits the counselor to focus on helping the client to develop more effective perceptions of himself and of his interaction with his environment. These are the primary purposes of any client-counselor encounter. Such self-knowledge on the client's part is fostered by appraisal and interpretive processes which delineate his development in the cognitive, affective, and motivational aspects of behavior. These in turn delimit and define any life choices he makes.

After the first chapter, an overview of preparation for counseling, the material divides itself into three areas: the processes of collecting and organizing data about the client from the many cultural sources which have influenced his development up to the time he comes for counseling; a discussion of how the counselor uses measuring devices which provide cross-sectional data to supplement developmental sources, with emphasis on interpretation to the client rather than on statistical and measurement concepts; and a consideration of the methods by which evaluation and improvement of the counseling process occur, i.e., research and supervision.

It is important for a counselor to select and organize data from many sources for counseling purposes. This appraisal helps him to understand the behavior of a given client *prior* to counseling and to check the validity of the client's statements *during* counseling against a societal evaluation of these same data. Obviously, some of these procedures will overlap counseling itself and should probably be considered a part of the counseling process. The initial interview is an example of this. Such an interview is a part of the preparatory process, as well as part of counseling itself. In like manner, any discussion of how information about the client's behavior is to be used in an interview cannot be separated completely from a discussion of how it is obtained, if the counselor is to have a full overview of the process.

Cases or persons described in this book are fictitious and any resemblance to actual persons is purely fortuitous.

The authors are greatly indebted to the following individuals and organizations who so generously allowed the use of their materials: Gordon Collister; Sidney Fine; E. J. Hankes; G. F. Kuder; The American Psychological Association; The American Personnel and Guidance Association; Columbia University Press; Holt, Rinehart & Winston, Inc.; Harper & Row, Publishers; the Educational Testing Service; Stanford University Press; the University of Minnesota Press; and the U.S. Department of Labor.

W. C. C.

N. M. D.

PREPARATION FOR COUNSELING

1

Overview

Counseling is the process by which a counselor assists a client to face, understand, and accept information about himself and his interaction with others, so that he can make effective decisions about various life choices. The bulk of counseling occurs in educational settings with clients whose behavior is within the normal range and who face the need to adapt to changes in ordinary living situations, rather than to produce deep-seated personality changes. In this way counseling differs from psychotherapy.

To provide counseling service to the large number of clients who can use it, the counselor needs to be as efficient and as well prepared as possible. He has to collect from many sources the data already available on a given client and decide what he can contribute to enhance the counseling process. He should be familiar with common sources of data and methods of checking, organizing, and synthesizing such data. He then is in a position to investigate the client's self-perceptions and client perceptions of society during the counseling process itself.

Individuals from many professions conduct interviews and advise others, but only an individual with special knowledge, skills, and education can prepare for and carry on a counseling interview. A unique combination of attributes is needed by the counselor in order to help a client make self-evaluations and changes in behavior based on these evaluations without telling the client what choices to make. The principal objective of this book will be to show how the counselor uses special training and skills to prepare for counseling with such clients.

The first task of the counselor and his helpers is to identify those who need help and make them aware of the means by which they can get such help. Then the helpers and the counselor must assist the client to develop a desire for change, without forcing particular choices or changes. The client should not only be aware of his needs but also want to meet them, if counseling is to be effective. This identification, and the development of readiness for counseling, involve sources of information and procedures that are supplied by a number of people cooperating with the counselor, such as support personnel or counselor aides, teachers, other school personnel, and other community workers. Whether these preliminary procedures are carried on in a school or in some other community agency, they center about collecting and organizing information about the individual and the cultural subgroups in which he functions. Such a task requires both an understanding of the cultural forces which have produced the current behavior of the individual (Hall 1966) and an understanding of how that individual can proceed to change his behavior as he desires.

The counselor does not always supervise or carry on these preliminary procedures; he frequently must ask others for the kind of information needed and show them how it can be used in counseling. If the persons who collect such data know why they are doing it, their contributions will be more useful to the counselor and the client.

Usually, educational, sociological, and psychological data have been collected from and are intended for use with groups. The same information and the same procedures for its collection can be adapted for use with the individual, but this changed frame of reference must be kept in mind in order that the full significance of the data, as it relates to the individual, is preserved in the course of collecting it.

It is the purpose of this book, therefore, to discuss how the counselor and others use these procedures to prepare for counseling. The procedures are often referred to as "tools and techniques of counseling." A *tool* of counseling is simply a device or instrument used to collect information, and a *technique or process* is the way in which the information is collected or used by the counselor. These procedures will be discussed as nearly as possible in the sequence in which the counselor would utilize them.

Upon entering a counseling job, the counselor's first move is to learn about those who will be the potential counselees. This is a problem of identification from records, observation, and measurement.

The first recourse a counselor has is to records maintained by the agency. In most instances, these records have been made for administrative purposes. It is the job of the counselor to assess their value for counseling and request any additional records or changes deemed necessary to give a more complete picture of his clients. The counselor should devise some system of organizing this recorded information about individuals in terms of potential vs. performance, so that those most in need of immediate help can be identified. This means the counselor must have some system of organizing information so that it can be evaluated in these contrasting terms. For the beginning counselor, some frames of reference for organizing data about the client will be presented. Experienced counselors usually prefer to develop a system of their own. The important thing is that some systematic approach be developed.

One hears statements that if a counselor does not practice a given orientation, such as that proposed by Rogers (1967), Krumboltz (1966), Blocher (1966), or the National Training Laboratories (Watson 1967a, b) his eclecticism means he has no organized theory of counseling or no established practices in counseling. On the contrary, there is no competent counselor who can maintain professional competence without a body of knowledge and its effective practice. Before a counselor can practice competently, he must have derived from his personal and professional experience a frame of reference within which he carries on his practice. Each in his own way varies from his peers, but each has his own systematic approach to counseling which guides his work with clients, determining the limits within which he functions and the tools and procedures he employs. There is no such thing as a competent counselor sans theory or systematic practice, but there are many competent counselors with an eclectic orientation.

It should be kept in mind that the recorded information used in an interview with a client may need to be modified from the form used by the counselor in his preliminary identification of potential clients from agency sources. However, the counselor may wish to develop one system which can be used for both purposes.

Two approaches to preparation for counseling are considered in the following chapters. Chapters 2 through 5 focus attention on the impact of the client's culture on his behavior and on the most common sources available to the counselor in his effort to collect and interpret such data to a client. Chapters 6 through 10 show how the counselor uses measurement processes to achieve this purpose. Most preparation for counseling involves a blending of both approaches.

CLIENT'S CULTURE AND BEHAVIOR

Hall (1959, 1966) has delineated the effects of culture on the development of the individual and on his attempts to communicate with others. He emphasizes the limits imposed by race, national origin, religion, and geography upon the development of the individual and upon his interactions with others. To these dimensions should be added the concept of the continuum created within each dimension by varying educational and socioeconomic status. The culture of the American Negro varies not only because he is in rural Mississippi, a recent migrant to a northern city, or a descendant of colonial servants in Boston or Philadelphia, but also in terms of his educational or vocational status in such a setting. If he is on welfare, or a school drop-out, his background and values are different than if he is a middle-class government employee with a high-school or college education or a member of a professional group, such as a lawyer or physician. The 1960 Census indicated that the American cultural groups with the highest proportion of children matriculated in colleges are of Hebrew, Chinese, and Japanese descent. This is bound to influence the culture of these groups and to modify, within the general culture, the status of individuals from such groups.

For this reason, developmental records, observations, interviews, and vocational experiences become important to the counselor in his attempt to help clients.

Observational techniques used to identify individuals in need of help include direct observation by the counselor and others, as well as the use of information contained in ratings and anecdotes. Observation by the counselor is directed toward finding evidences in an individual's behavior that counseling would be useful. Such observation needs to be carried on in a systematic fashion, with some sort of mental or actual checklist of types of behavior that would warrant a referral for counseling. Problems so identified may range from behavior indicating simple lack of specific information which can usually be supplied by the counselor, to behavior indicating somewhat involved problems of adjustment.

Observation requires training of the persons who are to do the observing. These observers must become familiar with the techniques they are to use. They must reach general agreement among themselves about their objectives and the descriptive terms they will use, if their observations are to be stable and capable of being combined into composite observations. Important characteristics in the behavior of a client during testing or interviews (discussed in Chapters 3 and 4) must be described carefully if observations made under these circumstances are to be usable to varied staff members.

As counselors turn more toward the use of cultural background as a basis for descriptions of behavior, rather than depending upon cross-sectional studies of the individual, the place of biographical information about the client assumes much greater importance. Such cultural data provide a developmental picture of the client which is more stable and explanatory of current behavior than any cross-sectional techniques can produce. All that cross-sectional data can do is describe the client at a given time. But when they are compared with developmental data, they can serve as a check on the validity and usefulness of the latter. As indicated in Chapters 3 and 4, biographical data, properly collected and interpreted, can show how and perhaps why present behavior developed. These data can take the form of a personal record completed for the counselor; relevant descriptions of cultural background written by sociologists and anthropologists; autobiographies, compositions, essays for classroom purposes, or other personal documents; case histories developed by social workers; and other collections of information about the individual and his subculture maintained over a period of time. The personal documents prepared by the client have the added advantage of showing not only what his behavior was, but also how he felt or still feels about such behavior. They often shed light on motivational aspects as well as feelings and emotions. Counselors need to stress this approach to understanding their clients much more. At the same time, the counselor must guard against letting such information cloud or bias his interpretations of current behavior. To do this, although he must be aware of past behavior, he must make only highly *tentative* assumptions from it which are easily modified by new information. For that matter, every assumption the counselor makes about a client should be a highly tentative and momentary assumption.

Another source of data about the client and his culture is the initial interview. Here the counselor has a chance to validate assumptions made from data which are already a matter of record and to add new information collected during the interview. In this interview, the counselor lays the groundwork for the relationships which are so necessary to successful counseling. In addition to making the client feel comfortable and willing to participate in the interview, the counselor is helping him develop the idea that counseling is of value. Kell and Mueller (1966) emphasize the interaction involved in this initial counselor-client encounter and delimit some of the negative and positive variables in this relationship. These are discussed in more detail in Chapter 4.

The counselor can enhance the client's participation in the counseling process by demonstrating a preliminary knowledge of the client and his environment which indicates competent preparation for the interview. After a brief period spent in putting the client at ease and developing a statement of the reasons why the client has come for counseling, the counselor can begin to verify and expand the information about the client which has been studied prior to the interview. As far as possible, the client should control the content of the material discussed, and the counselor should be concerned with methods of helping him express his needs or his reasons for wanting counseling. Then the counselor can indicate ways the client may receive help and begin to structure for the counseling interviews. Some counseling may take place in this initial interview, but primarily it is concerned with activities that are really preparatory to actual counseling (Bingham and Moore 1959; Kahn and Cannell 1957).

USE AND INTERPRETATION OF MEASURING DEVICES

In order to evaluate the data about group and about individual behavior that are basic to any counseling activity, the counselor must acquire a knowledge of statistics (Downie and Heath 1965). In Chapters 6 through 10, it is emphasized that the frame of reference in which the counselor uses statistics with individuals is somewhat different from that of other educational and psychological workers. In Chapter 6, it is pointed out that the counselor's purpose is to use statistics to help a client understand himself and the groups in which he functions. To do this, the counselor must be able to use statistics for organizing and explaining the data about the client's behavior. This is ordinarily done in terms of location in or divergence from the average group. Such divergence usually is sufficient to show the strengths and weaknesses that may need attention. However, this use of statistics also involves comparisons between individuals; therefore these two frames of reference for statistics, comparison with a group and the meaning of the data for a given client, must pervade each statistical inference the counselor makes. The chief purposes for which the counselor uses statistics in the ways indicated above are:

1. Directly for counseling the client or for referral reports.
2. Interpreting reports in the literature which will improve his effectiveness as a counselor.

3. Carrying on research which will contribute to the evaluation of counseling procedures or improve the effectiveness of counseling.

Statistics should be applied to all procedures and preparation for counseling, not just to tests used in counseling. Chapters 8 to 10 contain the kinds of standardized tests and self-rating scales that are the most common medium in which statistics are used. Such instruments have played a primary part in counseling up to the present time. Until counselors develop greater proficiency in using data from other sources, tests and inventories will continue to be a major source of information about clients. Actually, the chief value of tests lies in the data they provide which confirm information about behavior secured from other sources. In a few instances, such as vocational interest inventories, they provide data which can be secured in no other practical manner. Tests that can be administered and scored with relatively little training can also save the counselor's time when they are administered by clerical or other nonprofessional or support personnel.

This latter term, *support personnel*, is applied to assistants supervised by the counselor; they are also called *subprofessional personnel* or *counselor aides*. This is to distinguish them from teachers, social workers, and personnel in the health field, who are more frequently referred to as *para-professional workers* because they usually have preparation in a different profession and are administratively in a *staff* relationship to the counselor. Support personnel perform only those counseling tasks for which they are fitted. They are frequently persons with little or no formal preparation, but who are able to relate to a client in a fashion that helps promote his readiness for counseling or for making a behavioral choice, particularly clients from disadvantaged groups whose contact with a counselor may be difficult to initiate.

The more his procedures for collecting data can be adapted for use by technicians, the more effectively the time of the professionally trained counselor can be used. Tests are ordinarily used to support other sources of information about academic potential and performance, about special aptitudes, about vocational interests, and about personality traits and attitudes governing behavior. Chapters 6 to 10 show how tests provide cross-validation for other counseling procedures and, occasionally, new data about the client.

The counselor ordinarily evaluates academic potential in terms of cultural background, the family's socioeconomic level, school grades or marks, the judgments of teachers, tests of general intelligence, and multiple aptitude tests. The cultural background of the client indicates the expected general limits within which his academic aptitude will be found, as well as the kind of communication he will probably use to evidence this potential. The family's socioeconomic level is another dimension of the client's culture, one which indicates the limits within which his academic potential will be manifested, as well as the values and goals he will tend to set for himself. The average of his previous school marks is usually one of the best indicators of future academic performance. The use of marks in any given subject-matter area, however, is subject to considerable error and should be handled cautiously by the counselor. The teacher's judgment when used by the counselor should be tempered by the counselor's knowledge of the professional background, objectivity, and behavior of that teacher. Most teachers are capable of giving a good estimate of the academic potential of their pupils, at least for their own subject-matter areas.

Tests of general intelligence are subject to variation, both in terms of the kind of test used and the errors of measurement connected with any given test. Tests requiring timed performance and a high level of vocabulary or reading skills may present a different estimate of an individual's academic potential from that presented by tests which are untimed or nonverbal. An individual's cultural background and reading level may inhibit his performance on specific tests. For these and other reasons, the performance of an individual on tests of general intelligence will fluctuate and make an exact estimate of academic potential difficult or impossible. Teachers and counselors have been generally unsuccessful in getting this concept of variability in intelligence test scores across to parents and to the general public. It is vital that the counselor make sure his *clients* understand these facts. Many of these same defects of tests of general intelligence are also inherent in multiple-factor tests, even though multi-factor tests have been designed to overcome the most common faults of group intelligence tests (Samler, 1958).

The counselor not only evaluates academic achievement in terms of previous school marks and teachers' judgments, but adds other information about school projects, contests, and achievement test scores. In the initial interview, the counselor should also ascertain how the client *feels* about both academic potential and achievement. Frequently, the client's feelings about this may be at considerable variance with the evidence the counselor has collected. At this point, the procedures preliminary to counseling must include an attempt to understand those perceptions of academic performance which differ from the potential or actual performance indicated by the evidence. Such a process involves much more than just an interpretation of test scores. Differences between the indicated potential and the self-concept of the client, and between perceived and actual performance in a group, may be the basis for considerable time and effort in counseling. Until these discrepancies are clarified, understood, and accepted by the client, it is of little value to attempt to help the client evaluate future possibilities by discussing the meaning of school marks, other successes or failures in school, teachers' judgments, and achievement test scores.

In like manner, information about special aptitudes and abilities is collected and evaluated in the light of the client's perception of his special strengths and weaknesses. Sources of this information are all of the recorded data available to the counselor, including scores from previous tests. Again, the counselor needs to use these in the initial interview as a background against which to compare the client's statements in this area.

Concurrent with the counselor's evaluation of the client's potential, an evaluation of his interests (discussed in Chapter 9) is undertaken in order to narrow the areas of investigation. The counselor begins such an evaluation by collecting evidence (from the sources already described) which will shed light on what the client likes to do. Usually these data, when coupled with the client's own statements, are sufficient to give a fairly stable picture of his interests and to point toward highly promising areas of educational, vocational, and leisure activities. The client's statements about his interests alone, however, are frequently at variance with his previous behavior and with results from measures of interest. Thus it becomes necessary to know how a client feels about various interests, so that the counselor can understand and guard against misinterpreting the client's response sets or tendencies in the light of the total data about his interests and his scores from interest inventories. When these all present a congruent picture, the counselor can feel the client is on safer ground in making future life choices.

Chapter 10, which emphasizes the importance of the client's feelings and response tendencies, highlights the need for the counselor to make tentative interpretations about the personality traits and attitudes of the client. Many research studies show that these are the real reason behind the success of an individual in most of the activities that he undertakes. Knowledge of them is vital in helping the client to understand himself well enough to anticipate and predict his future behavior. Collecting data about the personality traits and attitudes of clients is, however, complicated by the fact that many persons who contribute data to these evaluations either lack training in making such evaluations or let their own personality traits and attitudes distort their evaluations.

Thus the counselor's task of helping the client create a consistent picture of behavior becomes a process of trying to eliminate or control all the inherent sources of distortion and of training persons to make observations and collect data without introducing any additional distortion. This process is discussed in Chapters 2 and 12.

EVALUATING THE EFFECTIVENESS OF COUNSELING

Chapters 11 and 12 review for the counselor two methods of evaluating the effectiveness of counseling: one involved in research processes and the other contained in supervisory practices.

Research obviously is related to the earlier discussion of the counselor's use of statistics in all the developmental and cross-sectional processes he uses to prepare for counseling. As is indicated in Chapter 11, the most common research activities of the counselor center about his attempts to:

1. Review the literature on counseling procedures.
2. Evaluate the effectiveness of supervisory practices.
3. Evaluate the usefulness of the specific procedures he practices as questions about these arise in his daily work.
4. Learn simple research techniques he can carry on himself.
5. Acquire a sufficient knowledge of computer processes so that he can rough out a proposed research design, check with experts on its feasibility, check the accuracy of his results, and interpret the meaning of those results.

In Chapter 12, the consequences of the pressing need for counseling activities is examined. Some counselors have had to undertake supervisory duties to help train persons with less preparation. In addition to this supervision of support personnel, the counselor is often supervised himself or is required to supervise counselors in practicum settings and to supervise other full-time counselors for whom he is responsible. Such supervisory activities involve two kinds of responsibility: one is to see that no practices occur which could be harmful to a client in any way; the other is to be of as much help, in a teaching sense, as possible, in order to promote the professional development of those he supervises. With both of these persons, the client and the person being supervised, the counselor has to produce a true learning situation, as free from threat and other negative affect as possible. This in turn requires that the supervising counselor's preparation for counseling be done for *two* other persons besides himself, and that he develop skills permitting him to function both as a teacher and as a counselor. If such supervisory practices are to be continued, an evaluation needs to be completed of their effectiveness in the counseling process.

Another issue, not covered in this book, is the place of group processes in the activities of the counselor (Glanz and Hayes 1968, Watson 1967a, b). If one considers group processes to be group information-giving designed to save the counselor's time and serve the needs of clients in as large groups as possible, then one course of action and series of skills is required. If one considers group processes to be group dynamics designed to serve several clients with similar problems, a different series of skills and procedures is essential. Actually, both of these group processes can make the work of the counselor more effective, but they require a different type of skill than those yet considered. Not only must the counselor have the preparation to be able to handle the forces operating in groups, but to be most effective the process must be accompanied by individual sessions with each group member. Group counseling cannot be looked upon as the panacea for the overworked counselor or the limited budget, but rather as a series of processes serving specific functions in counseling, which processes require a different kind of counseling competence and hence additional professional preparation. Giving information intelligibly and effectively in groups is not easy. Helping clients to interact with each other and to succeed in modifying their behavior in such interactions calls for a thorough understanding of, and the ability to control and utilize, the forces operating in groups, in order to promote behavioral change in the direction each group member chooses.

It is evident by now that two factors are paramount in determining how well the counselor is able to prepare to function in a counseling interview. One of these is the education and experience of the counselor. The other is his purpose in using the data.

From some discussions of counseling one gets the impression that successful counseling is a function of age—the older the counselor, the better the counseling—or that academic preparation is all that is necessary to become a counselor. Successful counseling is based upon a thorough knowledge of factors affecting individual behavior and the ability to help a client understand and accept these factors so that they may play an appropriate part in future behavior. The counselor acquires his knowledge and his skill through education and experience, and the relative importance of the two varies with the counselor. Some individuals who aspire to counseling may complete the necessary academic preparation, yet can never develop sufficient sensitivity to people, or sufficient objectivity, to become effective counselors.

The successful counselor must have enough academic preparation to use the procedures and preparation for counseling surveyed earlier in this chapter and to communicate the meaning of his client's behavior during counseling. In addition, such a counselor must be able to relate to clients in a manner that inspires confidence and trust, that respects the integrity and capacities of the client, and that minimizes the experiential biases of the counselor during counseling. While it is still difficult to spell out in detail the attributes which produce a successful counselor, it is possible to consider the absence of any of the above as negative factors that will prevent an individual from doing effective counseling.

The purpose for which the counselor intends to use the various kinds of data which are described in succeeding chapters will determine the precision with which the data are collected and interpreted. If the purpose is to use one or a few tools or techniques in the prediction of a specific act of the client, greater reliability and validity are required. If the purpose is to help the client develop an over-all understanding and acceptance of his behavior, less precision is required in any given tool or technique because each plays a lesser part in the synthesized picture of the behavior.

Thus it is evident that the importance of each of the procedures to be described in the following pages will vary—according to the needs of the client, the needs of the counselor, and the activities undertaken to satisfy these needs.

REFERENCES

Bingham, W. V., and Moore, B. V. 1959. *How to interview*. New York: Harper & Row, Publishers.

Blocher, D. H. 1966. *Developmental counseling*. New York: The Ronald Press Company.

Downie, N. M., and Heath, R. W. 1965. *Basic statistical methods*. New York: Harper & Row, Publishers.

Glanz, E., and Hayes, R. 1968. *Groups in guidance*. Boston: Allyn & Bacon, Inc.

Hall, E. T. *The silent language*. 1959. Garden City, N.Y.: Doubleday & Company, Inc.

———. *The hidden dimension*. 1966. Garden City, N.Y.: Doubleday & Company, Inc.

Kahn, R. L., and Cannell, C. F. 1957. *The dynamics of interviewing*, New York: John Wiley & Sons, Inc., pp. 3–91.

Kell, B., and Mueller, W. J. 1966. *Impact and change: A study of counseling relationships*. New York: Appleton-Century-Crofts.

Krumboltz, J. D., ed. 1966. *Revolution in counseling: Implications of behavioral science*. Boston: Houghton Mifflin Company.

Rogers, C. R., ed. 1967. *The therapeutic relationship and its impact: A study of psychotherapy with schizophrenics*. Madison: University of Wisconsin Press, 1967.

Samler, J., ed. 1958. *The use of multifactor tests in guidance*. Washington, D.C.: The American Personnel and Guidance Association.

Watson, G. 1967*a*. *Concepts for social change.* Washington, D.C.: National Training Laboratories, National Education Association. Published for Cooperative Project for Educational Development.

———. 1967*b*. *Change in school systems.* Washington, D.C.: National Training Laboratories, National Education Association. Published for Cooperative Project for Educational Development.

2

Records and Personal Documents

There is a trend in counseling toward the use of records and personal documents as longitudinal or developmental evidence of behavior, in contrast to dependence on cross-sectional methods that have been used in the past, such as information that has been secured from tests. In the past there has not been an adequate effort to keep records of individuals over their life spans. Lack of adequate school records forces school counselors to resort to testing and estimates based on current behavior. Lack of adequate work records has made job promotion a hit-or-miss affair based on subjective judgments that often could not be verified through objective data. Placement of clients from various state and community agencies has often been based on the counselor's hunches after a brief interview. But now attention is focusing on what usually has been referred to as the "life-history method." This should not be confused with the case history used in social work, which stresses environmental factors. The life history method stresses individual behavior and development.

Super (1957) talks about this as the developmental method or the theory of life patterns inherent in the "career-pattern" studies. Dailey (1958) has pointed out the limits of the trait-factor or actuarial method and suggests that "the assessment of an individual should be organized around (1) collecting a detailed set of facts regarding his past behavior; (2) translating that chronicle into an economic, specific and coherent 'theory' of the individual, and (3) basing the inferences of his future behavior upon a projection of these past trends as conditioned by probable future circumstances." Paterson (1957) lists a series of sources contained in records and personal documents from which developmental pictures of behavior have been secured and used in prediction of occupational success. It is the contention here that such an approach is the most reliable and valid one for helping a client to make *all* life choices, not just occupational choices.

The premise behind the life-history method is that present and future behavior is best explained by previous behavior. So this longitudinal approach is characterized by the collection, analysis, and summary of data that show the development of behavior. Allport (1942) refers to this as the study of "latent trends" within the individual which are evidence of major characteristics. This shifts the emphasis to the use of records and personal documents presenting data collected systematically over the entire life span of the individual. It also requires the education of counselors in the collection and interpretation of such data and the integration of the data with current cross-sectional techniques to help a client understand himself, evaluate his environment, and make choices for the future on the basis of his understanding and acceptance of what has been done in the past. So emphasis here upon records and personal documents is the emphasis upon client evaluation *by the client* assisted by the counselor making professional interpretations and statements of probabilities.

This approach has another advantage for the counselor. From these idiographic data which are collected on each individual, the counselor can accumulate what Allport refers to as "nomothetic" or "group" data. When the counselor collects information about the individual, it can be combined into nomothetic information about the various groups in which this individual participates, and therefore both kinds of information the counselor needs are available.

Historically, the first use of this method of any importance to the counselor is the study conducted by Sir Francis Galton (1892) of the outstanding families of England. His purpose was to show that it was not just one person, but a number of outstanding people in the same family, who made important contributions to English history. Terman (1925) used the life-history approach in studies of gifted children.

Personal documents were first used in a sociological study in 1920 by Thomas and Znaniecki (1959). In *The Polish Peasant*, they analyzed 763 selected letters to show typical family problems and individual problems. Allport (1942) refers to this as the first methodological use of personal documents. There have been a long series of psychological uses of auto-biographies. Some typical examples are William James' *Varieties of Religious Experience* (1929), Clifford Beers' *The Mind That Found Itself* (1948), and Helen Keller's autobiography (1903).

Along with this use of personal documents and historical records came the development of various forms of school records, beginning with Horace Mann and the Daily Register in the 1830's. This is still one of the major records of an individual's school history, even though it is only a record of attendance. About 100 years later, in 1930, the first cumulative record, developed by a committee headed by Ben D. Wood and E. L. Clark, was published by the American Council on Education.

In the earlier 1930's, a series of Employment Stabilization Research Institute studies was conducted at the University of Minnesota; these are discussed by Paterson (1957). They form the basis for approaches to mechanical, clerical, and business aptitude testing. These early studies also made use of all kinds of historical records and personal documents to predict occupational behavior. They contained information on home background, education, and training. They also included a detailed work history, the claimed interests of the individuals, information about their attitudes and motivations, general and special aptitude tests, trade, achievement, interest, and personality tests, and clearance reports from previous schools, employers, and social service agencies. Paterson compares this collection of information with a biographical data form and a brief interview by State Employment Service interviewers in the prediction of job success. The people using the life-history approach made more effective predictions.

The use of records and personal documents to get a description of people in terms of their life patterns is only half of the picture. Both Roe (1956) and Super (1957) point out that along with this increased use of records and biographical data, some sort of a description of life activities is needed. The kind of descriptive information about typical behavior collected by Barker and Wright (1951) and the studies of Fine and Heinz (1957) of occupational requirements, are examples of descriptions of life activities. Barker and Wright have tried to develop descriptions of typical daily behavior to show life activities, Fine and Heinz have made an attempt to describe jobs in terms of worker characteristics and trait requirements. They have attempted to organize this into a three-dimensional description called the Functional Occupational Classification Structure (see Chapter 5). When these descriptions of the individual and the description of the requirements for life activities are fitted together, individuals are better able to understand themselves and to make choices about common life activities.

RECORDS USED FOR COUNSELING

The counselor uses records to build up the longitudinal or developmental picture of the behavior of an individual. Records maintained over a long period will show how an individual's present behavior developed and, if enough personal documents have been collected, they can sometimes show why it developed as it did. In order to use records in this fashion, however, it is necessary to have clearly in mind the varying purposes for which records are kept, the content of records used with clients, and the way they are used in guidance and counseling. Records can be used to identify individuals who need counseling. Then, in counseling, they can be used to predict future behavior or to understand behavior so that the client can be helped to make changes if this seems desirable to him.

Purpose of Records

As previously indicated, the counselor uses records primarily to give a developmental picture of the individual. The counselor does this in order to help a client understand the amount, the rate, and the direction of growth that has taken place. For the client who is considering a career in journalism, it would be important to have samples of writing collected over a period of years, and a series of brief evaluations by teachers which would show growth in fundamental English skills and creativity. This, as well as other growth, would be evident if teachers saved typical samples of work from each year. With the present state of records in most agencies it would not be safe to assume that a person could not write well just because there is no evidence of this in the records. The counselor must show his colleagues how information about a client's strengths and weaknesses needs to become a matter of record, or they will not consider the data important enough to be collected, prepared, and preserved.

If this emphasis on contributing to records as a developmental picture of the client were stressed continuously, teachers and others who have contact with him would be more concerned about preserving information expressing a clear picture of behavior. This information could be used not only with the clients, but also with others who must work with him. Teachers could have a clearer picture of a pupil's behavior, which would permit them to make instruction more meaningful for a given pupil, whether this pupil were an average, or an exceptional child. The relationships that developed between teacher and pupil as they worked together to produce these records could improve the psychological field within which instruction and learning take place. School administrators could see the various ways in which a given client needs help in order to make school and other learning situations a more successful experience. As the administrator sees how records provide a more complete under-standing of the behavior of clients, the counselor would have to spend less time in explaining the need for different aspects of the counseling program. The administrator, through this better understanding of records, could provide more effective and understanding leadership for the record-keeping activities of the agency. As parents and relatives become aware of the ways in which information from records is used to help members of their families, they would be more willing to furnish useful information for these records and really help to keep such records current.

Understanding and purposeful contributions to records make the work of the counselor more precise, either in dealing directly with the client's needs in the interview or in making appropriate referrals to cooperating agencies. The data provided by records that have been collected with an understanding of their significance are more useful in research into the effectiveness of counseling and into ways of improving services to clients.

Content of Records

Traxler and North (1966) have provided one of the most comprehensive discussions extant in the use of records for guidance and counseling activities. Although they emphasize school records, the principles would apply to any agency. They list the following set of principles to govern the establishment and use of such records:

1. A comprehensive and detailed system of cumulative personnel records is indispensable for the proper functioning of the modern school.
2. The most important purpose of personnel records is to improve the instruc-tion and guidance of each individual pupil.
3. Records are needed that will be continuous over the whole history from the kindergarten to the junior college, and that will follow the child from school to school.
4. The personnel records for all pupils should be readily accessible to the

entire faculty of the school. . . . the freedom of use of the main records should not be impaired by the need for recording occasional confidential bits of information.

5. The records system should be simple enough and well enough organized so that the essential facts about any given pupil will be brought together on one central record card or set of cards in such a way that they may be grasped through a few moments of study by busy teachers and counselors who are not highly trained in interpreting records.

6. An attempt should be made to keep the records high in reliability and comparability by basing them as far as possible on objective data.

7. The records should be uniform in type throughout all the schools of the system.

8. The records system should provide for a minimum of repetition of items.

9. The building of a personnel record system for a given school does not begin with a consideration of the records themselves; it begins with a study of the nature and purposes of the school and of the pupil.

10. If a school adopts one comprehensive cumulative form as its basic personnel record, it should not only plan this form with meticulous attention to detail, but it should also carefully plan the forms which are to be used in collecting data which will contribute to the main record.

11. A detailed manual of directions should accompany the personnel records for the guidance of persons filling out or using the forms.

12. There is a natural and logical relationship between the information on reports made to the parents and the information recorded for purposes of permanent record; this relationship should be taken into account in planning both types of forms.

13. There is also a natural and close relationship between cumulative records and transcripts of school records which are sent to colleges.

14. A system of personnel records must not be static; it must be revised frequently, as a school's theory of education matures and its practices change.

15. It is imperative that a system of personnel records be associated with a program of teacher education in the use of these records.

If the primary purpose of records in guidance and counseling is to help the client grow in self-understanding, all records should be planned so that they present a clear picture *to the client* of the etiological aspects of behavior. If this is done, it will also be a relatively simple matter for teachers and counselors to interpret and use the records. It is probably best if records are maintained in three parts: (1) an administrative set of records which contain those data summarizing briefly the information about each client needed to establish and maintain administrative policies of the agency; (2) a cumulative collection of behavioral data available to all members of the agency; and (3) a confidential file of materials on specific clients to be released to others only with the written permission of the client.

In establishing a system of records, the counselor and the agency need to do two things. The first of these is to spell out clearly the agency policy on how these records will be maintained and the rules governing their release to personnel within and outside the agency. This is particularly important with records which are considered to be confidential. The second consideration should be for statutes governing the release of information from these records. A given state may have a law giving clients the right of privileged communication (Committee Report 1955), but the agency needs a ruling that such a right applies to their clients. In practice, few cases have developed which create a violation of an agency's promise about the confidential nature of records; at the same time the counselor should be aware that most records are subject to subpoena by a court, and govern the content of those records accordingly. For all these reasons it is essential that all agency personnel participate in the development of the system of record-keeping, in order that they understand the purposes and rules governing use of records.

There are certain data which are so private that they should never be made a matter of record. These data are often uncontrollable as far as limiting the persons who have access to them. So the counselor has to take other steps in his effort to protect his client in the present state of our legal system. In most states, a psychological counselor can be forced to testify in court. In other states there is a tendency to allow almost any citizen access to information in public agencies, including public schools, colleges, and universities, while at the same time limiting access to the same information for persons attending similar private institutions. The counselor must bear in mind that, except for those few states where such information about the client is protected and kept confidential by the law, these data should be maintained *only* in the memory of the counselor, if the client is to be protected fully.

Bristow and Proctor (1930) have presented a functional classification of high-school records which illustrates the limited use most agency records have for counseling. They list records under the following headings:

1. Registration and classification forms
2. Attendance
3. Routine permits and passes
4. Parental reports
5. Health and physical education records
6. Special and cumulative records
7. Reports to other agencies and colleges

It is evident that these records will have quite restricted value in preparation for counseling.

A much more valuable description of materials which should be included in school records is presented by Troyer *et al.* (1947). This report was constructed on the premise that an understanding of certain kinds of behavior is essential to work with pupils, and lists the following areas of information which should be included in records:

1. The student's home background
2. General abilities
3. Special abilities
4. Progress in skills and knowledge
5. Work experience, community service, and other activities
6. Quality of thinking
7. Special interests, attitudes, and beliefs
8. Social competence and emotional adjustment
9. Health, physical growth, and energy output
10. Genuineness of purpose, level of aspiration
11. Life values

These items, obviously more useful to the counselor and the client than the items in Bristow and Proctor's list, can be collected for the records from the following sources:

1. Personal data form completed by client
2. Autobiography of client
3. Other personal documents of the client, such as written school work, letters, and diaries
4. Case histories of social agencies
5. Anecdotal records
6. School marks, ratings, and follow-up reports
7. Records of excessive absence from school or work
8. Records of residuals of serious illness or accident
9. Employer's reports and ratings
10. Reports and ratings by supervisors of community activities, such as Scout or church leaders
11. Results of standardized tests and inventories
12. Sociometric data
13. Reports of specialists, such as psychologist or physician
14. Record of extra-class activities
15. Reports of conferences with parents and relatives
16. Reports of previous interviews

The sources of items included in the preceding list and the nature of items shown by Troyer and others indicate the differences between records prepared for use by a counselor and a client, and those prepared for administrative purposes. There is no reason why the agency records cannot embrace both purposes as long as the sources from which the records are collected provide for both kinds of use.

USE OF PERSONAL DOCUMENTS

It is obviously impossible for anyone to say or do anything which does not express something about himself and form a basis for hypotheses about future behavior. At the same time, very little has been done with psychological data of this sort. Casual conversation with friends and acquaintances reveals how little attention is paid to such data in daily life. Even the student doing graduate work in counseling tends to neglect these data unless they indicate highly abnormal behavior. This disregard of such personal or biographical data is partly a function of lack of training in their use, and partly due to a distrust of the candidness of the persons who write such documents.

More emphasis is being placed on the use of personal documents in the current educational programs for counselors, in conjunction with a renewed stress on the developmental approach to the study of the individual. Counselors are being shown what these data indicate and how they can be synthesized with other data for use with clients. Emphasis is being placed on the integration of personal documents into the rest of the cumulative record collected for a given individual. More often now, the counselor asks, "How do I discuss the meaning of these with a client?"

With the increased recognition of the importance of the relationship between counselor and client, and more information about the dynamics of behavior, the candidness of the client is recognized as a function of the timing with which the counselor puts the client into situations requiring candor, such as the writing of personal documents. The personal documents themselves vary, from the more common personal data or "biodata" form and themes or essay examinations through the autobiography, structured and unstructured, to the controlled diary intended for a given topic.

The Biodata Form

The biodata (biographical data) form is used more frequently as a new client comes to an agency. It deals with the more specific information about a client, such as identification or census data about client and family, educational background and aspirations, leisure-time activities, work experience, and vocational plans. Form 2.1 is a biodata form adapted for use at the high school level. Form 2.2 is intended for use with college students. Information similar to that contained on each of these forms is collected by most agencies. When the counselor does not have access to earlier records, the biodata form is quite useful in making tentative hypotheses about the client prior to the initial interview.

If the counselor knows the area in which the client lives, a street address permits tentative estimates of socioeconomic status and background. In states where religion and race are omitted from these biodata forms by law, a preliminary estimate can often be made on the basis of a street address. Depending upon the geographical region and whether the client's address is urban or rural, tentative conclusions about his background can be made on the basis of the size of his family and the occupation of his parents. The occupation of the parents, together with the length of time the family has lived in the United States, can often be a check on the academic potential of a client: A person of native American stock in a low socioeconomic area will probably have less academic potential than one from an area of high socioeconomic status. On the other hand, no conclusions can be drawn about recent immigrants, who may have come from almost any socioeconomic level in their native country, or about some disadvantaged groups, like American blacks.

Data about educational background can be analyzed in the same fashion. For instance, more meaningful estimates can be made about a client who says he was tenth from the top in a high-school class of 250 than can be made about a client who was fourth from the top in a class of five. And biodata about activities can give useful information about the girl stating an interest in engineering when they show she spends her leisure time building and flying model airplanes with motors.

The counselor who spends time learning to use these biodata forms can find considerable validation for data collected by other methods, as well as new data which the personal documents provide.

The Autobiography

The discussion that follows is specifically related to the autobiography, but much of the material applies to any writings of clients.

Autobiographies may be classified into two types—structured and unstructured. As Hahn and MacLean (1955) and Danielson and Rothney (1954) have pointed out, the unstructured form is most suitable in counseling when the major emphasis is upon social and emotional problems and the structured form is most useful when educational and vocational choices are to be made by the client. The unstructured autobiography is written in whatever form seems most suitable to the client. For educa-

Form 2.1

BIODATA FORM FOR HIGH-SCHOOL USE

PERSONAL RECORD

Name:
Address:
Phone:

This information will be released to no one without your written consent. When you wish to leave something blank, write **none**.

1. Personal data:
   Sex: _____ Age: _____ Date of birth: _____ Place of birth: _____
   Religious preference: _____ Height: _____ Weight: _____
   Physical disability? _____ Married: _____

2. Family data:
   Parents still married: _____ Separated: _____ Divorced: _____

Father	Mother
Age: _____	Age: _____
Job: _____	Job: _____
Grade completed: _____	Grade completed: _____
Birthplace: _____	Birthplace: _____

   Brothers and sisters:

Name	Sex	Age	Grade completed	Occupation

3. Education:
   Course taken: _____
   Approximate High-School average: _____
   Subjects liked: _____ Subjects disliked: _____
   What do you plan to do when you complete High School? _____
   _____
   _____

4. What do you like to do in your spare time?
   a. Hobbies: _____
   b. Training in music or art: _____
   c. Clubs and organizations: _____
   d. Offices held: _____
   e. Do you like to read? _____
   f. What books do you read? _____
   g. What magazines do you read? _____

h. What kind of group activities do you like? _____

_____

i. What sports do you play? _____

j. Varsity or intramural? _____

5. What occupation would you like to enter?

Job	Reason
a.	
b.	
c.	

Is this what your parents want you to do? Yes: _____ No: _____

What job would you like to be doing 10 or 15 years from now?

6. What kind of work have you done? Mark on-the-job training "X."

Job.   Time in months.   Did you like it?   Why?

7. What problems would you like to discuss with a counselor?

a. Job: _____ b. Education: _____ c. Relation with

others: _____ d. Finances: _____ e. Other: _____

8. Underline the traits in the following list which apply to you:
Persevering, friendly, patient, stubborn, capable, tolerant, calm, impetuous, pessimistic, bashful, self-confident, jealous, talented, quick-tempered, cynical, tactful, conscientious, cheerful, submissive, excited, irritable, anxious, poor health, nervous, easily exhausted, unhappy, frequent periods of gloom or depression, frequent day-dreaming.

Form 2.2

BIODATA FORM FOR COLLEGE USE*

GUIDANCE BUREAU

Personal Data Form

Case No. _____

Counselor _____

Date Returned _____

The purpose of this blank is to secure background information about you for use with tests results and interview information. Please feel free to answer as much or as little as you wish. However, the more completely you answer the items, the more useful the form will be for counseling. **No information about you will be released to anyone without your written consent.**

Final responsibility for decisions and plans always rests with the person being counseled. However, a discussion of your problems with a properly qualified counselor, coupled with such facts about your abilities, personality, and interests as can be gained by this blank, psychological tests, and interviews may enable you to make your decisions and plans more wisely than you could make them unaided. It is not to be expected that all problems will be solved by these interviews. Adjustment in and after school is a continuous process because of the changes within you and the changing conditions you must meet.

Name _____ Sex _____
        Last   First   Middle

Present Address _____ Telephone _____

Home Address _____

Height _____ Weight _____ Age _____ Date of Birth _____ Place of Birth _____

U.S. Citizen: Yes _____ No_____ Religious Preference: _____

Marital Status: _____ Dependents: _____

Spouse: Grade completed _____ Age: _____ Occupation: _____

Father	Mother
Name _____	Name _____
Job: _____	Job before marriage: _____
Grade Completed: _____	Job now: _____
Birthplace: _____	Grade completed: _____
Age: _____	Birthplace: _____ Age: _____

Parents still married: _____ Divorced: _____ Separated: _____

Brothers and sisters:

Sex (M or F)	Age	Highest Grade Completed	Occupation
_____	_____	_____	_____
_____	_____	_____	_____

---

*Adapted by permission of the University of Kansas Guidance Bureau, Lawrence, Kansas.

Name of high school? _____ Date of graduation _____

Course taken: (check one)   Subjects Liked   Subjects Disliked

    General _____   _____   _____

    Commercial _____   _____   _____

    Vocational _____   _____   _____

    College Prep. _____   _____   _____

Size of high-school senior class_____

Approximate high-school average _____

Rank in high-school senior class _____

Best subject _____ Mark _____

Poorest subject _____ Mark _____

College or special schools attended, including K.U., and also including special training in art, music, stenography, etc.

Name of School or College	Date Attended	Course Taken	Approximate Average
_____	_____	_____	_____
_____	_____	_____	_____
_____	_____	_____	_____

College Subjects Liked	Marks	College Subjects Disliked	Marks
_____	_____	_____	_____
_____	_____	_____	_____
_____	_____	_____	_____

What is (or was) your major? _____ What year are you in? _____

How many hours study do you put in during the week? _____

Are you engaged in any outside work while attending the University? _____

If so, what is the nature of this work? _____

How much time does it take per week? _____

Who is your employer? _____

Why did you decide to come to K.U.? _____

_____

What other type of training have you considered besides a college education?

_____

How does your family feel about college?

_____ Opposed to my going to college.

_____ Not interested in what I do.

_____ Leave choice to me.

_____ Wants me to go to college.

Sources of your financial support in college.

_____ Family

_____ Savings

_____ Part-time work

_____ Government aid

_____ Scholarship

_____ Other?

What kind of group activities do you like? _____

_____

_____

031677

_____

_____

What do you like to do by yourself? _____

_____

_____

_____

List in chronological order all your work experience to date including part-time or summer jobs.

Nature of Work	From To (Give month and year)	Salary
_____	_____	_____
_____	_____	_____
_____	_____	_____
_____	_____	_____

Which of these jobs did you like best? _____

Why? _____

Underline any of the following words which describe your general makeup:
persevering, friendly, patient, stubborn, capable, tolerant, calm, impetuous, pessimistic, bashful, jealous, talented, self-confident, quick-tempered, cynical, tactful, conscientious, cheerful, submissive, excited, irritable, anxious, poor health, nervous, easily exhausted, unhappy, frequent periods of gloom or depression, frequent day-dreaming.

From what person or other source did you hear of the Guidance Bureau? _____

_____

List any problems you wish to discuss with a counselor.

_____

If the problem(s) you wish to discuss with a counselor is not of an Educational-Vocational Nature it is not necessary to complete the remainder of this blank unless you so desire. If you do wish to discuss an Educational-Vocational problem, please complete the remainder of the blank following.

List in order of preference occupations in which you would like to earn your living. Do not consider abilities or job opportunities. Just consider whether you would be happy in the work.

	Occupation	Reason for Interest in Occupation
1.	_____	_____
2.	_____	_____
3.	_____	_____
4.	_____	_____

_____

What is your present vocational choice? _____

When did you make this choice? (give the year) _____

Why did you make this choice? _____

How certain are you that this occupation you have specified is the one you really want to prepare for:

Very certain and satisfied _____ Uncertain _____ Very questionable _____

How much information have you about the requirements of the vocation you are choosing? None _____ Some _____ Extensive _____

What vocation do (or did) your parents want you to follow? _____

Why? _____

If you were free of all restrictions (if you could do as you wish) what would you want to be doing 10 or 15 years from now? _____

_____

We are interested in determining why you have considered your present occupational choice. Below write all the things that have happened to you which you think might have influenced your vocational interests. If you need more room, use an additional sheet of paper.

_____
_____
_____
_____
_____
_____

Explain any diseases or physical handicaps that may affect your occupational choice:

_____

This space is provided for any additional information not covered in this form which you feel may be pertinent to your problem.

_____
_____
_____
_____
_____

tional and vocational counseling, usually more specific information is desired. An outline is presented to the client and he is asked to do his writing within that framework. Exactly what is contained in the outline depends upon the intentions and point of view of the counselor. In general, the client should be expected to cover such topics as vocational plans, economic problems, work experience, major likes and dislikes, and others. Form 2.3 is an example of such an outline.

The autobiography is more than a checklist completed by the client. It is hoped he will really describe pertinent behavior and values. For example, when he is talking about vocational plans, it is hoped that meaningful information about his level of aspiration will be given. Further, it is expected that more personal data and even more intimate information will appear here than would normally be obtained in an interview. However, this is probably related to the personality of the client, and may be true for some and not for others.

If the autobiography is to gather material of the type just described, it is felt that it should be written at the suggestion of someone associated with the counseling program. In schools these have been written in English classes as a regularly assigned theme, sometimes corrected, then rewritten, and then sent to the file in the counseling section. They are also often written in social studies classes. It seems that the introduction of the English teacher into the picture sometimes obscures and changes the material that is most suitable for counseling. It probably is more desirable to have valid autobiographies with a few grammatical errors and misspellings in them than literary masterpieces of no value to the counselor. It is hoped that the client will reveal things about himself. Thus it is necessary that the material covered be handled in a confidential fashion. In a counselor-client situation this is possible, in a classroom situation it may not be.

There is no agreement about how long such autobiographies should be. Certainly this is a function of what the counselor wants to know and the use to which the writings are put. Probably the best thing to do is to develop the outline so that the autobiography can be accomplished in about three-quarters of an hour.

This may best be written at the same time as the client's first regularly assigned session with the counselor. Some counselors have used the autobiography as a homework assignment. It is probably best to have it written in consultation with the counseling staff. If the papers are to be used for screening, this can be done easily by going through a pile and scanning. The counselor soon develops a system of organizing such data. If they are to be used in counseling, they should be filed and the information synthesized with other data immediately before the client appears.

A VOCATIONAL AUTOBIOGRAPHY

Follow the topics on this outline and discuss them in detail to show things about you which would be useful in making educational and vocational choices.

I. My present vocational choice is _____

  A. How long ago did I make this choice?

    1. What other choices have I made?

    2. Why did I make a change in my choice and how long ago?

  B. What things have influenced me in the choice of this occupation?

    1. Reading and other observation.

    2. Advice or suggestion of relatives.

    3. Advice of friends.

    4. Advice of teacher or counselor.

    5. It's the occupation of someone I admire.

    6. Good pay.

    7. I know I possess the aptitude to succeed in this job.

    8. It offers adventure.

    9. It will give me prestige in the community.

    10. Other influences.

  C. Why do I think I will be successful? What aptitudes and abilities do I have? Why do I think I possess these aptitudes and abilities?

    1. What about my scholastic aptitude? Where do I usually stand in my school or class group?

    2. Have I the ability to get along with others?

    3. Do I have skill with my hands? Have I won contests or awards?

    4. In what subjects do I do best? Poorest?

    5. What do my scores in aptitude tests indicate about my special talents?

  D. What do I know about this occupation and where did I get this information?

  E. What kind of education, training, and experience will I need to enter this occupation?

  F. My first year in this field I expect an income of $_____ per month. Five years after I have entered this field I expect to earn $_____. At the peak of my earning power in this occupation my salary should be $_____ per month.

II. My Work Experiences

  A. What are the jobs I have had, how old was I, who was my employer, what was the income I received, what was the type of work I did?

  B. Have these jobs influenced me in making my present choice of occupation?

III. My Hobbies

  A. What are my hobbies and other leisure activities which may have had vocational significance?

B. How have they influenced my present choice?

IV. What Vocational Interests Do I Have?

    A. In which of the following groups would I best fit from the standpoint of the things I like to do?

        1. Occupations involving mechanical and manual activities, such as mechanic, repairman, printer, farmer, occupational therapist, or dental technician.

        2. Occupations involving technical or scientific work such as engineer, physicist, draftsman, chemist, physician, architect, veterinarian, nurse, or dietitian.

        3. Occupations involving clerical or business detail activities, such as stenographic work, bookkeeping, cashier, or receptionist.

        4. Occupations involving business contacts with people, such as various fields of selling or politics.

        5. Occupations involving management, such as office or store manager, shop foreman, school administrator, or business executive.

        6. Occupations involving social service activities such as teacher, Boy or Girl Scout executive, personnel worker, religious or social worker.

        7. Occupations involving literary work, such as advertising agent, newspaperman, author, or lawyer.

        8. Occupations involving special artistic or musical activities.

    B. Why do I think I have these interests? (Sample answer is for occupations involving mechanical and manual activities.)

        1. My shop courses are interesting.

        2. My hobby is building a hot rod.

        3. I have a part-time job at a garage.

        4. I like to repair things.

        5. I read **Popular Mechanics**.

        6. My interest inventory scores are high in mechanical activities.

V. What personality traits do I have which will help me to do these things? How do I get along with people? Do I prefer to be with a few friends that I know quite well or am I comfortable in large groups of people? Can I convince people to do what I want? Would I be happy working alone?

In summarizing the use of this tool, Hahn and MacLean (1955) most precisely state:

The autobiography, sensibly used, offers the counselor in the secondary school and college a tool which meets most of the criteria of practicality and modest budget. It encourages counselee participation in the counseling process. It motivates serious consideration of common but troublesome problems. It imposes no heavy additional chores on instructional staff or counselor. It is low in cost. It aids in developing longitudinal histories so needed to implement our cross-section techniques of questionnaires and tests.

Riccio (1958) has listed arguments against use of the autobiography as:

1. There are questions about validity, reliability, and use.
2. Many students are unable to be candid.
3. The material often becomes quite complex.
4. There are frequent problems connected with interpretations.

At the same time he lists as some of the advantages:

1. Opportunity for students to tell about themselves, if they feel free to do so
2. Abundance of psychological material the autobiography provides
3. Provides information about a student's attitudes
4. The convenience with which the information can be secured

Other Personal Documents

A number of writers have discussed the use of *themes* and *subjective examination questions* as a common source of material for evaluating individual behavior. These are probably most useful in revealing personality dynamics and information about interests, goals, values, and attitudes, unless these elements are repressed because of poor teacher-pupil relationships. The teacher can summarize these and put them in the cumulative folder after the counselor has pointed out the kind of material which would be useful. Sims (1948) has discussed the use of essay questions as a projective device, dealing with the ways an individual reveals valuable information which is usable in the life-history method if collected in records.

Letters are other personal documents that can be analyzed for idiographic and nomothetic data, as illustrated by Thomas and Znaniecki (1959).

The *diary* is more frequently used as a controlled diary limited to a client's observation about a specific kind of activity, such as study or work habits. Except with younger children, diaries have to be used cautiously. They must always be treated as highly confidential material. Many individuals do not realize the extent to which they reveal themselves and need to be protected when such personal documents are used by others. Marbury (1948) discusses the use of children's diaries and themes. He says the diary should be a chronological account, over one or two days, covering what was done, with whom, and where. Properly structured by choice of topics or instructions, diaries can reveal highly useful background information about activities and family life which will form an important supplement to other data about the client.

A modern approach to records and their use has been initiated by Harcourt, Brace & World, Inc. They have inaugurated a service for handling information about students which uses optical scanners, data-processing cards, machine storage, and retrieval by computer "print-out." The data cover the student's and his family's background; his activities and interests; educational, occupational, and vocational information; and attitudes. These data are collected by means of an information booklet completed by the student and retrieved by a print-out for the student, or a print-out of selected data about the group furnished to the school system for one school or for the whole system. Such a process, while seemingly expensive, can be quite economical once a school system has planned its collection and use. The disadvantage is the time lapse that occurs between a decision to use the data and their retrieval.

IDENTIFICATION OF POTENTIAL CLIENTS

Earlier, it was mentioned that the counselor's use of records and personal documents in preparation for counseling would involve the identification of clients in need of help. This might mean using data from within the counselor's agency, such as the school, or it might mean recourse to other agencies. Such identification requires the development of some systematic approach by the counselor to the organization of data from records. A method contrasting various attributes needs to be devised.

Graphing Data

Darley (1945) has presented one way of contrasting information about academic potential and academic performance which has been modified and presented in the graph shown in Figure 2.1. The figure shows immediately that Individuals A and D are approximately equal in academic aptitude, but considerably different in academic achievement. To the counselor this suggests a number of tentative hypotheses worth investigation. Individual D may be a person for whom the method of evaluating academic aptitude was unsuitable, or the circumstances under which estimates of academic aptitude were collected may have been unusual in some way. If Individual *D* had limited reading skills and the estimates of academic aptitude required quite effective reading skills, and at the same time the estimates of academic achievement were based primarily upon performance in nonreading or nonverbal courses, such a discrepancy could occur quite easily. On the other hand, Individual *D* may be under considerably more pressure to make more effective use of his academic potential. In the first case, remedial reading procedures may be an outcome of counseling; in the second, counseling may involve learning to live under the psychological pressures contained in working at the top limit of capacity in academic situations. A review of the records should not only identify Individual *D*, but suggest reasons why such a discrepancy exists between potential and performance.

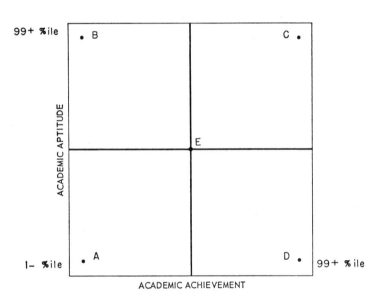

Figure 2.1

POSITIONS OF FIVE INDIVIDUALS RESULTING FROM
SCORES ON TESTS OF ACADEMIC APTITUDE AND
ACADEMIC ACHIEVEMENT

In like manner, the reasons for Individual *B*'s failing to achieve an academic level comparable to Individual *C* need investigation. Do these reasons include physical or psychological factors, or both? How can the counselor help? Records are the first sources of answers to these questions the counselor should be asking. While the situations of Individuals *B* and *D* more clearly need investigation, the counselor cannot afford to ignore Individuals *A, E,* and *C.* They would appear to be at an appropriate academic level, but contrasting data of another sort, such as that from social preference vs. social behavior, or interest vs. ability, may indicate ways in which Individual *A, C,* or *E* needs help from the counselor.

In addition to this method—the contrasting of two attributes of an individual in order to identify persons in need of counseling—information from sociometric devices may provide another way of extracting and organizing data from records to identify potential clients.

Sociometry

Sociometry is measuring social relationships. It is used to identify leaders, isolates, and rejects. Probably sociometric techniques have been used since people first began to study the behavior of the individual in groups. However, it was not until after World War I, when Moreno undertook his studies (1934, 1953) that any attempt was made to use these techniques systematically. Since that time he, Jennings (1958), and Northway (1952) have been the leaders in producing an important amount of organized information on the subject. Two other useful publications are Thorpe *et al.* (1959) and Gronlund (1959). In the short discussion that follows, an attempt will be made to show how the technique is used, how the data are collected and analyzed, and how the results of such sociometric evaluations may be used by the counselor to identify group leaders, isolates, and rejects who may need help through counseling.

General Nature of Sociometrics

As sociometrics are most frequently used, individuals are asked to respond to one or more very simple questions concerning other members in the group with whom they would like to carry on a specific activity. For example, suppose that a group is starting a project which is to be carried on by committees, or that the group is going to go on a trip, or going to have a party. Each person is asked to take a piece of paper and under his name place the numbers 1, 2, and 3. Then the person chooses, in order, the three members of the class with whom to carry on the proposed activity. (If negative choices are to be indicated, it is best to do this in private conversation with the person in charge.) It is obvious that sociometric techniques can only be used in groups where members are well acquainted with each other.

The data are specific to a single situation at a given time. The results of a sociometric test may be compared to a photograph. The status of each member of the group is shown as it existed on a certain day, perhaps even at a specific time during that day. Group relationships tend to shift and change, some groups more than others and certain aspects of groups more than others. Sociometry is useful in recording these group changes, but as Pepinsky (1949) has shown, this also makes it difficult to demonstrate the reliability of sociometric techniques.

For best results, the questions that are asked should be related to something that the group is actually going to do. If useful validity is desired, an effort must be made to see that the choices are carried out after they have been made by the group. The types of questions may vary, but most can be classified as involving social, educational, or physical attributes of the group.

There are two general methods used in analyzing such data for use in counseling. The first is to make a sociogram, as shown in Figure 2.2 (page 38). This figure shows the choices of 13 fourth-grade girls. In its simplest form, the sociogram consists of a group of circles, one for each member of the group, drawn on a large sheet of paper. Then the responses of the group are taken singly, and arrows are drawn showing the member chosen by each individual. An arrow is drawn from Chloe, whose first choice was Martha, to Martha, and a 1 placed near the head of the arrow to designate that Martha was first choice. Chloe's second choice was Bessie; another arrow is drawn to her circle, this time with a 2 appearing near the head. Finally Chloe's third choice, Elizabeth, is drawn and a 3 placed on it. It should be noted that Bessie and Elizabeth also chose Chloe, indicating a stronger relationship. In this way the responses of each student are tallied. Different colors are sometimes used, instead of numbers, to show the sequence of the choices.

This sociogram presents a picture of the group choices in reference to the question asked. Notice that Martha has been chosen more often than the other girls. She is referred to as a "star of attraction" or a possible leader. No one chose Jane, and she is referred to as an "isolate." If negative choices had been possible, Jane might have been a "reject." It will be noticed that there is also a small group within the group. This is in the upper right hand corner where Sadie, Sally, and Sue selected each other to as great an extent as possible. This small group is referred to as a "clique."

When the group is large, the construction and interpretation of a sociogram become almost impossible. Such data are almost useless for study in relationship to other variables.

The other method for handling the data gets around these objections. A worksheet similar to Figure 2.3 is set up on a large sheet of paper. Down the left-hand side are listed all the names of the members of the group. The same is done across the top. Under each name are columns

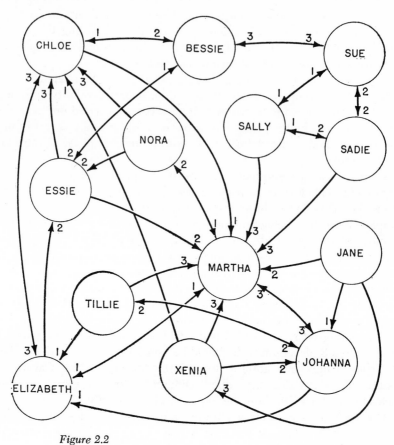

Figure 2.2

SOCIOGRAM SHOWING THE CHOICES OF
13 FOURTH-GRADE GIRLS

headed with 1, 2, and 3, to correspond to possible choices. The responses of the individuals are taken one at a time and entered into this chart. Suppose that Bessie's choices are considered. Her first choice was Chloe; her second, Essie; and her third, Sue. A check mark is placed under the name of each of these girls in the column for the appropriate choice. This is continued until all the choices are entered. Then the results are summed and the number of first, second, and third choices for each girl appears at the bottom. These may be turned into a numerical score by multiplying each first choice by 3, each second choice by 2, and each third choice by 1. Notice now that the scores run from 18 for Martha to 0 for Jane. A check on the accuracy of the work is that the sum of these scores should equal the number of individuals multiplied by 6. In this

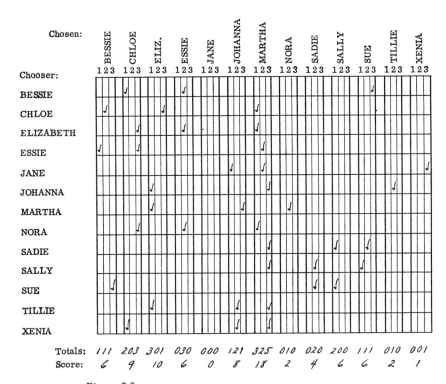

Figure 2.3

SUMMARY OF THE CHOICES OF
13 FOURTH-GRADE GIRLS

case, this comes to 78. It is possible to organize such a chart into quadrants to show the boys' choices of boys and of girls, and the girls' choices of boys and of girls.

Whether such choices are separated among first, second, and third choices and between sexes depends on the use to which the information will be put. There is evidence to show that such choices are temporary and less stable when made by socially extraverted individuals, who know more people, than when made by socially introverted individuals. The purpose for which these choices are made may affect their variability.

Using the Results of Sociometric Testing

Sociometric results merely tell or show the actual social relationships among a group. In the example, Jane was chosen by no one. Such a situation is not usually desirable. One of the functions of counseling is to help a client develop a healthy emotional life. Jane may be a girl who needs counseling. It is necessary to study Jane more closely and try to find out why she is not chosen by others. To do this, many of the other techniques available to the counselor may be used. Observation and anecdotal records, tests and inventories, information about the child's home, and the like could all be employed. In any group of average classroom size, there are apt to be several of these isolates. In the group shown in Figure 2.3, Xenia had a score of 1, having received one third choice. She and Jane and all other isolates must not be lumped into one group and treated similarly. Each is an individual with her own individual needs and problems. The situation of one will probably have little to do with the cause of isolation of any of the others. The major use of sociometrics is to *identify* the individual who may have problems and thus might profit from counseling.

Perhaps it could be said that all this is unnecessary, as any good observer knows the various types of leaders in a group and the ones for whom no one cares. This may be true, but research has shown that the opinions of many untrained observers are far from the actualities of the group structure, and this is probably true for many other group situations.

Besides contributing to the identification of individuals who may need counseling, sociometrics provide information that is useful in improving procedures for setting up groups. In addition to using this information in structuring projects and trips, data like these can be used in assigning individuals to halls and rooms in a dormitory, selecting adults for various types of work groups, or in any situation where individuals have to associate with others. But the main value of sociometric data to the counselor is as an indicator of persons with problems. Then the counselor can use other methods to explore causes of the problem.

Other Means of Identifying Clients

Texts describing various kinds of behavior can be used to secure a list of the kind of characteristics the counselor should use in identifying clients who need a certain kind of help. An approach to this problem by devising a brief list of behavior identifying various kinds of children at the elementary school level has been undertaken by Kough and De-Haan (1955). The counselor will need to supplement this with other sources, but it will serve as an initial list to use when scanning records and personal documents.

The counselor can also make his own checklist. Even though he has had considerable education in psychology and experience in counseling, it is well to have such a checklist, whether it is actually checked or only covered mentally. Such a procedure tends to increase the counselor's reliability.

This checklist could cover the topics indicated in the list by Troyer and others (1947), given earlier in this chapter. The counselor needs to ask such questions as the following:

1. What does the client's home background indicate about his behavior?
2. What do records and personal documents show about his level of abilities and achievement?
3. What do data about activities outside of school show about this client?
4. What interests, attitudes, goals, and values do they show?
5. What evaluation of social skills and personal adjustment can be made?
6. Are there any evidences of physical limitations or outstanding skills?

In these ways the counselor uses information from records and from personal documents to identify the clients who may need help. The next problem is to check and see which ones want help, and what can be done to promote readiness for counseling.

PREPARING COUNSELING DATA

The actual use of data from records and personal documents for counseling may require a somewhat different system of organization than for identification. Here the counselor has the choice of using a system which has already been developed, or of developing his own, unique system of organizing these data.

A new dimension has now been added to the accumulation, preparation, and use of data about the client. This has been provided through computers which store and retrieve such information. There are two general approaches in use. One is based on the storage and retrieval of information from documents or research for general professional use in counseling and personnel work, such as the Clearinghouses of the Educational Resources Information Centers (ERIC). The one devoted expressly to counseling and personnel work is located at the University of Michigan, where it was organized under the leadership of Dr. Garry Walz. Walz and Rich (1967) point out that the major objective of ERIC is to gather data from infrequently used sources of research, theory, and practice in order to store them more effectively, and make retrieval easier and more available to a greater number of users. An exhaustive, quantitative listing can be retrieved, or a qualitative list of limited relevance, but the process in either case requires that the user be competent to evaluate and synthesize the data to meet *his* specific needs.

Another type of computerized approach to client data is what has been referred to as a "regional" or "personal" data bank, exemplified by the work of Ellis, O'Hara, and Tiedeman (1967). They are trying to develop a system for storage and retrieval of vocational development information intended to serve the needs of a given individual at the junior or senior high-school level. Similar systems have been developed focusing on information about each pupil which is retrievable to meet either his needs or that of the school he attends (Carroll and Ellis 1965). Still a third system, devoted to the needs of the individual, is the attempt of the United States Training and Employment Service and the several state employment services to adapt computers to the needs of applicants for employment and employers seeking personnel (Golts 1966).

It is obvious that counseling in large agency settings will involve the cumulative storage in computers of data about each client, with counselor and client periodically deciding together when and what retrieval of data would be useful in the light of the current needs of the client (Loughary 1967). This does not mean an abrogation of the counselor's functions of data collection, storage, and retrieval; rather, it means he must familiarize himself with these processes and adapt them, along with his other professional procedures, to serve him and his client more parsimoniously. For those working in agency units too small to warrant such equipment, there may be the ultimate possibility of entering into a cooperative arrangement by making telephone or teletype connections with a distant computer. The teletype has been used in the California State Employment Service since 1964 in making placements of professional, technical, and managerial workers (Golts 1966), and since 1966 in placements of farm laborers (Geary 1967). A network of teleprinters connects 14 major offices which in turn are contacted by 50 smaller units via the telephone, so that an area of some 700 miles within the state is covered. All local offices, area offices, and the central office received copies, either by teleprinter or by mail, of the messages sent by teletype through the region. This provided a much more rapid and comprehensive coverage of the region for transmission of job-placement data.

The mobility of counselors also warrants that every counselor become familiar with these processes, for while he may not be able to use them in his present job, he may have to do so in his next one. Ten useful systems are discussed in a publication of the U.S. Department of Health, Education, and Welfare (1969).

SUMMARY

An attempt has been made in this chapter to show how the counselor's use of records to identify individuals in need of counseling and to help a client gain greater self-understanding may require different kinds of information. The work of Troyer and others points out the kind of information needed and possible changes in the way agency members contribute to agency records. Traxler has discussed the forms that records may take to meet unique needs of a given school and has illustrated a number of these. Such an emphasis highlights the need for accurate, objective, and directed observations by all personnel contributing to records. The next chapter will consider how these observations are achieved and the conditions which should exist if the observations are to be useful to the counselor.

REFERENCES

Allport, G. W. 1942. The use of personal documents in psychological science. *Soc. Sci. Research Council Bull.*

Barker, R., and Wright, H. F. 1951. *One boy's day: A specimen record of behavior.* New York: Harper & Row, Publishers.

Beers, C. W. 1948. *A mind that found itself.* Garden City, N.Y.: Doubleday & Company, Inc.

Bristow, A. B., and Proctor, W. M. 1930. Senior high school records and reports. *Junior-Senior High School Clearing House.* 4:410–32.

Carroll, J. B., and Ellis, A. B. 1965. *Planning and utilization of a regional data bank for educational purposes.* Cambridge, Mass.: Graduate School of Education, Harvard University.

Committee Report, Joint report of the APA and CSPA committees on legislation. 1955. *Amer. Psychol.* 10:727–56.

Dailey, C. A. 1958. The life history approach to assessment. *Personnel and Guidance J.* 36:456–60.

Danielson, P. J., and Rothney, J. W. 1954. The autobiography: Structure or unstructured? *Personnel and Guidance J.* 33:30–33.

Darley, J. F. 1945. *Testing and counseling in the high school guidance program.* Chicago: Science Research Associates.

Ellis, A. B., O'Hara, R. P., and Tiedeman, D. V. 1967. *A rudimentary demonstration for the information system for vocational decisions: Orientation, guidance scripts, test of occupational knowledge and a script writing language.* Cambridge, Mass.: Graduate School of Education, Harvard University.

Fine, S. A., and Heinz, C. A. 1957. The estimates of worker trait requirements for 4,000 jobs. *Personnel and Guidance J.* 36:168–74.

Galton, F. 1892. *Hereditary genius.* London: Macmillan & Co., Ltd. Reprinted 1952. New York: Horizon Press.

Geary, G. 1967. Teletype gets the job done. *Employment Service Rev.* 4:42–43.

Golts, E. 1966. Placement through automatic data processing. *Employment Service Rev.* 3:57–58.

Gronlund, N. E. 1959. *Sociometry in the classroom.* New York: Harper & Row, Publishers.

Hahn, M. E., and MacLean, M. S. 1955. *Counseling psychology.* New York: McGraw-Hill Book Company.

James, W. 1929. *The varieties of religious experience.* New York: Longmans, Green & Co., Inc.

Jennings, H. H. 1958. *Sociometry in group relations.* Washington, D.C.: American Council on Education.

Keller, H. A. 1903. *The story of my life.* Garden City, New York: Doubleday & Company, Inc.

Kough, J., and DeHaan, R. F. 1955. *Teacher's guidance handbook, Part I: Identifying children who need help.* Chicago: Science Research Associates.

Loughary, J. W. 1967. Will counseling be eliminated in the cybernation revolution? In *Preparing School Counselors in Educational Guidance.* New York: College Entrance Examination Board. Pp. 115–130.

Marbury, F. W. 1948. Studying the child's social world. *J. Educ. Sociol.* 21:535–543.

Moreno, J. B. 1934. *Who shall survive? A new approach to the problem of human interrelations.* Washington, D.C.: Nervous and Mental Diseases Publishing Co. (Revised ed., 1953. New York: Beacon Press.)

Northway, M. 1952. *A primer of sociometry.* Toronto: University of Toronto Press.

Paterson, D. A. 1957. The conservation of human talent. *Amer. Psychol.* 12:134–44.

Pepinsky, P. 1949. The meaning of "validity" and "reliability" as applied to sociometric tests. *Educ. and Psychol. Measmt.* 9:39–49.

Riccio, A. C. 1958. The status of the autobiography. *Peabody J. of Educ.* 36:33–36.

Roe, A. 1956. *The psychology of occupations.* New York: John Wiley & Sons, Inc.

Sims, V. M. 1948. The essay examination is a projective technique. *Educ. and Psychol. Measmt.* 8:15–31.

Super, D. E. 1957. *The psychology of careers.* New York: Harper & Row, Publishers.

Terman, L., *et al.* 1925. *Mental and physical traits of a thousand gifted children: Genetic studies of genius.* Stanford, Calif.: Stanford University Press.

Thomas, W. I., and Znaniecki, F. 1927. *The Polish peasant in Europe and America,* 2 vols. New York: Alfred A. Knopf, Inc. (1958. New York: Dover Publications, Inc.)

Thorpe, L. P., *et al.* 1959. *Studying social relationships in the classroom.* Chicago: Science Research Associates.

Traxler, A. E., and North, R. D. 1966. *Techniques of guidance.* New York: Harper & Row, Publishers.

Troyer, M. E., *et al.* 1947. Essential pupil-personnel records. Committee Number V Report. *Teachers Coll. Rec.* 48:269–86.

Walz, G., and Rich, J. V. 1967. The impact of information systems on counselor preparation and practice. *Couns. Educ. and Supervision.* 6:275–84.

U.S. Department of Health, Education, and Welfare. 1969. Computer-based vocational guidance systems, OE 25053. Washington, D.C.: Supt. of Documents.

3

Observation for
Counseling Purposes

Observation is a basic tool of the counselor and of those who furnish information for the counselor's use. Unless those who make the observations understand the frame of reference in which the observations are to be used, these data tend to be such a mixture of fact and subjective judgment that they are of limited value to the counselor.

Observations can be categorized in a number of ways, but perhaps the most useful categories for the counselor are "finding" observations and "directed" observations. *Finding observations* are those used in an exploratory or experimental situation to identify activities that are of importance to the observer. In counseling this means selecting activities that are important to the client being observed. When these activities have been singled out, any additional observations can be concentrated on such activities. These latter observations are then called directed observations. Thus *directed observations* are those where the observer's attention is pointed toward specific kinds of behavior. If the observations are described and recorded in a straightforward factual account, the counselor can use them to help clients become more aware of given facets of behavior.

Observations used in counseling come from many sources. The most important sources for the counselor are rating scales, anecdotes, psychometric situations, and initial interviews. These observations usually become a matter of agency record so that they are available to the counselor in preparing for interviews with clients. Unless sufficient preparation of observers has been carried out, the observations made are of limited effectiveness when the counselor is trying to piece together a picture of the behavior of a given client. A frame of reference is needed which will influence these observations in a way that makes them systematic and fairly objective. Such a systematic approach to observations can then be communicated to others during in-service training programs.

TRAINING OF OBSERVERS

The results obtained by many observational techniques are frequently of little value because of the conditions under which they were obtained. Observers collect data in a rather haphazard fashion, very often without any knowledge of what they are looking for or how to obtain the observations. If observations are to yield data of use to the counselor, certain procedures must be followed. Some books on personality go into this subject in great detail (e.g., Kleinmuntz 1967).

First, when personality is being studied by observation, the traits that are to be studied must be defined so that the observer knows exactly what he is looking for. This is most essential when there are two or more observers whose observations will later be compared carrying on activities with the same individuals. Very often it is said that the results obtained with observational techniques are unreliable, that they lack agreement from observer to observer. Discussion and agreement beforehand will go a long way toward rectifying this situation, and in the end such observations will be more meaningful and more useful to the counselor.

Second, observers have to be trained. To a certain extent this fits into what was first said. No matter what type of observational activity is carried out, training is essential. One method of training is to have two or more trainees actually observe or rate the same subjects for specific behavioral traits and then sit down with the supervisor and compare their results. Differences in observations or ratings are noted, and an attempt is made to find out why these discrepancies arose. Observers who are incapable of making accurate, factual, realistic, or unbiased records should be eliminated from the training. Included in this group are those whose physical or psychological traits prevent them from being trained to make usable observations. A simple way to illustrate the error that may creep into observational reports is for the leader to face away from the group *with his eyes closed* and appear to be looking out the window. Then the group is asked to describe the leader's behavior. Usually they will include the phrase "looked out of the window." This simple procedure makes it clear that the accurate and efficient observer describes only what he sees and makes no inferences beyond that.

Third, the trait studied must be of a nature that can actually be observed. It is relatively simple to observe acts of aggression by children. Such overt behavior on their part is common and more or less uncontrolled. But when dealing with adults or adolescents, observational methods are often far from satisfactory because the individual being observed so controls his behavior that his real feelings are not manifested by his actions. Very often, the observer is forced to make inferences about behavior on the basis of various cues that he picks up or *thinks* that he picks up. Observers do vary considerably in their ability to make inferences and in the frequency with which they make them. It follows, then, that personality traits that are evidenced by overt behavior are capable of being studied by observational techniques if adequate preparation is made by the observers.

Fourth, the use of "hardware" that is, audio or video tapes, cameras, and the like, provide better results than can be obtained by the use of the human senses and dependence on memory. Such devices record the whole picture at once, making it available for later study. In some situations, however, such devices act as intruders and affect what goes on, causing individuals to behave differently than they would if the recording machine were not present. There is also an ethical problem associated with the use of such devices without the subject's knowing about them or without his consent. If the circumstances allow, these aids to observation should be used whenever possible, but never without prior consent.

Fifth, a plan of observation should be established. Observations should be made at different times during the day, to control the effects of a particular time of day on a subject's behavior. If observations are made only before lunch, it follows that the records are basically those of a hungry subject. Usually the periods of observation should be short as well as rotated. Also, observational techniques produce best results when only one person at a time is observed.

Sixth, counselors should remember that the results obtained by observational techniques are only samples from a domain of behavior and that they must be supplemented by other information obtained by other methods.

In summary, it must be emphasized that all observational records are records of overt or manifest behavior. This is one of the chief weaknesses of such techniques. What a person does is seen and heard, but *why* he does what he does is not revealed. Little is learned, through observation, about the client's motivation, attitudes, plans, or conflicts. Of course, some inferences may be made about these basic aspects of personality, the knowledge of which is essential to the understanding of human behavior. From the results of observation, one can make inferences, but often these inferences are invalid. The techniques described in the following chapters, such as the use of the interview, standardized tests and inventories, and projective instruments, are all aimed at getting at some of these underlying aspects of human behavior. And it will be shown that each of these also has its limitations.

RATING SCALES

One of the chief observational techniques used to secure information about clients preliminary to counseling is the rating scale, which can be used to describe many facets of individual behavior, either in self-evaluations or in evaluations by trained observers. The self-evaluations usually take the form of adjective or problem checklists and of structured interest or personality inventories. Rating scales used by trained observers usually are for the evaluation of behavior for which more precise or more objective measures have not been developed, or are used to validate other measuring devices.

The counselor needs to be able to instruct raters, to organize and use ratings by others, to construct or to use data from instruments of self-rating, and to construct rating scales and use them.

Since the time of Sir Francis Galton, rating scales have been used to assess aspects of personality. After Galton's original work using rating scales in the evaluation of the vividness of imagery. Pearson next developed one for the assessment of intelligence. Acceptance by psychologists increased slowly until World War I, when scales were developed for rating the performance of officers. After World War I, rating scales were increasingly accepted by both industry and education in appraising various aspects of an individual's personality. Although today rating scales are more widely used in industry than in education—more precise evaluative devices and criteria have been developed in education—ratings still have many uses for the counselor, both in working with clients and in carrying on research.

Types of Scales

A discussion of all of the different types of rating scales is beyond the present scope. The most comprehensive summaries of previous work appear in Guilford (1954) and Symonds (1931). In the material that follows only the more frequently encountered types of scales will be covered.

Graphic Rating Scales

The graphic rating scale is one of the most commonly used types. On these scales, a trait is considered as a continuum, and descriptive terms are placed along it, as in the following examples:

How quiet is he?

Seldom speaks	Says very little	Carries on his part in a conversation	Talks more than his share	Talks constantly

Does he do the best quality of work of which he is capable?

Almost always	Most of the time	Sometimes	Seldom	Rarely ever

In using such a scale, the rater considers the individual being rated and places a mark along the line. This mark need not be placed over one of the descriptive terms. In scoring, a scoring scale with intervals on it may be placed along the rating scale and the rater's mark translated into a quantitative score. The gradations on the scoring scale may be as fine as desired by the scorer. Some rating scales have the line divided into pieces in line with the descriptive terms, and each of these segments or terms has a value.

Construction and General Use of Graphic Rating Scales

Here are a few rules which have to be followed in making rating scales:

1. Reach agreement among raters about meaning of terms to be used. Such words as *usually, frequently,* or *often* mean different things to different people. The best rule is to attempt to use quantitative rather than qualitative terms.
2. Keep the vocabulary as simple as possible. The same rules that apply when one is making a test or examination are relevant to rating scales.

3. Build scales for traits that can be observed. Many of the troubles with rating scales arise because the builder of the scale asks the rater to do almost impossible things. The trait being rated should be of such a nature that evidence can be observed. Ratings require that the rater observe and then make a judgment. These are both difficult tasks. It is much easier for raters to rate an individual on his promptness than on how his manners affect others. There are times when only very subjective ratings may be desired, but only skilled raters who are experts in the area should make such difficult ratings. There is some question whether even experts can carry on this type of rating with any sort of agreement.

4. It is probably best to have only one trait to a page. In practice this is rarely carried out. Nor is the suggestion that "desirable" and "undesirable" ends of the scale be alternated or randomized to prevent an individual's going down one side of the page marking all traits the same.

5. If possible, the use of extreme descriptive phrases or terms is to be avoided. When these are present, raters tend to mark nearer the middle and results are lacking in spread. The terms used at the end of the continuum should be such that they actually describe some individuals who are being rated.

6. The number of descriptive terms need not be the same for each scale. Sometimes fewer terms will function as well as many. These terms are merely guides, an indication of what a mark at certain points on a scale means.

Use of the Graphic Rating Scale

The use of graphic rating scales is usually rather easy, rapid, and straightforward. As with other observational techniques, any rater should have a period of training. In this training, major emphasis should be placed on the observational techniques used. Training two or more raters at once, having them carry on similar ratings, and then analyzing and comparing their results leads to more desirable ratings. The major problems that arise with the use of graphic rating scales are more or less common to all rating methods and are discussed later.

Paired Combinations

The other major type of rating in current use is called the *method of paired comparisons*. The rater compares each individual separately with every other individual to see which of them has more or less of the trait than the other individuals. It is apparent that with a sample of any size, the number of ratings make completion of the rating scale a burden for the rater, and that the analysis of the results becomes very laborious for the user of the scale. If there are 30 individuals being rated, the formula

$$\frac{N\,(N-1)}{2}$$

shows that 435 judgments would have to be made. Even with small numbers there is a tremendous amount of work involved. McCormick and Bachus (1952) conducted an experiment in which 50 workers were to be rated. The 50, paired each with every other, would result in 1,225 pairs. Patterns were developed for each person to be paired with 40, 35, 32, 25, 21, 17, 13, 9, and 7 members of the group. Performance rating indices were computed from these ratings and these indices were correlated with those obtained from the complete pairing. The correlation coefficients ranged from .99 to .86. From this it may be inferred that substantial reductions may be made in the number of pairings without greatly affecting results. For example, the correlation between 50 and 13 pairs per individual was about .93.

In another study, McCormick and Roberts (1952) again used the ratings of 50 employees by foremen, taking all possible pairs. Various patterns were developed, and the number of pairings were eventually reduced from 24 to 8. Reliability coefficients were computed and the following two findings reported:

1. The reliability of ratings obtained by partial pairings tends to decrease systematically with a reduction in the number of pairings.
2. For groups of 50, ratings based upon as few as 16 pairs per individual rater appear relatively stable (around .85). Research since 1952 has made use of McCormick and Roberts' findings, and now scales are so administered with good results.

A rating technique closely related to the paired-comparison method is the *forced-choice* technique. An example most familiar to counselors is the *Kuder Preference Record, Vocational* (1949, 1964). The items of this vocational interest inventory consist of groups of three, or triads, from which the individual selects the one liked most and the one liked least. These two choices must be expressed for each triad item, hence the "forcing." On some other inventories, four items are presented and the subject selects the two that describe him most. There has been a considerable amount of discussion as to whether two, three, four, or more parts are best for each item. To date this has not been decided. Travers (1951) feels that forcing an individual to make a choice about the item which is most like him and that which is least like him puts the rater into an unrealistic position in which he has no logical reason for choice. Wittenborn (1956) criticized Edwards' *Personal Preference Schedule* (1954, 1959) for using only two statements in each forced-choice item. Users of such inventories as the Kuder and the Edwards frequently notice that there is a resistance on the part of some individuals to complete items when they like none of the possible choices or none describes the individual. It is suggested that three or more responses are ideal for forced-choice items when, at the same time, the raters are instructed to select a statement that is most descriptive and one that is least descriptive of himself (Stewart 1945). Jarrett and Sharriff (1956) reported that when subjects were permitted to leave items unanswered in forced-choice scales, many did. They conclude that in the end substantially the same results are obtained as when clients are asked to answer all of the questions. This is open to question on several counts: (1) leaving items unanswered may be a response set or personality trait in itself; (2) leaving items unanswered may reduce reliability and validity; and (3) the effect of leaving items unanswered would vary with the affective nature of the items.

Users of forced-choice techniques claim that the various errors and biases discussed under graphic rating scales are controlled with this type of rating. In paper-and-pencil personality and interest inventories, which are actually self-rating blanks, it has been shown that the usual tendency is for the individual to make himself appear better than he actually is by selecting the items or marking the responses that are most socially acceptable. Frequently, clients consciously or unconsciously distort the results by the response set operating when the inventory is completed. Edwards (1954, 1959) has attempted to control this by having all the items on his inventory rated for social acceptability and by assembling pairs on the basis of equal social acceptability. Sisson (1948) noted that the use of these methods cut down on the ability of individuals to produce outcomes with either desired good or desired bad traits. In other words, the responses are harder to fake. Linden (1958) attempted to demonstrate this by making two experimental forms of the *Guilford-Zimmerman Temperament Survey*, one made up of three-response and the other of two-response items. These, along with the regular form of the inventory, were administered under a real and "fake" situation to a group of university students over the course of a semester. While his conclusions were not clear-cut, he noted a trend that suggested that items in the forced-choice form, especially the three-response items, reduced the influence of bias and made it more difficult to distort than the conventional personality inventory.

Errors in Ratings

Usually, in a discussion of rating methods, several common sources of trouble are noted. Among these are:

1. *The halo effect.* Very briefly, this is the tendency for a rater to rate an individual high on many or all traits merely because the rater considers the individual high on one trait. A student who is considered "good" by a

teacher, that is, who causes the teacher little trouble, is apt to be given spuriously higher ratings on other traits. A worker who plays poker with a foreman or supervisor may also be invalidly rated high on most traits because of the friendship. The halo effect can, of course, work both ways. Another student, for some personal reason, annoys a teacher: ratings of this student by the teacher would probably all be influenced in a negative fashion.

Much has been written on how to avoid the halo effect. The usual recommendation is that individuals should be rated on only one trait at a time. Other techniques, such as paired-comparison and forced-choice techniques, reduce this type of error.

Not all psychologists are in agreement that the halo effect is as important as some would have it. Johnson (1945) subjected a group of correlations obtained from a group of ratings to a factor analysis. In one of his studies, the factor analysis of an industrial merit-rating scale showed that almost all of the variability of the entire scale could be accounted for by one factor. The correlation among the traits is the result of this common factor, rather than the halo effect.

2. *The error of central tendency* is the tendency for raters to avoid a rating at the ends of the continuum. Many judges dislike to make extreme judgments. This results in evaluations near the middle. This can be reduced by avoiding extreme descriptive phrases at the ends of the continuum. Another possible method is to place the descriptive phrases at unequal intervals along the line. Those at the extremes can be closer together than those at the center.

3. *The error of leniency.* This is the tendency for raters to rate all individuals that they know above average or high on desirable or good traits. Guilford (1954) suggests that this type of error can be controlled by using only one unfavorable term and a series of favorable terms such as "fair," "good," "very good," and "excellent."

4. *Other types of errors.* Stockford and Bissell (1949) have discussed a *proximity error*, by which they mean that the closer the position of two traits on a rating scale, the higher the intercorrelation between the traits. Murray (1938) proposed a *contrast error*, by which he meant that raters tend to rate individuals in the opposite direction from the way in which they perceived themselves in reference to a trait. Thus a very precise or punctual individual would tend to rate others less precise or punctual. Raters low in a trait would tend to see others higher than themselves. Another type of error is referred to as the *logical error.* Certain groups of traits sometimes seem to be logically related in the minds of raters. Actually these traits are not related, but raters produce evaluations that are correlated. The effects of all of these different types of error may be reduced by the training of raters or by the use of improved, specific rating methods.

Reliability of Ratings

Since the 1920's, the psychological and educational literature has contained many studies on the reliability of ratings. To review them in detail is of limited value. In general they may be summarized by saying that the earlier reliability coefficients tended to run between .40 and .60. Symonds (1931) concluded that the typical coefficient was .55. Most of the earlier research then proceeded to focus on how ratings could be improved by the training of raters and by increasing the number of raters. It was shown that the reliability of ratings increased with the number of *different* judges; usually, two ratings by the same judge are no more reliable than one. Symonds stated that the pooled judgment of at least eight judges is needed to obtain useful reliability.

However, as Bradshaw (1930) showed, both the number of raters and the trait being rated affect the size of the reliability coefficient. He used a rating scale issued by the American Council on Education, with the results shown in Table 3.1.

Table 3.1

NUMBER OF JUDGES NEEDED TO SECURE
GIVEN RELIABILITY

Trait	.75	.80	.85	.90	.95
How does his manner and appearance affect others?	17	22	32	50	106
Does he need constant prodding or does he go ahead with his work without being told?	3	5	7	10	21
Does he get others to do what he wishes?	5	7	10	16	33
How does he control his emotions?	7	9	13	21	44
Has he a program with a definite purpose in terms of which he distributes his time and energy?	5	6	9	14	29

From F. F. Bradshaw, *The American Council on Education Rating Scale: Its Reliability, Validity and Use*, 1930. Used by permission of the Columbia University Press and the American Psychological Association.

Bradshaw's study very specifically points out the fact that some traits are a lot easier to rate than others. Notice that for the second trait only a small number of raters are necessary to produce pooled judgments of high reliability, whereas for the first trait a large number of raters were required.

Ratings now have much greater reliability than in the past. It is not unusual to have ratings with coefficients of reliability in the .80's and .90's. Such improvements have been brought about by the application of what has been learned about the use and construction of rating scales and by the careful instruction of those who make the ratings.

Validity of Ratings

Validity is studied by seeing how well the results on one of these rating scales agree with some outside measure, referred to as a criterion. Validity is usually expressed in terms of correlation coefficients, in this case the correlation between the ratings and the criterion. These validity coefficients tend to be between .40 and .60. All statements in Chapter 7 about validity coefficients apply to the use of rating scales. As in other types of observation, validity involves that of the observer, that of the individual being observed, and the activity being observed. All of these are involved in reported validities of rating scales.

Use of Rating Scales

It might be well to summarize here the uses that are made of rating scales. As already noted, they are widely used in self-evaluations, in both the areas of interests and of adjustment. This is one of the major uses in education. Another is the use of such scales as a criterion to validate other devices. In the past, rating scales were widely used in education for ratings of adjustment of students to be made by teachers. This use has to a great extent disappeared, except where instruction in making ratings has been developed, and been replaced by more precise and objective methods.

Counselors and teachers frequently use rating scales in filling out application blanks used by universities, business, and industry. Often these blanks conclude with a short scale which summarizes the applicant as a student or possible employee. Many of the reports to parents used in schools also have scales built into them. These reports cover a student's growth in getting along with others, leadership, and other personality variables or traits typically evaluated by teachers by the means of simple rating scales. In industry and the armed services, rating scales are extensively used in the rating of personnel by supervisors. Some corporations have all of their employees rated semi-annually or at least once a year. The results of these ratings are used for promotion.

Other rating scales, besides personality inventories, are useful in self-evaluation. When an individual uses one, he is forced to analyze himself. A certain amount of thought is apt to occur, and it may follow that there is a redirection of effort. Even when the individual does not fill out the scale, but is rated by others, much is to be gained by going over the ratings with the ratee. If this is done in a sound fashion and the ratee can accept the objectives of the ratings, he is frequently encouraged to move toward more socially desirable or effective behavior. The knowledge that there are to be periodic ratings also helps to keep a work group at a higher performance or behavioral level.

Sometimes ratings are combined with brief anecdotes describing the behavior that has been rated. Such a method combines the two types of observation and highlights the need for factual anecdotal records as a basic tool in evaluation and in counseling.

ANECDOTAL RECORDS

Beginning about 1940, teachers and counselors began to give serious attention to the use of the anecdote as a psychological technique (Jarvie and Ellington 1940) for appraising behavior. Since then much has been written about the best ways to use anecdotes and about their limitations.

In its simplest form an anecdote is a record of some incident of significant behavior. Anecdotes are written by anyone who has contact with the individual. The anecdote may be considered as a verbal photograph of behavior, usually recorded on a form provided by the agency. A typical beginning for such a form is a factual statement of exactly what was said or done. Space at the bottom or on the back is usually provided for the observer's interpretation of the behavior. Anecdotes should contain pertinent background information.

Hamalainen (1943) noted that the purpose of anecdotes was to:

1. Furnish the evidence needed for good cumulative records.
2. Substitute specific evidence for vague generalizations about human behavior.
3. Stimulate teachers to look for information that is useful in helping students achieve acceptable adjustments.
4. Contribute toward an understanding of an individual's basic personality.

Before a system of anecdotal records is instituted, a series of staff meetings should be held to discuss the purpose and use of these anecdotes. Understanding and acceptance by the staff are essential before such a system can be undertaken. When this hurdle is overcome, there should be sessions devoted to instruction in the actual writing of anecdotes. Writing anecdotes is not as easy as it sounds. Many staff members are prone to interpret a client's behavior in the light of their own attitudes and values. Actually, then, many anecdotes are more than records of behavior, because they tend to include a mixture of factual information, interpretation, evaluation, and condemnation. In the training session, attention must be directed toward preparing reports of significant behavior which are factual only. Instruction in writing anecdotes should emphasize that positive incidents are as important as negative ones. Frequently a system of anecdotes becomes nothing but a record of all the undesirable or anti-social behavior of individuals. Some agencies have gotten around this by insisting that for every negative anecdote written, a positive one must also be written. Sometimes two different colors of paper are used for each of the two types of anecdotes.

Whenever a group discusses anecdotes, the question is always raised about how many anecdotes should be written and how often. There have been decisions that each observer would write at least one anecdote per individual per week. This is probably not the best way to handle the writing of anecdotes. If the idea can be conveyed that when the observer sees significant behavior it should be recorded, there is no major problem. Of course, there may be cases in which no significant behavior is observed and no anecdotes written. Such a lack of significant incidents is important and should be noted in the records.

After the instruction, there arises an even larger issue about how the anecdotes themselves are to be handled. Unless something is done to treat the recording of anecdotes in a systematic fashion, the system will be mired under the weight of its own paper and paperwork. There are times when a teacher keeps anecdotes for personal use in evaluating students at periodic grade reporting, but this use of anecdotes will not be discussed. Interest centers on how anecdotes are used in an entire agency and how the results are made available and useful to the counselor.

There seems to be no question but that these anecdotes have to be forwarded to a central point. It is logical that this be the counselor's office. Many proposals have been made for the recording and summarizing of anecdotal data. To the writers it seems that one of the best methods is to draw up a summary record sheet on which are various traits, behavior patterns, or agency objectives. After each of these there are three spaces, labeled "weak," "average," and "strong." As the anecdotes arrive at the office, each one is evaluated. It may be noted that any one anecdote may contribute evidence about one or more of these traits or objectives. Then the anecdote is further evaluated as to whether this evidence can be classified as "weak," "average," and "strong" as far as the trait under consideration is concerned. If this is the first anecdote for this individual, then a "1" is placed in the appropriate cell. Each anecdote is classified on a summary sheet for a given individual as it is received. A continuous behavioral record is set up in this way. Growth, or regression, over a period of time is made easily apparent by the summary sheet for a given client.

There frequently arises a problem of how long anecdotes should be retained. There is often concern about this, especially when the material in the anecdote is deemed to be confidential by the writer. As indicated in the previous chapter, confidential material should be kept in a private office. Material gathered from anecdotes which is not confidential should be made part of the permanent record. Perhaps, at the end of a year, the summary sheets can be condensed into a brief verbal account of the individual's behavior over the year, and this shorter summary entered into the cumulative record. No attempt should be made to retain the complete anecdotes. After the initial evaluation of the anecdote has been made, all that remains is a note that the anecdote was evidence of the development or lack of development of a particular trait.

Evaluation of Anecdotal Records

Anecdotes offer continuous evidence of growth and behavior. Instead of the cross-sectional approach provided by many personality inventories and projective techniques, the use of anecdotes offers another longitudinal approach to the study of personality and adjustment. This is the more desirable type of information. Anecdotes include information from many sources: the classroom, playground, cafeteria, clubs, gymnasium, and all other facets of school life. Not only does the information come from many sources in the school or other agency, but it is gathered by varied personnel who have had opportunity to observe a given client. Anecdotal records are inexpensive when compared with other devices used in collecting information about behavior. Finally, it seems that the evidence obtained by the use of anecdotes is highly valid evidence, provided the gatherers of such information have been effectively trained. One of the major problems in obtaining evidence of behavior is that of obtaining valid evidence. Since anecdotes are records of what actually happened or did not happen, their validity is inherent.

On the negative side, there is no question that the writing of anecdotes is time-consuming. Many agency personnel feel they are overworked as it is, and case loads are increasing. However, there is the possibility that the writing of anecdotes might be substituted for some less worthwhile activity that such a worker has to carry on. Perhaps if these colleagues are really aware of the value of anecdotes, they might be more willing to produce and use them. The major obstacle to the use of anecdotes is that they require much staff time for recording and summarizing. This is certainly a valid argument. It is doubtful that ordinary clerical help are of much use here. To the writers, the evaluation and summarizing of these anecdotes are tasks for a trained worker, the counselor. Perhaps in the future, counselors will have less to do with administrative and clerical activities not directly related to counseling and will have more time to devote to their major work. Then certainly the daily batch of anecdotes could be readily disposed of in a brief part of each work day. Smaller case loads for counselors would also be useful in making it possible to set up a functioning system of anecdotal records. A procedure that is actually a modification of the anecdotal-record technique was described by Flanagan (1954), who named it the "critical-incident technique." Here the observer is interested only in certain types of behavior, rather than in behavior in general. The counselor, clinician, or personnel man decides what type of behavior he wants studied. For example, teachers may be requested to note all incidents of behavior that are good or poor examples of leadership, or a specific kind of group participation, or examples of whatever trait is to be studied. In industry, the foreman or supervisor similarly records incidents that illustrate either good or poor performance by each member of his staff.

SITUATIONAL TESTS

In the late 1920's, Hartshorne and May (1928) began to experiment with situational tests. Mostly they were interested in the trait of honesty, and so they set up what appeared to be routine classroom situations in which a subject had an opportunity to cheat if he so desired. For example, they had a test in which subjects were given a piece of paper with a dozen or so circles of varying sizes more or less randomly scattered over it. Subjects were to close their eyes, take a pencil and place a mark in each circle in numerical order, an almost impossible task unless one cheated.

In World War II, the Office of Strategic Services set up situations in which candidates for various types of assignments were tested to see how well they reacted to frustration and pressures. Candidates were given a task such as building a large cube out of pieces of wood resembling Tinker Toys or asked to get out of a difficult situation by getting over a 10-foot wall with a couple of props that would be of little use even if used correctly. Each subject was given one or two assistants, psychologists in disguise, whose actual role was to make the task more difficult for the subject to complete. They gave him poor or incorrect advice, they malingered, they heckled him—they did everything possible to keep him from getting the job done so they could observe his reactions to stress and frustration.

More recently, Bass (1954) has established what he refers to as "leaderless" group discussions for the observation of individuals in small groups. Groups are made up of individuals previously unknown to each other and given a rather mundane topic to discuss. In the course of the discussion various types of social behavior emerge, and soon evidence of leadership, such as cooperation, initiative, and other attributes, begins to emerge. The observer infers that the roles adopted by members of the group will be similar to those they play in natural groups. Stressful situations can also be set up, to observe the behavior of one member of the group in such situations.

OBSERVATION IN PSYCHOMETRY

The place in counseling where observation is very important—and is most frequently conducted in a disorganized fashion—is in the administration of tests. Psychometrics are often carried on by persons with limited training who do not realize the value of descriptions of the client's behavior during the testing and who are often unaware that the test score may be more representative of affect than of any cognitive factor. If it is a test designed to measure cognitive factors, the entire interpretation of the counselor may be distorted by the tester's failure to describe adequately the circumstances under which the test was administered and the condition of the client while taking the test. For these reasons it is essential that psychometrists be trained in observation as well as in the mechanics of test administration.

The person in charge of such training should begin by pointing out how the agency intends to use its tests and the necessity of strict adherence to the instructions given in the test manual. It should be explained that unless the test is administered in as nearly the same way as possible each time, the results might require a different interpretation each time and standardized, comparable results might become impossible. In like fashion, the person learning to administer tests must be shown that the counselor's interpretation of scores is based on how the client felt and responded while taking the test. If a description of the client's comments and behavior during testing accompanies a test score, the interpretation is much clearer to the counselor.

A simple observation, such as the time required to complete the *School and College Ability Test,* may be quite important for counseling inferences. Although the test is timed, most individuals complete it well within the time allowed. The counselor usually assigns a test of this nature when there is some question about the ability of the client to perform under speeded or timed testing conditions. Thus it is important for the counselor to know whether a client took all the time permitted or finished in advance, if a really meaningful interpretation is to be made. For this reason, psychometric observations should begin with an exact record of the day the client took the test, the time the test was started, and when it was completed. Even if this information is not furnished completely in records given to the counselor, it is then available for later reference in the agency files.

Irregularities During Testing

Aside from the more mechanical observations which are an important part of ordinary testing, occasional irregularities in psychometric procedure need to be recorded so that the counselor can account for them when he discusses his interpretation with the client. A simple example of this would be a record of the number of items left unanswered in each scale of the *Guilford-Zimmerman Temperament Survey*. If more than 3 items of the 30 in each scale are left unanswered, it is difficult to tell what the score means. However, if the counselor knows the number left unanswered, a tentative interpretation can be made. Assuming the raw score on the Sociability scale is 14 and that 5 items were left unanswered, the counselor can point out that the client's raw score is somewhere between 14 and 19 (a C-score of 3 to 5). This inference is possible because these items can only add to the raw score of 14 to the extent that they are scoring items; they are never subtracted to get a lower score. Since the profile of this test ranges from negative attributes attached to low scores toward positive attributes signified by high scores, information about omitted items can be quite important. Other examples of irregularities during testing would be administering a test battery in the wrong sequence, using the wrong time limits for a test, giving erroneous instructions prior to the test, and the sudden illness of a client during a test.

Other Factors Affecting Interpretation

In the light of their effect upon interpretation, the counselor should also have observations about the remarks of the client, his attitude, and indications of tension during testing. The physical condition of a client during testing can also be quite significant.

Value of the Client's Remarks

The client's remarks frequently indicate his approach to testing, and in this sense they should become part of the observations accompanying the test score or profile. If the client indicates a facetious approach to testing by joking with companions or ridiculing the tests, this may be a reflection of tension or of a lack of interest in the testing program. Either of these attitudes would affect the counselor's interpretation of the results. Remarks showing a tendency to hurry through tests may be indicative of results which are an underestimate of the client's potential. The client's remarks can also give the counselor a different view of the reasons a client has come for counseling. Because the counselor is more skilled than the psychometrist at establishing rapport, the client may relax and be much less anxious in the interview than during testing. In these ways, a psychometrist's record of the client's remarks during testing may become highly valuable to the counselor.

While it may seem simple to record remarks in a factual way which will recreate the meaning for the counselor, anyone who has attempted to reconstruct a counseling interview from verbatim typescript or tape recordings realizes how inadequate an actual record of remarks can be. The typescript does not show vocal inflection or subtleties of meaning created by tone or emphasis. The tape recording adds these to the counseling record, but still does not contain the meaning added by bodily posture and gestures. Only a sound film of the interview can recreate the scene in enough detail so that full meaning can be inferred, and even then both participants are not shown constantly.

For these reasons the psychometrist needs to give sufficient description of the circumstances in which the remarks occur that the meaning of the remarks is clear to the counselor reading such a record. This means that the psychometrist should be an individual who can describe objectively not only the actual statements of a client and the setting, but who can describe the mood and more obvious feelings of the client at the time. Was the remark a gripe about the test or an attempt to be humorous with the psychometrist? Not only is this ability to infer mood or feeling important to the written observation, but it dictates the proper response by the psychometrist in order to maintain rapport with the client.

Training in making observations about how a client seems to feel ultimately permits a clearer record of the client's physical and psychological condition.

The fact that a client took a test while obviously distressed by a cold or some other physical deterrent may cause the counselor to check such data against other criteria, and possibly arrange a retest if all the data are not congruent. To know that a client was highly irritated by the items on a structured personality inventory may add immeasurably to the counselor's understanding of the test scores and lead to a much less threatening discussion of results with the client. To know that a client is quite disturbed by his failure to finish the tests or by what seems to him to be poor performance will lead the counselor to a deeper insight into reasons the client is coming for help and to a better way of giving such help to the client. Evidence of other anxieties or tensions in the client during testing indicates other limits the counselor needs to place on the interpretation of the test results and on the interview.

These are some of the ways psychometric observations can really enhance the counselor's interpretation of the behavior shown by test scores and perform a real service for the client.

Lack of Agreement Among Test Results

Another kind of observation which the psychometrist should learn to carry on is that of noting the extent of agreement among test scores which research and counseling experience have shown to be related. A client may have a standard score of 50 on the Dentist Scale, 45 on the Osteopath Scale, and 5 on the Physician Scale of the *Strong Vocational Interest Blank for Men*. Both statistical research and counseling experience have shown that these three scores tend to be high or low *together*. When the psychometrist notes that the Physician Scale is not in agreement with the other two, steps should be taken to check this observation. The obvious first step is to rescore the three scales to see that they have been properly scored. (This assumes that the initial scoring included a preliminary scanning of the answer sheet to see that the items were marked properly by the client.) In most cases, such a procedure will show an error in scoring. Occasionally the lack of agreement has explanation only in the unique behavior of a given client. Persons training psychometrists in observation should be aware of common checks for agreement among test results and point them out to the persons being trained. Through efficient observations of this nature, much valuable counseling time can be saved.

OBSERVATION IN THE INTERVIEW

While the counselor's observation in the interview is continuous in effective counseling, it is of primary importance in the initial interview. When added to information from records, it is fundamental to the counselor's analysis and to his tentative hypotheses about the client. The initial impressions of both client and counselor can set the structure of future interviews. This first meeting often determines success or failure. The counselor needs to demonstrate to the client an ability to observe his behavior and integrate it into a coherent series of reflections and summaries which show that two-way communication is taking place. In this way, the client's confidence and respect are established and he can participate in the interviews in a more meaningful way.

Starting with such obvious factors as appearance and dress, the counselor notes and records vocabulary level and grammar, alertness of reaction to his statements, evidence of social sensitivity, ability to make self-evaluations in societal terms, balance of internal and external frames of reference, nervous mannerisms and degree of tension, flexibility or rigidity, and obvious omissions or gaps in the topics discussed. He also makes inferences about the client's goals and values. The counselor is trying to determine the congruence of the client's statements and his observed behavior. The client's level of awareness of self and environment will be a vital factor in the selection of the tools and procedures the counselor will use. The question to be answered by these observations is, "How do the data already available coincide with what this client says about himself?"

Client's Appearance

There are two reasons why an observation of the client's dress and appearance is important to the counselor. Dress can show awareness of and concern for reactions of others. It can also indicate how the client feels about himself. His dress shows the amount of conformity the client is willing to express and the importance he places on the opinion of others. For example, suppose in a given school girls wear hose and boys wear jackets and ties. The girl who does not wear stockings and the boy who comes to school without a tie are differing enough from the group so that the counselor needs to know why. Is it because the client is unaware of these rules of behavior? Are parents the cause of this difference? Is the client's difference in dress an expression of hostility toward the group? Do his long hair and beard represent an attempt to express conformity, or hostility toward authority? These are some of the questions prompted by such differences, and the counselor needs to seek answers to them if he is to be of maximal help to the client.

The client's general appearance may also be indicative of his feelings about himself. A sloppily dressed client is frequently expressing feelings of inferiority. Lack of concern about external appearance may be reflecting inner turmoil with which the client needs help. In many instances the counselor can secure cues to the success of counseling by observing progressive change in the client's dress or appearance. The counselor begins, in the initial interview, to establish the level of client norms for these external evidences of behavior, and develops through succeeding interviews a picture of how the client conforms to the group, how he differs in dress, and the meaning this has in the over-all picture of client behavior.

The Client's Vocabulary

The next aspect of the client's behavior which evidences itself in the interview is the way he communicates with the counselor. How extensive is his vocabulary, and what level of general intelligence does it indicate? What does his grammar indicate about his family's socioeconomic level? How does his vocabulary indicate the direction and extent of his interests? What does it show about the nature and amount of his reading?

The counselor who wishes to use the client's vocabulary as an indicator would do well to be familiar with one or more of the common lists of difficult words, such as that found in the *Thorndike-Century Junior Dictionary*. In such a list the number at the end of the definition indicates the difficulty of the word; usually, the lower the number, the easier the word.

A counselor gradually develops the ability to evaluate vocabulary and make inferences about the academic ability of clients from such evidence. This may agree with other evidence from records and biographical data, or it may indicate a need for individual testing in a further attempt to clarify the evaluation. The client's grammar and vocabulary may be a good indication of his socioeconomic status and give the counselor cues about family background which need to be investigated during the interview. If the counselor keeps in mind the general areas of vocabulary measured by a test like the *Michigan Vocabulary Test* and classifies the client's vocabulary into these areas, it is possible to develop a tentative pattern of his interests. Then it will be possible to get more detailed information about the way in which the client acquired his vocabulary. Was it through reading, through audio-visual activities, or through actual participation in gang or street activity? What does the client read, and how extensive is his reading? In the present culture so many vocabulary building activities are of an audio-visual nature or even nonschool-oriented that spoken vocabulary is not necessarily a measure of reading or writing skills. The counselor needs to clarify this, because a client with a reading or English handicap may function well in an interview but not in a classroom situation. The same client may be much more alert in the interview, where there is no struggle to understand the written word or to spell it. This alertness of the client may result in completely different data from those secured in the classroom or on standardized tests. A client who likes people but who does not like school is apt to be much more alert in an interview than a classroom. Conversely, the emotionally disturbed client may present a poorer picture in the interview than in the classroom, because this is a divergence from ordinary behavior requiring a greater effort to produce integrated behavior.

Client's Social Skills

The initial interview presents the counselor with an opportunity to observe the social sensitivity of the client. Is he poised and comfortable with the counselor, or ill at ease and unsure of how to behave? Does he make an effort to help the counselor develop a warm, friendly atmosphere, or must the counselor carry all the responsibility? Evidence that the client is aware of the counselor's feelings and of the physical comfort of the counselor can be an indicator that the client is able to relate well to people. Real social sensitivity is directly related to a client's ability to evaluate himself in societal terms and to evidence of a balance of internal and external frames of reference.

The client whose conversation and thoughts center on himself to the exclusion of others is demonstrating too much concern about personal activities for good mental health. Good mental health usually requires a balance of interests and activities which involve others as well as oneself. The client who is preoccupied with himself in the interview may be aware of societal values but frequently unable to apply them in self-evaluation. This is usually because there is too much threat to the self in facing these issues, and not because of fear of the counselor's reaction. As the counselor helps the client to understand the behavior in question, the client is able to reduce his concern about himself and develop more interest in relationships with others. This process eventually produces greater awareness of the activities that must be carried on in effective social relationships, and starts the client toward learning and practicing these skills. Before such a process can be initiated, the counselor must observe the present status of the client and decide what steps to undertake to help the client make any changes indicated *and desired.* By evaluating the client's behavior toward the counselor in the initial interview and later in other relationships with the agency staff, the counselor is able to form tentative hypotheses about the client's social sensitivity and ability to relate to others.

Client's Tension

The process of evaluating the client's social skills leads to a related facet of his behavior. This is the first opportunity the counselor has to observe nervous mannerisms and the ways a given client indicates and responds to tension. The female client who becomes preoccupied with a topic and begins to twist her hair around her finger, or chew on her glasses or her pencil, may be reflecting other behavioral needs than those she is describing to the counselor. In like fashion, the male client who clenches the arm of the chair or perspires considerably may be indicating tensions he is trying to conceal or control. The counselor needs to know how each client responds to tension in order to do an effective job of helping that client understand himself. The counselor also needs to have some concept of the reasons why a client is responding in this fashion. This means he must be able to distinguish between less important mannerisms, like autistic gestures, and the more important evidences the client displays of being under tension. Then the counselor is in a position to act to reduce this tension or to assume that the client is capable of handling it without help. The authors see one of the chief functions of the counselor as controlling the amount of threat and tension in the interview. By doing this, the counselor controls the climate or atmosphere in which the client functions and produces optimal learning conditions. Only through observation directed toward this end can the counselor begin to form estimates of the degree of tension present at any given moment.

Interview Topics

Usually the degree of tension is directly related to the topics the client is discussing at that time, although pauses for thought may also be fraught with considerable tension and the omission of topics may show an area capable of arousing anxiety within the client. Thus the counselor needs to note the relationship between the various topics discussed with the client and the amount of threat these topics present. If a client is able to talk about relationships with every member of the family except one, this may be a cue that such an omission reflects a topic the client is afraid to consider. It could also indicate that the family member omitted is of little importance to the client, but this is less likely.

The topics covered in the interview also reflect the client's goals and values. The client who constantly refers to jobs, income, and the things that could be done with money is presenting different goals and values than the client who is engrossed in scientific activities such as experiments in a home chemical laboratory or in collecting and classifying beetles. The client who shows an avid interest in mechanical activities, such as building and flying model planes or reconditioning old cars, is evidencing goals and values in considerable contrast to the client who is interested in people and in helping them through activities of a social-service nature. These interests reflect behavioral tendencies as well as probable educational and vocational choices. The counselor should investigate them to see if they are fundamental to the client's personality or temporary goals and values foisted upon the client by others. No matter what the topics discussed in the initial interview, they reveal something about the personality of the client. The counselor, by observation and classification, can collect data of value for diagnosis and counseling further with the client.

A comprehensive observation of the extent and nature of topics covered in the interview can also contribute to a tentative hypothesis about the flexibility or rigidity of the client. If the client is rigid, this limits the approach of the counselor and the tools and techniques which can be used to help the client. If the client is more flexible, as indicated by the topics which can be accepted and discussed in the interview, the counselor has less difficulty in controlling threat. It is easier then to create a conversational climate in which the client is freed to make positive changes in behavior, whether these changes are clarification of educational or vocational choices or changes in attitudes and values.

These are some of the ways in which observations in the initial interview can contribute to a more successful choice of ways in which the counselor can help the client deal with problems. They begin with an estimate of the readiness of the client for counseling, and they progress to the counselor's evaluation of the congruence between the content and the meaning of the client's statements, and how this agrees with other data. These observations, carried on in systematic fashion with the understanding and cooperation of the client, can lead to a diagnosis which allows for more effective procedures and more effective modification of behavior by the client. The more time the counselor spends in observation in the initial interview, the more time the client has to contribute information of value to the counseling process, because the counselor's understanding of the client's behavior usually develops more from the client's remarks than from the counselor's comments. This is one of the chief purposes of the initial interview.

SUMMARY

The observations used by the counselor, whether made personally or secured from others, are only useful to the extent that they are based on factual information. The observer must be capable of making realistic, factual observations, and be trained in proper observational procedures. To be valid, observations must center on determining specifically what is to be observed and the methods by which this is to be accomplished. The observations of greatest value to counseling are those secured through rating scales and anecdotes, and through those recorded during psychometrics and the initial interview. The counselor needs to convey to other observers the kind of information needed about client behavior and the way in which this information will be used.

REFERENCES

Bass, B. M. 1954. The leaderless group discussion. *Psychol. Bull.* 51:465–92.

Bradshaw, F. F. 1930. The American Council on Education rating scale. Its reliability, validity, and use. *Archives of Psychol.* 18:1–80.

Edwards, A. L. 1954, 1959. *Personal Preference Schedule manual.* New York: The Psychological Corporation.

Flanagan, J. C. 1954. The critical incident technique. *Psychol. Bull.* 51:327–58.

Guilford, J. P. 1954. *Psychometric methods.* New York: McGraw-Hill Book Company.

Hamalainen, A. F. 1943. *An appraisal of anecdotal records.* New York: Bureau of Publications, Teachers College, Columbia University.

Hartshorne, H., and May, M. C. 1928. *Studies in deceit.* New York: The Macmillan Company.

Jarrett, R. F., and Sherriff, A. C. 1956. Forced-choice versus permissive techniques in obtaining responses to attitude questionnaires. *J. Gen. Psychol.* 55:203–206.

Jarvie, L. L., and Ellingston, M. 1940. *A handbook of the anecdotal behavior journal.* Chicago: University of Chicago Press.

Johnson, D. M. 1945. A systematic treatment of judgment. *Psychol. Bull.* 45:193–224.

Kleinmuntz, P. 1967. *Personality measurement.* Homewood, Ill.: Dorsey Press.

Kuder, G. F. 1949, 1964. *The Kuder Preference Record manual.* Chicago: Science Research Associates.

Linden, J. D. 1958. The development and comparative analysis of two forced-choice forms of the *Guilford-Zimmerman Temperament Survey.* Ph.D. Dissertation, Purdue University.

McCormick, E. J., and Bachus, J. A. 1952. Paired comparison ratings, I: The effects of ratings on reduction in the number of pairs. *J. Appl. Psychol.* 36:123–27.

————, and Roberts, W. K. 1952. Paired comparison ratings, II: The reliability of ratings based upon partial pairing. *J. Appl. Psychol.* 36:188–92.

Murray, H. A. 1938. *Explorations in personality.* New York: Oxford University Press.

O.S.S. Assessment Staff. 1948. *Assessment of men: Selection of personnel for the Office of Strategic Services.* New York: Holt, Rinehart and Winston, Inc.

Sisson, E. D. 1948. Forced-choice: The new army rating. *Personnel Psychol.* 1:365–81.

Stewart, N. 1945. Methodological investigation of the forced-choice technique, utilizing the Officer Description and the Officer Evaluation Blanks. AGO, PRS Report no. 701.

Stockford, L., and Bissell, H. W. 1949. Factors involved in establishing a merit-rating scale. *Personnel.* 26:94–118.

Symonds, P. M. 1931. *Diagnosing personality and conduct.* New York: Appleton-Century.

Travers, R. W. M. 1951. A critical review of the validity and the rationale of forced-technique. *Psychol. Bull.* 48:62–70.

Wittenborn, J. R. 1956. A review of the *Edwards Personal Preference Schedule.* *J. Consult. Psychol.* 20:321–24.

4

The Initial
Encounter with
the Client

The initial encounter focusing on the needs of a normal client has at least four primary purposes. One of these is to establish a good working relationship between the counselor and the client which will last throughout counseling. Another is to validate and expand the developmental data about the client collected prior to the interview. A third is to observe the client directly and to collect information which will show his feelings about values, interests, attitudes, and goals. Last, this first meeting is used to establish the client's needs and the structure within which counseling will take place.

Interaction between the counselor and the client is the basic process underlying everything else in counseling. It tends to be a function of movement toward the answers to three simple, basic questions each must answer. These questions determine the personal and counseling frame of reference of both client and counselor:

1. Who am I?
2. How did I get this way?
3. Where do I want to go from here?

For the counselor, the answers to these questions determine the personal and professional values which underlie his orientation to counseling and which influence his proficiency. As the counselor understands and accepts these percepts, he makes them a part of his professional self. Blocher (1966, pp. 13–41) discusses the imperative nature of the counselor's responsibility to delineate and organize his personal and professional frame of reference. He functions more effectively when he is aware of his goals and his limits in counseling. Rogers (1967, p. 90) points out that the extent to which counselors are able to empathize and become congruent with the client's behavior in the interview is a major factor in the progress the client makes.

An interesting analysis of interviews by Truax (1963) judged clients more improved when their therapists were rated high on empathy, unconditional positive regard, and "self-congruence." Conversely, clients whose therapists were low on these three variables seemed to regress. This would offer support for the contention that the counselor's ability to establish clear, empathic communication and to focus on his client's behavior rather than on his own problems is essential to effective counseling. The counselor can then be more natural. In turn, the counselor's ability to focus on the client more completely affects the client's behavior, positive change throughout the counseling process, and the client's decisions.

For the usual client, the clarification of answers to the three questions listed above is the major reason he needs help from the counselor. As the client begins to understand, accept, and use information about his perceived self, he perceives also the goals he should be able to achieve; then the counseling process becomes not only an exploration of these goals, but their blending into the client's way of living. It is an exploration of what Tyler (1969, pp. 21–32) refers to as the "psychology of possibilities."

The counseling process is dependent on the consistent awareness, organization, and acceptance of the values of both counselor and client if the client is to be helped to become more aware of the conflicts or uncertainties which created the need for counseling and to carry on the decisions related to reorganization of behavior that is the primary purpose of counseling. Thus, the self-awareness of both counselor and client is a major factor in readiness for counseling. It involves a recognition of goals and possibilities as well as the desire to modify or to achieve them. As Blocher (1966, p. 157) has pointed out, until goals are formulated, counseling is ineffective.

COUNSELOR'S VALUES

Both Fiedler (1950) and Strupp (1955) have discussed the effect of professional experience upon the therapist, indicating that it reduces differences among therapeutic orientations. Strupp, and later Rogers (1967), further emphasize the effect of the therapist's personality upon the therapeutic process. Each of these three writers indicates that the effect of the neophyte's personality is more variable than that of the experienced therapist, and that variability in professional behavior does affect the client's choices and his progress.

The importance to the counselor of research data derived in a therapeutic setting must be questioned, however. Most of his clients are not concerned with the extensive personality changes inherent in the therapeutic situation. "Who am I?" to these clients means, "How am I different from other people in ways which will affect the life choices I must make?" This does not usually involve deep therapy, but rather clarification, synthesis, and a different emphasis of known data.

Hence, the effect of what Rogers (1957, 1961) has termed the "congruence" of the counselor may be infinitely greater to the client who is less preoccupied with internal problems and more concerned with his interaction with his environment. Rogers (1967, p. 76) has also said that the attitudes of both the counselor and the client become stabilized early and remain consistent throughout the relationship. Bandura (1956) has found a significant negative relationship between the anxiety level of the therapist and his therapeutic competence. How much more important, then, are the counselor's understanding and acceptance of himself in a counseling setting!

Thus, the emphasis upon the personal experiences of the counselor and the values these experiences have developed within him center about his interaction with his environment. Every reaction the counselor has ever had—to family, school, church, and community—has produced unique effects that determine the personal values with which he enters the interview. The depth of his insight into, and acceptance of, these reactions, and their subsequent effect upon his personal values, in turn determine the control he can exercise over them during his interactions with a given client. The vividness of a counselor's feelings about individuals with certain patterns of behavior, or certain ethnic, religious, or racial characteristics, can influence his interaction with them. The values the counselor attaches to religion or race and the objectivity with which the counselor can view these values limit his acceptance of differing values or characteristics in the client. The self-control the counselor exercises is part of the climate in which his client functions.

The counselor's personal values not only limit his relationship with a client in counseling; they also determine the kind and amount of formal learning he brings to his professional practice. If the counselor's frame of reference is in the authoritarian direction, a more permissive orientation will not only be somewhat objectionable, but usually professionally impossible to understand or achieve. If his personality leads him to work toward being a Rogerian, the eclectic use of counseling tools and techniques becomes difficult and sometimes impossible. The counselor's professional orientation is dependent upon who he has become, and therefore on what professional practices are possible without violating his basic personality structure. The degree to which he has been able to clarify, organize, and control his personal values influences the effectiveness of his innate potential for learning and, therefore, how much he learns about counseling as well as what he learns.

Consistency in the exercise of the counselor's personal and professional values as he works with clients whose behavior is within the normal range may be more important than the nature of his values. Rogers (1967, p. 92) says that "whether we are working with psychotics or normals, delinquents or neurotics, the most essential ingredient for change will be found in the (consistent) attitudinal qualities of the person-to-person relationship." Observation in classrooms and counseling settings also supports such an hypothesis. A given client learns in a variety of settings, but usually in the direction and to the degree that *he* determines. The counselor seems to function more to supply a climate that promotes or retards this learning than a climate that creates or manages it.

The counselor's experiences and values culminate in his choice of an orientation to counseling which is in harmony with them. He may elect an eclectic approach and borrow from many tools and processes, or' he may limit himself to one orientation. He may feel that a directive approach is most suitable to him, and so explore the possibilities offered by behavioral counseling or by some aspects of computerized counseling. He may choose to be quite permissive and elect a phenomenological approach.

The growing orientation to behavioral counseling (Krumboltz 1966) has brought a different focus to the consideration of counseling as a learning process. Knowledge of psychological conditioning has been brought to bear on the counselor's timing of reinforcement tailored to a given client's needs, so that that client can have the strongest support possible in modifying behavior. Various tools and processes have been adapted for behavioral counseling; for example, having clients read selected material, listen to audio tapes, watch films or video tapes, or use programmed instruction. Other procedures have been attempted to reinforce behavioral change, such as the "behavioral contract," role playing, a modification of Moreno's psychodrama called the "role shift," reemphasis of the timing of the counselor's "leads" or cues, and an adaptation of classical conditioning applications to counseling (Wolpe 1958; Wolpe, *et al.* 1964). Behaviorism seems most promising in areas of counseling either nonthreatening to the self, or when it is not essential that decisions be made entirely by the client.

On the other hand, the phenomenological approach to counseling seems more important when the client's self-enhancement is the focus, or when effective decisions have to be based on the client's understanding and acceptance of his environment and when the effect of his decisions upon that field need to be paramount in his awareness.

The counselor's choice of approaches will also vary according to whether the client's problem is primarily cognitive or affective and how the counselor perceives the client's values.

Success in an initial encounter may be determined less by the specific nature of the counselor's personal and professional values than by the degree to which he is able to control and use them in a systematic fashion. The counselor's personal needs and values must be consistent with the professional frame of reference he has developed during the theoretical and applied phases of his educational preparation, if his bias is to be controlled. The way these are blended into the personality of the counselor determines the approach he will take to establish a working relationship with the client, and will also determine many of the things which do or do not occur during their interactions.

CLIENT'S VALUES

In the same sense that the counselor's values are based on all the personal experiences that have preceded his initial meeting with a given client, the client's values are based upon the cultural forces he has experienced prior to such a meeting. Hall (1966) discusses this as man's perception of social and personal space, which he calls "proxemics." The impact which the client's perceptions of his racial origin, religion, family status, and other cultural factors have upon his development is tempered further by the effect his perceptions of himself, arising from his socioeconomic and geographic position, have upon them and upon his interactions within the varied cultural subgroups of which he is part.

Whether the American black is poor, of average income, or in an upper-income group determines in part his experiences as an individual in the United States. So does the section of the country in which he lives and whether he is an urban or a rural dweller. If he is able to fit easily into the general culture or must preserve his self-concept as a militant contributes to these forces acting upon him. The American Indian living in Oklahoma experiences a considerably different interaction with his culture than if he were living in New York State or on a reservation in the Southwest. The American of Puerto Rican, Cuban, or Mexican descent who is a physician, lawyer, or businessman also has different life encounters than does the slum dweller. The Catholic Irish or Italian American living in metropolitan Boston or New York has quite different experiences that one living in a small Southern or Midwestern community. The American of Jewish origin lives a different life than the American Gentile. The client who comes from a large family has experiences not possible for one who is an only child.

All these cultural dimensions interact to produce the unique perceptions of self and others that create the idiosyncratic value system of a given client. And his values and experiences, in turn, determine whether the client is apt to seek counseling or has to be sought and taught the usefulness of the counseling process in meeting his needs.

Amos (Amos and Grambs 1968, pp. 13–28) lists some of the problems of clients in low-income homes: cultural isolation, geographic isolation, minority group membership, unconnected physical and psychological disabilities, physical deprivation, great mobility and restlessness, poor housing and marginal living, inadequate social protection and social life, little parental encouragement to prepare for living, inability to communicate effectively, and immature or inadequate financial knowledge and practices.

The client coming from a low-income home usually has more immediate and temporary goals than the client from a middle-income home. School to him may not be seen as a means of upward mobility or of fulfilling a family expectancy, but rather as something to be endured until he is able to leave school, or work—which all too frequently means being on welfare because he lacks the skills to acquire and hold the jobs that are available. A job is seen as a way to purchase immediate benefits, not as a career. Often there must be an intermediate person who gets him to the counselor and tries to help the counselor understand that the values of such a client differ from those of the college-bound client or the client intending to follow a family pattern of union membership and middle-income employment.

As the client learns to organize, express, and accept or change these values during counseling, his life becomes more meaningful. He begins to spell out the nature of the answer to "Who am I?" and "How did I get this way?" In his interaction with the counselor he learns to be free enough to revise his values and to decide what he wishes to become. This is a major function of the counseling relationship.

CREATING A COUNSELING RELATIONSHIP

The first move in an initial meeting, after the client has been greeted and made physically comfortable, is to ascertain what he may have had in mind. During this discussion, a brief general description by the counselor will serve to make the client more aware of the possibilities available through counseling. Making the client aware that the counselor has taken the time to learn the key data about his development can facilitate this procedure. The counselor's attempt to make the client comfortable and somewhat relaxed is the first step in developing a good relationship.

The Counseling Relationship

The most important element in counseling is the relationship established between the counselor and the client. Tyler (1969, p. 61) calls this the first objective of an initial interview. Sometimes it seems that this relationship alone, without any of the other tools and procedures at the counselor's disposal, can account for much of the change that takes place in the client. Rogers (1967, p. 92) says that the research he discusses "would seem to justify an intensive focus on the interpersonal relationship as perhaps *the* most important element in bringing about personality change in any group" (of clients). Creating this relationship is a complex matter difficult to define, and Tyler (1969, p. 53) makes the important point that it is different (unique) with each client.

It is a professional relationship, different from that which exists between friends or relatives. It is based on the client's understanding that the counselor is an interested but relatively unbiased person with professional preparation and experience which fit him to help with the client's problems. It varies with the client's state and the nature of his problems. Again, Rogers (1967, 75–76) has said that neurotic clients seem to focus on self-exploration, while psychotic clients seem to focus on the formation of relationships. On the counselor's part, the relationship is based on a sincere desire to help by accepting the client as a person worthy of respect and as a person who possesses unused capacities for change when the counselor creates a climate where this change can begin. The relationship starts in the initial meeting, with the counselor and client learning to know one another.

Usually the client comes to this first meeting with little notion of what actually will occur. He wants to know how the counselor will try to help, but he may be quite reluctant to relax and discuss the circumstances which have culminated in this meeting with the counselor. The counselor is trying to put the client at ease, so that discussion and learning can take place. The counselor wants to learn in what ways it may be possible to help the client. The client wants to learn how the counselor can help and what this help will involve. He frequently also wants to know *why* the counselor wants to help. Each needs to learn enough about the behavior of the other so that these questions can be answered. Moreover, the behavior of each will be modified by the goals set by both client and counselor.

The counselor may begin by observing the ordinary courtesies. After introductions, he invites the client to sit down. Then he may talk about any interests noted in the information collected prior to the initial interview which do not appear to have a strong negative emotional value to the client. Usually some light remark or humorous comment begins this conversational part of the interview. The counselor's general rule in phrasing comments or in asking questions is ordinarily, "How would I like someone to say this to me?" or "How would I feel if someone said this to me in this way?" This is a good method of judging the amount of threat involved in comments and questions.

After the client has been made reasonably comfortable physically and psychologically, the counselor begins the process of creating a climate of confidence and trust. Whether it is called "rapport" or a "warm, permissive atmosphere," the relationship must be based on mutual respect and willing cooperation. This involves two moves on the part of the counselor. The first is a statement about the persons who will have access to the information discussed. This can have considerable effect on the topics discussed. The second is a brief description of the counseling facilities available to the client and the mechanics of the processes that will be carried out during counseling.

While this is going on, the counselor is also conveying to the client, by everything that is said and done, that the client is being accepted as a person worthy of respect and help. The counselor must therefore be able to like most people well enough to convey this impression. If he cannot feel this way about a client, that client should be transferred to another counselor immediately, for the counselor's negative feelings will pervade the interaction and obstruct the development of the counseling relationship. Whether his awareness of it is at a high level or not, the client will sense dislike and fail to react positively. For this reason the counselor needs to identify, at the initial meeting, those clients with whom it is not possible to work. It is often possible to reduce negative feelings if the counselor can recognize that the client acts in a given way only to maintain his present self-concept. It is the unusual client who deliberately acts at variance with society. The acts of the client are carried out because they are the best possible choice he can perceive at that moment. If they are unsuitable, the counselor must help the client to perceive this and, through an understanding of the conflicting values which cause them, to want to make a change to behavior more in harmony with society and with a changed self-concept, for this is the focus of the counseling process. As Hahn and MacLean (1955) have pointed out, it is the job of the counselor to open new doors with the client so that alternative solutions to problems are evolved. However, the counselor should never try to push the client through these doors.

To accomplish these goals, the counselor must help the client gain an increasing capacity to solve problems. The experienced counselor will readily admit that most clients are better able to solve their problems than would be expected. The client may not be keenly aware of it, but actually he knows more about his own personal attitudes toward the environment and about his interaction with it than the counselor can hope to know after a number of sessions. The acceptance by the counselor of the client's capacity to solve his problems in a fashion most suitable to himself is the essence of a sound counseling relationship. It makes possible the sharing of responsibility by the client and the counselor in the interviews. Furthermore, it makes no difference whether the client is 7 or 70, if this concept is used.

Counselor's Responsibility

The major responsibility of the counselor at the initial meeting is thus to prevent a situation where the client is so threatened that it is not possible for him to function well. At the same time some pressure must be present, or the client will fail to progress. This manipulation of threat and anxiety by the counselor presupposes training and experience of such a nature that he can estimate closely the amount of threat a client can handle, and increase or decrease it by the techniques used in the interview. Rogers (1961) has pointed out that mere recognition of feeling can frequently make those feelings easier to bear and to discuss. Often if a counselor says to a client, "You find it pretty difficult to talk about this," this simple indication of awareness of the client's anxiety operates to reduce the anxiety.

The acceptance of the client and of his statements in a matter-of-fact way can reduce the amount of threat the client is experiencing. The counselor's choice of words, as well as the unspoken attitudes he imparts, can have considerable effect on the increase or decrease of threat. To say to a client, "You are very determined," is much different, in the amount and kind of feeling it produces, than to say, "You are pretty stub-

born about this." The term "resolute" is a synonym for both, yet "determined" and "stubborn" have positive and negative meanings, respectively,
to most clients. The proper choice of words and attitudes expressed is
especially important in the initial meeting because it helps set the tone
of the relationship between the client and counselor, a tone which usually
pervades succeeding meetings.

A simple thing like looking interested in what the client is saying
increases the client's participation. If the counselor nods or tries in some
other way to show understanding of what the client is trying to say, this
seems to make it possible for most clients to relax and talk or act more
freely. Conversely, if the counselor looks out the window, stares at the
bridge of the client's nose, or even just closes his eyes, the client may
think the counselor uninterested, and become tense and have difficulty
in talking. For this reason the counselor needs to show in every way possible that the data the client is presenting are the primary center of his
attention. This in turn focuses the client's attention on the material being
discussed. Whether in an elementary school, as described by Hill and
Luckey (1969), or carried on with older clients, the purpose is the same.
As Tyler (1956) has pointed out, these same techniques of acceptance
also help to prevent reinforcement of the negative feelings the client
may be expressing. Because they convey to a client only that the counselor understands what is said, they permit the expression of client feelings without signifying the counselor's approval.

In the initial meeting, the phrasing of questions is of utmost importance. Usually the counselor wants the client to talk and expand on data
already available. Questions designed to accomplish this must be precise
and properly worded. One kind of phrasing will produce a "yes" or "no"
answer. Another kind causes the client to talk at considerable length. The
counselor must decide which is desirable and must phrase his questions
to produce the desired result. For example, the counselor may wish to
ask why the client came for counseling. If the counselor says, "Would you
care to tell me why you came here?" the client frequently responds by
telling why he or his parents came to a given city, agency, or school.
Whether this misinterpretation on the part of the client is a function of
emotional factors is immaterial. The concern here is with phrasing. If
the counselor says, "Would you mind telling me why you came to see
me?"—it produces a more precise phrasing which would secure the desired response. The function of the counselor in asking questions and in
making responses in the interview should not be just to make these statements understood. It should be to make questions and responses impossible to *misunderstand.*

Robinson (1950) has attempted to classify the counselor's remarks under the following headings, which he refers to as "techniques of leading":

1. Silence
2. Acceptance
3. Restatement
4. Clarification
5. Summary clarification
6. Approval
7. General leads ("What do you mean?")
8. Tentative analysis
9. Interpretation
10. Urging
11. Depth interpretation
12. Rejection
13. Assurance
14. Introducing new (and apparently unrelated) aspects of a problem

Three instruments used to evaluate the counselor's remarks in client-centered counseling are presented in Rogers (ed.; 1967). In this work, Truax (pp. 555–79) discusses a scale for rating empathy and one for rating "unconditional positive regard," while Kiesler (pp. 581–84) presents a scale for rating the counselor's "congruence."

Some leads which should produce answers of considerable length are:

"Tell me about the kind of subjects and activities you like in school." (This can be compared with the grades shown on the counselor's copy of the client's transcript.)

"Tell me how you got along with your brothers and sisters." (If this is asked toward the beginning of the meeting, it will usually produce only positive statements. If it is asked toward the end, it will produce both negative and positive responses.)

"What sort of things do you like to do for fun?" (This usually leads to statements which permit the counselor to ask further questions about group activities and solitary activities.)

"What sort of thinking have you been doing about the kind of jobs you would like to have?" (The counselor can check this against records of previous work experience, and against measured and stated interest.)

"Tell me about the things you do for fun that have interested you most." (This could offer leads into discussion of possible educational and job considerations. It could also offer leads to areas of reeducation for new jobs for the client with a disability or from a disadvantaged group.)

"Tell me about any suggestions your physician may have made about limitations on the kind of work and recreation you should consider." (In general the use of a question beginning with "Can you tell me . . ." produces a response at length. If the counselor had said, "Has your physician made any suggestions about the kind of work and recreation you should consider?" the client has a chance to give a "yes" or "no" answer.)

Conversely, if the counselor desires short answers, the same questions should probably be phrased as follows:

"What subjects and activities do (did) you like in school?" (If the counselor asks, "How do you feel about school?" the client is apt to reply by asking for clarification of the question.)
"How do you get along at home?" (this usually produces the response, "Fine!")
"What do you do for recreation?"
"What kind of job would you like?"
"What hobby do you like most?"

Thus the way the counselor phrases his leads determines much of the client's response. This is a vital part of the method by which the client's reaction is fostered so that the meeting can be more useful to him.

Client's Responsibility

The client also has some responsibilities in the counseling relationship. The first of these has been described by Robinson (1950) as "counseling readiness." This readiness for counseling involves two things. The first is the knowledge that some of his behavior is unsatisfactory; the second is a sincere, recognized desire to change. In addition to a willingness to change on the part of the client, he must accept the counselor's ability to promote such a change. The counselor can increase readiness for counseling, but he cannot create it. This is why it is usually easier to work with clients who come voluntarily for counseling. They tend to make more rapid progress than those referred by some authoritative source or by support personnel. Persons referred to a counselor in a ghetto agency may pose similar problems to those referred by a teacher or a school administrator. They usually perceive the counselor as another person in authority who will try to "manage" them for *his* purposes. It may be considerable time before they begin to realize that the counselor sees them as persons and is willing to help them find their solutions to problems. Readiness for counseling, in such cases must be fostered or stimulated.

Much has been made, in discussions of the interview, about the need for "frankness and honesty." Perhaps a clearer and more accurate term would be "candor," which implies frankness and an unreserved relationship without the value judgment implied by the term "honesty." Most clients are not deliberately deceitful, but they may be under too much tension to be completely candid with the counselor—or with themselves, for that matter. Until several meetings have occurred, the relationship may not be established enough for the client and counselor to be really candid with each other. The client actually may be more concerned with hiding from himself than with revealing himself candidly to the counselor. It takes time for the client to learn that the counseling session is one where it is no longer necessary to hide from himself or from another. Until this insight occurs, it is difficult for him to examine his goals, values, and attitudes and to realize that the situation is free from criticism or the need for fear. In the initial meeting, both client and counselor must curtail other activities and concentrate on this aspect of the counseling relationship.

The client has to recognize that the topics being discussed are not the responsibility of the counselor. A part of the development of a successful counseling relationship is the working out of these areas of responsibility between the client and the counselor. The topics discussed, as well as the extent of the discussion, are usually indicated as the responsibility of the client. The *way* in which these topics are discussed, the tools and procedures used, and the limits established within the interview are the responsibility of the counselor. If this division of responsibility does not emerge as the counseling progresses, the relationship is apt to be affected negatively.

Communication

The sharing of responsibilities is a part of the structure developed during the initial session and is a direct outgrowth of the ability of client and counselor to communicate with each other. Communication involves meaning expressed to one another by speech, gestures, facial expression, distance, or posture. This communication is affected by the words used, by emphasis, and by vocal inflection, but the meaning expressed reflects deeper elements of goals, values, and attitudes. This is why it is difficult to understand and evaluate all that happens unless one is actually present. As indicated previously, typescripts, audio tapes, films, and video tapes each have their specific limitations in conveying or preserving the *complete* interaction that occurs in the interview.

Part of the process of communication is the phrasing of counselor leads, but in addition the counselor must note the way in which the client responds to these leads and the information his response provides about his behavior.

It is important that the counselor check constantly on meanings abstracted by the client. This is an exceedingly difficult phase of the interaction, but a vital one. The counselor has to develop a dual skill in communicating: He must have the ability to present material precisely to a client to produce the desired response; he must also be able to understand surface content *and* the meaning behind the client's response. This is one of the reasons why extensive actual and vicarious experiences are necessary before the counselor can really understand what the client is saying and be able to see the world as the client sees it.

The counselor therefore must be a person with many levels of vocabulary. Professional terminology must be used in communication with colleagues in education, psychology, sociology, anthropology, medicine, social work, and rehabilitation. The same meanings often must be translated into the language of a factory worker or a fifth-grader in an initial interview. Successful counselors tend to develop a method of expressing meaning to clients which is simple and clear enough for every client to understand, yet does not sound patronizing or condescending. Such terminology also contributes to the consistency of the counselor's behavior and ease in remembering interview interactions for case notes. If the counselor cannot develop a basic vocabulary, the level of his language changes like the colors of a chameleon to meet the needs of each succeeding client.

THE VALIDATION AND EXPLORATION OF PREVIOUS DATA

Planning the Meeting

In order for the counselor to use the initial meeting to validate or expand and elaborate on data already collected on a given client, it is necessary to have some system of organizing information about the client (as described in Chapter 5) that will show easily the current knowledge about a client and the inadequacies or the discrepancies. Preliminary planning can only take into account the counselor's hypotheses about a given client's behavior based on knowledge about similar clients and on the limited specific information in the client's records. The counselor must plan the interview in terms of the tentative hypotheses these data permit, after a comparison with his own knowledge about the various groups within which the client must function.

Along with the validation of these data, the counselor will need to observe the unique ways in which a client differs from group norms of behavior and to modify his perceptions of and his tentative hypotheses about the client in the light of these unique differences. The beginning stages of the initial interview will usually produce statements about the client's purposes in coming for counseling, statements which may vary considerably from what the counselor anticipates on the basis of preliminary data. They may also vary considerably from the *real* purposes that are revealed as this first interview progresses.

The counselor's system of organizing the client's data determines the tentative hypotheses he develops about the client and indicates the kind of planning he must do in preparation. He must form some estimate of the level of general intelligence indicated by these data. This, in turn, establishes the methods and limits of communication that are to be used. The questions a counselor can ask and the information that can be given are partially determined by the intellectual level of the client as well as by the emotional impact they may have on the client.

Another limiting element in the counselor's planning is his preliminary estimate of the way in which the client views himself. If the preliminary data indicate preparation for occupations involving working with people and the client sees himself as one who has been unsuccessful in relating to others, this limits the approach the counselor can make in presenting and discussing these data. If the data indicate a need to help the client with personal problems and the client sees the interview as a place to discuss only educational or occupational data, this also limits the counselor. In similar fashion, the client's demonstrated readiness to accept or reject new ideas and his general adaptability may limit the degree to which the counselor can accomplish plans for the initial meeting. If these preliminary data also evidence what the client hopes to accomplish, this, too, can be a limiting element.

At the same time the counselor compares the preliminary data with the client's purposes. If the data are inadequate, then part of the initial meeting must be devoted to finding out whether it is a matter of incomplete information or whether there are real discrepancies between the client's goals and the information about him. If the client's goals include activities that involve meeting and dealing with people, and the data indicate behavior antithetical to this, the counselor's plans must take this into account.

Most of the initial sessions the counselor conducts will center about problems of an educational or vocational nature. This does not mean that these problems do not involve some rather strong feelings or that they are divorced from the rest of the client's field. It simply means that most data must be organized to solve rather mundane, practical problems. To do this the counselor usually follows some convenient outline and fills it in with data collected prior to the interview. Then, no matter in what order validating and new data are presented in the initial interview, they are fitted later into the outline. The client may present information about academic performance near the beginning, middle, and end of the interview, as the topics discussed develop logically and merge one into another in the natural sequence of a conversation. He may be able to make only positive statements about family members in the beginning but be able to be much more candid in expressing negative feelings toward the end of the initial session. Later, the counselor gathers and lists the new academic or family information, along with the rest of such data that have been collected previously from records and personal documents, in a synthesis of case data about a given client.

Any convenient list or outline of topics that suits a given counselor can be selected. One possible list (similar to the topics indicated in Chapter 2) is:

1. Elementary or high-school background
   a. Subjects liked best and marks
   b. Subjects liked least and marks
   c. Total grade point average
   d. Number in graduating class and client's position in this group
   e. Extracurricular activities
2. Family data
   a. Marital status and dependents
   b. Age, education, and occupation of spouse
   c. Present living conditions
   d. Present financial status with respect to schooling
   e. Age, education, and occupation of parents
   f. Exact nature of father's business
   g. Age, education, occupation of siblings
   h. Interaction with family
3. Leisure time activities
   a. Social life, actual and preferred (This includes religious activities, but do not ask about these: let client volunteer them.)
   b. Sports, participating and spectator
   c. Reading: books and magazines; be specific
   d. Hobbies: any consistent activities
   e. Organizations joined, current and past
   f. Experience in music and art
4. Course taken in college or technical school
   a. Subjects liked best; marks
   b. Subjects liked least; marks
   c. Grade point average or honor point ratio
   d. Extracurricular activities
5. Work and service experience
   a. Approximate number of months at each job
   b. Specific nature of job and duties
   c. Oral trade questions
6. Health and physical status
   a. Present disabilities; whether corrected, and how
   b. Long term illnesses; residuals

7. Client's feelings about environment
   a. Important areas above which were avoided in the interview
   b. Topics above which seemed to produce tension in the interview
   c. Feelings about home and family
   d. Feelings about school and teachers
   e. Feelings about job and fellow workers
   f. Readiness to participate in community social groups
   g. General attitude toward solitary vs. group activities
8. Would client be classified within the normal range of behavior?
   a. Diagnosis
   b. Suggested procedure
   c. Predicted results

All of the discussion about planning for an interview has been based upon the counselor's breadth and depth of knowledge about people as individuals and the way they behave in groups. Knowledge like that is acquired through experience with all kinds of people and groups. It involves scientific knowledge achieved in academic courses in the social and natural sciences, but it also includes vicarious and direct knowledge acquired from group work and group recreational experiences. The greater his background of understanding of his experiences with people, the better his preparation to understand what a client is trying to say. An understanding sensitivity to people is part of the empathic skill of every successful counselor. It should be noted, however, that this empathic skill is employed in a one-to-one counseling session; it does not necessarily follow that the counselor successful in one-to-one interviews is also successful in group activities.

DIRECT OBSERVATION OF THE CLIENT

As indicated at various points in this chapter, one of the primary purposes of the initial meeting is to explore the unique ways in which a given client differs from others in cultural background, behavior, personal interests, goals, and values. It is his individual differences in behavior that have brought the client to the first meeting. The variance of his behavior from societal values, or the unique needs they indicate, are the reason for counseling. The counselor uses the initial meeting as the first opportunity for direct observation of these differences and as an opportunity to collect new data on the client's behavior.

The first encounter is the point at which the counselor can begin to combine prior evidence of behavior with current observations to form an impression of *what* the client is doing. Usually the initial encounter also furnishes the first opportunity the counselor has had to understand and explore the *causes* of the client's behavior. At this session the counselor begins to experience with the client the feelings about self and environment which have resulted from the life values, interests, attitudes, and goals that the client has developed. In consequence, the counselor encourages the client to express these feelings and minimizes the amount of his own talk during the information-getting process.

Combining Interview Observations and Other Data

Until the initial meeting, the counselor's observations have been limited to looking through records and observations made by others to see how the client differs from the group. Now it is possible to make direct observations: to see, from the client's behavior and his talk what some of these differences are and why they have developed. As a counselor in beginning practicum once said, "I have had that boy in two classes, but this interview sure gave me a chance to get a different picture of him." Many clients reveal feelings in an interview which they have learned to conceal in other life situations. And the counselor has learned to make a different kind of observation in the interview from that practiced with colleagues, friends, or family.

The counselor, through experience, can learn to translate data from records into a picture of a client, but the face-to-face situation of the interview can add much to the picture. The notation on a folder that a high-school sophomore is 6 feet and 4 inches tall and weighs 200 pounds at age 16 is somewhat different from seeing the student filling the door of the counselor's office. Physical presence emphasizes data from records and makes them more meaningful.

A client may be quite friendly and relaxed when visiting with others in the outer office, but very tense and ill-at-ease in the counselor's office. The initial interview gives the counselor a chance to find out whether this difference is caused by inability to adjust in social situations involving peer vs. adult groups or whether it is related to the seriousness of the conflicts in values which have brought the client in for counseling. Such conflicts in values may produce tensions which diminish as the client learns that the interview is a place where no penalties are attached to the mention and discussion of the feelings involved in his conflicts.

Alert observation of any contrast between the client's talk and the counselor's visual observation can uncover important areas for remediation. A slight speech problem can pass unnoticed in many school situations, but not in the counseling session, where a trained observer notices it and explores with the client the possibilities for correction. Then referral to a speech specialist can be made and followed up by the counselor. This may seem an unreal situation, but actually it happens too often. In two recent cases of real speech defects, when teachers were asked about the clients, they thought in one case that it was a regional difference in accent, and in another that it was an affectation for status purposes.

The initial meeting gives the counselor a chance to get specific details about physical limitations. The notation on a health record of a high-school senior transfer that he developed arthritis in grade 6 is not very useful to the counselor. The sight of the boy in the outer office with his stiff bodily movements can immediately raise questions in the counselor's mind. Closer observation of enlarged knuckles and hunched shoulders gives evidence of some physical impairment, and the counselor needs to know more about this to furnish effective help to the client. As ordinary conversation makes it possible in the interview, the counselor asks the boy to tell about the arthritis and how it has affected his life. The boy indicates that there are certain sports which are difficult—such as golf, because it is hard to grip the golf clubs—so he engages less in sports and more in reading and study. Now the counselor sees as normal for this client the statement on the personal data form that he reads five or six books per week, which for most high-school boys would be atypical and possibly evidence a lack of social skills and group activity. Another significant item which appears in the initial interview is the fact that no one in any of the other four schools this boy has attended in three different states has mentioned the services available to him under state vocational rehabilitation. (This latter finding illustrates the lack of co-ordination among various counseling agencies and referral sources—someone should have checked this much sooner. Nor is this an isolated incident; all too often school counselors and other school personnel are unaware of such referral sources.)

As Tyler (1956) has pointed out, this phase of the initial encounter deals with "identifying psychological realities." In addition to the more obvious factors already mentioned, the interview is the first opportunity the counselor has to find out how the client feels about himself and his environment. When a client says, "I came to find out what my I.Q. is," the counselor cannot just give him a number. Professional responsibility requires that he find out why the client wants this information. The client may be seeking a way to excuse poor school work, or to show the counselor he feels inadequate at present, or the request may just be a screen to conceal the real reason for coming to the counselor. To give a number or a position in a normative group is not the professional response. The counselor needs to ask the client to tell more about why the intelligence test score is important. This leads to expression of the feelings which caused the client to come for counseling.

The counselor needs to use the first meeting to find out how the client feels, not just to collect a series of related facts which can be fitted into a case history or to dispense specific information without knowing how it will be used by the client Unless a client can learn to understand and accept the effect his feelings have upon his educational and vocational choices, his consideration of any activity is usually hampered by excessive anxiety. Part of the counselor's job is to distinguish between the normal anxiety or tension needed for learning and the abnormal anxieties which prevent learning.

In this process of getting to understand how the client's feelings and values affect his behavior, the counselor must make a tentative diagnosis of the behavior: that is, whether it is consistent and integrated enough for counseling to continue or whether a referral to some other agency is necessary. Unless the counselor can help the client reduce his anxieties to the point where new behavior can be learned, some other source of help will be needed. As Dragow (1956) has said:

Sometimes the client is so disturbed that he cannot be helped despite the fact that he presents problems which are usually dealt with in counseling. This distinction between the client and the problem he brings may explain why we are often successful in helping some clients with problems and fail to help other clients with the same types of problems.

Of course there are many other factors, besides the client's anxiety, that determine success or failure of counseling, but Drasgow's point is a good one for the beginning counselor to note. Unless the client's anxiety is optimal for learning, counseling tends to be ineffective.

Helping the client to reduce his anxiety may be the most important thing that happens in the initial encounter. A client may need to spend most of the time in this first meeting with the counselor in a discussion of the feelings which prevent successful school work, before it is possible to reach a point where an approach to educational or vocational choices is feasible. There may be several interviews in which counselor and client explore these feelings and their causes. On the other hand, the chance to relieve them in this first interview often makes it possible for the client to handle them alone in the future, so that they do not appear in succeeding interviews.

One of the problems the counselor faces is whether to let the client's feelings emerge, and to what extent, or whether it is better to temporize and see what happens in succeeding interviews. The counselor's decisions are determined by his education and experience, the purposes of the agency, the needs of the client, and the referral sources available. The counselor may decide not to permit the client's feelings to be discussed, or to limit the amount or kind of feelings which are discussed in the first interview. Sometimes a client will reveal too much in the first meeting and be unwilling to return. The counselor's decision will have to depend on tentative judgments about the client made on the basis of limited data. One of the factors which accounts for the all-too-frequent failure of clients to return for counseling is that such a decision has not been made soon enough. Tyler (1956) has said:

In some ways the counselor's task is harder than that of the psychoanalyst who aims to open up everything. The judgment as to which feelings should be recognized and which ignored is a very difficult one. A lifetime of practice is not enough for one to perfect the skill completely, but all of us can with concentration perform it moderately well.

STRUCTURING THE INTERVIEW

Some of the material on structuring which has been discussed previously will be considered only briefly here. Structuring occurs all through the initial session. It may be overt (formal) or covert (informal) at the discretion of the counselor, in the light of client need and comprehension. Structuring begins when the counselor greets the client and tries to create a satisfactory physical and psychological climate for the interview. In the process of doing this, the counselor ascertains the client's concept of what is going to happen and points out or implies what can actually happen. Blocher (1966, p. 158) defines *structuring* as "the process of communication and sharing expectations about the routine of the counseling process itself."

Overt Structuring

Overt structuring usually takes place as the client is informed about the various counseling processes that will be used in the course of any discussion of agency, legal, and ethical limits of counseling. For example, the counselor usually points out the available sources of information about the client, and sometimes indicates how they have been used prior to the initial interview. This permits the client to see what information the agency has and how it will need to be supplemented and expanded during counseling.

Within the limits created by differences between counseling orientations, the purpose of a counselor's lead is more often explained or evident to a client in the parts of the initial meeting centering about discussion of educational and vocational choices than in the parts dealing with feelings a client is expressing. The steps to follow after the initial session are also more apt to be openly delineated when educational and vocational problems are involved. These will include discussion of persons the client is to contact, a description of any tests he is to take, a statement of the additional information he must provide, and an explanation of the purpose of succeeding interviews.

In the beginning of the initial interview with adolescents or adults, the counselor usually tells the client about the routine the agency carries out with each client. If fees are charged, these are explained. Forms which must be completed are explained and their use illustrated. Most agencies have a control card for each client, similar to the one shown as Forms 4.1 and 4.2, which shows the steps involved in guidance and counseling. This is a useful device to indicate to a client the processes the agency carries on. Then, after the client describes his reasons for coming to the counselor, the counselor points out which of these procedures shown on the control card are applicable. The control card in Forms 4.1 and 4.2 is designed to permit the coding of the information it contains on computer cards for use in various types of agency research.

If it appears that another agency may be involved, the counselor can indicate how relationships with that agency will be handled, and what data might need to be released to another agency. At this point, the regulations of the counselor's own agency concerning the release of information and the release forms to be signed are often described to the client.

If the counselor has reason to expect that legal or ethical problems may come up in the interviews, this can be explained to the client along with a statement about the counselor's legal status (which in most states does not give clients the right of privileged communication). Unless a state grants privileged communication to the counselor's *clients*, the counselor can be required to testify in court about the content of counseling interviews, and agency records, including records of interviews, are subject to subpoena. The client should be informed of this as soon as the counselor has any intimation that such a situation can develop. Then the client is in a better position to decide what topics to discuss during counseling and the nature or extent of the discussion. The counselor should realize that even privileged communication is not intended to conceal a crime and that the law requires him to report contemplated or committed crimes revealed by a client, under penalty of becoming an accessory to them.

The counselor's agency itself may have established certain limits within which counselor and client must function. These need to be explained at the beginning of the initial meeting so that the client can decide whether topics coming under these limitations should be discussed. The limitations are apt to vary according to the needs and purpose of the agency, and therefore may not be clear to the client without an explanation.

For example, it may be agency policy to secure a written release from

FRONT SIDE OF AGENCY CONTROL CARD
DESIGNED FOR USE WITH IBM CARDS

Year	1	Case No.	2-5	Student No.	6-10	Name
Class	11	M F	Marital Status		12	Address
School	13	Changes	14	15	16 17	Phone
Age		Veteran □			18 19	Home Address
Referred by					20	
High School					21-23	
H.S. Graduation	24-25	Entered K.U.	26-27	Progress	x27	Physical Disabilities 28

Counselor	Interview	Counselor	Interview	Counselor	Interview	
29-31	PI 32	51-52		71-72		Referred to
33-34	CI 33-34	53-54		73-74		77
35-36		55-56		75-76		Testing
37-38		57-58				78
39-40		59-60				Method of Leaving School
41-42		61-62				Rec'd Degree from
43-44		63-64				
45-46		65-66			Remarks:	
47-48		67-68				
49-50		69-70				

(G-B Form, Rev. 57)

79
80

Form 4.2

BACK SIDE OF AGENCY CONTROL CARD SHOWING TESTS ASSIGNED AND DATE TAKEN

NAME...

Scholastic Aptitude Tests

.... American Council

.... Otis Self Adm.

.... Ohio Psychological

.... Wechsler-Bellevue

.... Miller Analogies

.... SCAT

Special Aptitude Tests

.... Minnesota Clerical

.... Psy. Corp. Clerical

.... O'Conner Finger-Tweezer

.... Minn. Spatial Relations

.... Paper Form Board

.... Bennett Mechanical (Form ....)

.... Dynamicube

.... Purdue Pegboard

.... EPSAT

Reading Tests

.... Coop. C2Y

.... Iowa Silent

Interest Inventories

.... SVIB-M

.... SVIB-W

.... Kuder Preference Record ....

.... Kuder Occupational Form D

.... Lee-Thorpe

Personality Schedules

.... MMPI

.... GZTS

.... EPPS

.... CPI

.... Study of Values

English

.... Coop. English ....

.... Michigan Voc.

Mathematics

.... K.U. Math.

.... Coop. Math. ....

Science

.... Chemistry Aptitude

.... Physics Aptitude

.... General Science

.... Natural Science

Foreign Language

.... Coop. Adv. Lang. ....

.... Coop. Elem. Lang. ....

.... Iowa Lang. Aptitude

History

.... Coop. Social Studies (Ach.)

Study Skills

.... Tyler-Kimber

.... Brown-Holtzman

.... Wren Study Habits

Batteries

.... Gen'l. Culture—I, II, III, IV, V

.... DAT—Verbal Reasoning
                        Numerical Ability
                        Abstract Reasoning
                        Space Relations
                        Mech. Reasoning
                        Cler. Sp. & Acc.
                        Lang. Usage

.... STEP—Read., Writ., Listen.,
                        Math., Sci., Soc. Stud., Essay
                        Writing

.... ITED—I, II, III, IV, V, VI,
                        VII, VIII, IX

.... Essential H.S. Content—Math.,
                        Sci., Soc. Study, Eng.

.... MAT—I, II, III, IV, V, VI,
                        VII, VIII, IX

Miscellaneous

....

....

Adapted by permission of the University of Kansas Guidance Bureau, Lawrence, Kansas.

the client before sending information to another agency. Or the agency may require a request from a potential employer before sending out information about the client's aptitudes. This limits correspondence to just those employers interested in the client, rather than sending information to every place the client applies for work. The same policy is usually followed in sending information to schools.

Ethical practices in counseling are fairly constant from agency to agency, however, and are usually demonstrated rather than explained. An example of this would be asking permission of the client before any recordings are made of the interviews. Sometimes it is necessary to make statements about the ethics involved in the way the counselor treats confidential data. The counselor should explain the differences between such things as test data collected by the agency for its own use or for referral purposes, and data collected by the counselor and the client solely for use in the interview. Usually data collected for use with the client are more confidential and are consequently handled differently from such things as scores on placement or selection examinations or data collected for upgrading in a job. Some tests may be given in order that the scores can be furnished to another agency, such as one offering services to the blind or another state vocational rehabilitation agency.

Overt structuring also includes a discussion of the persons the client will need to contact in the process of counseling. The counselor may ask the client to write and request that data collected previously be forwarded from another agency. The client may be asked to have summaries of previous interviews held in another agency forwarded for use in current interviews. Information about potential schools or potential employers may need to be secured by the client through direct contact with these referral sources. The client may agree to write for educational or vocational information. Many rehabilitation agencies make it a practice to have the client make the initial contacts between further schooling or future jobs. They feel the client assumes more responsibility for his progress if his own efforts have secured the placement than if the counselor has assumed responsibility for making the placement.

During the initial meeting and especially toward the end, the counselor may discuss appropriate tests with the client. Ordinarily the counselor is in a position to suggest that certain tests will best meet the client's needs for further information about himself; these suggestions are made and the client then decides whether such tests are worth taking, and which of several alternatives is best. For example, the counselor may say, "The *Strong Vocational Interest Blank for Men (SVIB)* will show you whether your interests resemble those of men in certain occupations," and will name the occupations in the *SVIB* in which the client has stated an interest. The counselor may explain further that the test contains items which the client marks "Like," "Indifferent," or "Dislike," and that it takes from 30 to 45 minutes, although untimed. Some counselors also like to point out to a client that for most useful results the client should do the test as rapidly as possible, because the more the client ponders responses, the more confused and possibly the less consistent and typical the resulting *SVIB* profile becomes. Scoring procedures for the *SVIB* may be pointed out to a client to indicate why there is a longer time lapse between the testing and the discussion of his scores than for most of the other tests he would take.

A counselor may point out that most of the personality and interest inventories a client takes will be more useful if the client completes them as rapidly as possible even though they are untimed—for the same reason given above for the *SVIB*. Conversely, the counselor explains that a power-type of intelligence test is intended to provide the best possible estimate of academic potential in untimed circumstances, and therefore will only be useful if the client takes as long as necessary to give a complete and thorough indication of his potential. Unless the client is willing to spend the necessary time on such a test, it is a waste of time for him to do the test.

In like manner the counselor describes the purpose and general nature of any other test that might be useful to the client. Which are assigned depends on the client, as does the way in which discussion of the test results is handled. If the client comes from a distance and is able to spend only one or two days in concentrated testing and counseling activities, the tests may constitute a single assignment. If the client is able to take them gradually over a period of time, one to two tests may be assigned and their results discussed before any other tests are assigned. The latter procedure gives the client a chance to see how a particular kind of information fits into his self-concept before a new and divergent kind of test information enters to complicate his thinking about himself and the interpretations of his test scores.

Frequently the structuring concerning tests can be handled in a group orientation to testing and counseling, but this needs to be reviewed in the initial interview also. Experience with group procedures followed by individual interviews has indicated that group orientation alone is not enough. Tyler (1956) has also mentioned the use of a brief written explanation of how the counseling service operates. Forms 4.3 and 4.4 are examples.

Toward the end of the initial meeting it is usually wise to review the procedures the client will follow later. If succeeding interviews have a stated time limit, this should be explained to the client. A counselor might say, "It is your job to make your next appointment as you leave each interview. Usually you will want to make it for the same time and

Form 4.3

INSTRUCTIONS FOR PRACTICUM COUNSELEES

This paper is to tell you of the procedure you will follow in your counseling program and remind you to be at the Guidance Bureau at _____ p.m. on _____.

The Guidance Bureau is in Room 116 on the main floor of Smith Hall (opposite the bus shelter). When you report there for your first interview, the counselor and counseling supervisor will review with you the material you have written on the enclosed Personal Data Form which you should bring with you to the first interview listed above. They will also go over with you any pertinent information which applies to your choice of education beyond high school or choice of a job after completing high school. After this is done, you will help them plan a testing program designed to help you answer questions important to you. The tests will vary according to the kind of questions you want answered and according to the college or job you are considering.

At the end of the first interview you can begin taking tests. The Guidance Bureau is open from 8 to 12 a.m. and from 1 p.m. to 5 p.m. You can take tests during these times as you desire. It is important that you complete these tests as soon as possible because the Guidance Bureau will be closed from August to September and your original counselor will not be here during that time. After you have completed the tests decided upon, you will return to discuss them with the counselor and counseling supervisor. At this second interview you will also be shown how to use the Occupational Information Library at the Guidance Bureau.

The total number of interviews will vary according to the information you wish. After these interviews we will send you a letter summarizing all the material we have covered. If you have no objection, we will send a copy of that letter to your high school. The information in your folder is considered strictly confidential and is released only with your express permission. Because you have volunteered in order to help us in our training program, **there will be no charge for these services.**

NAME _____

ADDRESS _____

PHONE NO. _____

ORIENTATION LEAFLET DISTRIBUTED TO CLIENTS

THE GUIDANCE BUREAU

The Guidance Bureau offers free counseling service to students. It is open from 8 a.m. to 5 p.m. on weekdays and until noon on Saturday. Any student may discuss his problems with a counselor. The counselor ascertains that the student can be profitably served by the Bureau or refers the student to the campus agency which is best equipped to help with the specific difficulty. Thus, there is little overlap with the regular academic advisement program, the Student Health Service, or other student personnel agencies.

The educational and psychological training of the counselors prepares them to help students collect and interpret information about themselves from many sources. These include tests, interviews, biographical information, and records. They vary with the needs of each student. Such sources provide information about abilities, aptitudes, interests, and personality to aid in making adequate choices of college majors and fields of occupations. They may also aid in the solution of personal problems allied to success in the University. A knowledge of strengths and weaknesses will permit the student to make the optimum use of opportunities while in college.

In the interpretation of these data the staff of the Bureau exercises discretion and professional judgment. Decisions are not made for students. Rather, students are aided in making their own decisions. Information about the student is released to no one without written permission. Counselees must arrange with their counselor if they wish information given to anyone.

The services furnished to students by the Bureau include aptitude testing, personal counseling with problems allied to academic success or failure, and counseling in regard to the choice of a suitable major or vocation. To use these services all a student has to do is make an appointment with a counselor through the Guidance Bureau Office either in person or by phone. In the first interview the counselor and the student decide which of the services of the Bureau will best meet the student's needs. This interview may last as long as one hour. If tests seem advisable, they are planned to meet the specific requirements of each student. Average time for most testing programs is from six to eight hours, arranged so that the tests can be fitted into the student's schedule. Succeeding interviews of one hour each are continued until the student has reached his objectives.

If the student is interested in investigating specific occupational fields, the counselor explains and illustrates the use of the Occupational Information Library. Here the student will find books on occupations which can be taken out for study, as well as files of unbound material and periodicals which can be used only at the reading tables.

In addition to these services offered free to students of the University, the

Bureau also offers its services to high school students and to adults interested in further education. The five dollar fee charged to high school students merely covers the cost of materials used. The services of the staff to high school students are considered a part of the free service offered to citizens of the state by the University. High school students should arrange for counseling through the principal of their own school. Adults pay a fee of twenty dollars, as do high school students from outside of the state.

Persons may apply by mail. Biographical information forms will be sent to them in advance so that they may complete the preliminary interview, testing, and the first counseling interview in two days spent at the Bureau.

Some of the questions asked about the Guidance Bureau are answered below.

1. What is the purpose of the Guidance Bureau?
   To counsel with University students who need assistance in making educational and vocational choices and in dealing with personal problems.

2. Does it cost the student anything to use the services of the Bureau?
   There is no charge made to regularly enrolled University students. High school students pay a five dollar fee and adults pay a fee of twenty dollars.

3. How may the services of the Bureau be secured?
   For vocational and educational counseling, it is necessary to register with the Guidance Bureau secretary for an interview. This interview will be held as soon as possible after registration. If a student has a particularly urgent problem, access to a counselor is usually possible on request. The student may ask for any particular counselor.

4. How long does it take to go through the Bureau?
   This depends upon the nature of the problem. Sometimes a single interview is enough. In other instances the counseling process may run over several months. The average calendar time is 3 or 4 weeks. When tests or inventories are used the average time for this is 6 to 8 hours, arranged at the convenience of the student.

5. When, during his school career, should a student receive the greatest benefit from Guidance Bureau assistance in the choice of an occupation?
   The Guidance Bureau has assisted freshmen, sophomores, juniors, seniors, and graduate students. However, first-year students may find the services of the Bureau of the most benefit. If a change of course should be decided upon by the student, it can then be made with the least loss of time.

6. Does a student have to take tests if he wishes to use the services of the Bureau?
   Not necessarily. For adequate vocational counseling some tests and/or inventories are essential. In the case of personal problems often none are used.

7. What is the purpose of taking tests?
   To gain information about interest, abilities, aptitudes, educational background, adjustment, and personality.

8. What is the purpose of an interview?

The first interview is primarily for the purpose of presenting the problem. Other interviews are to help the counselee understand his problem, understand any data developed through tests, inventories, or the counseling process itself.

9. Will the Guidance Bureau tell the student what occupation he should follow?

   No. It will assist in securing, analyzing, and interpreting data, but the choice is the student's responsibility.

10. What is the purpose of the Occupational Information Library?

   It is a special library of occupational information maintained by the Guidance Bureau. An effort is made to have available for current use the best available information on occupational trends, opportunities, remuneration, working conditions, and training requirements, for as many occupations as possible. When information needed by the student is not in the library the Guidance Bureau will make every effort to obtain it.

11. Who uses the Guidance Bureau?

   More than 10,000 students have come to the Guidance Bureau since its establishment for aid in vocational, educational, and personal problems.

Adapted by permission of the University of Kansas Guidance Bureau, Lawrence, Kansas.

same day each week, because this is easier to remember and it seems to be a good time for both of us." Or the counselor might say, concerning testing, "You can come in at your convenience and the girl in the main office will arrange for you to take each test as you have the time. I have told you how long each one takes. You can come in when you have that much time available, because most of them will take less than an hour. After you finish the test (tests), the girl will make an appointment for you to see me and talk about it (them)."

These are some of the more obvious ways the counselor can structure the counseling during the initial interview.

Covert Structuring

There are certain kinds of covert structuring which also go on. Throughout the interview, the counselor's responses and behavior show the client the climate that will prevail during counseling. Usually *covert or informal structuring* will include such things as the division of responsibilities between client and counselor; a demonstration of the counselor's professional capacities, of his attitude toward the client, and of the distinction between cooperative evaluation and the making of value judgments; and the presentation or discussion of data about the client.

As already observed, one of the aspects of counseling which is usually structured covertly during the sessions is the matter of division of responsibility between counselor and client. In most instances where a client goes to consult a specialist about a problem, the procedure involves describing the situation and letting the specialist decide what is to be done. For example, the person who is consulting a physician describes a series of symptoms and the physician prescribes treatment; the person with a legal problem goes to a lawyer for advice about how to handle it. Even parents and teachers have a tendency to tell children what to do instead of letting them make their own decisions. It follows that most clients coming to a counselor are inclined to describe the problem and wait for the counselor to tell them what to do.

It is difficult for the counselor to show the client that the interview is a sharing process. The counselor needs to get across the idea that his knowledge and skills are used to secure, organize, and interpret data about the client but that the decisions about his behavior that will be based on these data have to be made by the client. Sometimes this is handled overtly or formally, but usually it develops informally out of other activities. For example, the client may be discussing several possible subject-matter choices for a given school year and turn to the counselor with the question, "Which ones do you think I should take?" The counselor has a choice of several responses. One might be the simple reflection, "You would like to have me—someone else—make these choices for you." Others might be, "What do *you* think you should take?" or "Which ones would *you like* to take?" Responses like these, which either reflect the client's feelings or shift responsibility back to him, are a way of showing the client that he is the one who should make the choice, without harming the basic relationship between counselor and client.

Another client, who has been discussing a proposed plan of action, may turn to the counselor with the question, "What do you think about it?" The counselor can respond, "You're wondering what someone else would do about this," or "Someone else's opinion about this is important to you." Usually the counselor will avoid saying something like, "What I think is not important, it's your decision." This latter statement may be true, but it may have a negative effect on the relationship. Conversely, the counselor, who does not wish to reflect the client's feelings, may respond, "Have you considered what will happen if . . . ?" This makes possible the interjection of other information for the client's consideration without making his decision for him.

In these ways the counselor indicates to the client the division of responsibilities.

At the same time, such responses and other statements of the counselor are indicating that he accepts the client as someone worthy of help. Leaving the choices to the client emphasizes the counselor's belief that the client is capable of such decisions as these, and of similar choices. Thus, without saying so openly, the counselor conveys the impression of confidence in the client. But acceptance of what the client has said is not approval. For instance, if the client has just described some incident and expressed strong feelings about it, the counselor may say, "I can understand why you feel this way." Such a statement signifies successful communication between client and counselor, but it does not usually indicate approval.

The counselor's statements play as important a part in demonstrating his competence and responsibility as do any interpretations of data about the client or any direction of the client to appropriate sources of information or other agency contacts. Properly made, the counselor's responses convey to the client a knowledge of the client's strengths, which the client then begins to investigate and use.

At the same time, such statements provide a distinction between the value-judgments the client has encountered in other life activities and the lack of such evaluations by the counselor in the initial interview. Such phrases as "I see" or "I understand" not only reduce threat but create a different atmosphere than the usual "That's *good*" or "That's *bad*" heard in the rest of the environment. In a school situation the client is accustomed to being told that a score on a test is "good" or "poor." When a test score is discussed in counseling as being "higher than," "lower than," or "just like" most of the people who take the test, the client begins to see his strengths and weaknesses without psychologically cringing from someone else's value-judgments about them. Through this kind of interaction, in which value-judgments are left to the client, acceptance of weaknesses is made easier and the emphasis of strengths begins more quickly than in most life situations. Here the client is not being told "You are (or are not) able to compete with someone else"; it is evident, and the client can accept it as his other feelings make such acceptance possible. Such a process emphasizes the importance of the client's own value-judgments.

The inferences about the various things the client will do, made in the initial meeting, have a role in indicating that these activities are a part of the counseling process without their actually being listed in 1-2-3-4 fashion.

Another point at which the counselor usually prefers to avoid overt structuring is in the termination of the initial meeting. One way to do this is to summarize briefly the procedures the client will follow and then lean forward as if about to rise. Usually, if this is timed with some signal that the time has ended, the client will begin to make preparations to leave and, in succeeding interviews, will assume responsibility for this. When the counselor has someone to control his appointments, a call from the outer office saying the next appointment is waiting usually terminates the interview. Only in extreme cases will the counselor have to say, "I'm sorry, but this is all the time we can take today," and stand up to signify the meeting is ended. The termination of the initial meeting on schedule is important in structuring future interviews and helps to maintain a professional atmosphere in counseling.

SUMMARY

The discussion of the initial meeting with a client has centered around establishment of a counseling relationship, confirmation of data about the client secured prior to the interview, getting to know how the client feels about himself and his environment, and methods of structuring the sessions. It is obvious that these processes will vary with the age and needs of the client, with the personalities of both client and counselor, with the professional orientation of the counselor, and with the requirements of the agency for which the counselor works. Perhaps the best way to close is with a quotation from Tyler (1956, p. 473) with which she ends her article about the initial interview:

I wonder if other counselors would agree with me that the initial interview is the hardest part of our task—the part that demands from us the most intensive concentration. Each person constitutes for us a new adventure in understanding. Each is destined to broaden our own lives in directions as yet uncharted. Each initial interview renews our appreciation of the challenge and the fascination of the counseling task.

REFERENCES

Amos, W. E., and Grambs, J. D. 1968. *Counseling the disadvantaged youth.* Englewood Cliffs, N.J.: Prentice-Hall, Inc.

Bandura, A. 1956. Psychotherapist's anxiety level, self-insight, and psychotherapeutic competence. *J. Abnorm. & Soc. Psychol.* 52:333–37.

Blocher, D. H. 1966. *Developmental counseling.* New York: The Ronald Press Company.

Drasgow, J. 1956. Intake interviewing in counseling. *Personnel and Guidance J.* 35:100–102.

Fiedler, F. E. 1950a. The concept of an ideal therapeutic relationship. *J. Consult. Psychol.* 14:239–45.

———. 1950b. A comparison of therapeutic relationships in psychoanalytic, nondirective and Adlerian therapy. *J. Consult. Psychol.* 14:436–45.

Hahn, M. E., and MacLean, M. S. 1955. *Counseling psychology.* New York: McGraw-Hill Book Company.

Hall, E. T. 1966. *The hidden dimension.* New York: Doubleday & Company, Inc.

Hill, G. E., and Luckey, E. B. 1969. *Guidance for children in elementary schools.* New York: Appleton-Century-Crofts.

Kell, B. L., and Mueller, W. J. 1966. *Impact and change: A study of counseling relationships.* New York: Appleton-Century-Crofts.

Krumboltz, J. D. 1966. *Revolution in counseling: Implications for behavioral science.* Boston: Houghton Mifflin Company.

Robinson, F. P. 1950. *Principles and procedures in student counseling.* New York: Harper & Row, Publishers.

Rogers, C. R. 1957. Conditions of therapeutic personality change. *J. Consult. Psychol.* 21:95–103.

———. 1961. *On becoming a person: A therapist's view of psychotherapy.* Boston: Houghton Mifflin Company.

———, ed. 1967. *The therapeutic relationship and its import: A study of psychotherapy with schizophrenics.* Madison: The University of Wisconsin Press.

Truax, C. B. 1963. Effective ingredients in psychotherapy: An approach to unraveling the patient-therapist interaction. *J. Couns. Psychol.* 10:256–63.

Tyler, L. E. 1956. The initial interview. *Personnel and Guidance J.* 34:466–73.

————. 1969. *The work of the counselor.* 3rd ed. New York: Appleton-Century-Crofts.

Wolpe, J. 1958. *Psychotherapy by reciprocal inhibition.* Stanford, Calif.: Stanford University Press.

————, Salter, A., and Reyna, L. S. 1964. *The conditioning therapies.* New York: Holt, Rinehart & Winston, Inc.

5

Organizing
a Case Study
with a Client

Organizing with a client the data that will permit him to identify and take action about differences between potential and actual performance requires a systematic approach on the part of the counselor. He identifies clients who need help by contrasting information about the client's performance in academic, physical, vocational, psychological, and social areas of activity with indices of that client's aptitude in each of these areas. Then, he helps the client understand and use this information in a fashion that permits that client to make effective decisions about the possibilities open to him or to seek out the proper professional person to help him. Although the procedure will vary somewhat with each client, in general the process has to be consistent with the counselor's own frame of reference (discussed in the preceding chapter), and with the attitudes, goals, values, and interests of the client which are the primary determinants of his choices.

The processes of identification are similar, whether used for students or older clients in other settings. The major common element is that these processes are carried on with relatively normal individuals who are often unaware of the possible choices open to them and of the possibilities of professional help available to them. Hence the counselor's task may involve not only the identification of the kind of help the client needs, but also the promotion of his understanding that he needs such help. Depending on the setting, the counselor's role varies from that of a coordinator, or consultant, to an active counseling role. His functions vary from organizing and interpreting information to promoting the resolution of any conflicts within the client, or between the client and his environment, which do not require the deep or intensive treatment carried on in psychotherapy.

The theory and practice of counseling have progressed considerably since Parsons proposed a process of vocational self-evaluation, the Minnesota Employment Stabilization Research Institute Studies were carried on, and Bell wrote about "matching youth and jobs." Jordaan et al. (1968) and Patterson (1969) have reviewed that period in discussing the current status of counseling. The weakness of describing individuals in terms of traits and factors has been the omission of a description of the interaction of such elements in the total development of the individual. So the emphasis has changed to a self-psychology devoted to the study of how the individual interacts within himself and with his perceived world in terms of his "self-concept," and with how this has affected his development to the time he meets with the counselor.

Coincident with this transition was the research into career or vocational development theory described in detail by Osipow (1968). Out of the earlier work of Roe, Super, sociological studies of work, the attempted intrusion of psychoanalytic concepts, and the recent proposals of Holland (1966), described in Chapter 9, a gradual, but piecemeal and largely theoretical, approach to describing how an individual's choice of career occurs has been formulated. This is probably best typified by the proposals of Super et al. (1963) dealing with vocational development and the self-concept. Super, in this 1963 work, attempts to show that the individual's self-concept, formed by exploration, self-differentiation, identification, role-playing, and reality testing, is translated into occupational terms as each of these lifelong processes influences the approach or avoidance of occupationally related activities. To Super's proposals the writers would add the modifying effects of physical and psychological change during the years after 30, as proposed by Hahn (1963, 1967), if counselors are to think and work with individuals beyond that age and if vocational development is truly a lifelong process.

A third pathway into this vocational maze was opened by the work of the United States Training and Employment Service, particularly that of Fine and Heinz (1957), in developing a comprehensive system of describing people *in* jobs, and by experiments using computer programs to match people and jobs (Goltz 1966). This approach will be discussed in detail later in the chapter.

There are many gaps in the data describing how the development of an individual from birth to late adolescence determines what types of educational preparation he elects and what sorts of jobs he will seek. The counselor's function is to know how such theories bear on the collection, organization, and discussion of data with a given client so that he is free to make the most effective decisions about his future. The collection, synthesis, and interpretation of these data with the least amount of personal or social bias is the counselor's task in a case study with normal clients.

The counselor must be aware of the differing contributions which the available counseling tools and processes, old and new, will make to his usefulness to his client by providing information which will help promote the educational and vocational development of that client.

All of this he must synthesize with his own personal and professional principles: the frame of reference within which he organizes the educational and vocational case study to meet the needs of each client and those trying to help that client. For some clients the case study is extensive, for some only brief, but for each client it must fit and expand his own knowledge of himself and his future.

CONTENT OF THE CASE STUDY

The beginning counselor faces the problem of deciding what materials properly belong in a case study, how the case study should be organized, and how it should be used. The term *case study*, as ordinarily used, refers to the organization of all the information available on a given individual which is used for any specific purpose.

The amount of information and the nature of the information vary according to the purpose for which the case study is prepared. The most common purpose of a case study, as far as the counselor is concerned, is to collect information which can then be organized in a fairly simple fashion to be discussed with the client in order to help him to a more realistic self-concept or to direct his exploratory behavior. Much of the information that the counselor collects is designed for his personal use in understanding the client, or for helping the client understand himself. Usually, that information is not given the formal name of "case study."

Another factor that determines the content and scope of the case study is related to the competencies or skills of the counselor in collecting, organizing, and using information. The beginning counselor will obviously be more limited and must take more time to prepare and interpret his data than the experienced counselor who has developed a systematic approach. The purpose for which the case study is used has to be tempered by the client's needs, the counselor's needs, the needs of the counselor's colleagues or the client's parents, and by the needs of the so-called "referral agencies" to whom the case study may later be presented. Estimates of the kinds of case studies completed by schools and other agencies usually indicate that about 60 to 80 per cent of the cases in an agency dealing with the general public, such as the State Employment Service, a college personnel office, or a public-school counseling office, are centered about educational or vocational questions and predictions.

There really is no such thing as a purely educational or vocational question, because each individual varies enough that a counselor must consider a number of other intrapersonal and environmental interactions not directly rising from the educational or vocational problem. For example, the counselor may need to consider how this client feels about going to work. In a rehabilitation agency, the individual may have been on county welfare for two or three years and this has been more comfortable than seeking a job. The client has not had to worry about people seeing his disability or commenting on the capacities needed to meet a work situation. It is easier to stay home. It is harder to go out and compete occupationally. If county welfare is making payments to the client, he may not be willing to do this. So it may be pretty hard to talk about educational or vocational possibilities with this client until the point is reached where he is ready to consider them. A similar situation occurs in •a school setting. Until a given boy or girl gets to be a senior, no goals beyond high school or graduation from college may seem worth considering. They are in the far-distant future, and graduation from high school seems a long way off to a sophomore, as does graduation from college to a senior in high school. Therefore, the readiness of the client may be a factor in indicating what materials are to be included in a case study and how much a client's feelings about other elements of his life enter into educational and vocational considerations.

When the counselor works with clients who are not headed for college and who come from lower-middle to low socioeconomic groups, he encounters different types of problems and hence the need for different kinds of case studies. These clients do not usually come voluntarily to counseling. They need to be identified and routed to the counselor's office. They tend to be less verbal, particularly in the reading and writing aspects of verbality. Their entire motivational system is different from that of the other clients with whom the counselor works. Not only must the counselor identify them and get them to his office, but he must also open for them doors which his other clients usually open for themselves. He must help them develop long-term planning toward vocational goals they have not usually even considered. He must awaken and foster new self-concepts for these clients (Amos and Grambs 1968).

SYSTEMATIC CASE STUDY

The techniques that the counselor uses in preparing a case study come from a number of disciplines and professions. In psychology the counselor discovers techniques which will furnish information about individual behavior and its causes, because the function of psychology is the study of the individual. From sociology and social work come the techniques which permit the counselor to gather together information about the client's environment or background and its impact on that client. From education come a series of techniques which show how an individual learns and which assist the counselor in the process of helping the client learn. From medicine come the techniques that give information about physical capacities or restrictions which exist for a given client. From various government agencies come data concerning the world of work and the procedures for helping disadvantaged persons prepare for and secure work. These are the major areas from which the counselor has borrowed techniques of gathering, organizing, or using client information.

After the counselor's efforts have produced information, some method of organizing it must be selected. Williamson and Darley (1937) have suggested six steps in clinical counseling, which Hahn and MacLean (1955) discuss also. Those steps are: analysis, synthesis, diagnosis, prognosis, treatment, and follow-up. They also hold for the other three methods described in the rest of this chapter.

Analysis is the process of first studying over the data collected in the case study. *Synthesis* refers to the organization or the putting together of this information in some usable form. *Diagnosis* is the making of some estimate of causation and of the approximate nature of the problem, in the same sense that the physician makes a diagnosis. *Prognosis* refers to how the counseling processes may be useful for a client or whether a referral should be made to another agency. When the counselor's prognosis is that counseling can be of assistance, then the more specific questions concerning the techniques which will be useful depend upon the orientation of the counselor.

In *directive counseling*, the counselor participates more in decisions and bears a major part of the responsibility for counseling activities. In *client-centered or nondirective counseling*, the counselor bears less of the responsibility for interview topics and is more concerned with his relationship with the client, the atmosphere in which counseling takes place, and with reflecting to the client the real meaning behind what the client is saying. The *eclectic* counselor, who is somewhere in the middle of this continuum, would be choosing techniques and sharing responsibilities with the client according to that counselor's position on the continuum. If the counselor is more inclined toward a client-centered orientation, the process will be more Rogerian; if he is more inclined toward the directive approach, the tools and techniques chosen will be more in that direction and will consequently involve him in more responsibility for what is discussed as well as what is actually done in counseling. Perhaps this is an exaggeration of such differences, because (as pointed out in Chapter 4), experienced counselors tend to be more alike than different.

Treatment is what happens in counseling. This is the actual one-to-one or small-group process which the counselor and the client share. It may be just a few sessions or it may be many, and at the elementary school level it may not even be called "counseling."

The last step in the Williamson and Darley series, *follow-up*, is the one that is most frequently neglected. What happens to this particular client after counseling? In rehabilitation agencies, follow-up is a necessity, because such agencies get their funds from state and federal appropriations and they need to provide follow-up information to those governmental units. So they have to collect this information. In a school situation, there is not so much pressure to do it, although there is the same obligation to show what was done. If a school administrator is to get money for a guidance program, there must be evidence that the program is successful and is doing specific things. One function of the school counselor is to furnish this evidence, although when it has been neglected it is not altogether the fault of the counselor. If a counselor has to be responsible for 900 clients in a given year, instead of 300, not much time is available for follow-up. Some sort of follow-up is necessary, however, in order to justify the existence of a counseling program.

Whether the counselor uses Williamson and Darley's six headings for the systematic organization of case data or whether he uses some other system makes little difference, as long as the system is effective. The important thing is that an organized way of collecting, presenting, and using information about a given client is developed, one which the counselor can use comfortably as well as professionally. If the counselor feels at ease with this system in the counseling situation, the client will also be more at ease. In fact, the systems discussed here have considerable overlap.

At the elementary-school level, the chief function of the case study is to help the counselor and his colleagues identify boys and girls who need help, to indicate the type of help each needs, and to highlight any pre-ventive measures that need to be taken to eliminate serious difficulties in the development of each individual. This means that at least a rough case study needs to be developed for every elementary-school pupil so that the counselor and those who help him can pinpoint areas needing remediation and decide what resources are appropriate and available for such help.

If case studies of this nature are initiated as a boy or girl enters ele-mentary school, a real educational plan for that child can be initiated and work with him becomes preventive rather than crisis-oriented. While no guidance program can eliminate crises arising at some points in the development of given clients, these crises are less frequent or prolonged if boys and girls are helped to overcome deficiencies in their development as these deficiencies manifest themselves. The individual who learns to cope successfully with daily living is much better prepared to handle his own transition from elementary school to junior high or to make choices about what he wants to accomplish in school.

The elementary-school guidance worker trying to provide such help learns to prepare case materials to present to teachers, to parents, or to referral sources within the school system or in the community. This is where a single, simple form highlighting data about the client, so any of these individuals can review it quickly, can save considerable work. Forms 5.1 and 5.2 can be adapted for use in the elementary school and can present in simple fashion data concerning a client's academic, social, physical, and psychological progress.

The elementary-school guidance worker carrying out this work not only functions as a competent counselor and teacher, but also as a diag-nostician, coordinator, consultant, and referring agent (Hill and Luckey 1969). This poses another series of needs to be served by the case study.

As Patterson (1969, p. 28) has pointed out, counseling is based on the success of the interpersonal relationship in producing change in indi-viduals. He says:

We will realize soon, as has been the case with every other new method or technique in psychiatry and psychotherapy, that it is the basic human rela-tionship which is curative, or facilitative of positive personality and behavior change, and that it is this factor—call it the Hawthorne effect if you will—which is the effective factor in techniques of behavior modification.

As already indicated, counseling can be classified into at least two categories. The first of these, *preventive counseling*, encompasses the types of counseling where the client needs to be sought on the basis of his lack of awareness of what counseling can do for him. It involves identify-

Form 5.1

A SAMPLE PERSONAL DATA FORM
USING FICTITIOUS DATA

PERSONAL RECORD

Name:
Address:
Phone:

This information will be released to no one without your written consent. When you wish to leave something blank, write **none**.

1. Personal data:
   Sex: _m_ Age: _16_ Date of birth: _10/2/43_ Place of birth: _Anytown, Kansas_
   Religious Preference: _Protestant_ Height: _5'10"_ Weight: _165_
   Physical disability? _none_ Married: _no_
   School Grade _12_

2. Family data:
   Parents still married: _yes_ Separated: _____ Divorced: _____

Father	Mother
Age: _38_	Age: _38_
Job: _Tool + Die Maker_	Job: _Office Manager_
Grade completed: _12th_	Grade completed: _12th_
Birthplace: _Anytown, Indiana_	Birthplace: _Anytown, Kansas_

   Brothers and sisters:

Name	Sex	Age	Grade completed	Occupation
Henry	m	15	10th	Student

3. Education:
   Course taken: _College Preparatory no. and position in your class: 10th in 52_
   Approximate high school average: _B_
   Subjects liked: _math + Science_ Subjects disliked: _English_
   What do you plan to do when you complete high school? _Go to State University_

4. What do you like to do in your spare time?
   a. Hobbies: _Repairs on car-Build model train system-play chess or checkers_
   b. Training in music or art: _1 year piano-2 years mechanical drawing_
   c. Clubs and organizations: _Hot Rod Club, Eagle Scout- Rifle Club_
   d. Offices held: _Pres: Senior Class Pres: Hi-Y_
   e. Do you like to read? _yes_
   f. What books do you read? _Biography - Science fiction_

g. What magazines do you read? *Popular Mech- Hot Rod -Sports Illus -World News*
h. What kind of group activities do you like? *Scouting- Church, Sports*
i. What sports do you play? *Track & Basketball*
j. Varsity or intramural? *Varsity*

5. What occupation would you like to enter?

Job	Reason
a. *Engineer*	*Like math*
b. *Skilled mechanic*	*Father's job*
c. *College Teacher*	*Prestige*

Is this what your parents want you to do? Yes: __X__ No: _____
What job would you like to be doing 10 or 15 years from now? *College Teacher*

6. What kind of work have you done? Mark on-the-job training "X."

Job	Time in months	Did you like it?	Why?
Newsboy	*36*	*Yes*	*Exercise & money*
Grocery checker	*5*	*Yes*	*Meet people*
Gas station attendant	*5*	*Yes*	*Learn about cars*

7. What problems would you like to discuss with a counselor?
   a. Job: _____ b. Education: __X__ c. Relations with
   others: _____ d. Finances: __X__ e. Other: _____

8. Underline the traits in the following list which apply to you:
Persevering, friendly, patient, stubborn, capable, tolerant, calm, impetuous, pessimistic, bashful, self-confident, jealous, talented, quick-tempered, cynical, tactful, conscientious, cheerful, submissive, excited, irritable, anxious, poor health, nervous, easily exhausted, unhappy, frequent periods of gloom or depression, frequent day-dreaming.

Form 5.2

JOHN DOE'S ACTIVITIES

Nonlinguistic	Balance of Both	Linguistic
School Courses		
Liked math and science	10th in senior class of 52	
2 yrs. Mechanical drawing	B average in high school	
Dislikes English	College Prep curriculum	
School Extra-class		
Scouting		Pres. Hi-Y
Rifle club		Pres. Senior class
Hot Rod club		
Varsity track		
Varsity basketball		
Occupational Data		
Gas station attendant	Newsboy	
Wants to be engineer or skilled	Grocery checker	
mechanic	Wants to be college	
	teacher	
Leisure Activities		
Reads **Popular Mechanics** and	Reads **Sports Illustrated**	Reads biographies
Hot Rod	Reads science fiction	Reads **World News**
Builds model train system	One year piano lessons	Church group
Repairs own car		
Plays checkers and chess		

ing clients who need help and intervening directly with them to provide help. It is usually more of a preventive process, involved with problems of academic, vocational, social, physical, or psychological phases of behavioral imbalance. Preventive counseling occurs more frequently with younger clients and those from lower socioeconomic backgrounds; and its purpose is to reduce or eliminate minor difficulties before they can become of crisis proportions.

In contrast, *crisis counseling*, the kind of counseling where the client comes voluntarily for help, is apt to occur more frequently at the high-school, college, or adult level and to require more serious or involved counseling. The client has experienced enough difficulty in dealing with life situations that he wants to change his behavior, and he has become aware of the counselor as a source of help. In a sense, such clients are easier to help because of their awareness of their needs; yet the process is usually more complex and behavioral change more difficult. However, it is necessary before preventive counseling takes place.

PREVENTIVE COUNSELING

As a child enters school he faces a radically different environment which poses the need for more and more independent decisions. The understanding teacher must be aware of this and work carefully with the counselor in facilitating the process of growth toward independence. The teacher and the counselor in the elementary school are always on the alert to describe the child's behavior in developmental terms which reveal his success or lack of success in coping with his environment or with himself. Such descriptions reveal the need for and the kinds of intervention the school can provide.

It should be obvious to the counselor that each of these areas of the client's performance interacts and that it is impossible to separate them clearly and succinctly when exploring and describing his performance. For example, with the growth of audiovisual media centers and their importance in providing a complex of different ways for a person to learn, the academic skills of reading and writing have remained of prime importance, but new emphasis has been given the physical skills of watching and listening as a major part of the learning process. Hence any limitations upon sight and hearing dictate a different approach to a given pupil's education and the use of newer methods as part of the diagnostic and remedial process.

It should also be obvious that psychological factors play a part in the learning process, so that the diagnosis of academic differences (for varied clients) may involve an appraisal of the impact of emotional disturbance or of motivation toward school as a part of the estimate and description of cognitive functioning. In similar fashion, social interaction or lack of social skills may promote or retard the academic proficiencies of a client. While each of these areas is considered separately in the succeeding material, the counselor should bear in mind that the organization and appraisal of data about the client must take into account the complex interaction among these variables, often difficult to identify and to describe to the client or to others involved in the counseling process.

The Academic Area

As the child progresses in the elementary school he begins to acquire the fundamental processes which will not only facilitate his working toward fulfilling his academic potential, but which, it is hoped, will also be transferred to his life outside school, particularly his vocational activities. In the beginning these skills are manifested by aural and oral as well as nonverbal activities. The counselor is concerned with describing the pupil's potential for these academic skills as evidenced in the amount of sensitivity shown by teachers' and parents' descriptions, as well as by more objective measures. These he contrasts with any evidence of achievement he can secure from these same sources and from records.

Probably the most important academic skill, even now, is verbal communication through listening, talking, reading, and writing. An individual's ability to perform at his potential level, as well as his actual learning, are still highly dependent on this continuum of linguistic skills. The impression he makes on his teachers and others in the academic setting, and the resultant descriptions of his progress in school, are a direct function of such skills. Therefore the counselor and the teacher first explore evidence of the pupil's potential, as indicated by his spoken or written vocabulary, how rapidly he perceives and manifests understanding of relationships among learning variables, his aptitude test scores, and any other behavior expressing such potential. This information, about many pupils, is in turn contrasted with their achievement in spoken and written areas of language, as evidenced by school marks, achievement test scores, or descriptions of performance, in order to locate those persons who need some type of remedial instruction to improve their linguistic skills. At the same time, potential as evidenced by *nonverbal* aptitudes should be considered, to be sure undeveloped potential is not underestimated or overlooked—as it well may be in the case of recent immigrants or various other subgroups whose culture is based on a different language or on communication by nonverbal or oral means, such as those used by the American Indian, the American Black, or inhabitants of deprived areas such as Appalachia. In like manner, an appraisal of visual efficiency and of its place in verbal and nonverbal performance should be carried on. The appraisal of potential and actual performance in nonverbal school activities, such as watching visual media, working on science or arithmetic problems, art, music, or vocational projects, will frequently reveal other areas of weakness where remedial work can improve the performance. The instruments and procedures for evaluating the academic area are discussed in much more detail in Chapter 8.

The Physical Area

Earlier it was indicated that his physical condition plays a very important part in the learning process of any individual. Not only must the physically disabled or limited individual overcome his natural emotional reaction to a disability, but he must learn the limits within which he can perform as a result of his limitation. The counselor is not interested in past illnesses of the client, but rather he wants to identify which of these innate limitations or environmental circumstances have produced physical residuals which limit performance in school, work, or leisure activities. For the counselor, these residuals spell out the current or future conditions under which the client must perform, if they cannot be alleviated. To the extent that they limit the physical aspects of the client's performance, they become determinants of his educational and vocational choices.

The counselor not only must be aware of such limitations and help the client learn to cope with them effectively, but he must also know or discover referral agencies which will help the client do this. He is principally dependent on the available physical education or medical services in the diagnosis, description, and estimate of these limitations on the client's performance. This subject is discussed further in Chapter 8.

The Social Area

As in the case of each of the preceding areas of performance and those to follow, the social area interacts in various ways with each of the others. The social aptitude and performance of each client have a different valence in these interactions as academic, physical, psychological, and vocational aptitudes and performance make this possible. The major contribution of the counselor is to define and describe to the client his perception of and approach to his relationships with others—at home, in school, at work, or in other community settings. Each situation may disclose different social skills as the client perceives himself differently and functions differently in each setting. At home he may be quite comfortable or quite upset, depending upon whether his perceptions and the behavior he has developed to cope with them are effective and realistic or not. His school behavior may be quite opposite, because his perceptions, behavior, and degree of ease in the school setting are different from those at home. The same can be said about his work and his leisure social interactions. The counselor first needs to see whether these are consistent, reasonable, *and* satisfactory to the client. If they are, and the counselor can foresee no need for future change, then the client should be left alone. If they are neither consistent nor satisfactory to the client in any one of these areas, the counselor needs to help him decide what, if anything, he wants to do about changing his behavior.

The major discovery the client has to make is that his social behavior, unlike his intellectual potential or physical fitness, can become about what he wants it to be. If he wishes to engage in solitary activities, and is happy, this should be *his* choice. If he wishes to engage in many activities with people, he can acquire or improve the skills necessary to accomplish this in as gradual a fashion as he and his counselor work out. Within very broad limits, he can acquire the social skills he wants in any setting, provided his emotional and motivational condition permit him to choose the course of interaction he wants. If not, the counselor can help him work toward the psychological state where this is possible. More information about the devices and processes used to assess social skills is presented in Chapter 10.

However, the identification of such discrepancies is not enough. The counselor and the teacher must work with the client and his parents to help the client evaluate what change will mean to his behavior in and outside of school and to decide whether he wants to change. One-sided counselor's, teacher's, or parent's decisions to "change the client's behavior" are usually a waste of time and often produce negative effects. This is why the client's emotions and motivation are so important to the counselor. These psychological factors are most important in crisis counseling.

CRISIS COUNSELING

Psychological Factors

Cognition, or the ability to perceive and utilize relationships, has been considered in the discussion of activities defining academic aptitude and performance. The psychological effects of the client's emotions or feelings, and of his motivations, also need to be evaluated as part of the synthesis of data about the client. Thorndike (1918) said that things that exist, exist in quantity, and therefore can be judged, estimated, or measured.

This proposal is the basis upon which "appraisal programs" are started. Differences within and between individuals can be estimated, and therefore some system of organizing information about those individuals can be undertaken so that they can make educational and vocational choices. This applies to affect and motivation as well as cognition.

Some psychologists include emotions and motivation under affect. For the sake of clarity of discussion as well as more effective use in counseling, the two concepts will be separated here. Only emotions will be considered under affective behavior; motivational elements in behavior will be treated as a separate aspect.

Psychologists have had a difficult time convincing practitioners of the importance of the impact of emotions on *any* choices the individual makes. Freudian psychology, based upon the behavior of the abnormal personality, helped produce an antipathy toward any consideration of affect in teaching and counseling. This resulted in an overemphasis of emotional elements in behavior until counseling personnel accepted the importance of affect in the counseling process. Now it is one of the usual considerations of the competent counselor in his work with every client. Now one of the first questions he asks is, "How do this client's feelings about himself and his environment (or phenomenal field) support or detract from effective behavior?" Then he proceeds to help the client cope with his feelings and emotions to the extent that they do not prevent appropriate educational or vocational choices. Feelings and emotions, particularly as quantified by personality inventories, are still dirty words as far as parents, politicians, and the general public are concerned. It is essential that the counselor deal with them, but they should not be highlighted, and counseling procedures devoted to them should be carefully explained to clients or parents in advance.

Emotions or affect, as used here, mean any strong feelings relating to the self or the environment which determine in part how the client will react. The purpose in dealing with affect in counseling is to help the client to control it to facilitate, rather than impede, his functioning more effectively as a person. The instruments and procedures used to do this are described in much more detail in Chapter 10.

A third series of concepts concern *motivational* aspects of behavior, such as interests. The term *interest* refers to an individual's like or dislike for certain activities. It can refer to either educational or vocational pursuits or to leisure activity. It is possible to subdivide interests further, into stated interest and measured interest. *Stated interest* is "I want to be a nurse," "I want to be an engineer," "I want to be an auto mechanic." *Measured interest* refers to information shown by scores on inventories which reflect the relevant linguistic and nonlinguistic factors (discussed in detail in Chapter 9).

Other aspects of motivation, in addition to interests, involve attitudes, goals, and value systems. An *attitude,* as defined by English and English (1958), is "a persistent mental and/or neural state of readiness to react" to a certain object or class of objects—*as they are conceived to be,* not as they are. They define *goals* as "the end result, immediate or remote, which an organism is seeking." *Value* is defined by English and English as "an abstract concept, often merely implicit, that defines for an individual or for a social unit what ends or means to an end are desirable," while a *value system* is the "more or less coherent set of values that regulate a person's conduct, often without his awareness that they do so." It should be noted that these terms apply to social subgroups as well as to the individual. The assessment of these factors is discussed more extensively in Chapter 9.

Vocational Areas

Applying these psychological concepts to educational and vocational areas involves what Hahn and Brayfield (1945) called the "field and level concept." *Level* refers to the place in an educational or vocational hierarchy to which an individual may aspire. *Field* is the area, occupational or educational, in which an individual appears to have the best opportunities for success. This means the best combination of abilities, aptitudes, and interests. Consequently, one way of organizing educational or vocational information about individuals would be within this field-and-level concept. The level indicates whether the person should plan to be a semiskilled, skilled, technical, or professional worker. The field should be considered in the light of the linguistic and nonlinguistic continua dealing with interests, academic areas, academic skill, occupations, leisure activities, and so on. "Field" includes the activities of an educational and occupational nature which are carried out by an individual.

Subordinate continua can then be arranged in any order the counselor chooses. Those selected in Form 5.2 cover School Courses, School Extraclass Activities, Occupational Data, Leisure Activities. They illustrate one way in which the counselor could organize his data in preparation for counseling; because of the nature of Form 5.1, the topics are more limited than if all existing information were utilized.

Form 5.2 shows that most aspects of John's behavior are distributed about a central point, the nonlinguistic end of the major and subordinate continua. The counselor can see at a glance that most of the evidence points toward those educational and vocational choices that do not involve many linguistic factors. Now the evidence can be presented to John in an initial interview, and the counselor can check to see the amount and kind of effect these data have upon John.

There may be no negative emotional elements if John sees himself as a future engineer. There could be considerable psychological conflict if John sees himself as a future clergyman or journalist. Actually, most of the data in Form 5.1, and therefore in Form 5.2, present a congruent picture of John and one which the evidence indicates he can accept.

In such a case the counselor can make predictions of success in educational and occupational activities of a nonlinguistic nature. The counselor can point out to John that all three occupational choices listed in Form 5.1 are possibilities, but that the present evidence indicates greater chance for success in engineering or skilled mechanics than as a college teacher. It would also be possible for the counselor to explore with John the items in Form 5.1 that indicate this, and discuss what John could do if he wished to change his behavior to improve his chances of becoming a college professor or something not particularly indicated by present data. In these ways the counselor uses such data either for prediction or for helping a client to understand and change his behavior.

Interest Factors

Although some of the factors dealing with linguistic-nonlinguistic concepts in evaluating interests have been included in the organization of data in Form 5.2 and in Chapter 9, it may be useful also to describe them here. Cottle (1950) has proposed five such *interest factors*. They are described below as five subheads or continua which should be synthesized with data about aptitudes and abilities.

INTEREST FACTORS

Linguistic	*Nonlinguistic*
1. People and communication	Things and processes
2. Business contact	Scientific activities
3. Abstract, creative activities	Routine, concrete, organized activities
4. Social welfare activities	Nonsocial, mechanical activities
5. Prestige or status activities	Tangible, productive activities

The following elaboration of a linguistic-nonlinguistic system of organizing case data is based on research and counseling experience. It proposes a number of tentative hypotheses about the relationships that may exist between individuals and educational or vocational phenomena which need to be verified. These hypotheses are proposed here to illustrate the system rather than as established relationships.

1. The interest factor, *People and communication vs. Things and processes,* actually is a continuum ranging from the individual who deals only with people and communication, through individuals like physicians or physical

education teachers who deal with people from a scientific background (which would be nonlinguistic), to the engineer or various kinds of mechanics who would be placed somewhere near the nonlinguistic extreme of this continuum.

2. The second factor, *Business contact vs. Scientific types of activity*, appears time after time in studies of interest measurement and is self-explanatory.

3. The third factor, *Abstract, creative thinking* on the one extreme *vs. Routine, concrete, organized activities* on the other end refers to types of activity which do and do not require very much change or newness. These closely approximate descriptions of certain kinds of personality traits as well.

4. The fourth factor, *Social welfare activities vs. Nonsocial, mechanical activities*, is enough different from the first factor so that it needs to be considered by itself. Examples would be the people-related activities of a teacher, social worker, or counselor, as compared to the activities of the bookkeeper, custodian, or machinist.

5. The fifth factor, *Prestige or status activities* vs. *Tangible, productive activities*, represents the kind of work a manager, salesman, or public relations specialist might do, in contrast to the machine operator. The former need tangible evidence of success, in contrast to the machine operator, who knows at the end of a day that he has produced his quota of units and has more in his tool box or locker for tomorrow. The machine operator can count the things he produces and so has no need of mink or expensive cars to demonstrate that he is successful. The nonlinguistic worker can usually show the things that he does, the bridges he makes, the houses he builds, or the machines he produces.

These are different ways in which the behavior needed by people in jobs can be systematically described.

In the academic area, in like fashion, an illustration of *academic abilities* on the linguistic side of the continuum would be ability in languages, English and foreign, and the social sciences. At the other end of the continuum illustrating examples of nonlinguistic types of abilities would be mathematics, the physical sciences, and some vocational education. When *academic skills* are considered apart from academic subjects, such linguistic skills as reading, writing, spelling, and recitation might be listed in contrast to the nonlinguistic academic skills of computation, drawing, laboratory work, and class demonstration. This is another example of the interaction among these academic, vocational, and psychological variables.

Table 5.1 is an attempt to indicate examples of occupations on a *linguistic-nonlinguistic continuum* of behavior. It presents the occupations also in terms of level of education required.

The major linguistic activities, in order of complexity, are listening, talking, reading, and writing. The major nonlinguistic activities focus

Table 5.1

LINGUISTIC-NONLINGUISTIC BEHAVIOR RECOMMENDED FOR DIFFERENT WORK LEVELS*

Education	Linguistic Behavior				Nonlinguistic Behavior			
	Listening	Talking	Reading	Writing	Mechanics	Science	Math	Physical
Graduate work	Psychological counselor	Lawyer	Librarian	Historian	Engineering consultant	Biology professor	Physicist	Physical education professor
College	Social studies teacher	Commentator	Teacher	Newspaper reporter	Engineer	Chemist	Accountant	Coach or artist
Technical school	Stewardess	Office manager	Typesetter	Stenographer	Shoe repairman	Forest ranger	Surveyor	Professional athlete
High school	Telephone operator	Telephone solicitor	File clerk	Typist	Machine operator	Farmer	Cashier	Heavy machine operator
Less than high school	Counselors aide	Route salesman	Newspaper vendor	Stock clerk	Janitor	Veterinarian's asst.	Meter reader	Construction worker

* Occupational examples are listed in a category because their major behavior involves that segment, but other categories may also be descriptive of an occupation to a lesser degree.

around mechanical activity (which could really be subsumed under science but is separated for easier classification), science, mathematics, and physical activities. Most educational and vocational choices involve identifying and describing behavior in terms of these eight major categories, unless one is to get into as complex descriptions as those represented by the U.S. Training and Employment Service's *Dictionary of Occupational Titles* (1965).

The placing of an occupation in a given category in Table 5.1 means that the behavior represented by that category is a central aspect of the occupation. For example, in the Listening category at the College level is the Social studies teacher, who must do considerable listening. Whether this is a major requirement of the occupation for a given individual depends upon his training and personality. Some teachers might be more effective as talkers, and this would be their major classification, rather than listening. They would also be required to do considerable reading and writing. Thus most teachers would be required to manifest total behavior which is primarily linguistic in nature and which obviously involves communication with people. Even such workers as mathematics or science teachers, physical education teachers, or physicians must work with people in activities requiring a background of scientific or nonlinguistic knowledge. For this reason their occupations have to be classified toward the linguistic side of the middle part of the continuum while the Librarian is classified as an extremely linguistic occupation and the auto mechanic or plumber would be extremely nonlinguistic ones.

The purpose of such a system is to develop a method of simplifying and highlighting data about the client so that he can see how it fits into his process of making educational and vocational choices.

In Table 5.1, such linguistic occupations as teaching, law, journalism, selling, or management are occupations dealing with people and communication vs. the nonlinguistic skills needed in the natural sciences, mathematics, accounting, and chemistry. All of the latter group work primarily with things and processes, using nonverbal symbols as frequently as words. It is also possible to think of a "sub-sub" continuum, a more refined point of reference, when considering occupations. Teaching, for example, could be further subdivided, on a continuum of its own, from linguistic to nonlinguistic extremes. At the linguistic end would be the English teacher, the librarian, and the social studies teacher; the mathematics, science, and automobile mechanics teachers would be at the other end of the continuum. Probably the physical education teacher falls somewhere in the middle of the continuum. In like manner, the priestly and medical occupations could be placed along a continuum of linguistic to nonlinguistic jobs or specialties within the general professional classification. Probably even more minute subdivisions are possible, but they do not seem warranted by present data. The important point here is that customary occupational stereotypes actually vary considerably within an occupation.

In terms of leisure activities, reading on the one extreme vs. model building on the other would be examples of linguistic and nonlinguistic activities, respectively. Or parties emphasizing meeting and dealing with people vs. playing solitaire or even playing bridge in a foursome, might be examples of classifying leisure activities as in Form 5.2.

Linguistic activities are the kinds of activities that more women engage in than men in the United States. The nonlinguistic activities are more engaged in by men than women. In the past this has been described in terms of masculinity or femininity, but this has been a more *limited* concept than the one proposed here as a major educational and vocational continuum. Besides, the counselor who tries to explain to a high school boy that he has masculine interests, or worse yet that he has feminine interests, will find the atmosphere can get thick and warm for a few minutes. It is much simpler to explain to a male that he has linguistic interests centering around relationships with people and communication with those people. It is also easier to explain to a female that she has nonlinguistic interests centering around activities dealing with mathematics, or with scientific processes, or the kind of manual activities that a nurse in an operating room might perform. These are the more masculine types of activities and occupations as far as women are concerned, but when they are called nonlinguistic they have less emotional impact on the client and thus are easier to explain or to accept.

U.S.T.E.S. FUNCTIONAL OCCUPATIONAL CLASSIFICATION SYSTEM

For a number of years the United States Training and Employment Service (U.S.T.E.S.), through the activities described by Fine and Heinz (1957, 1958), has been working on a system for classifying occupations in terms of a number of components which make up a description of the occupations and which also include a description of the kinds of people who carry on these occupations. This constitutes still another system of organizing information about the individual in order to help in choice of education and a career. The 1957 publication by Fine and Heinz stresses the need for a single classification system for all workers and described a research program which culminated in the *Estimates of Worker Trait Requirements for 4000 Jobs* (U.S.E.S. 1956). These estimates provide profiles of six worker trait components required for 4,000 entry jobs. The components deal with training time, aptitudes, temperaments, interests,

physical capacities, and working conditions. In the 1958 publication dealing with functional occupational classification structure itself, two additional components, industry and work performed, have been added to the
previous six. Each of the components in the original description of 4,000
jobs was rated separately by different raters: four experienced and six
relatively inexperienced occupational analysts. All the analysts received
100 hours of basic training in the kinds of rating desired and in the background information and materials which would be used in analyzing the
samples of 4,000 jobs.

This approach was the initial phase in the most ambitious and elaborate system of presenting and organizing vocational information that has
been developed, the third edition of the *Dictionary of Occupational
Titles (DOT)* of the United States Employment Service (1965). In this
edition, the first complete revision of the *DOT* since it was published
in 1939, there are extensive job analyses, in terms of the workers' characteristics and the job requirements. More than 75,000 job studies were
made by job analysts in approximately 5,000 different establishments
throughout the United States. Approximately 6,000 new job descriptions
were added and about 7,000 were deleted as no longer appropriate, leaving a net of about 23,000 job definitions under 35,500 job titles. Volume
II deals with fields, or families of jobs, and levels or hierarchies within
each field.

The jobs, as already noted, are described in terms of the workers'
characteristics and the job requirements. The *workers' characteristics* are
identified and stated in terms of general educational development required and specific vocational preparation, minimum scores on the General
Aptitude Test Battery, interests important to the work, and temperaments identified with the work, as well as in terms of the essential physical demands of the work and any unusual working conditions. The other
series of components, the *industry or job requirements,* are described in
terms of the purpose of the work, material used, product, subject matter
or service performed, and generic terms used.

In Volume I each occupation is represented by a six-digit code and a
description, as in the following examples:

Teacher, Secondary School (education) 091.228. teacher, high school. Instructs
students in one or more subjects, such as English, mathematics, or social
studies, in private, religious, or public secondary school (high schools): Instructs pupils through lectures, demonstrations, and audiovisual aids. Prepares
teaching outline for course of study, assigns lessons, and corrects homework
papers. Administers tests to evaluate pupils' progress, records results, and issues
reports to inform parents of progress. Keeps attendance records. Maintains
discipline in classroom and school yard. Participates in faculty and professional

meetings, educational conferences, and teacher training workshops. Performs related duties, such as sponsoring one or more special activities or student organizations, assisting pupils in selecting course of study, and counseling them in adjustment and academic problems. May be designated according to subject matter specialty as Instructor, Typing; Teacher, Agriculture; Teacher, Commercial; Teacher, English; Teacher, Home Economics; Teacher, Language. See Volume II for additional titles.

Teacher, Elementary School (education) 092.228. teacher, primary. Teaches elementary school pupils academic, social, and manipulative skills in rural or urban communities: Prepares teaching outline for course of study. Lectures, demonstrates, and uses audiovisual teaching aids to present subject matter to class. Prepares, administers, and corrects tests, and records results. Assigns lessons, corrects papers, and hears oral presentations. Maintains order in classroom and on playground. Counsels pupils when adjustment and academic problems arise. Discusses pupils' academic and behavior problems with parents and suggests remedial action. Keeps attendance and grade records as required by school board. May teach grades from first to eighth in rural schools.

Counselor (profess. & kin.) II. 045.108. guidance counselor: vocational adviser; vocational counselor. Counsels individuals and provides group educational and vocational guidance services: Collects, organizes, and analyzes information about individuals through records, tests, interviews, and professional sources, to appraise their interests, aptitudes, abilities, and personality characteristics for vocational and educational planning. Compiles and studies occupational, educational, and economic information to aid counselees in making and carrying out vocational and educational objectives. Refers students to placement service. Assists individuals to understand and overcome social and emotional problems. Engages in research and follow-up activities to evaluate counseling techniques. May teach classes. May be designated according to area of activity as Counselor, College; Counselor, School.

The first three digits used in the descriptions are similar to those in previous editions of the *DOT* and represent the field of work, discussed earlier. In the first two definitions quoted, the first two digits, 09, represent "occupations in education"; the third digit describes the specific area within education, such as "college and university (090.)," "primary school and kindergarten (092.)," or "secondary school (091.)."

The last three digits of the code are referred to as "worker traits arrangements" and indicate the level of the occupation within the field, the higher numbers reflecting lesser or lower levels (as shown in Tables 5.2 and 5.3).

The last three digits in this system of organizing client information and job requirements make it possible also to describe job activities in terms of their relationship to data, people, and things as discussed earlier in the Functional Occupational Classification System and shown in Tables 5.2 and 5.4. Thus in the first two definitions given above, the last three digits (.228) are interpreted to mean that the occupation is classified as requiring the teacher to *analyze data* (2), the third highest or most complex activity in the category; to instruct people (2), the third most skillful process in the relationships-with-*people* category, and, has "no significant relationship" (8) to activities in the *things* category. These are considered to be the most occupationally significant elements in the entire description of the job and hence are highlighted in the code.

Table 5.2

DOT DESCRIPTIONS OF PRINCIPAL JOB ACTIVITIES IN
TERMS OF DATA, PEOPLE, AND THINGS°

Data (4th digit)	*People (5th digit)*	*Things (6th digit)*
0 Synthesizing	0 Mentoring	0 Setting up
1 Coordinating	1 Negotiating	1 Precision working
2 Analyzing	2 Instructing	2 Operating-controlling
3 Compiling	3 Supervising	3 Driving-operating
4 Computing	4 Diverting	4 Manipulating
5 Copying	5 Persuading	5 Tending
6 Comparing	6 Speaking-signaling	6 Feeding-offbearing
7⎫ No significant	7 Serving	7 Handling
8⎬ relationship	8 No significant	8 No significant
⎭ to data	relationship	relationship
	to people	to things

° From U.S. Department of Labor, United States Employment Service, *Dictionary of occupational titles* (Washington, D.C.: Government Printing Office), 1965, vol. II, Appendix A, p. 649.

The *DOT* (1965, pp. 649–50) further defines the categories of data, people, and things in Table 5.2 as follows:

DATA: Information, knowledge, and conceptions, related to data, people, or things, obtained by observation, investigation, interpretation, visualization, mental creation; incapable of being touched; written data take the form of numbers, words, symbols; other data are ideas, concepts, oral verbalization.

0. *Synthesizing:* Integrating analyses of data to discover facts and/or develop knowledge concepts or interpretations.

1. *Coordinating:* Determining the time, place, and sequence of operations or action to be taken on the basis of analysis of data; executing determinations and/or reporting on events.

2. *Analyzing:* Examining and evaluating data. Presenting alternative actions in relation to the evaluation is frequently involved.

3. *Compiling:* Gathering, collating, or classifying information about data, peo-

ple, or things. Reporting and/or carrying out a prescribed action in relation to the information is frequently involved.

4. *Computing:* Performing arithmetic operations and reporting on and/or carrying out a prescribed action in relation to them. Does not include counting.

5. *Copying:* Transcribing, entering, or posting data.

6. *Comparing:* Judging the readily observable functional, structural, or compositional characteristics (whether similar to or divergent from obvious standards) of data, people, or things.

PEOPLE: Human beings; also animals dealt with on an individual basis as if they were human.

0. *Mentoring:* Dealing with individuals in terms of their total personality in order to advise, counsel, and/or guide them with regard to problems that may be resolved by legal, scientific, clinical, spiritual, and/or other professional principles.

1. *Negotiating:* Exchanging ideas, information, and opinions with others to formulate policies and programs and/or arrive jointly at decisions, conclusions, or solutions.

2. *Instructing:* Teaching subject matter to others, or training others (including animals) through explanation, demonstration, and supervised practice; or making recommendations on the basis of technical disciplines.

3. *Supervising:* Determining or interpreting work procedures for a group of workers, assigning specific duties to them, maintaining harmonious relations among them, and promoting efficiency.

4. *Diverting:* Amusing others.

5. *Persuading:* Influencing others in favor of a product, service, or point of view.

6. *Speaking-Signaling:* Talking with and/or signaling people to convey or exchange information. Includes giving assignments and/or directions to helpers or assistants.

7. *Serving:* Attending to the needs or requests of people or animals or the expressed or implicit wishes of people. Immediate response is involved.

THINGS: Inanimate objects as distinguished from human beings; substances or materials; machines, tools, equipment; products. A thing is tangible and has shape, form and other physical characteristics.

0. *Setting Up:* Adjusting machines or equipment by replacing or altering tools, jigs, fixtures, and attachments to prepare them to perform their functions, change their performance, or restore their proper functioning if they break down. Workers who set up one or a number of machines for other workers or who set up and personally operate a variety of machines are included here.

1. *Precision Working:* Using body members and/or tools or work aids to work,

move, guide, or place objects or materials in situations where ultimate responsibility for the attainment of standards occurs and selection of appropriate tools, objects, or materials, and the adjustment of the tool to the task require exercise of considerable judgment.

2. *Operating-Controlling:* Starting, stopping, controlling, and adjusting the progress of machines or equipment designed to fabricate and/or process objects or materials. Operating machines involves setting up the machine and adjusting the machine or material as the work progresses. Controlling equipment involves observing gages, dials, etc., and turning valves and other devices to control such factors as temperature, pressure, flow of liquids, speed of pumps, and reactions of materials. Setup involves several variables and adjustment is more frequent than in tending.

3. *Driving-Operating:* Starting, stopping, and controlling the actions of machines or equipment for which a course must be steered, or which must be guided, in order to fabricate, process, and/or move things or people. Involves such activities as observing gages and dials; estimating distances and determining speed and direction for other objects; turning cranks and wheels; pushing clutches or brakes; and pushing or pulling gear lifts or levers. Includes such machines as cranes, conveyor systems, tractors, furnace charging machines, paving machines, and hoisting machines. Excludes manually powered machines, such as handtrucks and dollies, and power assisted machines, such as electric wheelbarrows and handtrucks.

4. *Manipulating:* Using body members, tools, or special devices to work, move, guide, or place objects or materials. Involves some latitude for judgment with regard to precision attained and selecting appropriate tool, object, or material, although this is readily manifest.

5. *Tending:* Starting, stopping, and observing the function of machines and equipment. Involves adjusting materials or controls of the machine, such as changing guides, adjusting timers and temperature gages, turning valves to allow flow of materials, and flipping switches in response to lights. Little judgment is involved in making these adjustments.

6. *Feeding-Offbearing:* Inserting, throwing, dumping, or placing materials in or removing them from machines or equipment which are automatic or tended or operated by other workers.

7. *Handling:* Using body members, handtools, and/or special devices to work, move, or carry objects or materials. Involves little or no latitude for judgment with regard to attainment of standards or in selecting appropriate tool, object, or material.

Isaacson (1966) has listed the terminal digits used in the *DOT* to show the level of complexity of some of the components of the data-people-things categories (Table 5.3).

In Table 5.4 are given several typical classifications as coded by the last three digits, to show how the user would interpret the code description of the job in terms of data, people, and things.

Table 5.3

TERMINAL DIGITS USED IN THIRD EDITION OF
DOT TO SHOW LEVEL OF COMPLEXITY IN
DATA-PEOPLE-THINGS HIERARCHY

.018	.101	.208	.328	.458	.582	.683	.780	.848
.021	.108	.228	.348	.463	.584	.684	.781	.858
.028	.118	.248	.358	.468	.585	.685	.782	.862
.031	.128	.251	.361	.478	.587	.687		.863
.038	.130	.258	.363	.483	.588	.688		.864
.048	.131	.261	.364	.484				.865
.051	.132	.268	.368	.485				.867
.061	.133	.271	.371	.487				.868
.062	.134	.280	.378	.488				.873
.068	.137	.281	.380					.874
.081	.138	.282	.381					.877
.088	.148	.283	.382					.878
	.151	.284	.383					.883
	.158	.287	.384					.884
	.168	.288	.387					.885
	.181		.388					.886
	.187							.887
	.188							

Reproduced with permission from L. E. Isaacson, *Career Information in Counseling and Teaching* (Boston: Allyn & Bacon, Inc.), 1966.

Table 5.4

INTERPRETATIONS OF SELECTED SETS OF THE LAST
THREE *DOT* CODE DIGITS: OCCUPATIONS ARE OF
A HIGH LEVEL OF COMPLEXITY OF OPERATION OR SKILL

Code	Data	Level	People	Level	Things	Level
.018	Synthesizing	High	Negotiating	High	N.S.R.*	Low
.825	N.S.R.*	Low	Instructing	High	Tending	Low
.572	Copying	Aver.	Serving	High Aver.	Operating Controlling	Aver.
.680	Comparing	Low	N.S.R.*		Setting up	High
.404	Computing	Aver.	Mentoring	High	Manipulating	Aver.

* No Significant Relationship.

All counselors working with clients about to enter the job market for the first time should make the effort to familiarize themselves with this tool of vocational counseling. It permits the counselor to work from the specific knowledge developed by professionals in the world of work rather than from a series of unfounded inferences gained from his own limited exposure in a much less current series of work experiences when he himself was younger.

There is a programed training manual for the *DOT*, to help individuals learn how to use the new system. This would permit a counselor to teach himself how to use the *DOT*. Further details of vocational appraisal are described in Chapter 8.

SOME SAMPLE CASE DATA AND QUESTIONS

The data in Form 5.3 are presented to give the beginning counselor some working data. Some of the questions a counselor could ask and answer are as follows:

1. What data shown in Form 5.3 indicate that this person may not be a good reader?
2. Is it possible that this person may be unable to learn to read better, or is there evidence that his academic potential would permit him to acquire better reading skills than are evidenced here?
3. Is it possible that this person may be having difficulty in school because he does not know how to study?
4. Are there any evidences in these data that this person may be so emotionally disturbed that he is unable to perform well in school?
5. Does the information contained in scores from the interest inventories indicate the kind of profile that would be expected of a person enrolled in an engineering curriculum and one who is apt to be happy and satisfied in the kinds of academic work required of such a curriculum?

This case illustrates five questions usually asked whenever any student is having difficulty in school. These questions center about academic potential vs. academic achievement, the reading and other study skills of the student, whether emotional disturbance is affecting performance, and the part that interests play in motivation for school.

The most probable interpretation of the above data might answer these questions in the following way:

The student would seem to have sufficient potential to function at the college level, if reading skills were improved. Other study skills would appear to be adequate and interest in the curriculum in which the student is enrolled would seem to offer adequate motivational factors. There is some question about the meaning of the personality inventory scores shown on the *MMPI*. These may be reflecting the normal concern an individual would have who is not getting along as well in school as he would like. The D and Pt scores would be indicating this type of pressure. It is difficult to tell from these scores whether the high F, Pd, Ma, and Si scores are a reflection of other personality difficulties or the concomitant of academic difficulty. The program the counselor undertakes will be modified by the interpretation placed on these latter scores in the light of other case data and in conjunction with the weak reading skills shown above.

Form 5.3

CASE OF MALE, AGE 18, FRESHMAN IN ENGINEERING

A.C.E.				Wechsler-Bellevue	98	Percentile Gen. Pop.
	Q.	64	Percentile National Coll. Fresh.			
	L.	5	"	Full Scale I.Q.	128	15–19 yr. olds
	T.	16	"	Verbal I.Q.	128	
				Performance I.Q.	125	
Coop. Reading C2	V.	27	Percentile Ent. Coll. Fresh.			
	S.	11	"	**MMPI**		**T score**
	C.	20	"	?		50
	T.	21	"	L		50
				F		60
Coop. English	U.	3	Percentile Ent. Coll. Fresh.	K		51
	Sp.	11	"	Hs		49
	V.	4	"	D		65
	T.	6	"	Hy		48
				Pd		64
Coop. Mathematics		31	Percentile Ent. Coll. Fresh.	Mf		50
				Pa		50
Iowa Silent		20	Percentile Coll. Fr.	Pt		67
Grade Equivalent		10.9		Sc		51
Age Equivalent		16.0		Ma		58
Tyler Kimber				Si		61
Study Skills		95	Percentile Jr. Coll. Students			

SVIB Men

Kuder Pref. Rec. B.M.		**A**	**Borderline B, B +**
Adult Norms		Engineer	Carpenter
		Prod. Manager	YMCA Phys. Dir.
Mech.	91 Percentile	Printer	Pres. Mfg. Concern
Comp.	86 "	Math-Sci. Tchr.	
Sci.	91 "	Policeman	
Pers.	40 "	Personnel Manager	**Rejects**
Art.	60 "		Artist
Lit.	5 "		City Sch. Supt.
Mus.	78 "		Minister
Soc. Serv.	10 "		CPA
Cler.	55 "	**B +**	Lawyer
		Chemist	
		Accountant	
		Office Worker	O. L. 18 Percentile Stanford Freshmen
		Purchasing	M. F. 83 Percentile College Males
		Public Admin.	I. M. 39 Percentile 18 yr. olds

Form 5.4

COUNSELING CASE

A.C.E. Psych.	Q. 74 Percentile Nat. Coll. Fr.		Otis S.A. Ment. Ability
	L. 32 Percentile		I.Q. 117 70 Percentile Coll. Stud.
	T. 54 Percentile		93 Percentile Unselected Adults
Coop. Reading C2	V. 6 Percentile Nat. Coll. Jr.		
	S. 13 Percentile		**MMPI**
	C. 22 Percentile		
	T. 12 Percentile		? 50
			L 50
Coop. English PM	U. 4 Percentile Nat. Coll. Fr.		K 48
	S. 1 Percentile		F 55
	V. 8 Percentile		Hs 52
	T. 2 Percentile		D 63
			Hy 52
Coop. Math B	96 Percentile Nat. Ent. Fr.		Pd 41
			Mf 80
Coop. Gen. Cult. X Total	21 Percentile Nat. Coll. Soph.		Pa 47
Curr. Soc. Prob.	30 Percentile		Pt 58
Hist. and Soc. Stud.	28 Percentile		Sc 49
Lit.	2 Percentile		Ma 50
Sci.	75 Percentile		Si 48
Fine Arts	2 Percentile		
Math	82 Percentile		
Minn. Clerical	No. 7 Percentile Employed Clerical Workers		
	Na. 5 Percentile		
Minn. Paper Form Board	91 Percentile Eng. Fr.		

Strong Vocational Interest Blank for Men

	A	**Rejects**
	Physician	Personnel Mgr.
	Engineer	YMCA Secretary
Kuder Preference	Chemist	City Sch. Supt.
Record	Farmer	Minister
Mech. 99 Percentile	Carpenter	Sales Mgr.
Comp. 99 Percentile	Printer	Real Estate Sales
Sci. 97 Percentile	Math.-Sci. Tchr.	Life Ins. Sales
Pers. 5 Percentile		
Art 73 Percentile	**B+**	
Lit. 1 Percentile	Production Mgr.	O.L. 3 Percentile Stanford Fr.
Mus. 5 Percentile	Y. Physical Director	M.F. 78 Percentile Coll. Males
Soc. Serv. 5 Percentile		I.M. 23 Percentile 20 yr. old men
Cler. 50 Percentile		

SUPPLEMENTARY DATA

This girl, who is a college junior wth a math major, came in either for help in choosing another major or for confirmation of the major that she has already selected.

She states that her high school graduating class was a group of 20 and that she was 7th in this group, with a B average. She then attended a junior college and maintained a B average there. In both high school and junior college she liked mathematics best and English least. Courses which she took in high school and junior college in math include elementary and advanced algebra, plane geometry, general mathematics, trigonometry, college algebra, solid geometry, analytical geometry, calculus I and II. She received A's in all of these except a B in trigonometry and in college algebra. She also has 12 hours of chemistry, 10 hours of physics, and is taking biology at the present time.

Activities that she likes are sports of all kinds. She reeled off a long list of all kinds of intramural sports which she likes to play rather than to watch. She would impress one as being a tomboy. Other activities that she likes are dancing and reading books, mostly popular fiction. She lives in a sorority.

When discussing other types of activities at the end of the interview to get an idea of her social ability, she mentioned that she belonged to a card club which they had called a "poker club" but in which they played all types of card games.

Work experience includes work as a typist for one month, work as a packer in a soap factory for two months; work for two and a half months in a powdered milk plant; and work as a girl scout and assistant girl scout leader. Her father, who is 70 and completed 8th grade, is a retired farmer. Her mother, who is 55 and completed 12th grade, is a housewife.

SVIB Women

A	Rejects	F.M. I—Percentile
Math Science Teacher	Home Economics Teacher	College Females
Physician	English Teacher	
	Social Worker	
	Social Science Teacher	
	YWCA Secretary	

The information shown in Form 5.4 can be highlighted by a number of questions that the counselor might like to ask. These questions are as follows:

1. What data from Form 5.4 would be indicating nonlinguistic factors as far as this individual is concerned?
2. If you had to discuss possible majors with this person in light of these scores, would you discuss engineering?
3. If you knew that this person was a second-semester college junior, would this make a difference in the possible majors you discuss?
4. When you look at the scores of the *MMPI* is there any scale which does not support choices of engineering or other nonlinguistic majors?
5. Would it help you to change the answer you made to question 4 if you knew that these data described a girl?
6. What additional data to support a nonlinguistic major are found in the Supplementary Data to Form 5.4?
7. What possible college majors would you suggest to this girl?

CASE OF WILLIAM ROE

Initial Interview with William Roe

This student was graduated second in a class of 20, from a 100-pupil high school (grades 9–12). He had a 90+ average, taking elementary algebra, plane and solid geometry, trigonometry, and college algebra. He also had general science and physics. He liked mathematics best and physics least. The reason for his dislike of physics was that he had a war-trained teacher who was not a science major.

In high school he played varsity football (2 yrs.), basketball (4 yrs.), and baseball and track (1 yr. each). He went out for basketball in college and made the B team. He was a Star Scout in high school.

We began by discussing his reading. He stated that he had always been a very slow reader, that he was supposed to wear glasses for poor vision but had never done so. During the interview he decided that probably his first point of procedure should be to go over to the reading laboratory and have a further check on his reading to see if corrective or remedial work were necessary. If results seem to indicate this, he also thought it might be wise to take a trip to either an eye specialist or to student hospital for a check on the glasses that he has at the present time, as they are five years old.

Much of the time of this interview was spent in developing rapport. The boy was rather reserved and quiet and did not contribute too much unless continually stimulated. He stated that he is having difficulty in chemistry, doing about F work at the present time. This would raise a serious question, coupled with his dislike for physics, about continuing in engineering. His ability in mathematics, however, seems to support some type of a mathematical background in further schooling and in occupations.

His college average at present is 1.4 (C+) with a D in inorganic chemistry. His mathematics grades were A's and B's.

He doesn't work outside school, using P. L. 550 funds and some savings to cover living costs.

His father is at present a second-class postmaster. Prior to this he was a superintendent of schools. He has a Master's degree. His mother, a housewife, is a graduate of a 3-year teachers' college course with a permanent certificate for high-school teaching.

He has three sisters. One, married, completed thirteenth grade. Another is in 14th grade at present. The third is in the eleventh grade.

He doesn't like social activities, except such sports as tennis and swimming. He reads one book every 2 months and likes *Reader's Digest*. He gave no clear picture of his leisure-time activities, either because he has no planned program or because of reticence. This was the only serious gap in the information which was evidenced during the initial interview.

Here are some questions the beginning counselor might answer from the data on William Roe:

1. What nonlinguistic factors appear in the initial interview notes?
2. What data could be considered evidence of his potential as a college student?
3. If he transfers out of engineering, what other majors might be considered?
4. What does the family data contribute to understanding the values to which this client has been exposed?
5. What do you know about his social skills?
6. What additional evidence would you want from a testing program?
7. What tests would you select to give such information? Would you assign these all at once or gradually?

When the counselor inspects the test data for William Roe, the following questions might be pertinent:

1. What evidence of poor reading skills exist? Do the scores on intelligence tests contribute evidence of poor reading skills?
2. Would you expect this client to be more successful at present in a liberal arts curriculum?
3. What about the ultimate choice of mathematics or science teaching? Do the two interest inventories agree about this? What attitudes do you suppose the family environment has created toward teaching?

SUMMARY PROFILE OF WILLIAM ROE

Name *William Roe*		Unit *Engr.*		Class *Soph.*		Sex *M*	Age *21*
Name of Test Form		*Score*	*Percentile*			*Norm Group*	
ACE Psych '41 Q '41 L-57		R98*	37 (Q,50;L,32)			N. Coll. Fr.	
Coop. Reading, Total C2T		S54*	37			N.E. Fresh.	
Vocab.		49	20				
Speed		55	35				
Compre.		59	56				
Coop. English, Total PM		S41*	6			N.E. Fresh.	
Usage		47	17				
Spell.		26	1—				
Vocab.		51	27				
Mathematics D-45		R60*	73			E. Coll. Fresh.	
Wechsler Bellevue Full	I.Q.	123	95			Gen'l Pop.	
Verbal		127				20–24 Yr. Old	
Performance		113					
Coop. Gen. Cult X							
Sci.		20	38			N. Coll. Soph.	
Math.		35	89				
Rev. Pp. Fm. Bd.		R47*	70			Engr. Fresh.	
Purdue Pegboard							
Right Hand		R12	8				
Left Hand		11	8				
Both Hands		10	17				
Total		33	3				
Assembly		8¼	65				
Minn. Clerical-Nos.		W82*	49			Adults Gainfully Occupied	
Names		61	32				
Iowa Physics Apt.		57	39			Engr. Fresh.	
Minn. Soc. Pref.		W125*	34			Minn. U. Students	
Minn. Soc. Behavior		W144*	67				

Kuder; Form BM, Adult Males.

Mech.	36 Percentile	Comp.	94 Percentile	
Sci.	40 Percentile	Pers.	87 Percentile	
Art.	11 Percentile	Lit.	52 Percentile	
Mus.	22 Percentile	Soc. Serv.	77 Percentile	
		Cler.	20 Percentile	

Strong:

	B+ *on*	B *on*	C *on*	
O.L. 28 Percentile	Prod. Mgr.	Printer	Artist	Minister
M.F. 35 Percentile	Math.-Sci. teacher	Policeman	Psychologist	Musician
I.M. 82 Percentile		Personnel Mgr.	Architect	Pres. (mfg.)
		Soc. Sci. Tchr.		Engineer
		Physician		Chemist
		Accountant		
		Dentist		
		Real Est. Salesman	City Sch. Supt.	

° *R, S,* and *W* show raw, scaled, and weighted scores.

CASE OF EDWARD DOE

Initial Interview Record of Edward Doe

This student is a junior in the College of Engineering, taking power plant work in the mechanical engineering sequence with a grade point average of 1.3 (C+). This does not appear consistent with placement examinations taken in the spring of 1948. Nor is it consistent with the fact that he was an aviation cadet and had completed pre-flight training just before the war ended and then was separated from service. For that reason additional tests of academic ability, in particular the Wechsler Bellevue, were planned, as was a retake on the ACE. He was graduated in a high school class of 75, approximately mid-way in the class, with a C average. He liked English least. He liked geography and mathematics best, but had only two years of mathematics in high school. He played varsity basketball and participated in varsity track for three years. He has had no musical training and no inclination toward music. He took one year of manual training in high school, consisting of one semester of mechanical drawing and one semester of shop work.

Here at college he likes mathematics and strength-of-materials courses best, although he failed the latter course last term. He likes English least.

Work experience includes work as an aircraft sheet metal worker for three years, work as a carpenter's helper for eight months, and Army training as an aviation cadet.

Leisure-time activities include various types of mechanical hobbies. He states that he likes to "mess around with mechanical things," such as building shelves, cabinets, and making photographic equipment for his new hobby of photography, developed since a baby boy was born. He states that he has no darkroom, that he only takes photographs.

His father, who is 48, completed fourth grade in the United States (born in Czechoslovakia) and is a shovel operator in a coal mine. His mother, who is 43, was born in the U.S., completed eighth grade, and is a housewife. He has one brother, 20, who completed one and one-half years at State Teachers College and is not in school at present; a sister, 22, who completed twelfth grade and is now a secretary in Kansas City.

His own family consists of his wife, who acts as a housewife and cares for his boy, who is 19 months old. She completed twelfth grade, worked as a secretary, and operated a lathe in an aircraft plant during the war. She was very active in 4-H Clubs while she was in high school. He made this latter statement as if he were quite proud of the fact that his wife had achieved quite a bit of distinction in this work in the state.

At the close of the interview we discussed tests he might take, how they could be useful, and when he would take them. He plans to investigate the power-plant-management and industrial-engineering options of the mechanical engineering program. His problems in adjustment seem an outgrowth of his academic progress and problems of academic choice.

Form 5.6

UNIVERSITY GUIDANCE BUREAU, SUMMARY PROFILE

Name. *Edward. Doe.* . . . . School *Engrg.* . . . Class *1965* . . . Sex *M* . . Age *24* . . .

	Date	Name of Test Form	Score	%-ile	Norm Group	1	5 10 15 20 30 40 50 60 70 80 85 90 95 99
Placement Exams	9/57	ACE Psych. Total	72	11	Nat. Coll.		
		Q	35	37	Freshmen		
		L	37	6			
	9/57	Coop. Reading Total	45	8	"		
		C 2 T Vocab.	45	10			
		Speed	48	14			
		(level. J.) Compre.	44	7	"		
	9/57	Coop. English Usage	43	9			
		PM Spell.	52	43			
	9/57	KU Mathematics	49	46	K.U. Students		
Scholastic Aptitude	2/62	ACE Psych. Total	90	34	Nat. Coll.		
		Q	52	84	Freshmen		
		L	38	6			
		WS IQ					
	2/6?	Wechsler-Bellevue. Full Scale	121 117	87	Gen. Pop.		
		Verbal	55 110		20-24 yr. olds		
		Perform.	66 121				
	2/62	Otis S-A Mental Ability	52	53	Coll. Stud.		
		IQ	110				
Achievement	2/62	Coop General Culture Total					
		I History- Social Studies					
		II Literature					
		III Sciences	24	50	Nat. Coll.		
		IV Fine Arts			Soph.		
		V Mathematics	30	84			
	2/6?	Iowa Silent Reading		5	13th Grade		
Specific Aptitudes	2/6?	Minn. Paper Form Board	54	81	Engrg. Sr.		
		Minnesota Clerical No.	185	94	Employ. Cler.		
		No.	166	90	Workers		
Personality	2/62	Minn. Soc. Att.					
		Soc. Pref.	137	54	Minn. U.		
		Soc. Beh.	156	83	Students		
Misc.							

Other Profiles   SVIBM *2/62* SVIBW   Kuder *2/62*   MMPI   GZTS *2/62*

Form 5.6

Other Data for Edward Doe

Kuder Preference Record, Form C		Guilford-Zimmermann Temperament Survey	
	Centile		Centile
Outdoor	59	G - General Activity	80
Mechanical	99	R - Restraint	20
Computational	46	A - Ascendance	42
Scientific	75	S - Social Interest	55
Persuasive	55	E - Emotional Stability	35
Artistic	88	O - Objectivity	50
Literary	1	F - Friendliness	57
Musical	21	T - Thoughtfulness	50
Social Service	55	P - Personal Relations	50
Clerical	14	M - Masculinity	98

Strong Vocational Interest Blank for Men

Group I

Artist	C
Psychologist (rev.)	C
Architect	B
Physician (rev.)	B
Dentist	B+

Group II

Chemist	A
Mathematician	C
Engineer	A

Group III

Production Manager	A

Group IV

Farmer	B+
Math. Science Teacher	B
Forest Service	B-
Army Officer	
Aviator	

Group V

Y.M.C.A. Phys. Dir.	C
Personnel Manager	C
Vocational Counselor	C
Soc. Science Teacher	C
City School Supt.	C
Minister	C
Social Worker	

Group VII

C.P.A. Partner	C

Group VIII

Senior C.P.A.	
Junior Accountant	C
Office Worker	B-
Purchasing Agent	C
Banker	C
Pharmacist	

Group IX

Sales Manager	C
Real Estate Salesman	B-
Life Insurance Salesman	C

Group X

Advertising Man	C
Lawyer	C
Author-Journalist	C

Group XI

President (Mfg. Concern)	B

OL 36 %ile Stanford Freshmen
MF 91 %ile College males
IM 10 %ile 24-year-old men

Some of the questions a counselor might ask after reading data about Edward Doe are:

1. How do the data about potential for school coincide between the initial interview and the first four scores on the Summary Profile? What does the Wechsler Bellevue Performance I.Q. indicate?
2. What tentative diagnosis about reading skills seems indicated? What data support this?
3. What test scores indicate problems of adjustment? Do these seem deep-rooted and serious? Why?
4. Do the interest inventory scores support continuance in engineering? Do they indicate a possible choice of production engineering over research and development? How?
5. As counselor, what other data do you think this client needs before making a choice of college major?
6. Are there any remedial or corrective measures you would suggest?

SUMMARY

As the counselor, through the use of records, biodata, observational techniques, or the initial interview, studies the things which a client has done, a pattern of behavior develops which usually shows a preponderance of skills and a preference for activities toward the linguistic or the nonlinguistic end of the continuum. The counselor who can organize data in this fashion has a convenient and practical way of helping a client to understand behavior, to accept such behavior as part of himself, and to make sound educational and occupational choices as a result.

Such systems of organizing data from records will have to be developed by the individual counselor in the light of personal needs and skills. Beginning counselors will find that some system of handling data develops without deliberate effort. They should be highly aware of this process at first, in order to evaluate how adequate their system is in terms of good counseling objectives and procedures. Only when this has been done can the counselor allow the process to take place at a low level of awareness.

REFERENCES

Amos, W. E., and Grambs, J. 1968. *Counseling the disadvantaged youth.* Englewood Cliffs, N.J.: Prentice-Hall, Inc.

Cottle, W. C. 1950. A factorial study of the *Multiphasic, Strong, Kuder* and *Bell* inventories using a population of adult males. *Psychometrika.* 15:25–47.

English, H. B., and English, A. C. 1958. *A comprehensive dictionary of psychological and psychoanalytical terms.* New York: Longmans, Green & Co., Inc.

Fine, S. A., and Heinz, C. A. 1957. The estimates of worker traits requirements for 4,000 jobs. *Personnel and Guidance J.* 36:168–74.

———. 1958. The functional occupational classification structure. *Personnel and Guidance J.* 37:180–92.

Garrett, H. E. 1946. A developmental theory of intelligence. *Amer. Psychol.* 1:372–78.

Goltz, E. 1966. Placement through automatic data-processing. *Employment Service Review.* 3:57–58.

Hahn, M. E. 1963. *Psychoevaluation.* New York: McGraw-Hill Book Company.

———. 1967. *Planning ahead after 40.* Beverly Hills, Calif.: Western Psychological Services.

———, and Brayfield, A. H. 1945. *Occupational laboratory manual for teachers and counselor.* Chicago: Science Research Associates.

———, and MacLean, M. S. 1955. *Counseling psychology.* New York: McGraw-Hill Book Company.

Hill, G. E., and Luckey, E. B. 1969. *Guidance for children in elementary schools.* New York: Appleton-Century-Crofts.

Holland, J. L. 1966. *Psychology of vocational choice.* Boston: Blaisdell Press.

Isaacson, L. E. 1966. *Career information in counseling and teaching.* Boston: Allyn & Bacon, Inc.

Jordaan, J. P., et al. 1968. *The counseling psychologist.* New York: Columbia University Press.

Osipow, S. H. 1968. *Theories of career development.* New York: Appleton-Century-Crofts.

Patterson, C. H. 1969. What is counseling psychology? *J. Couns. Psychol.* 16:23–29.

Super, D. E., et al. 1963. *Career development: Self-concept theory.* New York: College Entrance Examination Board.

Thorndike, E. L. 1918. The nature, purposes, and general methods of measurements of educational products. Bloomington, Ill. Seventeenth Yearbook, National Society for the Study of Education, Part II.

United States Employment Service. 1956. *Estimates of worker trait requirements for 4,000 jobs.* Washington, D.C.: Government Printing Office.

———. 1965. *Dictionary of occupational titles.* 3rd ed. vols. I, II. Washington, D.C.: Government Printing Office.

Williamson, E. G., and Darley, J. G. 1937. *Student personnel work.* New York: McGraw-Hill Book Company.

6

Statistics Used to Describe Groups and Individuals

In order to evaluate the data about groups and about individual behavior that are essential to any counseling activities, the counselor must possess a knowledge of statistics. In some ways the frame of reference in which the counselor uses these statistics is the same as that for other psychological or educational workers. Estimates of group behavior must be collected and interpreted so that a client is better able to understand the groups in which it is necessary to function. The client is helped to understand himself in terms of place in or divergence from the average group engaging in an activity. However, the frame of reference of the counselor differs also to the extent that part of the work with clients requires the use of statistics to organize and interpret comparative data about individuals. Thus it is essential that these two frames of reference for statistics, a comparison with a group and comparisons within a given client, are contained in almost every statistical inference the counselor makes.

These statistics should be used for all estimates of behavior in counseling, and not just for test scores. The chief ways in which a counselor uses statistics may be summarized as follows:

1. Directly, for counseling a client.
2. For referral reports about a client sent to other agencies.
3. In analyzing the results of tests given to groups. These results form a large part of the basis for counseling.
4. In interpreting reports in the literature so that such information can be used to improve the effectiveness of counseling.
5. In carrying on research which will evaluate counseling procedures or improve their effectiveness.
6. For reporting such research in the literature.

The brief introduction to statistics which follows is intended to emphasize the counselor's use of statistics and serve as an overview or refresher rather than as a basic source. It describes the purposes for which the counselor uses averages, measures of variability, and measures of relationship. A short discussion of sampling and the testing of hypotheses, as the counselor uses them in his frame of reference, will compose the last part of the chapter.

AVERAGES

The counselor is usually concerned with two averages or measures of central tendency. These are the mean and the median. The term *central tendency* is used because it describes the activities of the middle of the group.

The counselor is concerned with helping a client to identify and evaluate the distinctive characteristics or traits of the groups in which the client will function. To do this, the counselor and client must decide which of these groups are appropriate. It is not usually appropriate to compare a twelfth-grader with ninth-grade groups unless some sort of retardation makes it so. On the other hand, it is often logical to compare graduating twelfth graders with college freshmen, if this is the next group in which the twelfth-grader will compete. To make these comparisons and to choose appropriate norm groups it is necessary to describe the groups in terms of their central or average tendency and their deviation from an average.

The Mean

Suppose that a group intelligence test is administered to 40 individuals. There are two ways in which the mean score can be obtained. The scores could be added together and their sum divided by the total number of cases. This result is a value which is already familiar to the counselor, namely the *arithmetic average* or mean ($\overline{X}$).

Very often, when there are a large number of scores, it is an advantage to use another method in calculating the mean. The data are first entered in a frequency table. To construct a table like this, one follows several simple rules. In the first place, it is customary to have between 10 and 20 *intervals*, or divisions, in the frequency distribution. In order to arrive at such a distribution, an adequate size for the interval must be chosen. The interval size is determined by first obtaining the range of scores. The *range* is defined as the high score minus the low score.

How Numbers Are Regarded in Statistics

A digression to illustrate how each score is considered seems essential. Any number or score is thought of as being on a straight line or continuum. An example of this would be a score of 8. On this line or continuum the score 8 occupies the distance beginning at 7.5 and continuing *up to* 8.5. Each number has then a lower limit and an upper limit. The next number 9, really begins at 8.5 and continues *up to* 9.5. This is the way the counselor interprets scores and class intervals of scores. The score is considered a band on the continuum rather than a point.

When data are grouped, it is assumed that the values of the frequencies in any one interval will, when averaged, result in the midpoint of that interval. If this does not happen, slight discrepancies enter into the work. These discrepancies usually cancel out, that in one interval tending to balance that in another. To the extent that they do not, slight differences appear as a result of using the different methods.

The Median

The other measure of central tendency frequently encountered in counseling practice and research is the median. The median is defined as the point in any distribution with an equal number of cases on either side of it. It is the midpoint of any distribution.

The median for a set of intelligence test scores is computed in the following manner. If the total number of scores is 40, the median will have 20 scores on either side of it. The first step in obtaining the median is to divide the number of scores (N) by 2, or to take 50% of N. The median is halfway between the twentieth and twenty-first scores in this instance.

Use of the Mean and the Median

The mean is used when the data take on the shape of the normal curve, which is bell-shaped, tapering off in both directions. When data do not take this form, extreme scores tend to pull the mean in their direction and the result is a mean that does not give a realistic picture of the middle of the group. The median is not affected by these extreme scores. The top score could have any value, even in the millions, and the median would be the same. But a high score would have pulled the mean in the direction of that high score. The mean is also used for other computations. The median is purely an end in itself. It is a basic landmark in the distribution, but little can be done with it other than to show the exact midpoint. It is useful in counseling when distributions depart from normal, and the mean therefore would be misleading, or when a quick estimate of an average is needed.

VARIABILITY

Suppose there are two distributions. Both have a mean of 45. Both contain the same number of individuals, and both have been obtained by administering a test to these individuals. These two means tell very little about these two distributions other than that they have the same central tendency. Suppose that in one group the high score is 48 and the low score 42, and that in the other group the high score is 68 and the low score is 28. This gives an additional description of the two groups. One group has much variability and is said to be "heterogeneous." The other has little variability and is said to be "homogeneous." To describe a group adequately, it follows that a *measure of variability* is needed as well as a measure of central tendency.

The most widely used measure of variability is the standard deviation. The counselor needs to know how to use the standard deviation (S.D. or s) in order to describe the variability of a group and to interpret a client's position in the group in terms of such variability. The standard deviation is expressed in equal units of variability. Thus, if the standard deviation of the Otis is 12 I.Q. points and that of the Stanford Binet is 16 I.Q. points, an Otis I.Q. of 112 is interpreted as equivalent to a Stanford Binet I.Q. of 116.

Interpretation of the Standard Deviation

The standard deviation is always interpreted in reference to the normal curve, as shown in Figure 6.1. Notice that if a standard deviation is marked off on either side of the mean, 34% of the area of the curve, or 34% of the cases, are included between either of these points and the mean. The range of one standard deviation from both sides of the mean (2 standard deviations) includes 68%, or approximately two-thirds of the area, since it is assumed that the cases are equally spread over the entire area of the curve. Two standard deviation units on both sides of the mean (4 standard deviations) include approximately 95% of the cases. Three standard deviation units on each side of the mean (6 standard deviations) include practically all of the cases. Theoretically, the tails of the normal curve never touch the base line but extend to infinity in each direction. Three standard deviations on both sides of the mean include 99.74% of the area. This means that there are 13 cases in each 10,000 in each tail of the normal curve out beyond 3 standard deviations.

It is evident that 6 standard deviations cover the usual range of scores found in counseling. However, the relationships just described hold true only when the number of cases is at least 200. When the number of cases is smaller than 200, fewer standard deviations are needed to cover the range. As Dressel (1954) has indicated, in counseling it is customary to talk about being in, above, or below the average group. This average group is described in connection with the mean, as the middle two-thirds or the middle two standard deviations, one on either side of the mean. It is also described as the distance between the 16th and 84th percentiles. From this description it is easy to see why most people would fall in the average group on any given trait and why the best guess about the

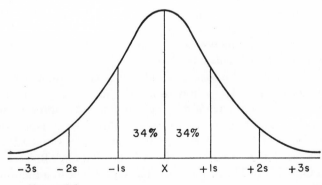

Figure 6.1

STANDARD DEVIATION UNITS AND THE NORMAL CURVE

amount of a trait which a client possesses is "an average amount." This is one of the reasons why the mean is the more widely used of these two measures of central tendency discussed here. When the median is used, the average group is considered to be the middle 50% of the distribution instead of the middle 68%.

MEASURES OF RELATIONSHIP

In dealing with test scores or academic grades it is frequently useful to determine the relationship between two or more variables or traits. The statistics used to measure these relationships are called *correlation coefficients.* Two of the most frequently encountered coefficients will be discussed here.

One of the questions a counselor is frequently called upon to answer is, "How are certain characteristics or traits related?" Another is, "How well will this estimate predict a given criterion of performance?" Still a third might be, "How consistent is behavior, or how stable is the characteristic?"

In order to answer such questions, the counselor must compute or interpret coefficients of correlation. The size of the coefficient indicates the degree of relationship between two traits. Height may be closely related to weight, but they are not the same. This relationship means that the taller an individual is, the heavier he is. In like manner, the coefficient of correlation shows how an estimate is related to a criterion of performance or how closely one estimate of behavior parallels another to show consistency or stability.

In size, the correlation coefficient ranges from +1.00 through 0.00 to −1.00. Both +1.00 and −1.00 indicate a perfect correlation or relationship. Such relationships are pictured in Figures 6.2 and 6.3. In Figure 6.2, notice that individual A is in the lowest position on both the X- and Y-axes. Individual B is in second position on the two axes. All other pairs of scores are arranged in the same way. The lowest on one test is the lowest on the second test. The second lowest on the first test is the second lowest on the second test. And so this goes for all of the other individuals. This illustrates a *perfect positive relationship.* Now notice Figure 6.3. Here individual A has the highest score on the Y-axis and the lowest score on the X-axis. Individual B has the second highest score on the Y-axis and the second lowest on the X-axis. All the remaining individuals continue this pattern. A situation like this illustrates a *perfect negative relationship.* Perfect relationships like these are not encountered in actual practice.

In educational and psychological estimates most of the relationships

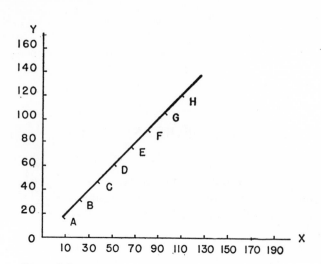

Figure 6.2

AN EXAMPLE OF A PERFECT POSITIVE RELATIONSHIP

are of a positive nature, but they frequently are far from perfect. The tallies in Figure 6.4 illustrate a fairly high positive relationship. Notice that the tallies no longer fall along a straight line, as they did in the previous figures. One can still see the *straight-line relationship,* but the tallies have spread out from it. The further they go from this imaginary line running through the center of them, the lower is the value of the correlation coefficient. When there is no relationship, the tallies are spread all over the diagram.

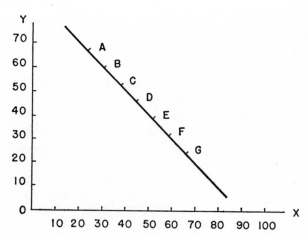

Figure 6.3

AN EXAMPLE OF A PERFECT NEGATIVE RELATIONSHIP

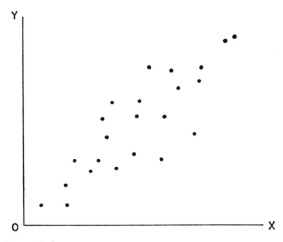

Figure 6.4

A RATHER HIGH POSITIVE RELATIONSHIP

The correlation coefficients to be discussed below are associated with a straight-line relationship. There are some situations when the relationship is not in a straight line, however. These relations are described as being *curvilinear* rather than linear. Such a situation is pictured in Figure 6.5. If one were to plot on one axis the ability to carry on physical activities, and age on the other, such a curvilinear relationship would result. This means that as one gets older one improves in a physical skill up to a certain point, and that, with continued age, one becomes

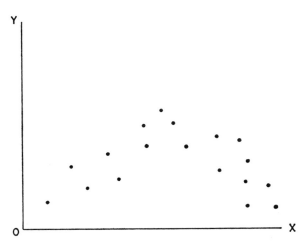

Figure 6.5

AN EXAMPLE OF A CURVILINEAR RELATIONSHIP

poorer and poorer in the skill as one's physical potential becomes more limited. When a relationship is found to be curvilinear, the two correlational techniques described below are not appropriate. The appropriate method for handling such data will be found in any elementary statistics book. It should be emphasized that curvilinear relationships are by no means rare and that it is always a good idea to do a little plotting of the pairs of scores before any correlations are computed.

The Spearman Rank-Order Correlation Coefficient

The *Spearman rank-order coefficient of correlation* is designed for use when there are a small number of cases (up to 35) being compared on two variables. The computational process is described in most texts on beginning statistics, such as Downie and Heath (1965) and will not be discussed here. The rank-order coefficient, *rho* or ρ, gives a close approximation of the Pearson product-moment correlation coefficient, most commonly used to indicate relationship.

The Pearson Product-Moment Correlation Coefficient

The *product-moment correlation coefficient* is intended for use when there are a large number of cases (more than 35) being compared on two variables. Its computation is laborious when done by hand, but relatively simple with a desk calculator and even simpler by computer. The description of the computational process is to be found in statistics texts like Downie and Heath (1965). This coefficient is the one most commonly cited in the literature, and the counselor should be familiar with its purpose and use.

The statistics discussed so far are referred to as *descriptive statistics*, since they are the ones that are usually used to describe a distribution of test scores in terms of characteristics of a group. In the pages which follow some other uses of statistics will be discussed along with the use of statistics when dealing with individual cases rather than groups.

SAMPLING STATISTICS

Most of the counselor's work is actually concerned with samples. An intelligence test may be administered to an eighth-grade class. This eighth-grade class is actually a sample of all possible eighth-grade classes in the local community, the state, or the whole United States. In like manner, one or two eighth-grade children could be held to be samples drawn from the population of all possible eighth-grade children in the United States. As already seen, statistics are used to describe these samples. Statistics in the e cases are really sample values. The numbers used to describe *total populations* are referred to as *parameters* instead of statistics. In much statistical work and research, the sample group is of value as a tentative way of describing the larger group or total population from which it came. For example, if research is started on a new reading method or test, or developing a new interest inventory, the findings might be a description not just of the sample, but of the population from which the sample was drawn. There are a few cases in which it might be possible to deal with populations rather than samples, but in most cases it is impossible to describe total populations.

Standard Errors

An example that illustrates this concept deals with the mental ability of all seventh-grade students in one or more states, each with large overall populations. To carry on this study it is necessary to develop and use a new intelligence test. For convenience, suppose that the samples are limited to a size of 25. In one community, using sampling procedures that will not be described here, the new test is administered to 25 seventh-graders. Suppose that the mean and the standard deviation for this sample are now computed. These are found to be 101.5 and 14.7, respectively, and, since they are used to describe a sample, are referred to as *statistics*. Now another sample is tested. This time the mean is 97.2 and the standard deviation is 12.6. Samples of this same size are tested until there are 300 samples. There are now 300 means. These 300 means may be averaged, and the standard deviation of the 300 means about the average mean computed. This average or grand mean may be taken as the best estimate that is available of the population or true mean. The standard deviation of the sample means about the population mean is given a special name and referred to as the *standard error*. All statistics have standard errors. To be specific, this one is called the *standard error of the mean* and the symbol for it is $S_{\bar{x}}$.

In a similar fashion it is possible to take the 300 standard deviations, find the average standard deviation, and then find the variability of these 300 sample standard deviations about this average. This standard deviation would be the *standard error of the standard deviation*.

In actual practice, the value for the standard error of the mean is computed with the following formula, using the data obtained from one sample:

$$s_{\bar{x}} = \frac{s}{\sqrt{N}}$$

The size of the standard error of the mean is inversely related to the size of the sample. The larger the sample, the smaller the standard error. This occurs because the larger the number of cases in any sample, the more reliable the statistics computed, that is, the less they will vary from sample to sample.

Suppose that a test has been administered and that the mean of the test is 48, the standard deviation 8, and N is 36. The above formula shows that the standard error of this mean is $8/\sqrt{36}$, or 1.33. Since standard errors are standard deviations, they may be interpreted in the same way. For this problem it is possible to say that 68% of future samples would be expected to fall within 1.33 units from this mean of 48. If N in the sample were 64, $S_{\bar{x}}$ would be $8/\sqrt{64}$, or 1.00. This illustrates the statements in the previous paragraph about the size of the sample.

All statistics have standard errors.

Confidence Intervals

One of the purposes of statistical methods is to make it possible to make statements or inferences about a population on the basis of sample values or statistics. This is generally done by setting up what is referred to as the "confidence interval." To illustrate this, suppose that a test has been administered to 324 individuals, resulting in a mean of 102 and a standard deviation of 16. The standard error of this sample mean is calculated as follows:

$$s_{\bar{x}} = \frac{16}{\sqrt{324}} = \frac{16}{18} = .89$$

When dealing with statistical inference or making statistical tests, the two levels ordinarily used are the 1% and the 5% level. If the 1% level is selected, it means that the chances are 99 in 100 that such an inference is true; at the 5% level, the chances are 95 in a 100 that something is so. Obviously the 1% level gives less opportunity for an event to occur by chance. Associated with each of these levels are two standard scores. *Standard scores,* known as z-scores, are scores that have been reduced to standard deviation units. A raw score which is exactly one standard deviation above the mean will have a standard score of 1, a raw score two standard deviations above the mean will have a standard score of 2, and so on. A standard deviation unit or standard score taken a certain distance from the mean in the normal curve always cuts off the same proportion of the area, or the same number of cases. When the sample is large, a standard score of 2.58 cuts off 99% of the area of the normal curve. Half of 1% of the area remains in each of the tails. This standard score then is to be associated with the 1% level. Similarly, a standard score of 1.96 includes 95% of the area measured off on each side of the mean. This score is associated with the 5% level.

The above technique works well when the sample is large. But when the sample becomes small, especially 50 or less, other values must be used for the 1 and 5% levels. These are obtained from a table of t ratios found in statistics books. The appropriate t-test is found for the sample size under consideration at a given level of confidence, and this value is put into the equations instead of 1.96 or 2.58.

MAKING STATISTICAL TESTS

Another very important and perhaps more frequently encountered use of sampling statistics is in the making of statistical tests. This is illustrated by the following data. Suppose that an experiment has been performed that produces the following statistics for two groups:

$$\overline{X}_1 = 78 \qquad\qquad \overline{X}_2 = 82$$
$$s_1 = 14 \qquad\qquad s_2 = 14.8$$
$$N_1 = 100 \qquad\qquad N_2 = 81$$

The two means differ, one being higher than the other. When there are differences, they may be either *chance differences* or real and *significant differences*. Looking at the above data will not reveal whether a real or only a chance difference is present. A statistical test must be applied to these data to determine whether a real difference exists.

In making a statistical test of this type, a null hypothesis is proposed. This is actually an hypothesis that no difference exists. For this problem the null hypothesis is that there is no difference between mean 1 and mean 2, or mean 1 is the same as mean 2. It is also the usual custom to decide ahead of time whether one is going to test the hypothesis at the 1% or the 5% level.

Now to continue with the problem. First the standard error of the mean is calculated for the two distributions:

$$s_{\overline{x}_1} = \frac{14}{\sqrt{100}} = \frac{14}{10} = 1.4 \qquad\qquad s_{\overline{x}_2} = \frac{14.8}{\sqrt{81}} = \frac{14.8}{9} = 1.64$$

Secondly, the standard error of the difference between the means is computed, using the formula for uncorrelated data:

$$S_{D_{\bar{x}}} = \sqrt{s^2_{x_1} + s^2_{x_2}}$$
$$= \sqrt{(1.4)^2 + (1.64)^2}$$
$$= \sqrt{1.96 + 2.6896}$$
$$= \sqrt{4.6496}$$
$$= 2.156$$

Finally, the standard score z is computed:

$$z = \frac{\text{Difference between the means}}{\text{Standard error of the difference between the means}}$$
$$= \frac{\bar{X}_1 - \bar{X}_2}{s_{D_{\bar{x}}}}$$
$$= \frac{78 - 82}{2.156}$$
$$= -1.855$$

The significance of z-scores of 1.96 and 2.58 has already been pointed out in the discussion of confidence intervals. The z found here is evaluated by using the same two standard scores. If z is equal to or larger than 2.58, the null hypothesis is rejected at the 1% level. This means that the chances are 99 in 100 that the difference in the data being studied is a real difference. Note, however, that there is still one chance in 100 that this difference could have occurred by chance. If the obtained z-score falls between 1.96 and 2.58, the null hypothesis is rejected at the 5% level. This means that the chances are 95 in 100 that the difference is a real one, or that there are 5 chances in 100 of being wrong about this real difference existing. Finally, if the z-score is less than 1.96, the null hypothesis is accepted for the experiment. Acceptance means that the data indicate that there is no difference between the two means.

In the problem a z-score of -1.855 was obtained. The minus sign is of no importance. With a z of this size the only conclusion that can be drawn is that "the null hypothesis stands." It was not possible to demonstrate any difference.

If the samples are small, less than 100 and certainly when less than 50, the technique is modified by making a t-test. This is done as above, t being the ratio of the difference between the means to the standard error of the difference between the means. For the problem worked here, the *t* would be 1.855, the same as the *z*-score. However, this *t* statistic is interpreted differently. Instead of using the 1% and 5% values of 2.58 and 1.96, a *t* table is used to compare the computed value with the 1% and 5% of *t*-ratio values for samples of various size. Most statistics books include this table.

If for any reason the data are correlated, the above method is modified by using the formula for the difference between the means for correlated data. The data are correlated when there are two sets of measurements of the same individuals, when there are brothers in one group and sisters in the other, or when some other relationship is known to exist between the groups.

It is almost impossible to read the educational and psychological journals today without a knowledge of these statistical tests. Here is an example from a widely read journal. Wright and Scarborough (1958) compared scores on the *Kuder Preference Record, Vocational,* of 125 men who were first tested as freshmen and then retested three years later as seniors. The results of their study are shown in Table 6.1. This table demonstrates clearly what happened to the inventoried interests of these college freshmen over a four year period. The greatest decline was in the

Table 6.1

COMPARISON OF INITIAL AND RETEST KUDER MEAN
SCORES FOR SENIOR MEN (*N* = 125)

	Initial	Retest	Difference	t
Mechanical	34.09	32.49	−1.60	1.74
Computational	22.56	20.98	−1.56	2.08*
Scientific	38.00	32.75	−5.25	5.64**
Persuasive	44.02	46.34	2.32	2.11*
Artistic	19.64	21.94	2.30	3.07**
Literary	20.28	22.20	1.92	2.82**
Musical	13.63	13.47	− .16	.30
Social Service	41.70	43.06	1.36	1.26
Clerical	37.78	36.74	−1.04	.96

° Significant at the 5% level.
°° Significant at the 1% level.
From J. C. Wright and B. B. Scarborough, Relationship of the interests of college freshmen to their interests as sophomores and as seniors, *Educ. and Psychol. Meas.*, 1958, **18**, 156. Used by permission of G. F. Kuder.

scientific area. Here the difference was significant at the 1% level. There was also a decline in computational interests. This difference, however, was significant at only the 5% level. There were declines also in three other areas, but none of these was significant. As seniors these students showed more interest in artistic and literary activities (1% level) and in persuasive activities (5% level). The increase in social service activities was not significant.

Summary

In this chapter, averages, variability, and measures of relationships were first discussed. These make up the part of statistics referred to as descriptive statistics. These statistics are used in describing samples or the relationships among samples. Next, consideration was given as to how inferences are made about populations on the basis of a sample. Tests for significant differences among samples were also discussed. These last two processes make up what is referred to as sampling statistics.

In the next chapter, specific use will be made of the statistics discussed in this chapter. Statistics form an important basis for counseling and personnel work. Test scores are also related to these statistics.

TYPES OF SCORES

In the educational and psychological world of today, many different types of scores are in use. It is impossible for all of them to be discussed in a book such as this. In the short discussion that follows, age scores and quotients, centile scores, standard scores, and grade placement scores will be covered. This will be concluded with a short discussion of norms.

Standard Scores

In recent years more and more authors of tests have turned to standard scores for reporting their test results. Standard scores come in a variety of forms. In this chapter the more widely used ones will be discussed. The *basic standard score z* is obtained by the formula:

$$z = \frac{X - \bar{X}}{s}$$

where all terms are as previously defined.

Suppose this is illustrated with a few test scores. In the distribution below, the scores are part of a larger distribution with a mean of 65 and a standard deviation of 10.

X	z
65	.00
75	1.00
55	−1.00
78	1.30
37	−2.80

The first of these scores has a deviation from the mean of 0. This results in a standard score of 0. The second score, 75, deviates by 10 from the mean. This, divided by the standard deviation, 10, results in a standard score of 1.00. By the use of the formula, the remaining standard scores are computed.

A little thought will show that the standard score is merely the raw score transformed into standard deviation units. These scores on different tests then show an individual's position with reference to the mean equated for differing standard deviations. Thus the standard score indicates comparable *positions* in two groups, not achievement in a subject. The first z-score in the example is at the mean, thus having no deviation. The second score is one standard deviation unit above the mean. Its standard score then is a positive one. Since 3 standard deviations measured off on each side of the mean will include practically all of the cases, it follows that in most distributions z-scores will range between +3 and −3.

These z-scores have two characteristics which make them cumbersome to handle: in any distribution approximately half of them are negative, and they are all decimals. To avoid these drawbacks, the standard scores are transformed either linearly or by using the normal distribution curve. In a *linear transformation*, a new mean is decided upon, and a new standard deviation. Suppose it is desired to set up a system of standard scores with a mean of 50 and a standard deviation of 10. Each z-score would be multiplied by 10 and added to the mean of 50. The scores then would fall between 20 and 80, and all could be rounded to the nearest whole unit. If they are normalized, the tables for the normal curve have to be used. But the results are about the same if the size of the sample is made up of several hundred individuals.

One familiar with the tests used by the Army in World War II knows that such tests as the *Army General Classification Test* have a mean of 100 and a standard deviation of 20. Tests used by the Navy had a mean of 50 and a standard deviation of 10. Other tests, such as the *College Entrance Examination Board* and the *Graduate Record Examination*, have means of 500 and S.D.'s of 100. Wechsler's current test of adult intelligence, the *WAIS*, uses I.Q.'s. But these I.Q.'s are standard scores with a mean of 100 and a standard deviation of 15. Each of the subtests of his scale has a mean of 10 and a standard deviation of 3. Scores obtained with Form L-M of the *Stanford-Binet* also are standard scores, with a mean of 100 and a standard deviation of 16. Series of group intelligence tests like the *Lorge-Thorndike* use similar deviation I.Q.'s, which are described later in this chapter.

Certain test publishers have also used "stanines" (standard nines) in reporting test results. Such scores as these have a mean of 5, and a standard deviation of 2, and range from 1 to 9. The percentage of cases in each stanine is always the same, that is, stanine 9 always includes the top 4% of the cases, stanine 8 the next 7%, and so forth. This is what makes stanine scores so easy to compute and use. Stanines are a very coarse scale. However, some authors have answered this objection by using a plus and minus sign with each stanine such as 5+, 5, and 5−. This results in 27 usable scores for each test. Other scales that are somewhat similar to stanines are Guilford's C-score, which has 11 units ranging from 0 to 10, and Cattell's "sten" (standard ten), which has a range from 1 to 10 with a mean of 5.5.

Since standard scores are equal units of measurement, they may be manipulated mathematically. This is not true of all test scores. Standard scores may be averaged, correlated, or treated statistically in any manner desired in research. Standard scores show where an individual falls in a distribution of test scores. For example, a standard score of $+1$ or one of 600 is at a point with 84% of the cases below it and 16% above it (refer to Figure 6.8). By using a table of the normal curve, the percentage of cases above or below any standard score may be ascertained. Standard scores from different tests administered to the same or to similar individuals may be compared directly. Suppose that two students, A and B, take a battery of tests and that on a verbal subtest they receive standard scores of 70 and 50, respectively; on a quantitative test, 20 and 60; on a test of spatial ability, 40 and 60; and on a test of clerical ability, 42 and 40. Each boy may be compared, first, to himself in respect to his abilities by using just his own test scores. Boy A is very high in verbal ability (top 2½%), above average in quantitative ability, and decidedly below average in both spatial and clerical abilities. Then the two boys may be compared to each other. A is superior on verbal ability, B is stronger on quantitative and spatial abilities. Neither is outstanding in clerical ability, each being about one standard deviation below the mean. With a little practice, the counselor can readily interpret all types of standard scores.

Centile Scores

Centiles, or percentiles, as they are sometimes called, are among the scores most frequently encountered and used by the counselor. In the previous section one centile score, the median, has already been encountered. It may be recalled that this was defined as a point which has 50% of the scores on each side of it. Now any other centile point may be so defined. For example, C_{33}, the thirty-third centile, is defined as that point in the distribution with 33% of the cases below it. Each of these centiles may be computed in the same manner as the median.

One could begin by taking 33% of the cases, then count up from the bottom, interpolate, and arrive at the value. Admittedly, this is a tremendous amount of work. Rather accurate results can be obtained, however, by setting up a *cumulative percentage or ogive curve* and reading the various points from this curve, as shown in Figure 6.6. On the vertical, or *Y*-axis are placed the percentages; on the *X*-axis, the scores. The ratio of the *Y*-axis to the *X*-axis is usually about 2 to 3. In putting the tallies into the graph, each of the cumulative percentages, *cP*'s, is placed above the value of the upper limit of its interval. After all percentages have been tallied, a smooth curve is drawn. This does not have to pass through all of the points. Ideally some should be on it, and equal numbers on each side of it.

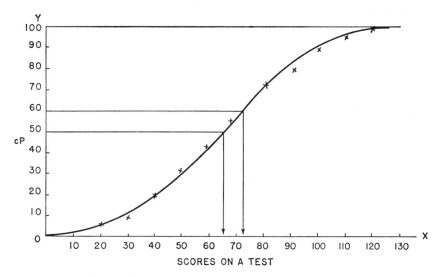

Figure 6.6

CUMULATIVE PERCENTAGE OR OGIVE CURVE

The reading of this graph is illustrated by showing how to obtain the median. Starting at 50% on the *Y*-axis, a straight line is drawn to the curve. From this point another line is drawn, meeting the *X*-axis at right angles. The point of intersection is the median. From the graph, this results in a median of about 65, which would be similar to that obtained by using the method discussed earlier in this chapter. In a similar fashion, the other 98 centile points may be read. To do this with any accuracy, a large piece of graph paper, much larger than Figure 6.6, must be used.

Despite the widespread use of centile scores, they leave much to be desired. The basic problem is that they are by no means equal units of measurement. Most of the data that are used in counseling tend to take the shape of the normal curve, with a large piling up of scores at the center. Note Figure 6.7; here a raw score of 72 is equal to the median.

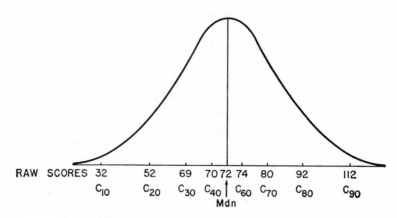

RAW SCORES 32   52   69   7072 74   80   92   112
C_{10} C_{20} C_{30} C_{40} C_{60} C_{70} C_{80} C_{90}
Mdn

Figure 6.7

DISTRIBUTION OF CENTILES

A score of 74 is the 60th centile. Actually there is no real difference or distance between a score of 72 and 74 but there is a difference of 10 centile points. Centiles, then, exaggerate differences at the center of the distribution. For all practical purposes, all of the various centile points in the center of a distribution may be considered as the same. On the other hand, the centile points in both tails of the distribution are much more spread out, hence larger. Anyone familiar with such profile sheets as that used with the *Kuder Preference Record* has noted this peculiarity of centiles.

The counselor might then justifiably ask why he should use these scores. They do reveal something about an individual's position in a group. But one must remember that many people use test results who know very little about tests and test scores. Centiles are rather similar to percentages in their appearance and are interpreted as such by the more naïve test users. This is particularly true of the orientation tests or entrance testing scores used on most university campuses. From the viewpoint of research these scores should be avoided. The research worker must go back to the original raw scores if the data that are to enter into the work are expressed in centiles.

It might be noted that a few of the centiles have special names. C_{25} is referred to as Q_1, the *first quartile*, and C_{75}, the *third quartile*, Q_3. C_{10}, C_{20}, and so on, are also known as *decile points*, with C_{10} being referred to as the *first decile*.

A related term that the counselor will encounter is *centile rank*. If a student has a centile rank of 90, this means that he surpasses 90% of those in the group upon whom the test was standardized. This individual is also at the 90th centile point.

Grade Placement Scores

Many tests used in the elementary school have their results transformed to *grade placement scores*. For example, a certain child has a grade placement score of 4.2 in arithmetic, 5.3 in spelling, 4.8 in reading, 5.0 in social studies, and so forth. Suppose now that this child is in fifth grade and that it is at the end of October. He has progressed then two-tenths of the way through fifth grade. His academic position is written as 5.2. Each of the above scores can then be related to 5.2. His spelling is about the same as the group average, his social studies and reading are a bit below, and his arithmetic is one year behind.

Such scores are very useful in going over test results with both parents and students. There is no type of score which is simpler or as easily understood. However, there are several problems associated with these scores. Grade-placement scores are constructed by administering a test to a large number of students, for example, in grades 3, 4, 5, and 6 in selected schools at a particular time of the year. The median or mean is then computed, and a graph is set up with a straight line connecting the four averages. Then the year along the base line is divided into tenths. From this graph, grade-placement scores in tenths of a year may be obtained. It is assumed that a child's growth is constant over a 10-month period and that no growth takes place during the 2 summer months. Any observer of child behavior knows that this is not so. Some individuals learn in spurts; some may have summer experiences that mean more educationally than a whole year's school work; others may go along in a mediocre way until certain insights develop, after which much learning takes place very suddenly. Human learning is never as smooth and constant as these scores would make it appear to be.

A second problem associated with grade-placement scores is the meaning of high and low scores. Very often one encounters data showing that a beginning third-grader is at 5.8 in reading, 6.4 in spelling, and 7.6 in language usage, or that some students in grades 6 or 7 have grade equivalents that place their achievement in the senior-high school range. It makes little sense to say that a third-grader is achieving at the junior-high school level or that a sixth-grader is operating at the tenth-grade level. Such scores are better interpreted by saying that the student is well-informed or very adept in the subjects tested. He has done well in previous school years, probably because he is bright, has had good teachers, and has been in effective learning situations. Low scores cause a similar problem at the other end of the scale. A fifth-grader who scores at 3.2 in reading is a very poor reader when compared to other fifth-graders. These low and high grade-placement scores are obtained by extending the line connecting the medians or means mentioned, both below and above the grades actually tested. All scores obtained outside these limits are extrapolated scores.

Grade-placement scores from different tests or test batteries are not directly comparable. Comparability would require that the norm for each test or battery be obtained from the same children within the same school. Obviously this is impossible. Since schools differ so in their educational philosophies, curricula, teaching, and in the makeup of the student body, scores obtained on different tests based on results in different school systems cannot be justifiably compared.

The elementary-school guidance worker will probably find that these scores, or similar ones called *age-equivalent scores*, are more frequently encountered than any other type discussed in this chapter. Age-equivalent scores are set up and used just as grade-placement scores are, and have the same limitations. The high-school counselor will have limited direct contact with these scores, but he may have occasion to use them when there is a continuous flow of student records between the elementary school and the junior and senior high schools.

Figure 6.8 shows the relationships among the different types of test scores.

Age Scores and Quotients

In the past, age scores and quotients were widely used and were very important in counseling. At the present time, mental age scores and ratio quotients, described below, are mostly of historical importance. In 1960, Form *L-M* of the *Stanford-Binet* appeared with standard scores in the form of deviation I.Q.'s. Up to that date the authors of the *Stanford-Binet* had been among the last using mental ages and ratio I.Q.'s in their tables of norms.

Among the earliest scores to appear were the *mental age scores* that Binet used in the second edition of his intelligence scale in 1908. With scales of this type each item on a test is given a value of so many months of mental age. An individual's score is merely the sum of the months of all of the items answered correctly. These may then be converted to years and months. For example, an individual may be said to have a mental age of 7-6, 7 years and 6 months. These tests were so developed that a mental age of 7 would be the mental age of the typical or normal child of 7 years. Such scales are difficult to develop, and over the years have tended to disappear from the scene. They were found typically in tests such as Forms *L* and *M* of Terman's *Stanford Revision of the Binet Scale*. There are also other indices similar to mental age, such as educational age, reading age, and the like.

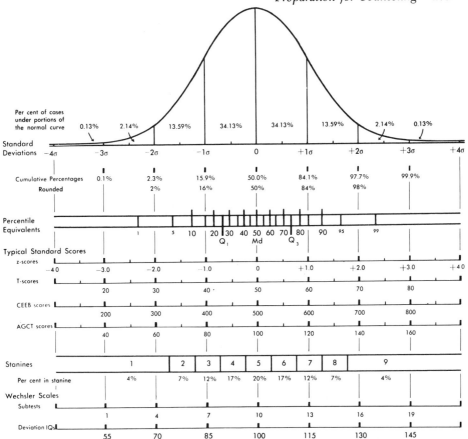

From The Psychological Corporation, *Test Service Bulletin,* no. 48 (New York, 1955).

Figure 6.8

THE NORMAL CURVE, CENTILES, AND STANDARD SCORES

Mental age was divided by chronological age, both in months, and the quotient multiplied by 100, to give the *intelligence quotient or ratio,* I.Q. On the *Stanford-Binet* the average I.Q. was approximately 100, and the standard deviation, though it varied at different age levels, was about 16, this being a sort of average among the different years.

Over the years, there was much discussion over the merits of the I.Q. First, I.Q.'s are not equal units of measurement. Second, the I.Q.'s of young people are quite different from the I.Q.'s of adults. It is generally accepted by psychologists that mental age continues to increase up through adolescence and then stops or slows down considerably in its rate of growth. Thus the numerator of the I.Q. ratio has a limit, whereas the denominator continues to increase. An individual would then, as he grows older and older, have a smaller and smaller I.Q. To prevent this, Terman (1937) used a constant chronological age of 15 years for all adults. From this it is seen that these adult I.Q.'s were quite different from those of young children. Finally, I.Q.'s obtained on different tests were not the same and could be compared only with difficulty.

When standard scores are discussed, a new type of I.Q. is now used. This is the *deviation I.Q.*, which has a mean of 100 and a standard deviation of 15 or 16 varying with the actual test. The old ratio I.Q.'s are now associated with only a few tests and batteries administered to younger children.

Change Scores

The user of tests frequently encounters another type of score that is referred to as a *change or growth score*. Such scores are obtained, for example, when students are given an interest inventory in grade 9 and the same inventory again in grade 11, when students are given a test at the beginning of a course and then the same test at the end of instruction, or when attitudes are measured at the beginning and at the end of a period of instruction. The basic purpose of all such measurement is to assess growth, change, or development. Differences between the "pre-test" and "post-test" scores are the change or growth scores.

If the measurements made are physical, the interpretation of these change scores is direct and uncomplicated, because the measures used to measure growth in height or weight are reliable. If it is found that Student *A* increased in height 4 inches during the period of a certain study and that student *B* grew 2 inches, meaningful statements may be made about the increments in height. However, psychological test scores always have a certain amount of unreliability (errors of measurement), and this leads to complications in the interpretation of change or difference scores. In the typical testing situation, both initial status and final condition are assessed by instruments that produce somewhat unreliable results. It has been shown that the higher the correlation between the initial and the subsequent test, the lower the reliability of the difference or change score. On the other hand, if the correlation between the initial and the subsequent test is lowered, the reliability of the difference scores increases, but the question next arises as to whether the two tests are measuring the same thing. To the extent that they are not, the difference scores become meaningless.

Another problem that arises with change scores is that frequently those individuals with the highest pre-test scores have the lowest change or growth scores. Various explanations have been made of this situation (Lord 1958). One is that the highest initial scores resulted in part from errors of measurement—luck in getting the correct answers. A second explanation is that the brighter students learn less. A third possibility is that the high initial scores have merely regressed toward the mean, a common statistical occurrence. Finally, imperfections or inequalities in the measurement scales may be such that a gain of 3 points at the high end of the distribution is the equivalent of a gain of 9 points at the lower end. There is probably some truth in each of these charges. Thus it is impossible to make statements about whether those who score high on an initial test gain more or less than those who score low, without detailed study of a specific situation.

These, among other problems, make the interpretation of change scores a complicated one. Solutions to some of the difficulties encountered with such scores (Harris 1963) are well beyond the statistical sophistication of the typical reader of this book. The counselor should be cautious in the use of such scores, always bearing in mind that they may not represent what they seem to.

Norms

A well-made test should have in its manual norms that are described in enough detail to enable the user to decide whether they are adequate and appropriate. The counselor will find that all tests are provided with norms. Some have been constructed with much time and care and at great expense; others seem to be constructed in haphazard fashion. A set of norms should provide any counselor with information about where his client falls on a particular test as compared to individuals similar to him in age, sex, educational level, and any other pertinent variable. The counselor will find that test manuals do contain national norms, regional norms, norms for different types of schools, for different curricula, and for clients with given attributes. However, very often the most effective norms that the counselor might use are the *local norms* constructed in his own agency. The counselor should be able to set up local norms in terms of centiles, stanines, or other standard scores.

The counselor may ask just what are adequate norms. Norms that fit this description are based upon a representative sample of individuals similar in specific attributes to those being tested locally. The publisher of the test should describe his sample in detail in the manual, and relate exactly how the sample was obtained. This will give the test user a chance to see whether or not the norms provided are suitable for his own group. Adequate norms should also be based upon a sample large enough to assure that the norms have reliability. Anyone who is willing to do some research on this topic will have little trouble in locating norms based upon as few as 15 individuals. While they may be the exception, such norms are still provided by some test constructors. Reliable norms should be based upon a large and representative number of individuals who have been selected by a scientific sampling procedure. Some test builders feel that the minimum number of subjects should be 200. But large numbers in themselves do not necessarily result in desirable norms. Some large numbers represent a large sample of individuals in one particular locality, and the norms may be utterly useless in other places.

The norms provided with tests should offer a variety of scoring possibilities. While standard scores are preferred, the user should be provided with centiles as well. If a test is an elementary-school achievement test, centiles or standard score norms should be provided along with the grade-placement norms. Norms should be so built that every raw score can be directly converted to a standard score or centile. When the test user has to interpolate each time he consults a table of norms, his work is slowed down considerably and the chance of making errors is increased.

It should be emphasized that in many situations and for many tests, the best norms are local ones. Research has shown that students in different schools and colleges, geographical regions, and cultural or disability groups differ tremendously on traits such as mental ability, socioeconomic status, occupational goals, and the like. When a college or university uses a test battery for the selection of new freshmen or graduate students, it has large enough samples to set up its own norms. Students applying as college freshmen or as new graduate students can have their test results compared to previous students in that school. Selection officers and counselors know from previous experience the types of scores necessary to success in their own institution.

Local norms have to be kept current. It is possible that the composition of a school may change in time, for example, when a new and large industry moves into a community. Curricula change, the organization of schools change, and the staff changes. Each of these may have an effect upon the achievement of the students or the type of students who attend the school. Hence, the newer students may perform differently on the tests. It should not be inferred, however, that all national norms are of little use to a given school. This is far from the truth. National norms on personality and interest inventories will often be more than sufficient for local schools. It is for achievement and aptitude tests, especially when the results are used for selection and admission, that local norms are most advantageous.

REFERENCES

Each of the following contains material on test scores in much greater detail than presented in this chapter.

American Psychological Association. 1966. *Standards for educational and psychological tests.* Washington, D.C.: American Psychological Association.

Downie, N. M. 1967. *Fundamentals of measurement.* 2nd ed. New York: Oxford University Press, Inc.

————. 1968. *The counselor and test scores.* Guidance Monograph Series. Boston: Houghton Mifflin Company.

————, and Heath, R. W. 1965. *Basic statistical methods.* 2nd ed. New York: Harper & Row, Publishers.

Dressel, P. L. 1954. Counseling caprices. *Personnel Guidance J.* 33: 4–7.

Guilford, J. P. 1965. *Fundamental statistics in psychology and education.* 4th ed. New York: McGraw-Hill Book Company.

Harris. C. W., ed. 1963. *Problems in measuring change.* Madison: University of Wisconsin Press.

Lord, F. M. 1958. Further problems in the measurement of growth. *Educ. and Psychol. Meas.* 18: 437–51.

Psychological Corporation. 1955. *Methods of expressing test scores.* Test Service Bull. no. 48. New York: The Psychological Corporation.

Terman, L. M., and Merrill, M. A. 1937. *Measuring intelligence.* Boston: Houghton Mifflin Company.

————. 1960. *Stanford-Binet intelligence scale: Manual for the third revision. Form L-M.* Boston: Houghton Mifflin Company.

Wright, J. C., and Scarborough, B. B. 1958. Relationship of the interests of college freshmen to their interests as sophomores and as seniors. *Educ. and Psychol. Meas.* 18: 153–58.

7

The Counselor's
Selection and Use
of Standardized Tests

INTRODUCTION

Standardized tests and the interview are the counselor's most frequently used tools. In this chapter there will be a discussion of how standardized tests are selected, and some remarks about their use. Scanning the catalogs of test publishers and bibliographies of tests reveals that there are a tremendous number of tests on the market. They range in quality from those that are unacceptable to those that are most desirable because they provide everything that is required of a satisfactory test. The major concerns here are the selection of tests for the entire counseling program and the considerations that will influence the counselor in choosing tests to be used with each individual client.

What are some of the problems encountered in selecting tests, and what are the various criteria applied to assure that the tests selected will be the most appropriate and useful ones? Tests selected for a counseling program are limited by the unique needs of that program and by the available tests which will meet those needs adequately. These tests are designed to furnish information about a client's aptitude or potentiality, his skills and abilities, his adjustment, and his avocational and vocational interests. They include tests of general intelligence, achievement, and special abilities, as well as personality and interest inventories.

In general, people do not understand most of the problems involved in the selection and use of tests. Counseling and testing agencies get letters constantly from people in various government services, public schools, private schools, and community agencies seeking advice about test selection. The letters usually ask, "What *test* shall we use in our program?" but they do not give any information about what the school or the agency is attempting to accomplish. Testing services also get numbers of letters, not just an occasional one, saying, "Please send us *The Aptitude Test.*" These letters are from administrators and teachers in public schools and community agencies, who should have learned that there is more than one aptitude test. They usually indicate little or no awareness of the problems involved in the selection and use of tests.

THE SELECTION OF STANDARDIZED TESTS

Since the counselor is a major user of the results obtained with tests, he faces the task of selecting the tests most useful for the agency. In recent years much has been written about what constitutes an effective or desirable test (American Psychological Association, 1966). In the following pages the various criteria that the counselor should have in mind in selecting tests will be discussed. The first two of these are of a technical nature and are called reliability and validity. However, little or no attention will be given to the various computing procedures necessary to determine reliability and validity coefficients. (Those counselors interested in such are referred to Downie and Heath 1965, or Guilford 1965.) The other criteria consist of the various characteristics of tests that may make them acceptable to both the counselor and client. Included are such things as time needed to administer the test, cost, ease of scoring, readability, and other related factors.

Reliability

Reliability, as used here, refers to the stability, consistency, or accuracy of the measurements made by a test. The reliability of a test gives the counselor an indication of the consistency with which a test measures whatever it measures. In test theory, every score is conceived as being made up of two components—one associated with an individual's true score, and a second brought about by the random errors of measurement. In actual practice, an individual's true score is never known, but methods have been established for determining the amount of variance associated with the error score. The magnitude of the error variance gives an indication of the reliability of measurement.

The error variance or variability of the error in a test makes tests unreliable. The greater such variance, the less reliable the test. Many factors enter into the creation of error variance. Among these are fatigue, illness, guessing, failure to follow directions, changes in an individual brought about by learning, incorrect timing of the test, improper instructions, and a host of other such conditions. More specifically, suppose that a client happens to be coming down with a disease that temporarily affects his performance. His illness has a unique effect upon this single test. The chances are good that the client's score will be lower than it would be if he were in better health. The basic characteristic of these *chance* contributors to error variance is that their results are random and not reproducible, that is, they are associated with a single administration of the test and not with a second. Other types of error variance may be associated with the administration of a test.

While chance errors are the most important ones affecting test scores, *constant errors* must not be overlooked. If men are being measured or weighed and the meter sticks or scales are out of order so that each individual is measured as 4 centimeters over his true height, a constant error is present. This error is the same for every one and will be repeated as often as the same measuring instruments are used. In testing, a repetitive misuse of norms or time limits, or wrong instructions may produce a constant error.

Both types of error cause the obtained scores to differ from the client's true scores. All scores are thus unreliable to a certain extent. When using tests it is only possible to get an *estimate* of a person's true scores. The size of these errors of measurement is indicated by the size of the test's standard error of measurement or its reliability coefficient.

The oldest coefficient of reliability, referred to as a *test-retest reliability coefficient*, is obtained by administering the same test to the same individuals twice. The correlation between the two sets of scores is then computed. If the time between the two administrations is very short, minutes or hours, subjects remember their responses made on the first administration and put the same ones down on the second administration, making the coefficient of correlation higher than it should be. On the other hand, when the interval between two testings is long, there is sure to be growth, decline, or other changes in the individuals tested which will lead to an increase in error variance and hence to a lower reliability coefficient. Most test makers no longer use the test-retest method, because much better techniques exist for determining the reliability of a test.

The second type of reliability coefficient is determined by calculating the scores made by a group of individuals on parallel or comparable forms of the same test. Two tests are considered to be *parallel* when they have equal means, equal standard deviations or variances, correlate equally with the same criterion, and are made up of the same type and number of items measuring the same content and objectives. When parallel tests are used, the effect of memory from one administration to another is ruled out. However, if the time between testings is long, the same problems arise as with the test-retest method. The best parallel-form technique is to administer the two tests several days apart. Parallel testing is one of the commonest methods now used. Whenever a test is a speed test or one in which speed plays a major role in an individual's score, this is the correct and *only* defensible method to use (see Downie and Heath 1965).

The third type of coefficient is obtained by analyzing data from one administration of a single test. Such coefficients are derived by manipulating responses to the items in one way or another and are referred to as *coefficients of internal consistency*. A common example of this index is the *split-half coefficient*. When this method is used, each test has to be rescored. A common method is to obtain a score on the odd items and one on the even items. These two sets of scores are correlated and the resulting coefficient corrected by what is known as the Spearman-Brown Prophecy formula. This is necessary because what has actually been obtained is the reliability of a test half the length of the original test, and the reliability of any test is a direct function of the length of the test. The longer the test, the higher the reliability, other things being equal. This correction consists of dividing two times the obtained coefficient by 1 plus the obtained coefficient.

Another coefficient of internal consistency is obtained by the use of the *Kuder-Richardson formula, number 20*. To obtain this coefficient the difficulty of each item on the test must be determined, difficulty being defined in terms of the proportion responding correctly to the item.

Coefficients of internal consistency must not be used with tests that are highly speeded. If they are, the results obtained are an overestimation of the reliability of the test.

The size of any reliability coefficient is also related to various factors. It has already been noted that the longer a test is, the more reliable it is. Of course, there is a limit to the length that one can make a test. After an optimum length has been reached, subjects become tired or bored, begin to guess or quit, and the reliability of the test decreases. Second, the size of the reliability coefficient is related to the similarity or dissimilarity of the group tested. If a group consisting of students in grades 3 through 7 is tested and the reliability of this test computed and then compared with the reliability of the same test administered only to fifth grade students, the first coefficient will probably be much higher. Reliability is also a function of the similarity or homogeneity of the items making up the test.

If the counselor asks just how high a reliability coefficient should be, the best answer is that no particular value can be singled out as a minimum. Reliability coefficients of standardized tests of intelligence, special abilities, and achievement tend to be over .90. Actually, as will be noted later, it is not reliability that is most important, but the validity. Tests must be reliable, but this is not the most important characteristic of any test. The counselor should pay particular attention to the use of subtests. On many standardized tests, the subtests are apt to be made up of a small number of items. These subtests are frequently unreliable, although the total test is very reliable. Diagnoses, predictions, and research made with these subtests are all apt to be worthless.

Finally it must be emphasized that tests are only pieces of paper and as such have no psychological properties. Whether a test is reliable or valid is to a great extent related to how, when, where, and with whom it is used. The author of the test usually does report a number of validity and reliability coefficients. But these were obtained when the test was used in a certain way. When the test user departs from the procedures outlined in the test manual, there is no telling what has happened to the reliability and validity of the test.

Some workers prefer to use the *standard error of measurement* in talking about reliability, rather than to use correlation coefficients. These standard errors of measurement or *standard errors of scores,* as they are sometimes called, are not greatly affected by the variability of the group tested. They tend in general to stay about the same throughout the range.

The standard error of measurement is computed by the following formula:

$$s_e = s\sqrt{1 - r_{tt}}$$

where:

$$s_e = \text{the standard error of measurement}$$
$$s = \text{the standard deviation of the test}$$
$$r_{tt} = \text{the reliability of the test}$$

Let us now illustrate the use of this statistic. Suppose that Willie obtains a score of 49 on a test. The standard error of measurement is computed for this test, and a value of 4 is obtained. This can be interpreted by saying that the chances are 2 out of 3 (remember that standard errors are standard deviations) that this score of 49 is within 4 raw score units of his true score. It follows, then, that the smaller the size of the standard error of measurement, the smaller the error component of an individual's test score, and then the more reliable any obtained score will be. Both the *Sequential Tests of Educational Progress (STEP)* and the *School and College Ability Tests (SCAT)* make use of this concept.

The user of *STEP* turns to a table of norms and, opposite each raw score value, finds a centile band instead of a single centile. This is actually a distance of 1 standard error of measurement measured off on each side of the client's obtained score. To quote the *STEP Manual for Interpreting Scores: Reading* (1957): "If the test interpreter assumes that students' 'true' standings lie somewhere within the percentile bands corresponding to their obtained scores, in the long run he will be correct in his assumption about 68 per cent of the time." The use of these bands should prevent any counselor from regarding scores as more precise than they actually are.

Figure 7.1 shows these centile bands for a student. The numbers below the figures represent the centile, 3 being the 30th centile.

Another use of the standard error of measurement is shown in Figure 7.2, a form used at the University of Kansas with placement examinations given to entering freshmen. The raw scores in each of the columns are 1 standard error of measurement from each other. Suppose a client has a raw score of 35 on the vocabulary subtest of the *Cooperative Reading Test*. A band could be marked off on each side of 35, extending from 32 to 38. The chances are 2 out of 3 that the client's retest score would fall between these two points, each 1 standard error of measurement from his obtained score.

As is readily apparent, the smaller the standard error of measurement, the more reliable the test, and hence the more confidence a counselor can place in any single score. It is assumed that an obtained score is close to the client's true score on any test. Since it is impossible to know an individual's true score, the band cut off by the standard error of measurement about an obtained score gives an indication of the range in which the true score may be. It might also be noted that standard errors of measurement are approximately equal, except in the extremes of the distribution. This statistic permits the counselor to tell how much a client's score will vary on tests by the size of the standard error of measurement. It also allows him to compare tests of a similar nature to see which one is more reliable and, hence, which one would be more useful.

EXAMPLE

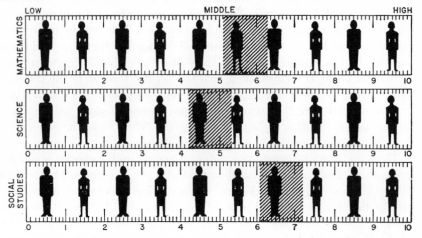

From Educational Testing Service, *Sequential Tests of Educational Progress: Manual for Interpreting Scores–Reading* (Princeton, N.J., 1957). Used with permission of the Educational Testing Service.

Figure 7.1

USE OF THE STANDARD ERROR OF MEASUREMENT
IN INTERPRETING SCORES ON *STEP*

"The shaded areas for Mathematics and Social Studies overlap; there is no important difference in standings on these two tests. The same is true of Mathematics and Science. However, the shaded areas for Science and Social Studies do not overlap. The student is higher in Social Studies than in Science ability, as measured by these tests."

Baxter and Paterson (1940) proposed a statistic, *the counselor's ratio,* given by the formula $\sqrt{1-r}$, to be used as is the standard error of measurement. The range of scores is multiplied by this counselor's ratio and the result divided by 2. This value, added to and subtracted from the obtained score, will show the band in which repeated measurements of the same individual will fall.

VALIDITY

The most important characteristic of any measurement or evaluative instrument is validity. If an instrument has no demonstrated validity, it has no use in a counseling program. A measuring device may be reliable, practical, and the like, but above all it must have validity; otherwise time is wasted in using it.

UNIVERSITY OF KANSAS

ACADEMIC PROFICIENCY
PLACEMENT EXAMINATIONS

NAME_____   SEX _____

COLLEGE_____   DATE_____

STEN SCORE	CENTILE RANK	T SCORE	ACE QUAN	PSYCH LING	EXAM TOTAL	COOP READING VOCAB	SPEED	COOP ENGLISH USAGE	SPELL	KU MATH	T SCORE	CENTILE RANK
		·84·							·45·	·77·	·84·	
		·82·	·79· ·77·		·176·			·160·			·82·	
9		·80·	·74·	·109·		·57·	·78·				·80·	
		·78·	·72·	·106·	·172·		·76·	·156·	·43·	·74·	·78·	
		·76·			·168·		·73·				·76·	
	·99·	·74·	·69·				·70·	·151·			·74·	·99·
8	·98·	·72· ·70·	·67· ·65·	·102· ·99·	·164· ·159·	·54·	·67· ·64·	·147·	·40·	·71·	·72· ·70·	·98·
		·68·	·62·	·95· ·92·	·155· ·151·	·52·	·61· ·58·	·142·	·38·		·68·	
7	·95·	·66· ·64·	·60·	·88·	·146· ·142·	·49· ·46·	·55· ·52·	·138·	·35·	·68·	·66· ·64·	·95·
	·90·	·62· ·60·	·57· ·55·	·85· ·81·	·137· ·133·	·43·	·49· ·46·	·133· ·129·	·33· ·30·	·63·	·62· ·60·	·90·
6	·80·	·58·	·53·	·79·	·129·	·41·		·124· ·120·	·29·	·62·	·60·	·80·
		·56·	·50·	·74·	·124·	·38·	·40·	·175·	·25·		·56·	
5	·70· ·60·	·54· ·52·	·48·	·71· ·68·	·120· ·116·	·35·	·37· ·34· ·31·	·110· ·106· ·101·	·22· ·20·	·59· ·55·	·54· ·52·	·70· ·60·
	·50·	·50· 47.98	·45· 64.05	10708	·111· 29.57	·32·	28.32	·97· 92.24	17.19	49.18	·50·	·50·
4	·40·	·48·	·41·	·61·	·103·	·27·	·25·	·88· ·83·	·15·	·46·	·48·	·40·
	·30·	·46· ·44·	·38· ·36·	·57· ·54·	·98· ·94· ·90·	·24· ·21·	·22· ·19· ·17·	·79· ·74· ·69·	·12·	·43· ·40·	·46· ·44·	·30·
3	·20·	·42· ·40·	·33· ·31·	·50· ·47·	·85· ·81·	·19·	·14·	·65· ·60· ·56·	·9· ·7·	·37· ·34·	·42· ·40·	·20·
2	·10· ·5·	·38· ·36· ·34·	·29· ·26· ·24· ·21·	·43· ·40·	·77· ·72· ·68· ·64·	·16· ·13·	·11· ·8·	·51· ·47· ·42·	·4·	·30· ·27· ·24·	·38· ·36· ·34·	·10· ·5·
		·32·	·19·	·36·	·59· ·55·	·10· ·8·	·5·	·38·	·2·		·32·	
1	·2· ·1·	·30· ·28· ·26·	·16· ·14· ·12·	·33· ·29· ·26·	·50· ·46· ·42·	·5·	·2·	·33· ·29· ·24·		·21· ·18·	·30· ·28· ·26·	·2· ·1·
		·24· ·22·		·23·	·37·	·2·		·19·		·15·	·24· ·22·	
0		·20· ·18·	·9· ·7·	·19· ·16·	·33· ·29·			·15· ·10·		·12·	·20· ·18·	

RECOMMENDATIONS :

HONOR ENGLISH_____ ENGLISH 1a_____ STUDY CLINIC_____ READING CLINIC_____

Figure 7.2

USE OF THE STANDARD ERROR OF MEASUREMENT
IN REPORTING TEST SCORES

At the present time psychologists recognize three types of validity: content, criterion-related, and construct (American Psychological Association 1966).

Content Validity

Content validity is associated most often with achievement tests. For example, it can be said that a test constructed to measure material in plane geometry is valid when it measures both the objectives and the subject matter content of the plane geometry course in an adequate fashion. It is not difficult to achieve this type of validity, although care is necessary in the construction of the test (Downie 1967, Ch. 4). Rating scales, checklists, and the like must also have this type of validity. The construction of these must also be careful.

Criterion-Related Validity

In the counseling situation this type of validity is the one most frequently encountered. No matter how long validity is discussed in classes, some counselors are still hazy about it. Validity, as far as the counselor is concerned, is how well this counseling tool predicts performance in a given activity. For example, the counselor is attempting to sit down with a client and, on the basis of test evidence, anticipate or predict future behavior. And how is this done? Usually the counselor does it on the basis of an instrument whose *correlation with some criterion of future performance* is known. The counselor knows the relationship between an intelligence test score and grades in school. The counselor knows the relationship between tests of ability and measures of interest. These relationships show the limits within which the counselor can predict performance. The other way in which validity can be shown is by *tests of significance.* If an experimental and a control group are compared in performance under specified circumstances, is the difference in performance of the experimental group greater than a chance difference? It should be noted here that it may be possible to show a statistically significant difference between groups which is not a practical difference usable in counseling.

To obtain validity coefficients which are related to a criterion, a test or battery of tests is administered and these test results are correlated with some other measure. The other measure, the criterion, is that which the test is supposed to predict. The criterion in counseling usually involves performance in a given activity. For example, scores on an intelligence test administered to entering college freshmen are correlated with the grade average or index that each student made during his first semester. This correlation coefficient is called a *validity coefficient.* Notice that the scores or data which are the criteria are collected in the future. Other examples of criterion measures frequently encountered are amount of sales, number of units produced, supervisor's ratings, accident rate, or spoilage of materials.

It was previously noted that reliability coefficients of standardized achievement tests tended to run above .90. This is not the case with validity coefficients. The typical validity coefficient for predicting academic grades is in the .50's. Very seldom is a validity coefficient above .70 found. A little thought will show that the reason is that the criteria used are far from perfect. Take grades, for example. Is mental ability the only factor that enters into grades? Certainly interest and motivational factors are very important. Then there are the idiosyncrasies of the various teachers, the attitudes of the student toward the instructor and vice versa, and a dozen other things that enter into the grade that any student receives. The same is true of the criteria used in industry. Suppose that the criterion is the number of units made by the workers in a given period of time. First, an assumption has to be made that the motivation of each worker was the same. Of course, this is far from the truth. Then there are the peculiarities of the different machines—speed, general state of repair, and the like. Light, noise, relations with fellow workers, and the availability of materials, each in its own way, may affect production. In all prediction or validation of this type, the major problem is finding suitable criteria. The criteria themselves must be reliable and valid. It might be noted here that content validity is used for achievement tests because there is no adequate criterion available either at the time of testing or at any reasonable future time.

As already noted, validity coefficients are used in predicting future performance. On the basis of an intelligence test score, a college freshman's first semester average is predicted. With a test of manual dexterity a person's performance on a particular job may be predicted. The use of validity coefficients in the prediction of individual performance is the next topic. It is necessary to use what is known as a *prediction equation* (see Downie and Heath 1965, or any elementary statistics book). Little time will be spent talking about the derivation of prediction or regression equations. For example, data might be collected on the entering freshmen of the current year, and then this regression equation might be used to predict the performance of those who enter the following semester or the following year. It seems that most institutions tend to attract the same sort of students year after year; hence the prediction equation may be used in this way. It may be recalled that when the correlation coefficient between two variables, using the Pearson r as described in the last chapter, is computed, an assumption of a straight-line relationship between the two variables is made. This prediction equation is the actual equation of a straight line.

Suppose that, on the basis of data collected, something like this results:

$$Y' = .041 \, X + .24$$

Suppose that Y' stands for the predicted grade point average and that X is the intelligence-test score. Then the predicted grade point index is equal to 0.41 times the intelligence test score plus a constant of .24. Suppose that on a certain intelligence test a student obtains a score of 100. When this is substituted into the equation, his predicted grade point average is 4.34. Actually this is too simple to be true; it would only be correct if there were a perfect relationship between the two variables, that is, when r is equal to 1.00. To make predictions of this type, the straightforward approach has to be modified and a probability statement made about the prediction.

To do this requires that first a statistic known as the *standard error of estimate* be computed. The formula for this is as follows:

$$s_{yx} = s_y\sqrt{1 - r^2_{xy}}$$

where:

$s_{yx} =$ the standard error of estimate in predicting criterion Y from predictor X
$s_y =$ the standard deviation of the criterion measure
$r_{xy} =$ the validity coefficient

Suppose that as a result of substituting the proper values into the equation, a standard error of estimate equal to .3 is obtained. Remember that a standard error is a standard deviation and is interpreted as such. Then it can be said that, for any given X-score, the chances are two out of three that the predicted criterion score would be in the band made up of the Y' score obtained from the regression equation plus or minus the standard error of estimate, in this case three tenths. For the specific example, it follows that when a student has a score of 100 on this intelligence test, the chances are 2 out of 3 that his predicted grade point average will fall between 4.04 and 4.64, the predicted value, ± 1 standard error of estimate. A statistics book will show how this can all be done graphically by drawing the regression line and then constructing a parallel line on each side of this 1 standard error of estimate distance from the regression line. Then, for any given X-score on the bottom of the graph, the range where two-thirds of the predicted values on the Y-variable for that score will fall may be obtained.

Sometimes counselors, when they talk about the predictive capacity of a test, refer to an index of *forecasting efficiency E*. This is obtained by the use of the following formula:

$$E = 100 \left(1 - \sqrt{1 - r^2_{xy'}} \right)$$

where all terms are as previously used. Suppose that for a specific situation a validity coefficient of .40 is obtained. Substituting the values of the present example into the formula, one obtains:

$$E = 100 \left(1 - \sqrt{1 - .40^2} \right)$$
$$= 8.3\%$$

This is interpreted by saying that, with this test, predictions can be made 8.3% better than chance or 8.3% better than with no test at all. Values like this may be computed for each and every validity coefficient. A few of the more frequently used ones are listed below:

r	*E*
.80	40%
.70	28.6%
.65	24%
.60	20%
.55	16.5%
.50	13.4%
.45	10.7%
.40	8.3%
.35	6.3%
.30	4.6%

The counselor will find that for *E* to be large, in the 90's, the validity coefficient, also has to be large. As already noted, this is seldom so.

The counselor needs to consider the percentage of forecasting efficiency for a given validity coefficient before deciding what predictions can be made. Suppose a correlation of .35 between a given instrument and a criterion is significant. The counselor still is not going to be able to predict much from it. This is a prediction that is 6% better than chance (Bingham 1937, pp. 258–59). Chance should produce 50 right and 50 wrong predictions. Splitting the 6% improvement in half, and adding to the 50 right and subtracting from the 50 wrong will give the change in prediction with use of such an instrument. The counselor would be right 53 times, and wrong 47 times, out of every 100 predictions made with this device. He will not know which of the 47 times a wrong prediction was made until afterwards. It does not increase the counselor's predictive capacity very much and it is necessary to ask, "Is this worthwhile?" Cottle (1951) has discussed in detail these problems of forecasting efficiency and the selection of tests.

The counselor should memorize the percentage of forecasting efficiency for validity coefficients of .80, .70, .60, .50, .40, and so on. This tells him quickly how much error is still involved in a prediction. Even if there is a correlation between an intelligence test and class grades of about .68, which results in a percentage of forecasting efficiency of 26%, when the counselor tries to use this to predict grades, it only gives about 63 right out of every 100 predictions.

Predictive ability is usually increased by using more than one variable for the predictor. Instead of using only intelligence test scores as the predictor, the counselor might use a combination of high-school grade point averages, scores on a mathematics test, scores on an English or reading test, a score from an interest inventory, and the like. Usually four or five variables constitute the maximum number which are entered into this type of equation which is known as a multiple regression equation (see Guilford 1965).

By now the reader has probably felt that this is a rather bleak picture and has begun to wonder about the fundamental usefulness of tests. In most situations counselors are not concerned with an exact score or grade point average. They are much more interested in questions such as, "Will this student pass or fail?" "Will this employee succeed on the job?" "Will this student become a superior student and thus merit a scholarship?" This is a sort of group prediction, and standardized tests help very nicely in predicting when used in this manner. Anyone who uses tests will soon see that they are of limited use in telling whether a given person is going to score at the 40th, 50th, or 60th percentile on a test. Statistically, there is little difference between these three centile points. Nevertheless, the odds are against a person who scores at the 5th centile on the test receiving a score at the 95th centile on the criterion, if the test is a valid one. The following material from *Bulletin No. 45* of the Psychological Corporation (1953) illustrates the effectiveness of tests, when 191 eighth-grade boys took the *Verbal Reasoning Subtest* of the *Differential Aptitude Tests (DAT)* battery at the beginning of a school term. These measures of verbal ability were compared with grades received in a social studies class at the end of the term. There were 76 students found to have earned grades of D or lower. This was 40% of the entire class. Using chance estimates, 40% of those at each test score level (low, medium, or high) would be expected to obtain grades of D or lower. The correlation between the two variables was found to be .61, which results in an index of forecasting efficiency of about 20%. The data in Table 7.1 show quite a different picture, however. Now it is clear that the test is a

Table 7.1

CHANCE EXPECTATIONS AND ACTUAL PERFORMANCE IN
A SOCIAL STUDIES CLASS IN RELATION TO
DAT-VERBAL REASONING SCORES

DAT Verbal Reasoning Test Score	No. of Pupils	% expected by chance to earn D, E, or F	% actually earning D, E, or F
26–up	19	40	6
18–25	49	40	14
10–17	60	40	36
2–9	63	40	73

From The Psychological Corporation, *Better than chance*, Test Service Bulletin, no. 45 (New York, 1953).

good predictor of grades in social studies. Instead of 40% of the highest-scoring pupils receiving low grades, as would be expected by chance, only 6% are found there.

Some psychologists use expectancy tables (Tiffin and McCormick 1965) to show the effectiveness of a test in prediction. In its simplest form such a table looks like this:

Intelligence Test Score	Percentage Making C or better first term
140+	97
130–139	93
120–129	82
110–119	72
100–109	48
90–99	31
80–89	18
less than 80	4

An entering student with a score of 132 on this intelligence test could be predicted to be at least a C student.

In selection procedures using tests, a chart like Figure 7.3 may be set up. In this figure the test scores have been placed on the X-axis and the criterion, "pass–fail" or "succeed–not–succeed," on the Y-axis. A line has been drawn above a score of 70 on the X-axis, the cutoff point. Individuals scoring higher will be admitted; those scoring less will be refused admittance. The variable of success has been placed on the Y-axis. The horizontal line is drawn at the point separating success from failure. Any individual tallied in either the upper right cell or the lower left one is classified as a "success" or a "hit." It was predicted that these individuals would succeed in one case or, in the other case, fail, and this they did. The lower right-hand cells include the failures for whom success was predicted because they scored above the cutoff score. Those in the upper

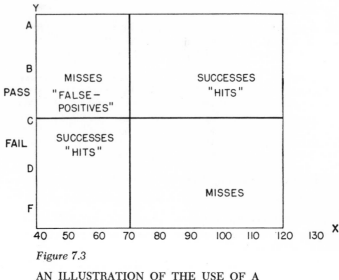

Figure 7.3

AN ILLUSTRATION OF THE USE OF A
CUTOFF POINT IN SELECTION

left-hand cell are also misses, but they are of a less serious nature. For these failure was predicted, but they succeeded. Such are referred to as "false positives." In actual practice, the cutoff score is moved around, depending on the number that one wishes to select, the drop-out rate, or some other element. In industrial selection, the number of job applicants would affect the location of the cutoff point. For a thorough discussion, see Tiffin and McCormick (1965) or *Double-Entry Expectancy Tables* (The Psychological Corporation 1966).

Construct Validity

To determine whether a test has *construct validity*, an investigation is made of those qualities measured by the test. By this is meant the degree to which certain explanatory concepts or constructs are related to performance on a certain test. One simple method of studying construct validity is to correlate the scores on a test or inventory with those obtained with other tests purportedly measuring the same thing. For example, a newly developed test of spatial perception should be more highly correlated with other tests of spatial relationships than with a vocabulary test or a test of numerical reasoning. One expects tests of a similar nature to be more highly correlated with each other than with dissimilar tests.

Basically, studies of construct validity are attempts to check on the theory underlying a test. This is done by going through the following procedures. First, the investigator asks what behavior might be expected from those who score high or low on a certain test. If the test is an interest inventory, he might hypothesize that socioeconomic differences or differences in training are related to different interest profiles. Second, data are collected to test various hypotheses. Finally, the data are analyzed to see if an inference can be made to explain the behavior of the subjects as measured by the inventory. In this case, if the scales of the inventory differentiate between students in different training programs, then construct validity has been demonstrated. In practice, the counselor, unless he is building a new test or inventory, will have little contact with construct validity.

Face Validity

Although face validity is a term frequently used, it really has nothing to do with validity as discussed above. A measuring instrument is said to have *face validity* when the individual taking the test goes away feeling that the test was appropriate for the reason he had in taking it. It really may have no validity, but it seemed reasonable, fair, and related to the examinee's future. Thus, it had face validity. This is most important when dealing with adults. Face validity and content validity are frequently confused. A test constructed to have content validity has true validity. Face validity is superficial and meaningless.

Homogeneity and Validity

During World War II there was much research carried on in the construction of a test battery for the selection of aircraft pilots. To become a pilot, a trainee had to pass a series of hurdles made up of educational attainment, intelligence, and physical health and stamina. As a result of this testing, pilot trainees made up a rather homogeneous group. When the scores on these tests making up the battery were correlated with a criterion of success, the validity coefficients tended to be very low, some close to zero. At one time a group of unselected trainees was put into training. The validity coefficients for this heterogeneous group were of the usual size (Thorndike, 1949).

While on the subject of validity, reference should be made to another term that is being encountered more and more in research, and that is *cross-validation*. Very briefly, this means to try the experiment or study again with another group and to see if the results are the same. Many of the studies in clinical psychology and some in counseling psychology are of no value, chiefly because no research worker bothered to cross-validate them.

SUMMARY OF VALIDITY

It must again be emphasized that validity coefficients, like reliability coefficients, are basically correlation coefficients and as such are affected by the variability of the group used in any particular study. In general, the greater the variability in the groups, the higher the validity coefficient. The counselor should consider this when he tries to evaluate statements about validity found in the test manuals.

It was noted that validity coefficients tend to average about .50 and that most reported in the research literature fall within the band .40–.60. The counselor might ask how large one of these coefficients should be to be considered useful. The best answer is that any that predict better than chance may be used. There are no absolute values to give. As with reliability, test results are most valid when the test is used as recommended by the author. Any deviations from the instructions in the manual, such as using the test with a different group, changing the directions, or altering the time, leave no other choice than to revalidate the instrument.

Considerable time has been spent discussing certain aspects of validity and reliability. These are the two characteristics a test must have above everything else. However, when the counselor is selecting tests for professional use, there are some other points which must be considered. All of these other characteristics might be considered part of the practicality of a test. In the material which follows, brief comments will be made about the more important phases of these characteristics.

THE USEFULNESS OR PRACTICALITY OF STANDARDIZED TESTS

Ease of Administering

The tests used by the counselor should be such that they can be administered by an individual with a minimum of training and instructions. Frequently, teachers and others with limited psychological training have to help in the collection of test data and other material. Any competent teacher can administer the modern group tests with valid results, if he is willing to read the manual ahead of time and follow directions exactly. Most individual tests, on the other hand, require a trained and experienced administrator, and they are frequently so time-consuming that they have limited use in the counseling program. A clerical worker who is conscientious can be trained in a limited time to administer most of the common group tests.

Ease of Scoring

Many agencies do not have budgets large enough to facilitate the scoring of tests by either a rented scoring machine or sending the answer sheets for scoring to a test publisher or test-scoring service. These tests have to be scored in the agency by agency personnel. One way for the counselor to antagonize colleagues is to add to their already heavy schedule and duties the job of scoring group tests. One way to avoid this difficulty is to buy tests which are so-called "self-scoring." Such tests have carbons in them, and to obtain a score all one has to do is open the test booklet or the answer sheet and count the number of marks that fall within the small blocks or other designated areas. At the present time, the California Test Bureau has a patented answer sheet called *Scoreze* and Houghton Mifflin Company has had self-scoring tests on the market for many years. Even though these are a little more expensive, in the small school system the extra two or three cents expended per student for these special answer sheets will be repaid, and more, by the improved attitudes of the teachers toward the counseling program. The choice of machine-scored tests whose stencils can be used for hand-scoring machine answer sheets also cuts down scoring problems. Another factor in ease of scoring is to have the hand-scoring key exactly opposite the answer space. The choice of tests without weighted scoring can decrease scoring problems, if this is about the only difference involved in the choice.

With the application of the computer to test scoring, much of the drudgery has been eliminated. All of the work is done very rapidly, and the complete scoring of complex tests like the *Strong Vocational Interest Blank (SVIB)* becomes a simple matter. Not only are tests scored, but the means and standard deviations of the tests or subtests are provided, reliability coefficients are computed, item-analysis data are tabulated, and, for some tests or inventories, profile sheets are printed. So successful has this scoring by computer been that many test-scoring centers have been established, by both universities and the publishers of standardized tests. For a moderate fee any user of tests can have his tests scored and analyzed by one of these centers.

Ease of Interpretation

The tests used by the counselor should be such that it does not require three additional psychology courses in order to find out what the results mean. Many tests have very straightforward and adequate information in the manuals to facilitate scoring and interpretation. The meaning of projective techniques and other individual tests, however, is still highly controversial in spite of the amount of research and training that has been expended upon their use (Patterson 1957). It is these techniques that require the most extensive training.

Probably the best way to begin learning how to interpret tests, after basic instruction in evaluation, is to take the test oneself and have it interpreted by a competent counselor. This will familiarize the beginning counselor with the items and with a general interpretation. Then the beginning counselor needs to study the manual to see how the test author proposes the test be used, and with what groups. At this point the counselor should begin to use and interpret the test under supervision.

Frequently the counselor will find that what appears to be an appropriate test has no norms for the individuals and the groups with which it must be used. The only recourse is to collect scores on a large enough group so that appropriate norms can be developed. Until this happens, interpretation must be delayed or must be highly tentative.

Costs

Most counselors find that they have to look in every direction in order to keep testing costs down. Saving can be most easily accomplished by purchasing the nonconsumable or reusable editions of tests with separate answer sheets. Then there is no telling how many times the test booklets themselves may be used, providing the test administrator takes care to see that the booklets are handled as they should be.

The counselor should determine ahead of time the maximum number that will be tested with a specific test at any given time. Buy this number plus several extra test booklets. There are many tests that are used very infrequently. A couple of test booklets and a package of answer sheets is more than adequate for these. The counselor can also cut costs by setting up a testing program that fits local agency needs rather than buying the packaged program offered by some publishers. This requires a knowledge of tests and of the local situation. If the counselor cannot do this, it is better not to use tests until he learns how to choose and tailor the testing program to fit local needs.

There is another point that merits attention. There are times, especially after the counselor has gained some experience, when it will be obvious that an inexpensive, short test will do as good or even a better job than an expensive time-consuming battery. This is especially true of some of the tests used in the prediction of academic success or success of a job.

General Suitability

A major problem associated with the selection of tests is their suitability for the clients involved. Basically, this comes down to whether or not the language of the test is too difficult for the examinees and whether the person taking the test is like the group on which it was standardized. Studies of the vocabulary level of standardized tests (Forbes and Cottle 1953) have revealed that the level of reading difficulty varies considerably from test to test. If a client is a poor reader or a very slow reader, the majority of the available standardized group tests are not for him, because time, related to speed and efficiency of reading, is an important element in determining the score.

Currently, much is heard about how tests are unfair to this or that group. Usually these are minority groups in our culture. Charges are made that certain tests favor the urban individual over the rural, the white over the black, or the younger man over the older. Unfortunately, there is considerable truth in these charges. If every individual in this country had an equal opportunity to learn, obviously tests would be much fairer to all. However, since there seem to be no drastic changes imminent in many educational programs in the *immediate* future or in the desires on the part of many individuals to utilize present educational offerings, people from different backgrounds will continue to perform differently on standardized tests. From this it follows that the counselor will have to become adept in interpreting test scores in the light of what he knows about the cultural background of each individual client. Scores obtained with a 19-year-old black trainee with a sixth-grade education from a lower-class home have to be considered differently from those of a 19-year-old white or black youth from a middle or upper-class home. The intelligent *use* of tests by the counselor will lessen considerably the number of incidents ascribed to so-called biased tests.

Time

Probably the best tests to purchase for a school are those that can be administered within a school period. Other agencies must judge the time that can be taken in terms of the client's and counselor's available time, especially if either must travel any distance for testing. The counselor must remember that there is more to testing time than the time needed to complete the items. The materials have to be passed out and collected, directions have to be read, and often sample exercises are worked and corrected. The nature of the group or individual being tested causes the time spent on these preliminaries to vary considerably. Tests with parts having short time limits, such as 4, 5, 8, and 10 minutes, require the use of a stop watch—and still no two administrators get exactly the same timing. This produces part of the error in testing and reduces a test's validity and reliability.

There are some longer tests which have been constructed so that half the test may be administered in one session of about 50 minutes' duration and the other half in another similar period at a later time. Some counselors do not like to break up the test this way. They feel the individual is really not the same individual during each of the testing sessions. Also, when there are such interruptions, clients tested in groups are apt to talk about what was on the test.

Use of Parallel Forms

It is very useful to purchase tests which have parallel forms. Sometimes there is a question about whether a test score is a valid measure of an individual's ability. The first score may be verified by administering the second form of the same test. Some test publishers have three or four forms of the same test. One form can be used one year, and another form can be used for the same individual or group the next year. Often a test can be used at different levels.

Most of the newer tests are built in levels, the usual number being five or six. These levels usually cover measurement of aptitudes and abilities from kindergarten through high school, and several cover a year or two of the university. There are two reasons for considering tests in these series. First, there is apt to be a relationship between the scores made on the tests at the different levels that is higher than the relationships obtained when tests by different authors are used at different levels. This is true because the general structure of the test seems to be the same from level to level. Second, there are times when it is convenient to have a more difficult test at hand to administer to a given client when the test administered to a group was too easy. If a test is too easy, especially a test like an intelligence test, the examiner does not get a measure of the real ability of the client tested. This works in the opposite direction, too. If a test is too difficult for some clients, a better measure of aptitude or ability may be obtained by using an easier test from a lower level.

THE CLIENT AND TEST SELECTION

Earlier in the chapter, mention was made of selection of tests by the client. In some counseling situations, the client is allowed to select the type and number of tests that he is to take. At the other extreme he has no say; all clients take virtually the same tests. Those who argue that the client should get involved in test selection maintain that such behavior leads to stronger motivation of the client to do as well as possible on the tests because he understands why he is taking them and understands how the results will be meaningful and helpful to him in solving his problems. Those who argue against this practice maintain that the offering of a choice of tests is more expensive in both time and money, and also that clients are either not informed enough about tests or are too involved with their problems to know which tests would be helpful. It should be noted that the decisions being mentioned here are related to the generic *type* of tests to be taken—aptitude, achievement, interest, personality, and so forth—not to the specific tests that might be used. It is assumed that these have already been selected by the staff doing the counseling and are available for use.

THE USE OF STANDARDIZED TESTS

From the viewpoint of the counselor, there are six major uses of tests. A very common one is the *confirmation of diagnoses or decisions* which have been made. For instance, a teacher considers a boy or girl as being capable of A's, B's, or C's, in terms of experience with that boy or girl. This needs to be validated independently. So a test of general intelligence is administered, to get some idea of how near right the diagnosis is. Or it may be obvious that a given pupil does a superlative job as far as the local school is concerned, but it is hard to tell how that individual will compare with people in other schools over the nation. So the person is asked to take scholarship examinations, to secure a comparison with pupils from other schools. These are two examples of the use of a test to confirm a diagnosis, judgment, or decision that has been made.

A second purpose is *to save time and to correct errors of omission.* If a counselor does not have time to sit down with a client and talk long enough to know whether psychiatric help is needed, an intermediate step might be to have someone administer the *Minnesota Multiphase Personality Inventory (MMPI).* This reduces the amount of time spent with that client. The same is true of other tests. Rather than sit down and pick out, piece by piece, information about vocational interests from a client, it is simpler to give an interest inventory and check it against other case data. If the counselor does not have adequate school records, it may be necessary to use tests to make up for the lack of information over the previous 10 or 12 years. Tests are also used to repair omissions by any agency that may not have adequate records of what a client has done before being referred to that agency, or in the school that gets a new pupil with no accompanying records and does not know what to do about placement or referral.

A third use of tests, the most logical and the least often suggested, is *to get information that cannot be secured in any other way*. If the counselor wants to know the status of an individual's inventoried interests, the client can be given an *SVIB* or a *Kuder*. The easiest way to find out how this individual's interests compare to those of engineers is to give him a *Kuder Form DD*, which has scales for mechanical and electrical engineer, or an *SVIB*, which has a scale for engineer. Then it is possible to see how this client's interests compare with those of people working in that occupation. If the counselor wants to find out how the person compares with other scholarship candidates in a state or in the entire United States, the only way to find out is to give the client the same scholarship test taken by others in the state or the nation. The counselor may have a pretty good idea of how the individual, and others in the school, compare with people across the nation, but unless they perform on the same test there will not be objective evidence. This is the most logical and justifiable use of tests.

A fourth purpose of testing is *to secure information for referral to other agencies*. Very frequently other agencies prefer certain tests be administered before an individual is sent to them for help because they do not have the resources to handle such testing.

Fifth, tests are used in the *prediction of future behavior*. In educational and vocational counseling it is frequently important to predict what an individual will do or will be like. Many standardized tests are quite useful in developing such a prediction.

Sixth, and last, tests are used in *evaluating a client's present status*. This includes his achievement, abilities, and personality make-up. In general, it might be said that tests are basic in the evaluation of the strengths and weaknesses of the individual client.

LIMITATIONS OF TESTS

A major limitation in the use of tests is that errors associated with testing cause any obtained test score to be only an estimate of an individual's true score. This was discussed earlier in the chapter.

Another problem also has to do with error. A low test score is of less value in the prediction of what an individual can do than a high score. For example, suppose an individual's score on the *SCAT* is at the 90th centile for college freshmen. There may be just as much error involved in this individual's score as there is with an individual at the 10th centile.

But it is possible to predict more about what the person with the 90th centile score will do in college than the person with the 10th centile score. The reason is that, even though the score at the 90th centile is an underestimate, it is still possible to predict that the individual should get A's and B's with the appropriate motivation. What is apt to happen to the individual at the 10th centile is less clear. He may have been sick the day the test was given, or a fraternity brother may have said, "Don't make a good score on this or they'll expect you to get A's and B's." Any number of things may have happened to reduce the score unnaturally. If the counselor predicted that the individual would not be able to do college work, the prediction could be in considerable error. Both predictions contain errors, but one is more usable for prediction of successful college performance than the other.

Here it would be advisable to refer to longitudinal data for validation of the test score, because over a long period of time the errors involved in longitudinal data are more apt to cancel out than they are in one short test. Similarly, the average of all high-school marks is a better index of what an individual should do, or a better predictor, than his scores in one subject. Actually, then, the trend in programs of guidance services is toward the use of more longitudinal data, properly collected and interpreted, and supplemented by the judicious use of tests.

The *judicious use of tests* is a function of counselor development. A counselor passes through three stages in learning to use tests. In the first stage, he discovers tests, jumps up in the air, and says, "Oh boy, this is it! This gives me all the information I need." Stage two develops when the counselor discovers tests will not give the information desired, and so decides that they are no good and that he will not use them. Some counselors never grow beyond this stage! The third stage occurs when the counselor learns what can and cannot be done with a given test. These stages might be called "discovery, disillusionment, and maturity" in the selection and use of tests.

In the third stage the counselor understands what tests can do, what they cannot do, and uses them properly to get the information wanted to help any client. In order to do this, he must go through a rather arduous apprenticeship in the use of individual and group tests. It is necessary to learn the theory and the practical, applied phases of psychometric techniques. Then the beginning counselor is ready to interpret tests to individuals in the practicum courses in counseling. This has to be done under supervision, if the counselor-in-training is to profit from it as fully as possible. Picking out a test in the agency situation and using it without instruction or supervision is fraught with too many perils for both the counselor and client. The counselor can pick up a test manual and read it, but it will not give all the background information that people who have used the tests professionally over a period of years can give.

People who use tests professionally often fail to write down their experiences, and many of these experiences involve subliminal cues. These experiences are such that counselors are hesitant to put them on record, because they are only very tentative hypotheses. For example, on the *"Psychopathic deviate (Pd)"* score of the *MMPI*, the test maker and the test user have only dealt with the meaning of a high score as indicating dislike of rules, regulations, and having to conform. They do not go on to point out, in the first place, that the person may conform and that his high score may reflect covert resentment. This is more apt to be the case with girls, because they are conditioned to be "good girls." A boy is more apt to react overtly. A high score may reflect, for boys, a tendency to rebel openly to rules and regulations; and with girls it may not. There is another element involved here, however—a low score on the *MMPI Pd* scale has no meaning as far as the test makers and the manual are concerned because the test was constructed to show only the meaning of a high score. Yet use has indicated that the individual who gets a score one standard deviation below the mean is apt to be a very rigid person. Such a person sets up high standards or goals for himself and his acquaintances. These individuals make their own lives and the lives of their acquaintances miserable, by the fact that they are always critical about not meeting such standards. A person who has rather strict moral or religious principles might also get a low score on the *MMPI Pd* scale.

These are the kinds of things that are not written in periodicals or manuals, because they are considered hypotheses too tenuous to be published without research validation or empirical data. Instead, they are passed on orally in a supervised practicum situation.

Some of the other limitations of tests center around the kinds of information tests can give. Tests can give information about *aptitude or potentiality* or they can give information about *present skills or ability.* Actually, tests of general intelligence include both aptitude and ability. A certain amount of what is being measured by an intelligence test involves previous learning, and is therefore a measure of skill or capacity. It also involves seeing relationships which have not been encountered previously and this, of course, would measure aptitude or potential. There is no measure of scholastic aptitude available at present which does not include some type of prior learning. When it is a tool for predicting future performance, the test is one of scholastic aptitude. If the same test is used to measure present status, then it is a measure of ability, or achievement. If the same test were used to diagnose weaknesses, it would be a diagnostic test. If used to show the need for or the results of remediation, it would be a remedial test. The same test can be used for all of these purposes. That is why it is difficult to discuss the material and information in a clear-cut manner. Included in these tests of achievement are structured personality inventories, because these are a measure of current social skills—the ability to deal with people and the ability to live with oneself, both of which are aspects of social ability. A third kind of test is the *interest inventory*. These inventories are closely related to the structured personality inventory, but tend to be measuring different things. Interest inventories are considered indicators of possible satisfaction in vocational or avocational activities.

Cautions Concerning the Use of Tests

Some individuals come to the counselor to take tests believing that the tests themselves have all the answers to problems. "If I could take some of those aptitude tests and one of those interest inventories, my problems would be all over." This is not an unusual attitude, but it should be apparent to the counselor by now that all tests are fallible instruments. As pointed out previously, there may be a wide difference in the performance of any individual on the same or parallel tests from time to time. If, then, only one evaluation of a personality trait is available for an individual and if this happens to be a test score, the counselor must be very cautious in the interpretation of this test score. In other words, the counselor should not place too much reliance upon one score. It is good procedure to use several intelligence tests, several interest inventories, and so on, in the same counseling program, or to validate test scores against other data about the client. The more information that can be obtained about the individual, the better the counseling tends to be.

Test scores are apt to be interpreted frequently without consideration of the motives of the individual who was tested. The counselor is apt to assume idealistically that each client is strongly motivated and did his best in the testing situation. Nothing is actually farther from the truth. There is all sorts of evidence that the motivation of test takers varies considerably. It is very difficult to know exactly what the individual has in mind when taking a test. There is strong evidence, also, that the social class status of an individual has a lot to do with motivation and performance on tests (Eells *et al.* 1951). It seems possible to get greater motivation, and thus more valid test results, when dealing with children from middle-class homes. Taking tests and striving to do well on them is an accepted pattern of middle-class culture, and children copy their parents' attitudes and behavior. Obviously, this is evidence that many tests have a bias favoring middle-class children. As a matter of fact, one might generalize by saying that most of the tests used favor the urban, white, middle-class child, *but this is no reason for avoiding their use.*

Test scores certainly, then, cannot be interpreted singly or without other types of information. They are pieces of the picture of an individual and a very important part of this picture, but they have to be integrated with the other information into what is hoped will be a meaningful whole. Too much reliance must not be put upon test data. The counselor must learn the value, and even more important, the limitations of test scores. He will need to continue to use the tests available until more appropriate tests or other sources of information about clients are available to him.

Fallacies Concerning Tests

It probably would be a good idea to review briefly the fallacies concerning tests that are discussed by Hahn and MacLean (1955; used by permission). The first one listed is *belief in tests.* The competent counselor does not believe or disbelieve in tests. Such a counselor knows what a test can do and what it can not do. This is not a matter of faith but of professional experience and competence. The second is the fallacy of *simplicity.* Test results look simple. A series of scores on the *DAT* furnished by a state-wide testing program appears pretty simple to interpret. But when the counselor starts thinking in terms of patterns of scores and differences between the scores on parts of the battery, the meaning that this has for a client in a given high-school is nowhere near as simple as it looks.

The third fallacy is that of *test labels.* Just because a test is called a test of "critical thinking" does not mean that it is. A test labeled "achievement" may be used to indicate need for remediation and the progress of remediation, rather than achievement. Allied to this is the matter of *named scales or keys.* For instance, on the *SVIB* one of the three non-occupational scales is a so-called Occupational Level score, which is supposed to show whether a client will perform at the professional level in occupations. Research has shown that engineers tend to score low and persons in managerial occupations score high. Such a score is a function of the field or area of the occupation, rather than the level of the occupation. A high Occupational Level score is secured by marking few items in the "Indifferent" category. Another example of false labels is the Interest Maturity scale of the *SVIB.* It has been found that people score high on the Interest Maturity scale if they like more things than they dislike (Rhodes 1956). Engineers tend to score low on it. This does not mean that they are immature in their interests. It means they dislike more *SVIB* items than they like. The T399 form of the *SVIB* has eliminated this scale. Empirical observations during counseling and knowledge of published research are necessary to bring real meaning to the named scales of the *SVIB* (see Chapter 9).

A fifth fallacy centers about the *prestige of the test author*. Just because a prominent and accepted psychologist produces a test is not evidence that it is a good test. The chances are that it will be excellent as far as the statistics and the production of the test are concerned, but there is no guarantee that it is valid for the purpose for which it was constructed until research into its validity is reported in the literature. It is probably safe to assume, however, that it is a better test than one an author lacking in measurement experience and training might produce.

Another fallacy is the matter of *generalizing* from a known test to a similar test, or from a sample similar to the test norm group to one which is not like the standardization group. For example, the *SVIB* has been on the market for years and counselors have learned how to use it. Kuder published what is called the *Kuder Preference Record-Occupational, Forms D* and *DD*. This interest inventory uses occupational criterion groups similar to the *SVIB*. Its ability to differentiate between people in a given occupational group and other groups *appears* similar to the *SVIB*. The test description seems as if it could be used in the same fashion as the *SVIB*, but when a counselor tries to use it in a counseling interview and compare the interests of clients in mechanical engineering on the *Kuder* with those of the same clients on the engineering scale of the *SVIB* there appear to be discrepancies. This may be a function of differences in coverage of the two tests, differences in criterion groups, or differences in the interpretation of a score for a given individual due to errors discussed earlier in this chapter. Research based on a study of the relationships between the two instruments is needed before a counselor can make statements to a client about it. A counselor cannot assume, because of experience with the *SVIB*, that it is possible to move immediately into competent, effective use of the *Kuder-Form D* or *DD* or even *SVIB T399*.

The other fallacy of generalization applies to a test developed with a given group. Counselors often assume it will be useful with another group which actually may not be at all similar. When writing theses, most persons state in the last chapter, "The results of this study apply only to the sample on which it was done or performed, and generalizing to similar groups is dangerous until the same information has been collected on those groups." The counselor cannot know what scores on such a test mean for freshmen in a given college or university until a sufficient, consecutive series of samples of such freshmen has been tested, and the results reported and norms derived. If a counselor tests a ninth-grade group with certain results, there is no guarantee that last year's ninth grade or next year's ninth grade will show the same results. Probably it will, but the counselor must check before making the assumption or using the information for all three groups in a similar fashion. The counselor working in a rehabilitation agency will often assume that tests used with the general population apply equally well to the disabled clients with whom the agency deals, or that the scores of clients with various kinds of disabilities have the same meaning. This is not so. For example, Phillips and Wiener (1947) have presented evidence that various disability groups have scores on the *MMPI* related to their disability or disease. The rehabilitation counselor may find that test scores indicating concern about physical health are natural to various disability groups and not abnormal concerns, as they would be for others. Tests used with the disabled may require separate standardization, and frequently may need to be considered in the light of the psychological disturbance accompanying the disability. Whether working with general population or specialized groups, the counselor cannot generalize that test scores derived on other groups apply until local use indicates that this is so.

The seventh fallacy Hahn and MacLean state is that *validity and reliability do not apply to tests alone.* These concepts apply to every tool the counselor uses in counseling, and to the counselor also. Research should be conducted to show the validity and reliability of the counselor, as well as all the tools used in a program of guidance and counseling.

TESTS AND BATTERIES

There are two types of tests available: single tests, based on a specific norm group for each test, and batteries of tests which are based upon the same norm group for all the tests in the battery. These batteries are discussed in Samler, ed. (1958) and in Chapter 8.

Single tests include the kinds discussed above: aptitude, ability, achievement, and interest inventories. The most commonly used single tests are tests of general intelligence. These tests of general intelligence include four different kinds, as will be shown in the next chapter. First is the speeded or time-limit test, an example of which is *SCAT.* On such a test an individual has to perform specific tasks within given time limits. These tests do not work well for the individual who is slow either physically or psychologically. He should be given a power test, which is the second kind of general intelligence test. Examples are the *Ohio State Psychological Examination* or the *California Test of Mental Maturity.* No time limits are set on the power test, so slow individuals may take as long as they require to do the best job they can. A third type of test is the oral, nonreading test which is read to a client by the examiner. A test like this is the *Binet* or the various forms of the *Wechsler*. A fourth type is made up of nonreading *and* nonverbal tests, either for groups or for the individual. There are a number of tests which now have nonverbal parts. An example is the nonverbal part of the *Lorge-Thorndike Intelligence Test*. Nonverbal tests do not use words at all, instructions read by the examiner being the only verbal part. Thus there are two kinds of tests of general intelligence that do not involve reading.

The growth of the test batteries from the various factorial studies and the fact that all the tests in one battery are based upon the same norm group, representative samples from the national population, makes them more usable than single tests combined into a battery. For example, *SCAT* has national norms for college freshmen. The *Minnesota Clerical Test* has all kinds of norms, but those that are most commonly used are the norms for employed clerical workers or adults gainfully occupied. How can a score for employed clerical workers or a score for adults gainfully occupied be compared with a score for entering college freshmen? How can the score on *SCAT* for *one* group of entering college freshmen be compared with the score on some of the *Cooperative Achievement Tests* based on *other* groups of college freshmen? Are the samples from the same sort of groups, or are they different? This is unknown. There is no way of determining the relationships among the different norm groups except to *hope* that they are fairly similar. With a test *battery* this is no problem because the norms are established with the same group. These tests are mostly a result of factorial analysis and for the most part have limited overlap. In that sense they are better tests, because the older tests, developed singly, have a considerable amount of overlap. In addition, the tests in new batteries have lower correlations among the parts of the battery and a high correlation with a criterion. Sometimes the same criterion, such as success in school, is used for a measure of numerical aptitude, a measure of verbal aptitude, and a measure of spatial aptitude. This gives more comparable information per unit of testing time.

In summary, there are three advantages in limited overlap among tests: lower correlation with other tests in the battery, a higher correlation with criteria, and more information per unit of testing time.

Another advantage, which is obvious but often overlooked, is the fact that these tests are created on a statistical rather than an empirical basis. The earlier tests were constructed on the basis of the kinds of items that the test author *hoped* might differentiate. New tests are a result of analyses showing the kinds of items that *will* differentiate for a given purpose. Thus it is possible to know, when constructing the test, that it will do certain things. Two examples of these batteries would be the *DAT* and the *General Aptitude Test Battery (GATB)* of the United States Training and Employment Service, both of which are discussed in the next chapter.

Actually there are different levels of professional competence and professional pride among the test producers, and it is necessary to evaluate the kinds of tests that are being put on the market (see Super 1957).

Information About Tests

Frequently the counselor has to purchase tests for professional use or needs some information about tests which appears in research or about the scores which appear in agency records. Many times the counselor is approached by others in the agency for information about the interpretation and selection of tests. The counselor, then, should have ready information about tests. Perhaps the best sources of this information are the *Mental Measurements Yearbooks* compiled under the direction of O. K. Buros (1949, 1953, 1959, 1965). Although there have been six of these yearbooks published to date, the earliest one appearing in 1938, the counselor will find that most of the information needed is found in the last four. These yearbooks are made up of sections covering the various types of standardized tests. For each of the tests discussed, there is information about content, level, forms, and other data concerning the basic structure and use of the test. This is followed by critical evaluations of the test written by several experts who are in a position to make valid remarks about the structure and use of the test. About the latter third of each of these yearbooks is made up of summaries of research using various tests. In using these yearbooks it is a good idea to start with the 1965 edition, the sixth one, and see if there is any information available about the test under consideration. There may be, and there may also be references to similar entries in earlier editions of the yearbook about the same test.

In addition to the *Mental Measurements Yearbooks*, Buros published a volume entitled *Tests in Print* (1961). This book serves as an index to the five older yearbooks, listing all tests that were then obtainable and referring to the yearbook in which they were reviewed. About a fourth of the book is made up of listings of tests which are out of print. Buros has also included in this volume a directory of test publishers and distributors throughout the world.

In addition to Buros' publications, information about tests is continually appearing in several journals with which the counselor should be familiar. *The Personnel and Guidance Journal, The Journal of Counseling Psychology, The Journal of Educational Measurement,* and *Educational and Psychological Measurement* contain information about and evaluations of new tests from time to time. Studies using tests in counseling research are often published in these journals as well. About every three years the *Review of Educational Research* publishes an issue completely devoted to the research of the previous three years on intelligence tests. Similar issues cover achievement tests, personality evaluation, statistics, and other topics of interest to counselors. *The Journal of Applied Psychology* is another journal which is more or less devoted to research using tests or other evaluative techniques; however, the majority of the studies in this journal are related to industrial situations. Material on tests used in vocational guidance also appears in *The Vocational Guidance Quarterly*. The counselor should probably begin research on a topic pertaining to tests or testing by referring to the annual index in *Psychological Abstracts*.

Finally, the information of the test publishers themselves about tests should be considered. Each of the large test publishers puts out an annual catalog which all agencies should receive. In these will be found the basic information about the tests published. All publishers offer specimen sets of their tests, either for a nominal sum or free. It is best to obtain some of these specimen sets and look them over carefully before purchasing any test. The specimen sets usually contain a copy of the various forms of the test, a manual, scoring keys, and often research information about the test.

The test publishers also put out from time to time short bulletins which contain much useful information about tests. The major ones are:

Test Service Bulletins, published by The Psychological Corporation, 304 E. 45th Street, New York, N.Y., 10017.
ETS Developments, The Educational Testing Service, Princeton, N.J., 08540.
Test Service Bulletins, Harcourt, Brace & World, Inc., 757 Third Ave., New York, N.Y., 10017.
Educational Bulletins, California Test Bureau, Del Monte Research Park, Monterey, Calif., 93940.

A postal card to any of these publishers will put the counselor on the publisher's mailing list, and the agency will then receive new catalogs and bulletins as they appear. All of the material that the counselor will then receive should be read with the realization that these publishers are trying to sell something.

Listed below are the addresses of the other major test publishers. These are their home offices. In their catalogs many of them list regional offices, from which it is more convenient and less expensive to order materials.

American Guidance Service, Inc., 720 Washington Ave., S.E., Minneapolis, Minn., 55414.

The Bobbs-Merrill Company, Inc., 4300 W. 62nd St., Indianapolis, Ind., 46206.

Bureau of Educational Research and Service, East Hall, State University of Iowa, Iowa City, Iowa, 52240.

Consulting Psychologists Press, Inc., 577 College Ave., Palo Alto, Calif., 94306.

Harper & Row, Publishers, 49 E. 33rd St., New York, N.Y., 10016.

Houghton Mifflin Company, 2 Park St., Boston, Mass., 02107.

Institute for Personality and Ability Testing, 1602 Coronado Dr., Champaign, Ill., 61822.

Psychometric Affiliates, Chicago Plaza, Brookport, Ill., 62910.

Science Research Associates, Inc., 259 E. Erie St., Chicago, Ill., 60611.

Sheridan Supply Co., Box 837, Beverly Hills, Calif., 90213.

C. H. Stoelting and Co., 424 N. Homan Ave., Chicago, Ill., 60624.

Western Psychological Services, 12045 Wilshire Blvd., Los Angeles, Calif., 90025.

Much can be learned about tests by studying them systematically. The counselor should be well grounded in psychometrics. But practice with and the use of tests are basic to learning about them. It is a good idea to summarize information about tests on a form such as Form 7.1. A large amount of the information concerning tests discussed in this chapter is summarized in this form. The beginning counselor may effectively learn about tests by taking them under the same conditions as a client would, and by having a more experienced counselor interpret the scores. As he studies each test, pertinent information may be summarized from the manual (see Linden and Linden 1968).

In the next three chapters, various kinds of tests are described and reviewed for the counselor approaching their use. Whether the tests scores are found in the client's records, or the tests are taken between the initial interview and counseling interviews or interspersed among counseling interviews, the following chapters of review information concerning tests should prove useful to the beginning counselor. These chapters should be considered a review of the more commonly used tests rather than a coverage of all tests available to the counselor.

Form 7.1

FORM FOR EVALUATING STANDARDIZED TESTS

I. Preliminary Data: Name of test _____

Author _____ Publisher _____

Parallel forms available? _____ Is test part of a series? _____

Cost per test _____ Type: Individual _____ Group _____

Use suggested by author _____

II. Validity Indices   Number and Type   Criterion   Adequacy of
                   of Subjects   Criterion

_____   _____   _____   _____

_____   _____   _____   _____

_____   _____   _____   _____

_____   _____   _____   _____

III. Reliability   Number and Type   Method Used   Other Data
     Coefficients   of Subjects

_____   _____   _____   _____

_____   _____   _____   _____

_____   _____   _____   _____

_____   _____   _____   _____

IV. Details of Administration: Untimed _____ Timed _____ Under 25 min. _____

Under 45 min. _____ Under 90 min. _____ Over 90 min. _____.

Materials needed: Stop watch _____ Electrographic Pencil _____

Special answer sheet _____ Punch board _____ Punch _____

Extra paper for working problems _____ Other materials _____

Special training needed? Yes _____ No _____ Type _____

Number of subtests and subscores _____ Purpose of these _____

V. Method of scoring: Hand scored _____ Machine scored _____ Either _____

Self-scoring _____ Scoring stencil _____ Strip key _____ Scoring time

per test _____ Can it be scored by client? Yes _____ No _____ Weighting

system used? Yes _____ No _____.

Norms: Reported for what grades, groups, sex, and so forth _____

_____. How reported? IQ's _____, Centiles _____, Standard

scores _____ Other _____. Adequacy of these norms _____.

VI. Minimal interpretation needed:

_____ By psychologist only

_____ By counselor with psychometric training

_____ By an instructor with no psychological training

_____ By client with explanation

_____ By client without explanation

VII. Recommendation: By whom recommended? _____

For what group? _____ For what purpose? _____

References _____

_____

_____

VIII. On the back of this sheet write a short summary and evaluation.

Adapted from W. C. Cottle, A form for evaluating standardized tests, *Occupations*, 1951, 30. Used by permission.

REFERENCES

American Psychological Association. 1966. *Standards for educational and psychological tests and manuals.* Washington, D.C.: American Psychological Association.

Baxter, B., and Paterson, D. G. 1940. A new ratio for clinical counselors. *J. Consult. Psychol.* 5:123–26.

Bingham, W. V. 1937. *Aptitudes and aptitude testing.* New York: Harper & Row, Publishers.

Buros, O. K. 1961. *Tests in print.* Highland Park, N.J.: The Gryphon Press.

———, ed. 1949. *The third mental measurements yearbook.* New Brunswick, N.J.: Rutgers University Press.

———. 1953. *The fourth mental measurements yearbook.* Highland Park, N.J.: The Gryphon Press.

———. 1959. *The fifth mental measurements yearbook.* Highland Park, N.J.: The Gryphon Press.

———. 1965. *The sixth mental measurements yearbook.* Highland Park, N.J.: The Gryphon Press.

Cottle, W. C. 1951. A form for evaluating standardized tests. *Occupations.* 30: 184–94.

Downie, N. M. 1967. *Fundamentals of measurement.* 2nd ed. New York: Oxford University Press, Inc.

———, and Heath, R. W. 1965. *Basic statistical methods.* 2nd ed. New York: Harper & Row, Publishers.

Educational Testing Service. 1957. *Sequential Tests of Educational Progress: Manual for interpreting scores*—Reading. Princeton, N.J.: Educational Testing Service.

Eells, K. E., *et al.* 1951. *Intelligence and cultural differences.* Chicago: University of Chicago Press.

Forbes, F. W., and Cottle, W. C. 1953. A new method for determining the readability of standardized tests. *J. Appl. Psychol.* 37:186–90.

Guilford, J. P. 1965 *Fundamental statistics in psychology and education.* 4th ed. New York: McGraw-Hill Book Company.

Hahn, M. E. and MacLean, M. S. 1955. *Counseling psychology.* New York: McGraw-Hill Book Company.

Linden, J. D., and Linden, K. 1968. *Tests on trial.* Guidance Monograph Series. Boston: Houghton Mifflin Company.

Patterson, C. H. 1957. The use of projective tests in vocational counseling. *Educ. and Psychol. Meas.* 18:533–51.

Phillips, E. L., and Wiener, D. N. 1947. Relationships between selected disability and disease groups and the *MMPI. Amer. Psychol.* 2:274.

Psychological Corporation. 1953. *Better than chance.* Test Service Bulletin no. 45. New York: The Psychological Corporation.

————. *Double-entry expectancy tables.* 1966. Bulletin no. 56. New York: The Psychological Corporation.

Rhodes, G. S. 1956. An investigation of response sets in the *Strong Vocational Interest Blank* for men and response set effects on scores on selected *SVIB* scales. Ed.D. dissertation, University of Kansas.

Samler, J., ed. 1958. *The use of multifactor tests in guidance.* Washington, D.C.: The American Personnel and Guidance Association.

Super, D. E. 1957. The multifactor tests: Summing up. *Personnel and Guidance J.* 35:576–77.

Thorndike, R. L. 1949. *Personnel selection.* New York: John Wiley & Sons, Inc.

Tiffin, J. and McCormick, E. J. 1965. *Industrial psychology.* 4th ed. Englewood Cliffs, N.J.: Prentice-Hall, Inc.

8

Evaluation of Abilities and Aptitudes

The words "ability" and "aptitude" are frequently encountered in the counselor's literature. In the past there has been considerable confusion between the two terms, which were used very loosely and often interchangeably. *Aptitudes* may best be considered, in the words of Hahn and MacLean (1955), as: "latent, potential, undeveloped capacities to acquire abilities and skills and to demonstrate achievement." Tests are constructed to measure these latent capacities, and on the basis of their scores, predictions are made of future performance or behavior. As already noted, however, an intelligence test, which in many cases is a measure of achievement, is used to predict scholastic performance or success. As an evaluation of an individual's current mental status, this test may be looked upon as a test of ability.

When used to predict future behavior, this test becomes an aptitude test. Similarly there are tests of typing ability, musical ability, artistic ability, and the like. Many times, perhaps most typically, these are used as aptitude tests. Even an achievement test such as one constructed to measure high-school mathematics is commonly used in the university to predict performance in mathematics, science, or engineering courses. The line which separates ability from achievement is a thin one. Both are probably the result of the developments of aptitudes by training and learning. In the discussion that follows, tests which measure current status will be referred to as tests of *ability, or achievement*. The use to which these tests are put will determine whether or not they are aptitude tests.

A discussion of abilities may be separated into two parts. First there is general ability, or intelligence. Theories about its nature and components will be discussed. The other abilities are referred to as special abilities. Of this type there are many. In the discussion that follows, attention will be given only to those that are encountered in the usual counseling situations—mechanical, clerical, artistic, and musical ability. It should also be strongly emphasized, again, that tests are only one method used in collecting information about these abilities. It is granted that they are very useful, and even suspected that they are the easiest way of obtaining information about abilities. But they are not the only way, and the alert counselor is always looking for other bits of information with which to do a better job of evaluating abilities.

All information about aptitudes and abilities needs to be synthesized into a meaningful pattern for use with the clients in the counseling interviews. The cross-sectional data described in this chapter form an important part of the counselor-client evaluations which result in life choices. A central part of these data is that describing a client's general ability to perform life tasks. Thus it is essential that the counselor consider the meaning of general ability, ways of evaluating it, and how it can be used in the counseling interviews.

GENERAL ABILITY

Usually general ability is referred to as *intelligence*. Many have become dissatisfied with the term "intelligence" because it means different things to different people and thus becomes difficult to use. Frequently intelligence is called "academic or scholastic ability," or even "book-learning ability." There is justification for this when it is considered that these intelligence tests are used, most typically, in schools to predict how well an individual will learn in an academic situation, that is with books.

Definitions of intelligence by psychologists have been many and varied. About 60 years ago, Binet defined intelligence as the capacity to judge well, to reason well, and to comprehend well (Goodenough 1949). The editors of the *Journal of Educational Psychology* published some definitions of intelligence from a symposium they conducted (1921). Some follow: Dearborn, "The capacity to learn or profit by experience"; Henmon, "Capacity for knowledge or knowledge possessed"; Terman, "The ability to think in terms of abstract ideas"; Pintner, "The ability of the individual to adapt himself adequately to relatively new relations in life"; and Thorndike, "Intellect, as the power of good responses from the point of view of truth." Stoddard (1943) proposed one of the most comprehensive definitions: "Intelligence is the ability to undertake activities that are characterized by difficulty, complexity, abstractness, economy, adaptiveness to a goal, social value, emergence of originals, and to maintain such activities under conditions that demand a concentration of energy and a resistance to emotional forces." Wechsler (1944), in the book about his intelligence test for adults, described intelligence as the "global" capacity of an individual to act purposefully and to deal effectively with his environment. Garrett (1946) described intellectual capacity as the abilities demanded in the solution of problems which require understanding and the manipulations of symbols. Goddard (1946) conceived of intelligence as the availability and use of one's past experience for the solution of immediate problems and the anticipation of future ones.

All of these definitions may be classified into two general types. The first includes definitions related to the ability to carry on abstract thinking, the ability to manipulate symbols, or the ability to learn materials of a verbal nature. The other category includes the definitions that consider intelligence as the ability to adapt to one's environment. Stoddard's definition is the best of this type. It follows that, since a definition such as Stoddard's is so complex that it is all but impossible to construct a test to measure such a comprehensive concept, test makers have concentrated on measuring the other type of intelligence.

The early tests, such as Binet's 1905 scale, were based upon no theory of intelligence. They were essentially trial-and-error attempts that differed from their predecessors in that they seemed to work. This early test of Binet's was immediately followed by two revisions that were considerable advancements over the 1905 scale. Psychologists all around the world became interested in Binet's work, and soon translations of his tests or adaptations began to appear in various countries, the most notable being Terman's *Revision of the Binet-Simon Intelligence Scales (1916)*. This test was made up of items arranged in age levels. Each item was worth so many months' mental age and an individual's score on the test was the sum of the months received for responding to an item correctly. Such a scale is referred to as an *age scale*. Mental age was divided by chronological age to give the I.Q.:

$$I.Q. = \frac{MA}{CA}(100)$$

The 100 was introduced to remove the decimals. A test like this is labeled an *individual test* because it can be administered to only one person at a time.

In 1917, the United States entered World War I and for the first time an attempt was made to measure extensively the mental ability and other characteristics of a large group of men. A group of psychologists was asked to construct a test which could be given to a number of individuals at once. The results of their efforts brought forth the first practical intelligence test, the *Army Alpha*. This test, which could only be used by draftees who could read and write English, was soon followed by the *Army Beta*, the first nonverbal group test designed for illiterates and non-English-speaking personnel. At the end of the war both industry and education began to use these intelligence tests, this use continuing to the present.

The early tests, now referred to as "old-type" tests, typically resulted in one score that was translated into an I.Q. They were made up of a series of items such as word meaning, arithmetic problems, number series, analogies, same-opposites, and the like. The items were in random order as far as content was concerned, but they were usually arranged in order of difficulty with the easiest item first and each succeeding item more difficult than the one before it. Such an arrangement of mixed items in ascending order of difficulty results in a test described as a "spiral-omnibus test." Tests which resulted in more than one score did not begin to appear until the 1930's when Thurstone's (1938) work was beginning to have effect. Since then the majority of these tests measure certain aspects of intelligence, or factors, as Thurstone called them. Instead of one score being derived from a test, a profile of several factors may result from this new type, or at least a total score that is broken down into parts: a verbal score; and a nonverbal score which is also called a "quantitative" or "performance" score. Thurstone's original test was the *Chicago Test of Primary Mental Abilities*. Other tests of this type are the *Cooperative School and College Ability Tests (SCAT)*, the *Army General Classification Test (AGCT)* administered to millions of draftees in World War II, the *Lorge-Thorndike Intelligence Tests*, and the *Holzinger-Crowder Uni-Factor Tests*.

Theories of Intelligence

Spearman (1904) was the first to propose an acceptable theory of intelligence. His theory is referred to as the "two-factor theory" because he stated that intelligence was made up of a *general factor g* and other *specific factors s.* According to this theory, two tests correlate because they both contain some of the g-factor, and the larger the amount of this factor in common between the two tests the larger the correlation between the two. Spearman stated that this g-factor was a particular type of mental energy that could be used in making comparisons or in drawing inferences. In the years following, Spearman had to revise his ideas to make way for other factors that he referred to as *group factors.* These group factors may be common to two or more tests but not to all tests under consideration at one time. They received labels such as "mechanical," "arithmetical," "musical," "logical," "psychological," "perseveration," "oscillation," and "will." Spearman's ideas are still followed by many British psychologists in describing and measuring intelligence.

Vernon (1961, 1965) proposed that, along with the g or general factor, there were *two major group factors,* the verbal–educational group and the spatial–practical–mechanical group. He noted that the first of these usually included *minor group factors* such as number, divergent thinking, word fluency, and scholastic factors. The second group factor included psychomotor, perceptual, physical, mechanical, and spatial factors. Vernon (1965) added that there were various cross-links, as in the case of mathematics and science, both of which depend upon mathematical ability and spatial perception, or, as in verbal tests, which combine both verbal ability and perceptual speed. At the lowest level in his hierarchy he placed what he called *specific factors.*

In the United States, T. L. Kelley and L. L. Thurstone have been the pioneers in developing theories of intelligence. The approach in this country is to conceive of intelligence or of "the organization of mental life," as it is sometimes called, as being made up of a group of factors. Thurstone (1938), after administering a large number of tests to a group of high-school students, was able to identify statistically, by factor analysis, a group of factors that he called *primary mental abilities.* These are:

V   Verbal: understanding ideas expressed in words
N   Numerical: the ability to carry out the four fundamental arithmetic
    processes
R   Reasoning: problem solving
S   Spatial: the ability to perceive spatial relationships
P   Perception: perceptual speed
WF Word fluency: the ability to write and speak with considerable ease
M   Memory

Six of the above factors (omitting P) are published as the *Chicago Test of Primary Mental Abilities.* The SRA *Primary Abilities Test* contains only five of the factors, M being omitted as well as P.

Guilford (1959, 1966) outlined a new *three-way organization* of mental ability. He set up a three-dimensional model with Operations on one side, Products on a second side, and Contents on a third. The first of these, *Operations*, contains five categories: Cognition, Memory, Divergent Thinking, Convergent Thinking, and Evaluation. The second, *Products*, includes six categories: Units, Classes, Relations, Systems, Transformations, and Implementations. The third, *Contents*, has four categories: Figural, Symbolic, Semantic, and Behavioral. The five categories of the Operations dimension of the block intersect the six categories of Products, which in turn intersect the four categories of Content. This results in 120 cells, $5 \times 6 \times 4$, each of which represents a factor, ability, or type of task that may appear on an intelligence test. According to this system, any test item would then have three terms to describe it, such as "cognition, units, and symbolic." An item illustrating the ability to "cognize symbolic units" is one which asks a subject to rearrange the following letters to make a real word—g o n l o m. Guilford (1966) stated that he had named 75 of the 120 cells in his model. Actually he has demonstrated the existence of 80 abilities, but a small amount of duplication reduced the number to 75.

Guilford and his students are the strongest advocates of a multifactor approach to describing intelligence. However, American psychologists are far from agreement on such basic ideas as this. For example, McNemar (1964) protested that the factor analysts had fragmented mental ability into more and more factors of less and less value. Such statements as McNemar's are based upon the fact that much of the research done with multifactor tests has pointed out that only one or two of the factors contribute anything to the prediction equation. Usually the verbal part of the battery is the most important one in prediction. The same results can be obtained with one of the older, shorter tests. That is, the older, shorter, and more economical test works better in actual practice than the long, detailed, time-consuming multifactor test. There will be more discussion of this later, when some of the multifactor batteries are discussed in detail.

As Vernon has pointed out, while the multifactor approach has been favored by most American test theorists and builders, counselors and others who use tests for making practical decisions seldom use this approach. Despite the writings and assertions of Thurstone, Guilford, and others, in which it is claimed that general intelligence is too vague and complex a concept to be meaningful, counselors go along their merry way, administering the familiar and simple group tests of intelligence that are basically measures of *g*. Vernon noted that the chief concession that is made to the factor analysts was to divide total scores into separate verbal and quantitative parts. Research shows that intercorrelations among tests that comprise a battery tend to be high. This indicates the presence of a general factor g which is very difficult to ignore and very useful in the counseling situation. As a result, the user of tests feels that he can do his job better with a simpler test that measures g. The British, of whom Vernon is very representative, look upon factors as merely a classification of similar tests and only that. Some American writers, on the other hand, seem to feel that factors such as Thurstone's are basic components of mental organization, as are elements to a chemist.

The Measurement of Intelligence

In the past, considerable confusion and disagreement existed as to exactly what intelligence tests measure. If one looks at the types of items that appear on many of them, there is a very obvious conclusion. Consider the items: "If two pencils cost five cents, how many pencils can be bought for 35 cents?" "Who is the President of the United States?" "A word meaning the same as eulogize is . . . ." and the like. These items measure the results of learning, or achievement. An intelligence test of this type, then, is an achievement test. The score that an individual obtains is greatly affected by his interaction with his environment. It is important for the counselor to remember that the client's background includes not only the school but the home and community as well, because much learning takes place in home and community activities—in certain social classes, and not in others. These tests, then, do *not* measure innate ability. They measure the effects of learning upon a native ability. It follows, then, that the user of the tests has to make the assumption when using them that each child has had an equal opportunity to learn. A little thought reveals that this assumption is never fully justified, not only because of the inequalities of the schools, but also and chiefly because of the gross and glaring differences in the homes and communities from which children come. The psychological literature of the past is full of studies of the backwoodsmen of Kentucky and Virginia, the canal-boat children of England, and the changes brought about in the measured intelligence of American Blacks when they move to northern cities from the rural South. Children from these barren environments do poorly on intelligence tests, mainly because they live in a different culture from the one in which the tests have been standardized. Therefore the counselor must adjust his interpretation of a test score in terms of differing cultural backgrounds of clients.

Closely related is the effect of parental occupation upon the intelligence tests scores of children. Terman (1937), in the *Manual* for his revised *Stanford-Binet Scale*, showed the effects of the socioeconomic status of parents on the intelligence test scores of children. He found that the mean I.Q.'s of 10-to-14-year-old children of different social classes were as follows: Professional, 118; Semiprofessional and managerial, 112; Clerical, skilled trades, and retail business, 107; Rural owners, 92; Semi-skilled, minor clerical, minor business, 103; Slightly skilled, 101; and, Day laborers, urban and rural, 97. The greatest mean difference here is 26 I.Q. points between children of professional people and those of farmers who own their land. Terman showed similar differences in children of three other age groups among these same social groups. Eells and others (1951), in a major study conducted at the University of Chicago, evaluated the effects of social-class membership on more widely used group tests. They found that on some of these tests every single item had a bias which favored the child from the middle-class home. Their work resulted in a test known as the *Davis-Eells Games* (1953), which attempts to measure mental ability by ruling out the effects of class membership. The counselor must take test bias into account in interpreting and using test scores with any client.

R. B. Cattell (1960) issued *Culture Fair Tests,* which were revisions of his earlier *Culture Free Tests.* It was claimed that these tests were relatively free of dependence on school achievement, socioeconomic status, and other aspects of the environment that may affect test scores. It was also held that such tests had a high saturation of the general factor *g.* Research carried out with these tests, however, has shown that they have been only partially effective in eliminating cultural biases. In some studies, individuals in drastically different cultures have produced similar results; in other studies, actual differences were found. These tests are supposed to measure latent ability, unmodified by learning. It has been argued that a knowledge of this latent ability is of no practical importance. All individuals have to function in a given environment under certain conditions. It is important that a counselor know where any individual stands among others in his actual environment. It is exceedingly practical, from the counselor's point of view, that evaluations of subjects be made which take these cultural influences into account. Perhaps attempts to produce culture-free or culture-fair tests are efforts to attain goals that are of little value to the daily user of tests. A better procedure would be to establish appropriately varying norm groups, such as urban whites, urban blacks, rural whites, rural blacks, Indians on or off reservations, and the like.

Stanley and Porter (1967) make a point which is highly pertinent to counselors. In a study comparing correlations of scores on the College Entrance Examination Board *SAT-V* and *SAT-M* vs. college grades of blacks in predominantly black colleges with *SAT* scores vs. grades of whites in predominantly white colleges, they found that while scores of blacks tended to be lower, the *predictive validity* (or counseling use) of these scores was not significantly different for black males, black females, and white males. The predictive correlation for white females *was* significantly higher, however. Cleary (1966) reports that she was able to predict grades for blacks and non-blacks about equally well in two of three integrated colleges she studied. This appears to mean that while there may be social or cultural differences in the general level of scores on such tests, they can still be used *effectively to predict performance in school* for blacks as well as whites.

In addition to the effect of background of the individual being tested on test results, there is also the effect of motivation. This is related to a certain extent to the social class to which the individual belongs, for the individual from the middle class comes from a background where the emphasis is on striving and attaining success. It might be expected that he will do his best to work up to capacity on a test. Lower-class children are apt to see little value in tests or in anything associated with school. There is usually no evidence about just what their test score measures. It follows, then, that a counselor has to use extreme caution in interpreting their scores. The best thing to do is to interpret any such score in the light of all other information available about a student. Also, the counselor must remember that there are error factors even in the best of intelligence tests. Actually, these tests are most valid when they are used to measure the mental ability of urban, white, middle-class American children between the ages of 7 and 16.

Scores from these tests are reported in I.Q.'s, centiles, or standard scores. As pointed out when scores and norms were discussed previously, I.Q.'s have little meaning when used for adolescents and adults. Another problem that has concerned psychologists for a long time is the constancy of the I.Q. In earlier times there were those who thought that it was stable or constant throughout life. Then there were the environmentalists who argued that placing any child in a desirable environment would bring about a significant increase in measured intelligence. Stoddard (1943) presents a good picture of the research basis of these ideas. The whole question was whether measured intelligence was the result of factors inherited from parents or the effect of being in a desirable environment. Today the argument has quieted down and most psychologists take a middle-of-the-road approach, saying that both inheritance and environment are important and that what is measured is the effect of both. As far as the stability of the I.Q. or the intelligence test score is concerned, it is now felt that if a child's intelligence is measured at the age of 6 or older, this measure is a reliable measure of what he will be like in later years. There will of course be variations, but these are slight. If the individual stays in the same sort of environment, he will obtain about the same scores on subsequent forms of the same test, the variation being a function of the standard error of measurement. Even a great change in environment will bring about increases of only a few points. Tests administered before the age of 6 are apt to be more unreliable, and the younger the child at the time of testing, the more unreliable the test (P. Cattell 1947). It must also be noted that I.Q.'s from different tests are not the same. The means of all may be 100, but the standard deviations will vary. For example, the standard deviation of the Binet is 16; of the Otis, 12. Thus the counselor interprets a Binet I.Q. of 116 as equivalent to an Otis I.Q. of 112.

Types of Intelligence Tests

The simplest classification that can be made of intelligence tests is that of group and individual tests. Group tests are by far the more common. *Group tests* may be administered to one or more persons at once. The responses to the items are recorded either on the test booklet or on a special answer sheet. An *individual test*, on the other hand, is administered orally to one individual at a time and responses to every separate item are recorded by the examiner. Most of the tests that the counselor uses are group tests.

Group Tests of Intelligence

Group tests may be further divided into two types, one-score tests and those which provide results in terms of many scores, or a *profile*. The *one-score test*, as previously pointed out, is the older of the two. Such tests as the *Otis-Lennon Mental Ability Tests*, the *Henmon-Nelson Tests*, and several short tests used in industry, such as the *Wonderlic Personnel Test*, and the *Purdue Adaptability Tests*, are of this type. The older tests produced results that were expressed in I.Q.'s. Some of the newer ones use both standard scores and centiles in reporting scores. Such tests as these are usually short, with about 30 to 45 minutes being the maximum testing time. Several, such as the *Wonderlic*, are very short, requiring only 12 minutes of working time. They are very useful with groups in elementary and high schools, and in industrial situations, especially for average individuals. Brighter students or older individuals need more difficult tests. When these tests are used with college students, for example, there is a tendency for the scores to cluster near the top. Such tests are said to have "low ceilings." Also, individuals who are considered dull or of below-average mental ability cannot have valid estimates of their mental ability made with these tests, for they are slow or retarded in reading, and speed is an important factor.

As pointed out previously, the work of the Thurstones led the way in the construction of *tests with more than one score*. In the most general form such tests are composed of a verbal and a nonverbal part, resulting in two scores and a total score. A few go further than this and break mental ability down into component parts. It must be pointed out that all of these tests are not based upon the results of factor analyses, as was Thurstone's *Chicago Test of Primary Mental Abilities.* In the next paragraphs several of the more widely used tests of this type will be mentioned.

In 1955 the Educational Testing Service issued the first forms of the *SCAT* to replace a test, the *American Council on Education Psychological Examination (ACE)*, that had been used for many years with high-school upperclassmen and entering college freshmen. The *SCAT* differed from the *ACE* in that it covered five levels: intermediate grades, upper grades, junior high school, senior high school, and college freshmen and sophomores. The test was made up of four parts that resulted in a verbal score *V* and a quantitative score *Q.*

SCAT: Series II, published in 1967, is a complete revision of the earlier *SCAT.* Like its predecessor it measures verbal and mathematical ability, but it provides three scores, *V*, *Q*, and a total. The number of parts was reduced to two, and the administration time was reduced to 40 minutes, making the test much more amenable to use in the public schools. The new form is available at the same five levels as the original *SCAT.* Like the *ACE*, it is a good predictor of academic success.

Another test series that can be used throughout the school is the *Lorge-Thorndike Intelligence Tests* issued by Houghton Mifflin Company. This test consists of six levels: I, for kindergarten and grade 1; II, for grades 2 and 3; III, for grades 4 through 6; IV, for grades 7–9; V for grades 10–13; and *H* for college freshmen. The tests covering the first two levels are essentially nonverbal. At the three highest levels the tests are made up of two parts, a verbal and a nonverbal series. The test authors recommend that Level IV be reserved for the general run of the population and Level V be used with high-school graduates. The results are expressed in I.Q.'s, but these I.Q.'s are of the standard-score type. A multilevel edition appeared in 1964 for grades 3–13. This battery has both verbal and nonverbal parts, each made up of a series of subtests. An edition such as this provides for greater flexibility in the testing program and makes using the test less expensive in terms of student costs.

In 1963 the California Test Bureau published a revision of the *California Test of Mental Maturity.* This series of tests consists of 8 batteries: (0) kindergarten and grade 1; (1) grades 1–3; (1*H*) a transitional form for between grades 3 and 4; (2) grades 4–6; (2*H*) a transitional form for grades 6 and 7; (3) grades 7–9; (4) grades 9–12; and (5) grade 12, college students, and adults. Like the earlier editions, it has a *Long Form* and a *Short Form*, taking two and one class periods, respectively. These forms yield a language, nonlanguage, and a total score. A detailed profile shows the individual's performance on each part of the test. Scores are reported in deviation I.Q.'s.

While these batteries with all their details and elaborate profiles seem ideal and useful, it must be remembered that the reliability of any test is directly related to its length. On some of these tests the number of items in the various subtests is small. This results in subtests with little or no reliability, whereas the total test score, or the scores based upon the two parts (verbal and nonverbal), may be highly reliable. In many cases the subscores are of no value and should not be considered in counseling. There is even evidence that the use of more than the total score adds little or nothing to the prediction of academic success (Super 1956d).

There are several tests that were constructed for the *top part of the distribution of mental ability.* Level I of the *SCAT* is one example. Another test, used with high-school seniors and university freshmen, is the *Ohio State University Psychological Examination,* which is available from Science Research Associates. This test is almost unique in that it is a power test, that is, there is no time limit, but most individuals complete it in less than two hours. The test is entirely verbal. It is an excellent predictor of the grades of college freshmen. Another test, on an even higher level, is the *Miller Analogies Test* (available through The Psychological Corporation to certain counseling and testing bureaus) which is made up of 100 analogy-type test items. Certain universities use it in the selection of students for graduate work. Validity coefficients resulting from the use of this test have tended to be very low. There may be two reasons for this: the fact that grades in the typical graduate school tend to be very restricted in their range; and the homogeneous nature of the graduate student group. It may be recalled that the more restricted the range of the group, the smaller the size of any correlation coefficient. Terman developed another high-level test, the *Concept Mastery Test* (available from The Psychological Corporation). This test resulted from his study of gifted individuals and is similar in part to the Miller, in its makeup and use. Batteries such as the *Graduate Record Examination* and the *College Entrance Examination Boards* also contain high-level intelligence tests of a verbal and quantitative nature.

Of all the tests already mentioned and discussed, the majority may be classified as being *verbal* or mostly verbal. By this is meant that to respond to the item the examinee has to manipulate words. The other type of group test is called *nonverbal.* When taking these, the examinee manipulates geometrical figures, mazes, figure analogies, and the like. Such tests are used with those who have language or reading handicaps or, in some cases, with those who do not speak English, as was the *Army Beta* of World War I. They are used in the schools, chiefly with children in the primary grades (e.g., the *Lorge-Thorndike Tests,* already mentioned) and with others who have reading problems or who have been raised in an environment of such a nature that taking an ordinary verbal test would be to their disadvantage. Similar in their function to these nonverbal tests are other tests known as *performance tests.* Usually these are individual tests in which the client has to complete tasks such as mazes, formboards, or building designs with colored blocks. Such tests are usually reserved for the physically and mentally handicapped. These batteries or tests result in I.Q.'s, but they are apt to be considerably different from those obtained from verbal tests. A typical correlation coefficient between the two types of tests would be somewhere around .50. The counselor will make limited use of performance tests.

Individual Tests

Individual tests are administered to only one person at a time. There are two widely used individual tests. The oldest is the *Stanford-Binet,* now in its third revision (1960). This battery consists of a series of tests that start at age 2 and go, by either half-years or whole years, up to the adult ages. Administration, scoring, and interpretation of the test require special training in which tests are administered and scored under supervision. The results are either in mental ages or I.Q.'s. The test is highly verbal. This, and the fact that it was standardized upon children and adolescents in school, limit its use, especially with adults. The test is now most frequently used in clinical settings such as child guidance centers, and by school psychologists.

Wechsler (1939) introduced the *Wechsler-Bellevue Intelligence Scale,* an intelligence test for adults standardized upon adults. The scale was made up of two parts, verbal and performance, the latter being a collection of many of the performance tests that had been used by psychologists for many years. In 1955, a revision, the *Wechsler Adult Intelligence Scale (WAIS),* was produced; however, there is little difference between the two editions except that a few of the tests were lengthened. Wechsler also has developed the *Wechsler Intelligence Scale for Children* (1949), similar in content to his other scales and for use with children from ages 5 to 15. In 1967 he published the *Wechsler Preschool and Primary Scale of Intelligence (WPPSI),* intended for ages 4 to 6½ years. This overlaps somewhat with the lowest range of the *WISC.*

Since World War II these Wechsler scales have been widely used in both clinics and counseling centers. A lot of pointless research has been carried on with the sub-scales of these tests—pointless because it was based upon tests with such a small number of items that reliability was nonexistent. Many counselors have recommended that clients take the test. In some schools all clients were automatically administered this test when they appeared for counseling. The writers feel that such a practice is a waste of time and money. There is no evidence that the individual tests are any more useful or effective with the average client in educational and vocational counseling than any of the group tests. Until any real value is shown to result from the use of these tests with all clients, they should be reserved for individuals who cannot be adequately appraised by the use of the group tests, usually individuals at the extreme ends of the continuum of intelligence, and those with reading, language, physical, or cultural handicaps. A bright child has a chance to be more adequately measured on the *Stanford-Binet* because of the higher ceiling of the test, and the lower levels permit more effective appraisal as well.

Use of Intelligence Tests in Counseling

Intelligence tests, along with other evidence of mental ability that will soon be discussed, probably find their greatest use in the prediction of educational and vocational success. This is not surprising when it is considered that one of the major goals of counseling is educational and vocational adjustment. These tests are also used in identifying the superior students for awards, scholarships, or for more advanced and strenuous academic programs. At the other extreme, these tests are used in a diagnostic manner along with reading, study skills, performance, interest, and personality tests to see if the reasons for a student's failure can be identified on an *intelligence test.*

There is a question about whether a client should be told his exact score. The general feeling is that it should not be done. But this refers only to the exact scores. What was said earlier about the standard error of measurement is one reason for not handing out these tests scores indiscriminately. Each score is unreliable to a certain extent, and thus is too indefinite to be a label put on clients unless it is combined with other evidence. And then the I.Q. is no longer the major factor.

However, if the counselor accepts as one of the major aims of counseling that clients obtain information about themselves and their own strength and weaknesses, it follows that they must have some information about where they stand on the continuum of intelligence. It is hoped that on the basis of the information brought out in the counseling situation the client will be able to put all the details together and come to a logical decision about himself and his future. This is impossible if the client knows nothing about his mental ability. So, instead of being told or given specific scores, the client should be informed about scores on rather broad bands into which the continuum of intelligence has been divided, such as "in the top 10% of your freshman class," "in the bottom 25% of high school seniors," "very superior when compared to high school seniors in this curriculum," "below the average group" or "below the mean when compared to other engineering freshmen." There is no need for this method to be too threatening when the client is in the lower half of the average group or in the lowest 16%. Usually the client knows this, and a way can be found to say it if the counselor is alert. More appropriate norm groups can also be chosen, and these may provide fairer and more meaningful comparisons for the client. Then comparisons can be made without creating a feeling of despair.

In using intelligence test scores, it is a good idea not to place too much reliance upon scores from a single test. In the ideal testing program the client is tested at different intervals, and usually there are one or more scores from the same test series that can be evaluated to give a better idea of his mental ability than would be obtained from a single score. The ideal use of intelligence tests in schools is to administer such tests at the end of the 3rd or 4th grade, this followed again, in grade 5, by another form of the test, as a check upon the previous one. Then a test should be administered at the beginning of junior high school, and again at the beginning of senior high. It is also recommended that there be additional testing in the senior year, when there is an intensification of the counseling process for both educational and vocational purposes. In general, intelligence tests should be administered at the transition points in the educational program. In other agencies, sufficient intelligence test scores should be secured that, together with other evidence of intelligence, they will give a stable estimate for counseling purposes.

Again the reader should remember that these scores of mental ability must be interpreted in the light of other information collected about the client. Psychologists consider individuals in parts or segments of behavior when testing and evaluating them. Often, when results are considered, there is a tendency to overlook the fact that information about some of these parts is not consistent with that about the whole individual.

Other Evidences of Mental Ability

Considerable space has been devoted to the use of tests in the collection of evidence on mental ability. It must not be overlooked that there are other ways in which such information may be collected, very important among which is the use of observational techniques. Ratings are used to appraise how an individual solves problems, shows evidence of creativity and original thinking, or carries on any activity involving mental ability. Probably better than the use of these rating scales is the use of a system of anecdotal records (see Chapter 3). Well-written anecdotes are filled with information such as that mentioned about rating scales. Another source of information about mental ability is in the questions that individuals ask. This is particularly true of younger children, for it seems that in many schools, as children grow older, they become conditioned to asking certain kinds of questions or toward not asking questions at all. The judgments of competent teachers also provide excellent information about students' mental ability. Rating scales and anecdotes involve these teachers' judgments to a great extent.

There are many bits of additional evidence that the counselor might look at which offer suggestions as to the client's mental ability. Some of these are noted below. The client's age may be compared with his grade placement in school. The amount and the type of reading done offer valuable insights. Certain hobbies, such as playing chess and working complicated puzzles, aid in identifying the brighter individuals. The counselor may note the rapidity with which the client "catches on" in the interview. Samples of the client's writing containing material which offers a chance to be creative or to organize material are also good indicators of higher mental ability. Rank in graduating class is also important, but the counselor must consider the size of the class. This information is very important when the client was graduated in a large class, but it is of no value when the graduating class consisted of only a small number of individuals. A comparison of grades obtained and the number of activities carried on by a student is also useful. Finally, such factors as the socioeconomic status of the family, the occupations of the parents and siblings, the education of the parents and siblings, and the like may also contain valuable information. The counselor must recognize that all of these may not provide valid information about the mental ability of all individuals. An individual from a minority group should not have some of these applied to him.

Another important source of information about general ability, or intelligence, is the grades that students receive in their academic courses. Earlier it was noted that marks in school correlate highest with intelligence tests and for that reason the tests are known as tests of book-learning ability. The counselor must accept grades for what they are. They are apt to be unreliable, for there are any of a number of different things that go into the makeup of grades given by any one teacher. When one compares grades from one teacher with those from another, or compares grades among members of different departments or schools, the variability of the grades becomes even greater. However, when all grades are taken for any given individual, they tend to cancel out the idiosyncrasies of a given teacher and to give a rather accurate picture of the individual's mental ability. However, the accuracy is frequently limited by differences in motivation among individuals. Inequalities between academic potential and grades are most frequently encountered when contingency or motivational factors, such as attitudes and interests, play a vital part. It is not unusual to find one of the brightest individuals in a school, office, or factory failing or being dropped because of poor work. In such cases the counselor needs other evaluative devices. Grades are not the only measure of school achievement available, for there is a large series of standardized achievement tests that provide valid and reliable measures of academic attainment. Grades should be compared with achievement test scores to see whether the teachers' estimates coincide with a more objective measure of classroom performance. These achievement tests will be discussed next.

ACHIEVEMENT TESTS

Standardized achievement tests are the most plentiful of the many standardized tests. An *achievement test* is a test that is used to measure the outcomes of learning. While most of them are associated with classroom learning, this does not have to be the case. Achievement tests fall into two rather large groups, the *elementary school batteries* and the *specific subject matter tests* used in high schools and colleges. Especially important among the latter are reading tests. All produce highly reliable results when used correctly. They are so constructed that they possess content validity. Before such tests are purchased they should be examined carefully to see how well they cover the content and the objectives of the courses taught in the schools where they are being used. Many times there is a rather wide discrepancy between local practice and what the tests measure. The extent of this discrepancy governs the validity of the tests. In the discussion that follows, several of the more widely encountered batteries and tests will be described. The counselor interested in others should see the catalogs of the various test publishers or Buros (1949, 1953, 1959, 1965).

Currently, the widely used elementary school batteries are the *Metropolitan Achievement Tests, Stanford Achievement Tests* (both published by Harcourt, Brace & World, Inc.), the *Iowa Every Pupil Tests* (Houghton Mifflin Company), the *California Achievement Tests* (California Test Bureau), and the newest, the *Sequential Tests of Educational Progress* (Educational Testing Service). While these batteries, in general, cover the elementary grades up to junior high school, the last two differ in that they may be used with high-school students and those in the first two years of college. Generally, these batteries measure reading skills, language usage or communication skills, arithmetic skills, and work-study skills. Some of the older ones test content, such as history, literature, and geography, but the trend is away from this toward a concentration on the more permanent results of the educative process, such as the ability to use data and apply principles.

At present, three series of achievement tests are used with students in secondary and higher education. One of the oldest is the group known as the *Cooperative Achievement Tests* (Educational Testing Service). These tests are of two types: general proficiency, as in mathematics; and the regular tests associated with specific academic course subjects like plane geometry. These tests have a reputation for excellent construction and norming. A second group is the *Evaluation and Adjustment Tests* (Harcourt, Brace & World, Inc.). This is a series of well-constructed tests for each of the secondary academic subjects. Finally there are the *Iowa Tests of Educational Development* (Science Research Associates). This series differs from the others in that no attempt is made to measure the various academic subjects. There are nine tests in this battery, bearing such headings as Understanding of basic social concepts, Interpretation of reading materials in the natural sciences, General vocabulary test, and Uses of sources of information.

The results of such tests are useful to the counselor in various ways, an important one of which is prediction. A common problem of the high-school and university counselor is assisting the client in making vocational plans. For example, achievement tests and course grades in mathematics and physical science would be most useful in making a prediction about success in engineering, or even in discussing the feasibility of the study of engineering with a client who is considering engineering as a vocation.

Achievement tests are also useful in the diagnostic work of locating weak areas. This is especially true of reading. It is not at all unusual to find that some students are doing poor or failing work merely because they are poor or slow readers. The counselor must not overlook this fact, and in all such cases reading disability must be considered as a potential source of the difficulties. At other times, mathematics and English tests may serve a similar need in their respective areas. The counselor or teacher may also use an achievement test in a given subject to determine weak areas in need of remediation *within* the subject field. Thus achievement tests can be used for predictive, diagnostic, or remedial purposes. In general, the counselor should use these tests to evaluate, with the client, his individual strengths and weaknesses in the academic subjects in the way that best meets the client's needs. Proper use would then result in better educational preparation and better vocational adjustment for the client.

SPECIAL ABILITIES

In contrast to general ability or intelligence, there is a group of abilities equally important in counseling, referred to as special abilities. Five of these are: mechanical, clerical, artistic, musical, and physical ability.

Field and Level Concepts

Order is introduced into the area of abilities and their use in predicting educational and vocational success by what is known as "field and level concepts." It would be impossible to set up tests for the thousands of different occupations that exist in the United States. Many can be classified as being in the mechanical area, or field. To be successful in these occupations one has to have one or more of the mechanical skills or traits. Individuals with these skills, however, do not all work at the same level. Some are trained, and perform, at the professional level, whereas others do semiskilled work. To a great extent the amount of general ability one possesses more or less determines at which level he is going to perform.

In one of the earlier classifications of fields, Paterson, Gerken, and Hahn (1941, 1953) constructed the *Minnesota Occupational Rating Scales (MORS)* in which they set up the following abilities:

1. *Academic.* The ability to understand and manipulate ideas and symbols.
2. *Mechanical.* The ability to manipulate concrete objects, to work with tools and machinery, and to deal mentally with mechanical movements.
3. *Social.* The ability to understand and manage people, to function well in social relationships.
4. *Clerical.* The ability to handle numbers and names accurately and rapidly.
5. *Musical.* The ability to sense sounds, to image these sounds in reproductive and creative imagination, to be aroused by them emotionally, and so forth, and finally the ability to give some form of expression in musical performance or in creative music.
6. *Artistic.* The ability to create forms of artistic merit and the capacity to recognize the comparative merits of forms already created.
7. *Physical.* The ability to perform physical tasks.*

The fields that are used with the *Minnesota Occupational Rating Scales* are named exactly as are the seven abilities listed above. Practically all

---

* This and the following lists of levels were adapted, with permission from D. G. Paterson, C.d'A. Gerken, and M. E. Hahn, *Revised Minnesota Occupational Rating Scales* (Minneapolis: University of Minnesota Press, Copyright 1953).

occupations can be placed into one of the above fields or in a combination of two or more of them.

The same authors set up four occupational levels which may be generally classified as follows:

Level A. Professional, Semiprofessional, and Executive occupations. The top 10% of the population, except in the last three fields, where it is 4%.

Level B. Technical, Clerical, and Supervisory. 15% of the population.

Level C. Skilled tradesmen, low-level, low-grade clerical workers, and the like. The middle 50% of the population.

Level D. Unskilled workers. The bottom 25% of the population.

The authors describe the intelligence or the academic ability associated with each of these levels as follows:

Level A. Superior abstract intelligence with training equivalent to college graduation from a first-class institution or two or three years of college, or to that of executive of a moderately large business. Ability for creative and directive work is implied.

Level B. High average abstract intelligence with training equivalent to high-school graduation and/or technical school or junior college.

Level C. Average abstract intelligence with training equivalent to vocational high school. Work demanding specialized skill and knowledge; tasks mostly of a concrete nature requiring specialized training.

Level D. Low average or slightly below average abstract intelligence with training equivalent to eighth grade or less. Work demanding a minimum of technical knowledge or skill but may involve special abilities, such as dexterity in the performance of repetitive routine work.

In the area of mechanical ability, examples of types of work in each level, as listed by the same authors, are:

Level A. Machine designer, mechanical engineer, toolmaker, civil and electrical engineers.

Level B. Draftsman, engraver, bricklayer, auto mechanic.

Level C. Boiler maker, tire repairer, shoe repairer.

Level D. Telephone operator, wrapper, bench assembly worker, day laborer, lawyer, writer, and public officials in nonmechanical occupations.

The main purpose of this chapter is to show the counselor how he can obtain information that will enable him to do an adequate and valid job in organizing information about clients. The *Minnesota Occupational Rating Scales* enable the counselor to have ready access to an analysis of the minimum levels of the various abilities that are required for more than 400 occupations. For example, they indicate that an automobile salesman should have the following profile: Academic ability, level *B;* mechanical ability, *C;* social ability, *A;* clerical ability, *C;* and artistic and musical abilities, *D.* The *Minnesota Occupational Rating Scales* contain a listing of jobs that require *A* and *B* levels in the different fields. The information contained in the *MORS* is probably of very limited use even to the beginning counselor. It is included here to illustrate one of the earlier approaches to the organization of data about the client.

A more elaborate technique (discussed in Chapter 5) was developed by the U.S. Department of Labor (1965, 1966) and published in the third edition of the *Dictionary of Occupational Titles (DOT).* Part I of the *DOT* contains the listing of 35,550 job titles which are classified into 10 major categories. These jobs are also, in Part II of the *DOT,* grouped according to 22 workers' traits, using general education required, specific vocational preparation, aptitudes, interests, temperament, and physical demands of the work. Examples of some areas or groups are art, clerical work, machine work, medicine and health, and transportation.

In Part II of the *DOT* (1965, pp. 652–56), there appears a listing and descriptions of the contents of each of the traits. A brief enumeration follows:

I. GENERAL EDUCATIONAL DEVELOPMENT (*G.E.D.*)

Level 6. Apply principles of logical or scientific thinking to a wide range of intellectual and practical problems. Deal with nonverbal symbols and a variety of abstract and concrete variables.

Level 5. Apply principles of logical or scientific thinking to define problems, collect data, establish facts, and draw valid conclusions. Interpret an extensive variety of technical instructions.

Level 4. Apply principles of rational systems such as bookkeeping, electrical wiring systems, house building, etc., to solve practical problems. Interpret a variety of written and oral instructions.

Level 3. Apply common-sense understanding to carry out instructions furnished in written, oral, or diagrammatic form. Deal with problems involving several concrete variables in or from a standardized situation.

Level 2. Apply common-sense understanding to carry out detailed but involved written or oral instructions. Deal with problems involving a few concrete variables in or from standardized situations.

Level 1. Apply common-sense understanding to carry out simple one or two-step instructions. Deal with standardized situations with occasional or no variation in or from these situations encountered on the job.

Examples of the above, in terms of mathematical development, are as follows:

Levels 6.⎫ Apply differential and integral calculus, factor analysis, and so
    5.⎭ forth, to original and complex situations.

Level 4. Perform ordinary algebraic and geometric procedures in standard, practical situations.

Level 3. Make arithmetic calculations involving fractions, decimals, and percentages.

Level 2. Use arithmetic to add, subtract, multiply, and divide whole numbers.

Level 1. Perform simple addition and subtraction, read and copy figures, count and record.

SPECIFIC VOCATIONAL PREPARATION (S.V.P.)

Level 1. Short demonstration time.

Level 2. Short time, up to 30 days.

Level 3. Over 30 days, up to 3 months.

Level 4. Over 3 months, up to 6 months.

Level 5. Over 6 months, up to 1 year.

Level 6. Over 1 year, up to 2 years.

Level 7. Over 2 years, up to 4 years.

Level 8. Over 4 years, up to 10 years.

Level 9. Over 10 years.

II. APTITUDES (*Apt.*)

G   Intelligence: general learning ability.

V   Verbal: the ability to understand the meaning of words and to use them.

N   Numerical: the ability to perform arithmetical operations rapidly.

S   Spatial: the ability to comprehend forms in space and to understand the relationship of plane and solid objects.

P   Form perception: the ability to perceive pertinent detail in objects or in pictorial or graphic material.

Q   Clerical perception: the ability to perceive pertinent detail in verbal or tabular material.

K   Motor coordination: the ability to coordinate eye and hands or fingers rapidly and accurately in making precise movements with speed.

F   Finger dexterity: the ability to move fingers and to manipulate small objects with the fingers rapidly and accurately.

M   Manual dexterity: the ability to move the hands easily and skillfully.

E Eye-hand-foot coordination: the ability to move hand and foot co-ordinately with each other in response to visual stimuli.

C Color discrimination: the ability to perceive or to recognize similarities or differences in colors.

A subject's measured amount of each of the above aptitudes is carried out according to the following 5-point scale:

1. Top 10% of the population: possess the trait to an extremely high degree.
2. Top third less the top 10%: above average.
3. Middle third: average; possess trait to a medium degree.
4. Bottom third less the bottom 10%: below average.
5. Bottom 10%: possess negligible amount of the aptitude.

III. INTERESTS (*Int.*)
A positive preference for an interest on the left-hand side implies a rejection of the interest on the right-hand side.

1. Situations involving a preference for activities dealing with things and objects.

2. Situations involving a preference for activities made up of business contacts with people.

3. Situations involving a preference for activities of a routine, concrete, organized nature.

4. Situations involving a preference for working with people for their personal good—in the social welfare sense.

5. Situations involving activities that result in prestige or the esteem of others.

6. Situations involving a preference for activities concerned with people and the communication of ideas.

7. Situations involving activities of a scientific or technical nature.

8. Situations involving activities of an abstract or creative nature.

9. Situations involving activities nonsocial in nature, carried out in relation to processes, machines, and techniques.

0. Situations involving activities that result in tangible, productive satisfaction.

IV. TEMPERAMENTS (*Temp.*)
Expressed in preferences for the following:

1. Situations involving a variety of duties characterized by frequent changes.
2. Situations involving repetitive or short-cycle operations carried out according to set procedures.
3. Situations involving doing things only under specific instructions, al-

lowing little or no room for independent action or judgment in working out job problems.

4. Situations involving control and planning of an entire activity or the activities of others.
5. Situations involving the necessity of dealing with people in actual job duties beyond giving and receiving instructions.
6. Situations involving working alone in physical isolation from others, though the activity may be integrated with that of others.
7. Situations involving influencing people in their attitudes, opinions, and judgments about ideas or things.
8. Situations involving performing adequately under stress when confronted with the critical or unexpected or when taking risks.
9. Situations involving the evaluation of information against sensory or judgmental criteria.
0. Situations involving the evaluation of information against measurable or verifiable criteria.
X. Situations involving the interpretation of feelings, ideas, or facts in terms of personal viewpoint.
Y. Situations involving the precise attainment of set limits, tolerances, or standards.

V. PHYSICAL DEMANDS (*Phys.*)
  S — sedentary
  L — light
  M — medium
  H — heavy
  VH — very heavy

By type of activity involved in the job:

1. Lifting, carrying, pushing, pulling.
2. Climbing and/or balancing.
3. Stooping, kneeling, crouching, and/or crawling.
4. Reaching, handling, fingering, and/or feeling.
5. Talking and/or hearing.
6. Seeing.

VI. WORKING CONDITIONS
1. Inside, outside, or both.
2. Extremes of cold plus temperature changes.
3. Extremes of heat plus temperature changes.
4. Wet and humid.
5. Noise and vibration.

6. Hazards.

7. Fumes, odors, toxic conditions, dust, poor ventilation.

An example of the use of these traits is given, using a clerical group and a professional group.

SECRETARY GROUP

Profile

I. *G.E.D.* 3

II. *S.V.P.* 5,4,6

III. *Apt.*   **G,V,**N S,**P,Q** **K,F,**M E,C

(Level) 3,2,4   4,2,2   2,3,3 5,5

IV. *Int.* 3,6

V. *Temp.* 3,Y,2

VI. *Phys.* L; 4,5,6

The significant aptitudes are in bold type. In this case, the significant aptitudes are **G, V, P, Q, K,** and **F.** These are the ones that are occupationally significant for this specific group, i.e., they are basic and essential to average successful performance in this area. Nor all the aptitudes in bold face are necessarily required for each job within a "worker group," but some combination of them is essential in every case. The aptitude profile means that a worker in this group should be in the middle third of the population in general intelligence, have above-average Verbal ability, Form perception, Clerical perception, and Motor coordination, and be in the middle third in Finger dexterity and Manual dexterity. The other aptitudes are not necessary for successful work performance in this group. General educational development is at level 3, requiring, mathematically, the ability to manipulate decimals, fractions, and percentages. Specific vocational training varies from 3 months up to 2 years. The worker in this group should be interested in situations involving activities of a routine, concrete, organized nature, and also in situations involving contact with people and the communication of ideas. By temperament, he should like to work in situations in which he does things under specific instructions allowing little or no room for independent action, situations involving the precise attainment of set limits or standards, and in situations involving repetitive or short-cycle operations carried out according to set procedures. The physical demands of jobs in this group are light, demanding reaching, fingering, talking, hearing, and seeing.

GUIDANCE AND COUNSELING

Profile

I. *G.E.D.* 5,6

II. *S.V.P.* 7,8

III. *Apt.*   **G,V,**N S,P,Q K,E,M E,C

(Level) 1,1,3   4,4,4   4,4,4   5,5

IV. *Int.* 4,6,5,8

V. *Temp.* 5,9,4

VI. *Phys.* S,L; 4 5, 6

Since it is presumed that the reader of this book is either working or planning to work in guidance and counseling, the interpretation of the above profile is left to him.

In the *Supplement to the DOT* (1966) is presented a structured summary of individual physical demands, working conditions, and training time for each of the jobs defined in Part I of the *DOT*. While this uses only part of the data given for the various groups in Part II of the *Dictionary*, it is a concise summary for the use of the counselor whose clients have questions about vocational choice.

Although schemes like this make occupational counseling look very simple and straightforward, it must be emphasized that excessive caution must be used in interpreting and applying such information. Job descriptions are composite descriptions of jobs as they may typically occur, rather than as they are actually performed in a certain establishment or locality. The traits and characteristics named are suggestions to be explored in the counseling situation. A counselor should not give a client a battery of tests, then go looking for an occupational profile that seems to fit best the client's test pattern, and then recommend that he make that occupation his vocational goal. Rather, the complete picture of behavior collected for an individual includes all the possible educational and vocational placements, in the proper field and at the proper level.

MECHANICAL ABILITY

Over the past half-century the psychological literature has included much speculation and theorizing about the nature of so-called "mechanical ability" or "mechanical aptitude." Actually, no progress was made in identifying and describing the nature of this ability until Thurstone's method of factor analysis was applied to the materials used to evaluate it. One of the earlier factor analyses was made by Harrell (1940). As a result of administering a battery of tests of mechanical ability and including information about such variables as amount of schooling, ratings of job performance, and the like, he analysed mechanical ability into these factors: (1) verbal; (2) spatial; (3) agility, i.e., manual dexterity; (4) perception; and (5) youth, i.e., inexperience. Wittenborn (1945), in a similar analysis of test data collected at the University of Minnesota, isolated six factors: (1) spatial visualization; (2) stereotyped movement of the wrist and forearm; (3) scholastic ability; (4) manual dexterity; (5) perceptual speed; and (6) steadiness. Guilford (1947, 1948) showed that mechanical ability, on the basis of factor analyses of data used in the U.S. Army Air Force testing programs, was made up to a great extent of two factors, mechanical information and spatial visualization. Other factors, similar to and more numerous than Harrell's, were also present. The research carried on in the Division of Occupational Analysis of the War Manpower Commission (1945) based on the factor analysis of 59 tests revealed or suggested the following factors: (1) a verbal factor V; (2) a numerical factor N; (3) a spatial factor S; (4) a factor designated O, apparently general intelligence; (5) a perceptual factor P involving the use of geometrical figures; (6) a second perceptual factor Q, related to words and numbers; (7) an aiming factor, related to accuracy and exactness of movement A; (8) a speed factor T; (9) finger dexterity F; (10) manual dexterity M; and (11) a logical-reasoning factor L. In later work, the U.S. Training and Employment Service continued to use the factors V, N, S, P, Q, and M. The O factor was replaced by one called General intelligence G. The speed factor T and the logical reasoning factor L were dropped. The aiming factor was replaced by a factor called motor coordination K. Two other factors, eye-and-foot coordination E and color discrimination C, were added. These are the factors which are used in the general category of Aptitudes in Part II of the U.S. Department of Labor's *Dictionary of Occupational Titles* (*DOT*, 1965).

Usually, any discussion of mechanical ability is broken into several of these subdivisions or factors. Super and Crites (1962) have separate chapters on manual dexterities, mechanical aptitude, and spatial visualization. Bennett and Cruikshank in their monograph (1942) set up three categories: (1) the capacity to understand mechanical relationships; (2) manual and finger dexterity; and (3) motor abilities of strength, speed of movement, and endurance. The discussion that follows will consider spatial visualization, dexterities, and mechanical information.

Spatial Visualization or Spatial Perception

Tests that measure spatial visualization require that the subject visualize the putting together or the taking apart of geometrical forms or objects. In the earlier tests, this ability was measured by the speed and accuracy with which pieces were inserted into a board. This technique has been largely superseded by tests known as paper form boards, in which all the maneuvering is done mentally.

One of the earlier and more widely accepted devices used to measure this ability was the *Minnesota Spatial Relations Test* (C. H. Stoelting Co.). This instrument is made up of two sets of two boards, each about three feet long and one foot wide. From these boards have been cut, usually in sets of three, circles, triangles, squares, and objects of irregular shape. Boards A and B use 58 of these cutouts in common, and the other two boards, C and D, are completed by the use of another set. The subject stands in front of the board and tries as rapidly as possible to insert each piece into its correct position. The four boards are completed and scored, either by counting the results of the first board as practice and letting the score consist of the number of seconds required to complete the other three boards together, or by counting the number of seconds required to complete all four boards.

As these tests are individual tests and require a half-hour or more for administering, they have been replaced to a large extent by a test known as the *Minnesota Paper Form Board* (The Psychological Corporation). This 64-item group test has a time limit of 20 minutes. Each item consists of a geometric design which has been cut into pieces. Following it are five geometrical figures, one of which can be correctly visualized mentally from the pieces shown in the main part of the item. Another paper-and-pencil test is the *Space Relations Test* of the *Differential Aptitude Test* (*DAT*, The Psychological Corporation). In this test, the stem of the item consists of a two-dimensional design or pattern followed by a series of three-dimensional objects. The examinee has to decide how many of these latter objects are the result of the folding of the original two-dimensional surface.

Research with these tests has shown that they are useful in predicting success in courses in mechanical drawing, machine-shop work, dentistry, and art. Therefore, the chief use of these to the counselor is for counseling with clients about technical courses, engineering courses, and drawing and art training.

Dexterities

Under dexterities are included the grosser arm movements, referred to as *manual dexterity*, and the finer ones, known as *finger dexterity*. The measurement of these abilities is more or less restricted, by their very nature, to individual performance tests. Super and Crites (1962) recommend the use of the term *arm-and-hand dexterity* to separate manual dexterity from wrist-and-finger or finger dexterity.

The most widely used measure of manual, or arm-and-hand, dexterity is the *Minnesota Rate of Manipulation Test* (Educational Test Bureau). This consists of a board about 3 feet in length and 1 foot across, from which 60 circles have been cut out in four equal, parallel rows. In the first part of the test, Placing, the subject is to place the circles from an arranged pattern on the table into the board. The second part of the test, Turning, requires that the subject, using a standardized technique, turn each of the circles the other side up. Usually four trials are administered for each part of the test, the first one being optional as a practice trial or as part of the total score. This test has been used to select bundle or parcel wrappers.

Finger dexterity is measured by the use of pegboards, two commonly used ones being the *Purdue Pegboard* (Science Research Associates) and the *O'Connor Finger-Tweezer Dexterity Test* (C. H. Stoelting Co.). A pegboard consists of a piece of wood or metal into which holes have been drilled. With the fingers alone or with a pair of tweezers, the subject inserts pegs into these holes as rapidly as possible. The wooden *Purdue Pegboard* differs from most in that there is first a trial for the right hand, then one for the left hand, followed by both hands simultaneously, and finally an assembly test in which small objects are assembled out of pegs, washers, and collars.

Research with these instruments indicates that they are most useful in the selection of individuals for semiskilled jobs, such as assembling small objects, packing, and sorting. Their major use, then, has been industrial. In the counseling situation they may be used in negative fashion, for advising students *against* considering technical training in courses such as watch repairing, tool-and-die making, lens grinding, typing, and even such professional occupations as dentistry and medicine.

Mechanical Information

In the earlier days of testing and counseling, mechanical information was measured by individual tests such as *Stenquist's Mechanical Assembly Test* or, later, the *Minnesota Mechanical Assembly Test*. In both of these the examinee was confronted with a metal box consisting of a series of metal bins, in each of which was a disassembled mechanical object such as a mousetrap, door latch, clamp, or bicycle bell. The client was given a fixed amount of time to reassemble each object.

These tests have been replaced by paper-and-pencil tests such as the *Bennett Test of Mechanical Comprehension* and *The Test of Mechanical Reasoning of the DAT* (both published by The Psychological Corporation). In both tests, the emphasis is upon the general principles of mechanics, information about tools, and some of the elementary principles of physics. For example, two shears are presented, and the question is asked which is the better for the cutting of metal. Or there are arrangements of gears and cogs on which the direction of the rotation of one cog is noted, and the examinee has to figure out the direction in which another cog or gear is turning.

Counselors will find tests of this type useful in counseling students about technical or vocational training. In some agencies there has been the unwarranted assumption that if an individual can do nothing else academically, he can always be put into a shop course to be trained. This makes no more sense than putting all individuals into any other field, or area, or curriculum. There should be appraisal and selection before individuals enter technical training, because field and level, as determined by skills, aptitudes, and interests, are just as important there as in any other area.

There are several tests that cannot be classified into one of the three above areas; rather than measuring one aspect of mechanical ability, they tend to cut across abilities and measure two or more of them. Probably the most frequently encountered of these is the *MacQuarrie Test of Mechanical Ability* (California Test Bureau), a booklet made up of seven subtests measuring one-hand manual dexterity, spatial visualization, and perceptual speed and accuracy. Another is the *SRA Mechanical Aptitude Test* (Science Research Associates) which has sections covering mechanical information, spatial visualization, and shop arithmetic.

Other Sources of Information

Valid evidence of mechanical ability is available from sources other than these standardized tests. A very important one is the individual's hobby or spare-time activities. It is obvious that the boy who tears down and rebuilds old cars, constructs scale models of vehicles or machines, or designs and draws mechanical things possesses mechanical ability. Other evidence comes from grades in shop courses or certain academic courses such as physics and drawing. On-the-job performance on mechanical jobs or tasks is valid and useful information, if described in sufficient detail so that the counselor can evaluate it. A filling-station attendant who just pumps gas does not get the same mechanical experience as one who also repairs cars. Closely related to such evidence as this is the type of part-time job that a student might have in his spare time or during the summer vacation. However, it is a good idea to ascertain whether or not the client has been free to make his own choice of jobs or courses, and also whether or not other possibilities were available.

There are other characteristics and skills that should be considered with mechanical ability in certain types of vocational counseling. For example, there is the entire problem of vision. Good eyesight has a lot to do with certain types of work. Then there is color blindness, which limits or changes training in many skilled and unskilled occupations. This is usually measured by a series of plates like the Ishihara plates, which consist of a background of small circles of one color, usually a light or pastel one. Into the center of this background a number has been traced in another color. The client goes through the plates, reading the numbers. The presence and degree of color blindness are determined by the client's responses to these numbers. Another good test of color blindness is the *Farnsworth Test of Color Blindness* (The Psychological Corporation). It measures three kinds of color blindness. Color blindness will limit a person in mechanical work like telephone installation or welding: the telephone wires are connected according to colors, and the welder tells how hot the flame is by the color of the flame. In a similar way, hearing and tests for hearing are important in other types of vocational planning and training. They function as negative indicators. Lack of the trait measured will limit an individual in performing particular mechanical activities. However, possession of the trait without defect does not insure success in mechanical tasks.

CLERICAL ABILITY

Clerical ability, like mechanical ability, is not a single unitary trait but a complex of different abilities, skills, and interests. One of its major components is the ability to handle or to manipulate words and numbers accurately and rapidly. Basically, this is nothing but accuracy of perceptual speed. With this is associated skill in arithmetic, especially in the four basic arithmetical processes. Clerical ability also involves knowledge of good English usage, that is, the rules of grammar, punctuation, spelling, and sentence structure. In certain clerical positions a good vocabulary is also essential. Since many clerical workers operate typewriters and various office or business machines, manual and finger dexterity are important in certain clerical tasks. There is no single test that measures all these different abilities and knowledges. The following discussion will include several of the widely used tests of clerical ability along with some of the other evidences of this ability for which the counselor should watch.

Tests of Clerical Ability

Probably the most widely used test of clerical ability is the *Minnesota Clerical Test* (The Psychological Corporation). This short test is made up of two parts—number checking (8 minutes) and name checking (7 minutes). Items like the following make up the entire test:

$$
\begin{array}{lll}
87694 & X & 87694 \\
5468926 & & 5469826 \\
\text{John J. Smith} & & \text{John F. Smith} \\
505 \text{ Lingle Ter.} & X & 505 \text{ Lingle Ter.}
\end{array}
$$

The examinee proceeds through the test as rapidly as possible, placing an X in the space between the pairs that are similar. The test measures only perceptual speed and accuracy.

Norms are provided with the test for grades 8 through 12, gainfully employed adults, general clerical workers, and clerical workers in specific occupations, such as accountants, bookkeepers, and shipping clerks. Age seems to have little effect upon scores except for the usual slowing up in middle age. Research reported in the *Manual,* and by others, shows that scores on the test are not affected to any extent by clerical experience. Sex differences (in favor of women) are significant, requiring the use of separate norms for men and women. An inspection of the norms shows that only 21% of employed male clerical workers exceed the median of female clerical workers. Andrew (1937), the author of the test, reported a correlation of .66 between number checking and name checking. Darley (1934) reported the reliability of the two parts of the test to be .76 and .83, respectively. As Super and Crites (1962, p. 168) have pointed out about the parts, since their intercorrelation is lower than their separate reliabilities, one of them is measuring something not so well measured by the other. This was shown to be intelligence; of the two parts of the test, name checking correlates higher with intelligence than number checking, .37 and .12, respectively, with a homogeneous group, and .65 and .47 with a heterogeneous group (Super and Crites 1962 p. 168).

Another clerical test is the *General Clerical Test* (The Psychological Corporation). This is a much more comprehensive test than the *Minnesota Clerical Test* and is made up of nine subtests. The first two subtests, Checking and Alphabetizing, are measures of perceptual ability. The three subsequent tests, Arithmetic reasoning, Computation, and Location of error, produce a numerical score. The last four tests, Spelling, Reading comprehension, Vocabulary, and Grammar, provide a verbal score. Another simple, short perceptual test is the *Clerical Speed and Accuracy Test* of the *DAT* battery.

The validity indices of all of these tests are of the usual magnitude when results are correlated with such criteria as grades in commercial courses and accounting. Hay (1943) showed correlations of .51 and .47 between the two parts of the *Minnesota Clerical Test* and the speed of posting ability of bookkeeping machine operators. Blum and Candee (1941) showed correlations of the two parts of this same test with the output of packers in a department store to be .57 and .65, respectively. In summary, these and other studies (Super and Crites 1962) show that clerical tests predict very well grades in commercial and related courses, success on business-machine operating tasks and on various packing and inspecting tasks.

Just as with mechanical ability, there are other sources from which valid evidence of clerical ability may be obtained, to supplement that obtained from these tests. First among these is grades in commercial courses in high school and such specialized courses in commercial skills as might be learned in a commercial trade school or at the college level. Certain hobbies might also be evidence of clerical ability, e.g., keeping track of statistics of athletic teams. Other evidence might come from some on-the-job tryouts on various clerical jobs or part-time work programs in vocational education. Types of after-school or summer jobs held by individuals might also offer evidence. There is also a group of aptitude and ability tests for specific types of skills, such as shorthand and typing, that can be administered for more specific information about clerical ability. These are often referred to as *proficiency* tests.

Use of Evidences of Clerical Ability in Counseling

The concept of level may be applied to the use of information about clerical ability, just as it is with mechanical ability (Paterson, Gerken, and Hahn 1941). *Before tests of clerical ability are used, measures of general ability must have been made.* The top level A requires superior general intelligence, usually accompanied by a college degree. Included here are such workers as accountants, actuaries, statisticians, and top-level secretaries (top 10% of the group). At level B, the technical level, high-school graduation or equivalent specialized training in commercial skills is required. In this group are bookkeepers, secretaries, and operators of various business machines. Here the next 15% of the workers are found. At level C, the routine clerical level, very little training is needed. Jobs included here are those of file clerk, mail clerk, retail sales clerk, and operators of simple machines such as ditto machines and mailing machines. Here is the middle 50% of the distribution of clerical ability. Many individuals possess sufficient ability to operate at this level.

In using data on clerical ability, the counselor must associate general ability with it, first keeping in mind that some of the top positions in the clerical field require a college degree or more. It must also be remembered, as Hahn and MacLean (1955) point out, that this field of work is to a great extent a woman's world. However, this does not preclude males, especially if they are skillful and highly intelligent. Confidential secretaries to the presidents of corporations, or to corporation boards of directors or trustees, are most frequently male clerical workers. The same writers point out also that since there is a rapidly increasing movement from hand work to machine operating in this field, the counselor must be alert for new job openings. It might be added that he should also be aware of the various types of clerical jobs that are disappearing because of the increasing use of business machines. New developments in automated or computer business processes are increasing jobs at the *B* level, for programming of automated equipment, and there are more mechanical jobs at the *B* level, to repair such machines. There is a tendency for a considerable decrease in *C* and *D* level clerical jobs as a result of automation and computers. For example, one plant at Camillus, New York, does practically all the national clerical work for Sylvania Electric Company. This trend is also developing in the mechanical field.

ARTISTIC ABILITY

Artistic ability, like those previously discussed, is also made up of various skills and abilities (Meier 1942). In the *Manual* accompanying *The Meier Art Tests, I: Art Judgment,* Meier states that there are six factors involved in this ability: manual skill, energy output and perseveration, aesthetic intelligence (spatial and perceptual ability), perceptual facility (the ability to observe and reproduce sensory experiences), creative imagination, and aesthetic judgment. Only the last of these is measured by Meier's test. Hahn and MacLean (1955) consider aesthetic intelligence, as they label this field, to be divided into four parts, each requiring a greater amount of this ability. These divisions are: appreciation, interpretation, creativity, and analysis. The last two include the research scholars and high level critics.

Tests of artistic ability may be broken into two types: tests of artistic or aesthetic judgment and tests of creative ability. The most widely used test of the first type is *The Meier Art Tests, I: Art Judgment* (Bureau of Educational Research Services, University of Iowa, or The Psychological Corporation). This test is made up of 100 items consisting of pictures of works of art from all parts of the world, and of such a type that they can be generally considered as being timeless. Each item is made up of two parts, one a reproduction of the art as the author originally created it, and the other the same piece of art but with a certain aspect of the work changed. The student's attention is focused on this part of the picture, and he has to decide which of the two he prefers. His score is the number of times that he selects the work as the artist created it. Scores on this test have been shown to correlate in the .40's with grades in art school and with ratings of creative artistic ability.

In 1963, there appeared a second test, *The Meier Art Tests, II: Aesthetic Perception* (Bureau of Educational Research, University of Iowa). This test contains 50 items, each containing a work of art presented in four different ways: first, the original as created by the artist; and three other versions varying in form, design, and light-and-dark pattern, or a combination of these three qualities. The client studies the prints, noting how the versions differ in unity, proportion, form, and design, or how they vary as satisfactory wholes. Then he ranks each part of the item on a scale, placing the one that is most aesthetic at the top and the one that is least aesthetic at the bottom. The author provides tentative norms based upon a large sample of high-school students taking art, and also upon a second large group of college and adult subjects. The test is followed by a third test, of creative imagination. The three tests, used together in a battery, provide a measure of the basic elements comprising aesthetic sensitivity.

Another approach was made by Graves with the *Design Judgment Test* (The Psychological Corporation) which uses geometric designs and lines in shades of gray and black. Most of these are arranged in pairs as on the *Meier,* and the examinee goes through the booklet marking the one preferred. Art teachers were used to judge which was the best drawing on each page. Little research has been done with this instrument. Downie, in an unpublished study, found that the correlation between scores on this test with those on the *Meier,* of 45 university students in a course in psychological testing, was approximately .40.

When tests of artistic ability are used, the individual is given various things to do to see if actual drawing, sketching, or painting skills are present. One of these tests, the *Knauber Art Ability Test,* contains 17 parts in which the examinee has to reproduce a drawing from memory, shade compositions, draw objects asked for, create abstract designs, and do similar things. A similar test is the *Lewerenz Test in the Fundamental Abilities of Visual Art* (California Test Bureau). A different approach was made by Horn (1945). The chief part of his test consisted of 12 cards, each bearing lines arranged in various ways. The examinee uses these lines as starting points about which he has to construct a picture on each card. The scoring of all these tests of artistic ability is very subjective, as in most of them the work done by the examinee is compared with prepared scales and evaluated by finding the item on the scale that comes closest to the examinee's drawing. The drawing is then given this value.

Other Evidence of Artistic Ability

It is felt by the writers that the best information about a client's artistic ability is obtained by having some of his work evaluated by an expert or two. Usually on university campuses there are such people in one of the schools who will be very willing in helping the counselor and the client in making such product evaluations. Two evaluations are better than one, for one is apt to reflect the bias of the individual judge that causes him to be overcritical of art that deviates from his own school or standards. Prizes and awards from art shows, or even the showing of work in shows, certainly indicate the presence of ability. Tests of spatial relations, finger dexterity, and color blindness offer some evidence of various aspects of this ability.

Use of Data About Artistic Ability in Counseling

Using the *Minnesota Occupational Rating Scales,* the field of art can be divided into three levels, and into a fourth, nonartistic. At level *A,* the professional level, a high degree of creative skill is required. This is the top 4% of the distribution, and it includes professional artists, sculptors, etchers, and art teachers. Level *B,* containing those below these professionals but above the ninth decile in ability, requires a fairly high degree of artistic ability along with some originality. Commercial art workers, as well as magazine illustrators, advertising-layout men, landscape gardeners, interior decorators, and various types of designers are included. Level *C,* crafts and mechanical work, includes all those above the first quartile in artistic ability. This is the level of the craftsman—sign painter, draftsman, potter, weaver, and others.

Tests of artistic ability may frequently reveal individuals who have hidden talents. They are perhaps *more useful* in pointing out those who have very little or no artistic ability. In general, it seems that very high scores or low ones should be considered as the significant ones when these tests are used.

MUSICAL ABILITY

Of the few tests which have been constructed to measure this ability, Seashore's *Measures of Musical Talent* (The Psychological Corporation) has been most widely used and has had the largest amount of research conducted with it. Seashore started working with this test during World War I and spent the rest of his life, while at the University of Iowa, experimenting with it. Seashore (1939) considers the traits involved in musical ability as manual skills, energy output and perseveration, creative imagination, emotional sensitivity, and those abilities measured by his tests.

The Seashore battery consists of three 78 rpm records, each having a test on both sides and measuring pitch, loudness, time, rhythm, timbre, and tonal memory, or one 33⅓ rpm long-playing record with three tests on each side. The items are presented in pairs, and the examinee has to evaluate if the second is louder than the first or the same, or which note has been changed in a series. The records may be used with individuals from grade 5 on up. When used with younger children, the results are frequently of no value because one has to listen carefully to the records in order to complete the test. Younger children have difficulty listening as do some adults, especially those with little musical ability. The administration of the test requires about an entire class period. Practice is given at several points on each record, until everyone understands exactly what he is to do, and then the test for the record is administered. Some counselors prefer to shorten the process by using the tests of pitch, tonal memory, and rhythm as negative indicators, omitting the balance of the tests.

The reliability of the different tests varies between the .60's and the high .80's. For example, for adults the lowest reliability coefficient is .62 (timbre) and the highest, .88 (tonal memory). The second lowest value at this age level is .74.

Validity has been mostly determined by correlating results with criteria such as grades in music courses, completion of a period of training, and ratings of musical ability. Correlation of Seashore scores with grades in music courses has produced coefficients ranging between .30 and .59. The most noted study, using completion of training, was that of Stanton (1929), who over a period of years administered the Seashore battery to more than 2,000 entering students at the Eastman School of Music. The results were filed unseen by members of the staff. Stanton set up a rating system on the basis of the Seashore scores, intelligence test scores, and teachers' ratings by which the students could be classified as "safe," "probable," and so on. Later she showed that 60% of the "safe" group were graduated, 42% of the "probable," 33% of the "possible," 23% of the "doubtful," and 17% of the "discouraged." In her study, Stanton made no attempt to isolate the importance of the intelligence factor. In general, however, the Seashore seems able to distinguish those who have musical ability from those who do not. It separates professional musicians from amateurs and beginners. Interestingly Fay and Middleton (1941) have shown that those who prefer classical music make higher scores on pitch, rhythm, and time subtests than those who prefer jazz music.

A more recent test of musical aptitude is the *Gordon Musical Aptitude Profile* (Houghton Mifflin Company). The purposes of this battery are said to be to provide students and parents with objective information concerning a student's musical ability, to evaluate the musical aptitudes of groups of students, and to encourage musically talented students to participate in the musical organizations of the school. The battery consists of three tests: Tonal imagery *T*, Rhythm imagery *R*, and Musical sensitivity *S*, each of which consists of two or three subtests. The tests are made up of 250 short selections composed by the author for violin and cello and recorded by professional artists on high-fidelity magnetic tape. The tests were validated by correlating scores obtained on this test against judges' evaluations of tape-recorded musical performance of students. The resulting coefficients were reasonably high. In a longitudinal study of three years' duration conducted with students in grades 4 and 5, scores on this battery were correlated with ratings of tape-recorded selections prepared in advance with the teacher's help, against such recordings prepared without the teacher's help, with tape-recorded performances of sight-reading material, with teachers' ratings, and finally with scores on an achievement test in music. The correlations, respectively, were .49, .52, .51, .37, and .61. When students in this study were retested after a one year interval in which they underwent intensive musical training, the mean gain on the 250 exercises was less than 5 points and the reliability correlation between the two sets of scores was .80.

The Drake Musical Aptitude Test (Science Research Associates) measures musical memory and rhythm and is used to evaluate a subject's potential for a musical career. This battery is recorded on two 33⅓ rpm discs that require two 30-to-40 minute periods for administration.

As with the artistic field, the judgments of experts are most useful and important in evaluating the musical ability and potential of a client. In most cases, it does not take long for one of these judges to decide whether or not an individual has the ability needed for professional training.

Use of Musical Ability Tests in Counseling

Only individuals in the top 4% of the musically able can operate at the professional level. In this small group are the concert artist, composer, soloist, conservatory teacher, and director. The technical and lower professional level, making up the remainder of the highest 10%, includes arrangers and critics of music, music teachers in grade and high school, orchestra members, and the like. Here is the professional musician, of average or above-average musical talent, a high degree of technical knowledge, and well-developed musical discrimination. The third level, from the first quartile to the ninth decile, includes musical repairmen, instrument testers, clerks in music stores, and music retailers. A small amount of training, but a greater amount of technical skill and general information about music must be possessed by those who operate at this level.

The counselor might use the results of these tests in the same way as the results of tests of artistic ability. Low scores will point out those who have little musical ability. High scores may or may not be indicative of musical ability. But these high scores merit further investigation. Scores in between are of limited significance.

PHYSICAL ABILITY

Information about physical abilities and health is most important to the counselor. Records of the client's physical development and health should always be available. In this case the counselor is a user of material collected by others, not an information gatherer. However, things may come up in the counseling interview that offer insights into physical status or show the need for proper referral to investigate or remedy conditions that have gone undetected. In the text following, the types of information that the counselor should have will be noted.

Physical or Medical Examinations

Physical or medical examinations are conducted by a physician, usually periodically, being given at the beginning of school, at the end of the primary grades, and at the commencement of both junior and senior high school. In most places these are carried out by the family's personal physician, and the results are filed in the student's school folder. The examinations are carried out more frequently for certain individuals, such as members of athletic teams, individuals who work in the school lunchroom or cafeteria, those who have a record of a chronic disease or disability or who have been out of school a long time as a result of a long illness or an accident, and any others who in the judgment of teachers, administrators, or counselors should have one. Results of dental examinations conducted by the school dental hygienist should also be a part of the medical record. Reports of school nurses are also to be included.

Health Histories

A record of diseases and disabilities is usually gathered from an interview with a parent at the time a child is starting school. Information is added as the individual progresses through school.

Screening Tests

Screening tests are probably the most commonly employed practices used in evaluating health and physical status. In most schools these tests are an annual event, especially in the lower grades. They are conducted by both the teacher and the school nurse. Most typically, they consist of tests of vision, hearing, and speech, along with measurements of height and weight. The dental examination is usually conducted at this time also.

Physical Tests

The physical education department has a large battery of tests that are useful in evaluating physical development. These are tests of strength, capacity, and endurance. While the results of these tests may not be available to the counselor in the cumulative record, there is no reason why they cannot be; better still, the physical education instructor should prepare a summary of his evaluation of the physical development of each individual, as revealed by these different tests.

Observational Techniques

The classroom teacher is in the best position to gather information about physical health, and to record and report such data. One method applicable here would be anecdotal records. The classroom teacher is also the source of most of the referrals in relation to the student's health.

In using data about the physical ability of the client, the counselor is most concerned with outstanding professionals as well as residuals of illness, accident, or limitations produced by insufficient physical development.

MULTIFACTOR TEST BATTERIES

Both the factor-analysis work of Thurstone and the experiences gained in the construction and use of tests in World War II in dealing with military personnel led to the development of what are known as multifactor batteries. Typically these consist of six or more of the various types of tests that have already been discussed. Usually, the tests included in these batteries are representative of the various mental abilities and are comprehensive enough to be used in the consideration of many different occupations. These tests may be constructed upon the basis of an analysis of the various workers' requirements of different jobs. In using the tests, the counselor or personnel worker works in terms of test battery profiles, this being merely an analysis of the client's or job applicant's strong and weak points. In some of these batteries the majority of the tests are the results of factor analyses. However, this is not true of all of them.

Basically, there are two types of multifactor batteries. One is of a general nature, used in counseling individuals when all capacities and traits are being considered. This is used when students and workers are just entering the world of work. The other type is made up of batteries specific to a given purpose. For example, there are batteries constructed for the selection of students for medical school, law school, dentistry, teaching, and other professions.

Batteries such as these are expensive in both time and money. Usually they take a full day to administer, and the cost is correspondingly high. Usually, the cost of the battery for professional schools is borne by the individual taking the examination. Moreover, there is evidence that predictions as good or even better than those made with the multifactor tests can be made with a short intelligence test. On the positive side, there is no question that these are well-made tests and usually interesting to the examinee. Situations are offered which are unusual and intriguing. Some, such as the dental-school batteries, have increased their validity through the use of manipulative tests that correspond to activities carried on by dentists. Specific evaluations of the different batteries will be made as each is discussed. The general type of battery will be discussed first.

General Multifactor Batteries

The most important of the general multifactor batteries, to the high-school and college counselor, is the *DAT* which was made available for use in 1947 by The Psychological Corporation. This battery is made up of eight tests assembled in seven separate booklets, the last two of which are combined into one or into a two-booklet form (Bennett 1955, 1956). The 1963 edition is made up of eight tests that yield nine scores. These tests are: (1) Verbal reasoning—the understanding of and reasoning with words; (2) Numerical ability—numerical computation and reasoning; (3) Abstract reasoning—reasoning by the use of designs and geometric symbols rather than by the use of words; (4) Clerical speed and accuracy—a perceptual test similar to the *Minnesota Clerical Test;* (5) Mechanical reasoning—a test similar to the *Bennett Test of Mechanical Comprehension;* (6) Space relations—visualization of three-dimensional figures from a two-dimensional pattern; (7) Language usage I—spelling; (8) Language usage II—sensitivity to correctness of expression, punctuation, and word usage. The ninth score, an index of Scholastic ability, is obtained by summing the Verbal reasoning and the Numerical ability scores. This latter score is the equivalent of scores obtained with the usual group intelligence test (Bennett *et al.* 1963). The Verbal, Numerical, Spatial, and Abstract reasoning tests are designed to measure Thurstone's factors V, N, R, and S. The Clerical test is a test of speed and accuracy in perceiving symbols, and the remaining three tests are actually achievement tests, measuring the results of learning that took place either in school or elsewhere.

This test battery was basically designed as a tool in the educational and vocational counseling of high-school youth. Norms are also provided for eighth-grade students, and some universities are employing the battery in their counseling activities, using norms that have been developed locally. The tests are so built that any one of them may be administered easily in a class period. The *Manual* recommends several sequences for the administration of the tests in giving students the entire battery. However, whether there is a reason for any sequence (other than the prevention of boredom) or whether any given consequences issue from not following these patterns has not been demonstrated. Many agencies use only those pieces of the battery that the counselor and client feel are appropriate to the immediate needs of the client.

The 1966 revision of the *Manual* contains a summary of about 4,000 validity coefficients. Super (1956a) recapitulates many of these data by saying that the *DAT* tests do a good job of predicting grades in English, social studies, science, and mathematics. They seem to measure that which is needed for success in such courses, namely general ability or intelligence. In commercial courses, the Numerical and Language-usage subtests are good predictors for bookkeeping and typing courses. Scores on the Space relations subtests were to some extent related to grades received in vocational shop courses.

Bennett (1955, 1956) summarized a long-range study done with the *DAT*. Scores of about 1,400 students who had taken the battery when it was being developed or when it first appeared were reexamined in the light of their status 7 and 8 years later. He showed that those students who had graduated from college tended to be superior on the basis of all tests given to the high-school group of which they had been a part. As might be predicted, this superiority was most noticeable on the Verbal reasoning, Numerical reasoning, and Language-usage subtests. Students who had some years of college fell between the group that was graduated from college and that which had had no further education beyond high school. Students who attended special schools tended to score near the mean of their high-school group, and students who had no more education beyond high school were slightly below the over-all average for high-school students. Bennett also analyzed the scores of the individuals on the basis of the occupations that they were currently pursuing. His findings were in line with expectations: Engineers were considerably above average on all tests, individuals in the technical trades tended to fall around the mean; and those in the semiskilled and unskilled occupations tended to fall a bit below the group average on the various subtests.

A second multifactor battery is the *General Aptitude Test Battery* (*GATB*) issued in 1947 by the U.S. Training and Employment Service (see Dvorak 1947, 1956). The current revision of the battery consists of 12 tests that are used to measure nine aptitudes. These are:

G: Intelligence. Measured by Test Nos. 3, Three-dimensional space; 4, Vocabulary; and 6, Arithmetic reasoning.
V: Verbal aptitude. Test No. 4, a vocabulary test.
N: Numerical aptitude. Test Nos. 2, Arithmetic computation; and 6, Arithmetic reasoning.
S: Spatial aptitude. Test No. 3, Three-dimensional space.
P: Form perception. Test Nos. 5, Tool making; and 7, Form matching.
Q: Clerical perception. Test No. 1, Name perception.
K: Motor coordination. Test No. 8, Mark making.
F: Finger dexterity. Test Nos. 11, Assemble; and 12, Disassemble.
M: Manual dexterity. Test Nos. 9, Place; and 10, Turn.

Eight of the above tests are paper-and-pencil tests. The last four, 9, 10, 11, and 12, are individual performance tests. An examination of the subtests reveals that they cover the major factors and skills that are required to a greater or less extent in the majority of occupations. Lacking are tests of rather specialized abilities such as art and music, and also tests of mechanical information such as the *Bennett* or the *Mechanical Reasoning Test of the DAT*.

Norms are presented in terms of aptitude patterns for different occupations, giving cutoff scores for the three most important aptitudes required for any family of similar occupations. Suppose that a family of occupations requires Intelligence *G*, Spatial aptitude *S*, and Form perception *P*. Minimum cutoff scores are then provided for these three aptitudes for different positions within the family of jobs. Profiles of individuals are compared. The U.S. Department of Labor's *DOT*, Part II (1965) lists the different aptitudes and the level of aptitude required for each job.

Although this battery was developed for use in government-operated employment services, especially as an aid in placing the new and young worker who has had no vocational experience, the battery has been offered for use with high-school and college students. There are high schools in which the graduating seniors are given the battery as an aid in planning their life's work.

A third battery is the *Guilford-Zimmerman Aptitude Survey*, the GZAS (Guilford 1956). The GZAS (Sheridan Supply Co.) is made up of seven subtests: Verbal comprehension, General reasoning, Numerical computations, Perceptual speed, Spatial orientation ("the ability to form an awareness of the spatial order of things perceived visually"), Spatial visualization, and Mechanical knowledge. Guilford (1956) showed that the first six of these have factorial validity (a type of construct validity) and that the Mechanical knowledge test was built to have content validity.

The battery was constructed for use with high-school and college students. When scores on different subtests were correlated with freshman grades made in college, correlations of the following magnitudes were obtained: Verbal comprehension, .46; General reasoning, .34; Numerical computations, .28; Perceptual speed, .16; Space orientation, .10; Spatial visualization, .17; and Mechanical knowledge, −.07. Notice that the first three—the ones usually included in a test of general intelligence—were the important ones in predicting.

Other multifactor batteries are the *Flanagan Aptitude Classification Tests, FACT,* published by Science Research Associates (Flanagan 1957); the *Holzinger-Crowder Unifactor Tests,* published by Harcourt, Brace & World, Inc. (Crowder 1957); the *Segal-Raskin Multiple Aptitude Tests,* published by California Test Bureau (Segal 1957); and the *SRA Primary Mental Abilities,* published by Science Research Associates (Thurstone 1957). In general, these are similar in content and in recommended use to those already described. Super and Crites (1962, pp. 329–30) recommend only the *GATB* and the *DAT* as being developed enough for extensive use.

Evaluation of Multifactor Batteries

Super (1949) wrote that "The day of the publication of isolated tests of single aptitudes will no doubt soon be past." That he was not alone in holding this attitude is shown by other writers of that period (see Anastasi 1954, and Cronbach 1949). However, in less than 10 years, Cronbach was writing in the *Annual Review of Psychology* (Farnsworth and McNemar, eds. 1956), "while factorial scores may be useful for a theory of abilities, as soon as testers make inferences to behavior in significant situations, they encounter the same trouble as personality assessors." (That these troubles are tremendous will be pointed out in Chapter 10.) In a series of articles beginning in the September, 1956, issue of the *Personnel and Guidance Journal* and continuing with an article on and an evaluation of a particular multifactor battery in each of nine subsequent issues, and concluding in the September, 1957, issue of the same journal, Super and one of the authors of each of the batteries presented descriptions and criticisms of each battery. These will now be examined.

In the first of these articles, Super (1956d) offers a general discussion of multifactor batteries and what they should do. He notes that: (1) they should describe the makeup of the student or client; (2) they should predict what he will be like and what he will do in the future; (3) they should be timeless; and (4) they should be "multipotential." An examination of the current batteries reveals, he continues, that they do describe, they are timeless to a certain extent, and that they are multipotential. He feels that they fall down when it comes to prediction, especially differential prediction. In the construction of each of these batteries an attempt was made to arrive at factorial purity, providing for each battery factors, or "aptitudes" as they are called by some, of psychological meaning and importance. These different factors contribute to success in a variety of situations or occupations, to any of which the factor in question may be related. Super states that these factorial tests are pure, abstract, and general in nature. In tests used in specific situations, when the test is a miniature of the job, the elements common to or specific to certain jobs give these tests higher validity coefficients than would be obtained from the general factor test in the same situation.

In his critique of the *DAT*, Super (1956*a*) notes that grades in English are well predicted by scores on the Verbal reasoning, Numerical reasoning, Abstract reasoning, and Spelling and Sentence subtests of the battery. The same subtests also predict grades in social studies, mathematics, and science. In other words, the tests do an adequate job in predicting success in the usual academic grades, but not in any differential manner. This may, however, be due to the criterion rather than a defect in the tests. Those tests that measure intelligence predict success in the academic subjects. This was also true of the *Guilford-Zimmerman.* Super further notes that Numerical reasoning and Language-usage scores predict bookkeeping grades and typing grades. Scores on the Spatial reasoning test also predict shop grades to a certain extent. Thus, if all that is desired is prediction of academic success, why not use a simple, short, and economical intelligence test which saves both time and money?

In the subsequent articles, Super shows that the other batteries are no better and frequently worse than the *DAT* in differential prediction (1956*b, c;* 1957*a, b, c, d, e*). In the final article (1957*f*), he summarizes by stating that the *DAT* and the *GATB* are judged ready for use in counseling at the present time. He found the *FACT* perhaps ready for limited counseling. The *Guilford-Zimmerman, Holzinger-Crowder,* and *Segal-Raskin* batteries were judged to be still in the research stage. Two batteries, the *SRA Primary Mental Abilities* and the *Factored Series* (King 1957), were dismissed as not having "stood the test of time or the scrutiny of science." In using these batteries, the counselor must remember that validation is to a great extent still to be desired. Super notes that these tests and their publishers do a fine job of demonstrating content, concurrent, and construct validity, but have frequently not enough information about predictive validity, which is related to the counselor's chief job.

Another major study concerned with the use of the aptitude test batteries was conducted by Thorndike and Hagen (1959). The test battery used in this report was that given to aviation cadets in the Army Air Corps during World War II. The battery, made up of 19 parts, yielded 20 scores covering areas that may be broadly grouped into five abilities:

(1) General intellectual; (2) Numerical; (3) Perceptual and spatial; (4) Mechanical; and (5) Psychomotor. A Biographical Data Blank, in addition to yielding two of the above scores, provided data against which to analyze both test scores and data about the criterion. This battery, in one form or another, was administered to approximately 500,000 Air Force personnel in World War II. The men first had to pass a stiff physical examination, score at or above a certain score on a test of general intelligence (the *Aviation Cadet Qualifying Examination*), be single, and between 18 and 26 years of age. It follows that they were a select group.

Thorndike and Hagen selected a sample of 17,000 of these trainees who took the tests at about the same time during 1943. Approximately 12 years later, the men were sent a short questionnaire covering educational and vocational activities since their separation from the Air Corps. The items on the questionnaire were related to the following criteria: monthly salary; number of men supervised; a self-rating of success and one of job satisfaction; a rating of both vertical and lateral mobility, the latter being a measure of job stability; and finally, length of time in occupation. The ratings of mobility were derived by judges from responses made to items on the questionnaire. About 70% of the sample returned the completed questionnaire.

As a result of their study, Thorndike and Hagen showed that there were real and logical differences among various occupational groups. For example, college professors were shown to be about .75 of a standard deviation above the over-all mean on General intellectual ability, about .4 of a standard deviation above the mean on both Numerical and Perceptual ability, about .3 of a standard deviation below the mean on Mechanical ability, and at the mean on Psychomotor skills. Artists and designers were shown to have means very similar to the group means on all abilities except Perceptual, on which their mean score was about .5 of a standard deviation above the group mean. Other occupations, such as clergyman and real-estate salesman, showed profiles that were quite flat. In other words, some occupations were shown to require very special abilities and others to have no special requirements in terms of the abilities studied in this research. It should also be noted that there was considerable variation within any specific occupational group, in terms of the five abilities studied.

An analysis of the Biographical Data Sheet showed that the various occupational groups differed in background as well as on ability test scores. The item on this data sheet that made the most discriminations was the one that asked if the trainees had any previous college education. This single item differentiated 54 occupations at the .01 level of significance and 10 at the .05 level. An analysis was made to see how well each of the 112 items on this sheet differentiated among the various occupations. For example, 74 of the items differentiated college professors significantly, either positively or negatively, from other occupational groups at the .01 or .05% level. College professors showed a history of verbal and intellectual activities (positive discrimination) and one of low activity in sports and mechanical activities (negative discrimination). (See the discussion of the linguistic-nonlinguistic continuum in Chapter 5.)

The final conclusion of the study, based upon some 12,000 correlation coefficients, was that success in an occupation cannot be predicted either by these aptitude tests or by the items on the Biographical Data Sheet—or, at least, not when these data were analyzed against the criteria previously mentioned—a finding that created quite a stir when it was first made public. It may be well to remember the limitations of the study pointed out by Thorndike and Hagen. They emphasize that the individuals in this study were a select group to begin with, and they present evidence to show that the more successful tended to return the questionnaire. Second, other aspects of personality, such as interests, attitudes, and over-all personal adjustment, were not studied. These so-called "nonintellectual factors" have much to do with vocational success. A third problem arose from the fact that, even if occupational groups bore similar titles, such as college professor or lawyer, many different types of college professors and lawyers were included. Each of the different occupational groups was quite heterogeneous. Finally, the authors discuss the criteria of vocational success used. It so happened that these criteria were those most readily available; it does not follow that they were the best or were collected in the most dependable fashion. They conclude their discussion of limitations of the study by saying:

As far as we were able to determine from our data, there is no convincing evidence that aptitude tests or biographical information of the type that was available to us can predict degree of success within an occupation insofar as this is represented in the criterion measures that we are able to obtain. This would suggest that we should view the long-range prediction of occupational success by aptitude tests with a good deal of skepticism and take a very restrained view as to how much can be accomplished in this direction.

In the light of the limitations of the study that Thorndike and Hagen themselves point out, the present writers wonder if it can really be said that occupational success cannot be predicted. Perhaps a test battery administered to predict occupational success, rather than success in air-crew training school, and used in conjunction with other nonintellectual predictors, may present different results. The evidence is not yet conclusive.

BATTERIES FOR SPECIFIC OCCUPATIONS

As pointed out earlier, there are a large number of batteries that have been constructed chiefly for the selection of students for the study of medicine, dentistry, law, and the like. The counselor will have little opportunity to use these batteries, but it will certainly fall upon him to advise others to take them. The distribution of such tests is, as it logically should be, restricted. The test batteries are usually administered one or more times a year at certain examination centers. Individuals who plan to take them sign up in advance, pay a fee, and at that time or later are sent an admission card to the testing session. Sample items, and a general discussion of the battery, are given to the student at that time. These tests, in their format and content, are apt to be very similar to the multifactor batteries just discussed, but they include materials or tests specific to the profession for which they were constructed. In general they are made up of tests of abilities and achievement tests. In the paragraphs that follow, a few will be described.

For many years the Association of American Medical Schools has supported the construction and use of a battery for the selection of medical students. At the present time the *Medical College Admission Test* (issued by the Educational Testing Service) is made up of two parts, a test of ability and another of achievement. The first is made up of tests measuring verbal ability, and a single test of quantitative ability; the second is made up of two subtests, one measuring the understanding of modern society and social concepts, and the other covering premedical school science.

Similar to this are the batteries used in dental schools, except that they are apt to have added tests of spatial relationships and manual and finger dexterity. This is frequently done by having the examinee carve objects out of a block of chalk. As might be expected, batteries used in law schools emphasize the verbal aspects of mental life. Typically such tests measure vocabulary, reading comprehension, interpretation of data, or evaluation of arguments. Tests used for engineers put stress on numerical computations, problem solving, formulation, and achievement in the basic physical sciences. *The National Teachers Examination* (Educational Testing Service) is composed of a morning examination covering professional interests (educational psychology, child development, measurement, guidance, and so on), general culture (history, literature, fine arts, science, and mathematics), English expression, and nonverbal reasoning. The afternoon session is devoted to an examination covering the examinee's two major teaching specialties. Other batteries are used for the selection of students for both the undergraduate and graduate phases of higher education. The three most widely used of these batteries are discussed below.

The *American College Testing Program Examination* (*ACT*, Iowa City, Iowa) is a battery of tests constructed for use with either entering college freshmen or with transfers from junior colleges to four-year institutions. This battery consists of four tests that yield five scores: English usage, Mathematics usage, Social science reading, Natural science reading, and a total or composite score. The battery, which requires slightly over 3 hours for administration, is offered four times a year at various centers throughout the country. Each test is a measure of the student's prior educational development. For example, the Mathematics usage test measures the student's use of mathematical principles in solving quantitative problems and in the interpreting of charts and graphs. Two types of items are included in this test: reasoning problems based upon timely situations, and formal exercises or problems in arithmetic, algebra, and geometry. The reading tests measure the student's ability to evaluate and interpret reading matter in the natural or social sciences. About a quarter of the items in each reading test measure his knowledge of important facts and concepts, but the general emphasis is upon interpretation and understanding. The mere memorization of factual information is not rewarded. Scores on the tests are reported as standard scores with a mean of 15 and a standard deviation of 5.

The tests of this battery are expertly made. The various types of reliability coefficients computed for the battery are all high. Intercorrelations among the four tests are in the .50's and .60's, high enough to suggest that the counselor be cautious in making differential predictions upon the basis of these scores. Content validity was built into the construction of the tests. Criterion-related validity is based upon the relation of the four basic *ACT* scores to the four corresponding high-school grades and with freshman grades. The multiple correlation coefficients are typically in the .60's.

The publishers of the battery have assembled an outstanding group of tests that offers competition to the tests of the *College Entrance Examination Board*. They are educationally sound in their construction, and built according to the specifications of well-made tests. The reporting services and the materials presented for the administration and use of the battery, such as manuals and bulletins, are all very good. The test makers provide a continuing research service for the users of the tests.

The *College Entrance Examination Board Tests* (*CEEB*), published by the Educational Testing Service, consist of two basic parts, a scholastic aptitude test and a series of achievement tests. *The Scholastic Aptitude*

Test (*SAT*) provides two scores, verbal and mathematical. The verbal score is based upon sentence completion items, analogies, antonyms, and reading comprehension; the mathematical part is made up of essential arithmetic operations, these giving way to more difficult reasoning problems requiring the application of algebraic and geometric concepts as the test goes on. Scaled scores are provided, with a range from 200 to 800, a mean of 500, a standard deviation of 100, and a standard error of measurement of approximately 30. Test-retest reliability and measures of internal consistency are both high, and intercorrelation between the two parts is, like that of the *ACT*, in the .50's and .60's. Much research related to the prediction of college success has been carried on with this test since it first appeared in 1926. It has been shown to be about the best predictor of the grades of college freshmen. The verbal score is a better predictor in liberal arts colleges; the mathematics score, better in engineering schools.

This battery, like the *ACT*, is well constructed, with adequate and precise norms. The services provided to both students and schools using the tests are similar to those offered by the *ACT*. In structure and content this test is more similar to the conventional intelligence test, the *ACT* being more of a modern achievement test. The line separating intelligence tests and achievement tests is thin and tenuous, however, and actually there is no point in arguing whether or not this difference has any significance. Like the *ACT*, the *SAT* is administered four times a year in centers across the country; in addition, overseas centers have also been set up. Both batteries, in summary, are well made, and well administered. The results of both are handled efficiently and effectively. There is a question of whether two such batteries are needed. The existence of the two requires that some students take both, for the students are never really sure just which one will be required by the colleges to which they apply. There has been consideration of the establishment of equivalency tables between the scores of the two batteries to prevent this duplication of time, effort, and money.

The other part of the *CEEB* consists of a series of 15 achievement tests covering the usual high-school academic subjects. Each candidate selects from one to three of these tests, as the college to which he is applying for admission specifies. Some schools use the *SAT* scores in selecting their freshmen, and then suggest that those who are admitted take certain achievement tests later in the spring, just before the completion of their high-school course. The results of the achievement tests, such as English, languages, mathematics, or sciences, are used in the placement of the new freshman at the appropriate levels in his new college courses. It has been found that these achievement tests contribute very little to the prediction of academic success when the scores obtained on them are entered into the regression equation. What is measured by these tests is also measured by the parts of the *SAT* and by the elements that went into the determination of the student's high-school rank; thus they offer nothing that is not already in the regression equation.

Similar in makeup to the *CEEB* is the *Graduate Record Examination* (*GRE*), also published and distributed by the Educational Testing Service. This battery, used for the selection of students by graduate schools, is made up of an aptitude test that yields both a verbal and quantitative score, a series of "advanced tests" in special curricular areas, such as physics and psychology, and three area tests—humanities, natural science, and social science. Many graduate schools require that the applicant take only the aptitude part of the battery, which in the opinion of experts is a well-constructed test of high-level scholastic ability. Its usefulness as a predictor of success in graduate school has been variable. Some studies have shown that it has no validity, others that it does a respectable job of prediction. Since graduate schools vary so much in their programs and in their criteria of just what constitutes success in graduate school, this is not surprising. This test is best used when the various schools and departments in any graduate school use their own criterion or criteria of success in evaluating the validity of the battery. The administration of the tests, reporting of results, and research with the battery are all handled by the Educational Testing Service in the same fashion as this organization handles the College Boards.

SUMMARY

The counselor, in reviewing the scores of aptitude and ability tests found in the record of a given client, may wish to go over these scores during the initial interview and discuss with the client any additional information needed to supplement such data in later counseling interviews. This means the counselor must not only be able to interpret the test scores which are a matter of record, but must be in a position to recommend appropriate counseling tools which will provide the additional data needed during counseling.

In addition to test scores, the counselor must be able to evaluate and use other evidences of aptitudes and abilities from agency records and from other community sources. This has been largely overlooked in the past, but is coming to have increasing importance for the counselor and the client.

REFERENCES

Anastasi, A. 1954. *Psychological testing*. New York: The Macmillan Company.

Andrew, Dorothy M. 1937. An analysis of the *Minnesota Vocational Test for Clerical Workers: I and II*. *J. Appl. Psychol.* 21:18–47, 139–72.

Bennett, G. K. 1951. *Counseling from profiles: A casebook for the Differential Aptitude Tests*. New York: The Psychological Corporation.

————. 1955. *The DAT: A seven-year follow-up. Test Service Bull.* no. 49. New York: The Psychological Corporation.

————. 1966. *Manual for the Differential Aptitude Tests*. New York: The Psychological Corporation.

————, and Cruikshank, R. M. 1942. *A summary of manual and mechanical ability tests*. New York: The Psychological Corporation.

————, et al. 1956. The *Differential Aptitude Tests:* An overview. *Personnel & Guidance J.* 35:81–91.

Blum, M. L., and Candee, B. 1941. The selection of department store packers and wrappers with the aid of certain psychological tests: II. *J. Appl.* 1961.

Buros, O. K. 1961. *Tests in print*. Highland Park, N.J.: The Gryphon Press, 1961.

————, ed. 1949. *The third mental measurements yearbook*. Brunswick, N.J.: Rutgers University Press.

————. 1953. *The fourth mental measurements yearbook*. Highland Park, N.J.: The Gryphon Press.

————. 1959. *The fifth mental measurements yearbook*. Highland Park, N.J.: The Gryphon Press.

————. 1965. *The sixth mental measurements yearbook*. Highland Park, N.J.: The Gryphon Press.

Cattell, R. B. 1960. *Culture Fair Intelligence Tests*. Champaign, Ill.: Institute for Personality and Ability Testing.

Cattell, P. 1947. *The measurement of the intelligence of infants and young children*. New York: The Psychological Corporation.

Cleary, T. A. 1966. *Test bias: Validity of the Scholastic Aptitude test for Negro and white students in integrated colleges*. Educational Testing Service Res. Bull. RB-66-31. Princeton, N.J.

Cronbach, L. J. 1949. *Essentials of psychological testing*. New York: Harper & Row, Publishers.

Crowder, N. A. 1957. The *Holzinger-Crowder Uni-factor Tests. Personnel and Guidance J.* 35:281–86.

Darley, J. G. 1934. *Reliability of tests in the Standard Battery*. Bull., Empl. Stab. Res. Inst., no. 4. Minneapolis: University of Minnesota.

Davis, A., and Eells, K. 1953. *The Davis-Eells Games.* New York: Harcourt, Brace & World, Inc.

Downie, N. M. 1967. *Fundamentals of measurement.* New York: Oxford University Press, Inc.

Dvorak, Beatrice J. 1947. The new USES General Aptitude Test Battery. *Occupations.* 26:42–44.

———. 1956. The General Aptitude Test Battery. *Personnel and Guidance J.* 35:145–52.

Eells, K., *et al.* 1951. *Intelligence and cultural differences.* Chicago: University of Chicago Press.

Farnsworth, P. R., and McNemar, Q., eds. 1956. *Annual review of psychology.* Stanford, Calif.: Annual Reviews.

Fay, C. J., and Middleton, W. I. 1941. Relationship between musical talent and preferences for different types of music. *J. Educ. Psychol.* 32:573–83.

Flanagan, J. C. 1957. *Flanagan Aptitude Classification Test. Personnel and Guidance J.* 35:495–503.

Garrett, H. E. 1946. A developmental theory of intelligence. *Amer. Psychol.* 1: 372–78.

Goddard, H. H. 1946. What is intelligence? *J. Soc. Psychol.* 24:51–69.

Goodenough, F. 1949. *Mental testing.* New York: Holt, Rinehart & Winston, Inc.

Guilford, J. P. 1947. The discovery of aptitude and achievement variables. *Science.* 106:279–82.

———. 1948. Factor analysis in a test development program. *Psychol. Rev.* 55:79–94.

———. 1956. The *Guilford-Zimmerman Aptitude Survey. Personnel and Guidance J.* 35:219–23.

———. 1959. Three faces of intellect. *Amer. Psychol.* 14:369–79.

———. 1966. Intelligence: 1965 Model. *Amer. Psychol.* 20:20–26.

Harrell, T. W. 1940. A factor analysis of mechanical ability tests. *Psychometrika.* 5:17–33.

Hahn, M. E., and MacLean, M. S. 1955. *Counseling Psychology.* New York: McGraw-Hill Book Company.

Hay, E. N. 1943. Predicting success in machine bookkeeping. *J. Appl. Psychol.* 27:483–93.

Horn, C. A., and Smith, L. F. 1945. The *Horn Art Aptitude Inventory. J. Appl. Psychol.* 29:350–59.

Intelligence and Its Measurement (symposium). *J. Educ. Psychol.* 1921. 12: 123–47.

King, J. E. 1957. The *Factored Aptitude Series of Business and Industrial Tests. Personnel and Guidance J.* 35:351–58.

McNemar, Q. 1964. Lost: Our intelligence? Why? *Amer. Psychol.* 19:871–82.

Meier, N. C. 1942. *The Meier Art Tests: I, Art Judgment.* Iowa City, Iowa: Bureau of Educational Research Services.

————. 1963. *The Meier Art Tests: II, Aesthetic Perception.* Iowa City, Iowa: Bureau of Educational Research Services.

Paterson, D. G., Gerken, C. d'A; and Hahn, M. E. 1941. *The Minnesota Occupational Rating Scales.* Chicago: Science Research Associates.

————. *The Minnesota Occupational Rating Scales.* rev. 1953. Minneapolis: University of Minnesota Press.

Seashore, C. H. 1939. *The psychology of music.* New York: McGraw-Hill Book Company.

Segal, D. 1957. The *Multiple Aptitude Tests. Personnel and Guidance J.* 35: 424–31.

Spearman, C. 1904. General intelligence objectively determined and measured. *Amer. J. Psychol.* 15:201–93.

Stanley, J. C., and Porter, A. C. 1967. Correlations of scholastic aptitude test score with college grades for Negroes versus whites. *J. Educ. Measmt.* 4: 199–218.

Stanton, H. W. 1929. *Prognosis of musical achievement.* Eastman School of Music, Studies in Psychology, no. 1.

Stoddard, G. D. 1943. *The meaning of intelligence.* New York: The Macmillan Company.

Super, D. E. 1956a. Comments [on the *DAT*]. *Personnel and Guidance J.* 35:91–93.

————. 1956b. Comments [on the *GATB*]. *Personnel and Guidance J.* 35: 152–54.

————. 1956c. Comments [on the *GZAS*]. *Personnel and Guidance J.* 35: 223–24.

————. 1956d. The use of multifactor test batteries in guidance. *Personnel and Guidance J.* 35:9–15.

————. 1957a. Comments [on the *Factored Aptitude Series*]. *Personnel and Guidance J.* 35:358–60.

————. 1957b. Comments [on the *Flanagan Aptitude Classification Test*]. *Personnel and Guidance J.* 35:504–7.

————. 1957c. Comments [on the *Holzinger-Crowder Unifactor Tests*]. *Personnel and Guidance J.* 35:287–88.

————. 1957d. Comments [on the *Multiple Aptitude Tests*]. *Personnel and Guidance J.* 35:432–34.

————. 1957e. Comments [on the *Tests of Primary Mental Ability*]. *Personnel and Guidance J.* 35:576–77.

————. 1957f. The multifactor tests: Summing up. *Personnel and Guidance J.* 36:17–20.

————, and Crites, J. O. 1962. *Appraising vocational fitness.* New York: Harper & Row, Publishers.

Terman, L. M. 1916. *The measurement of intelligence*. Boston: Houghton Mifflin Company.

————, and Merrill, M. A. 1937. *Measuring intelligence*. Boston: Houghton Mifflin Company.

————. 1960. *The Stanford-Binet Intelligence Scale: Manual for the Third Revision, Form L-M*. Boston: Houghton Mifflin Company.

Thorndike, R. L., and Hagen, E. 1959. *10,000 Careers*. New York: John Wiley & Sons, Inc.

Thurstone, L. L. 1938. *Primary mental abilities*. Psychometric Monographs, no. 1.

Thurstone, T. G. 1957. *The Tests of Primary Mental Abilities. Personnel and Guidance J.* 35:569–77.

U.S. Dept. of Labor. Manpower Administration. 1965. *Dictionary of occupational titles*. vol. II. *Occupational classification and industry index*. 3rd ed. Washington, D.C.: Government Printing Office.

————. 1966. *Selected characteristics of occupations (Physical demands, working conditions, and training time): A supplement to the DOT*. 3rd ed. Washington, D.C.: Government Printing Office.

Vernon, P. E. 1962. *The structure of human abilities*. 2nd ed. London: Methuen & Co., Ltd.

————. 1965. Ability factors and environmental influences. *Amer. Psychol.* 20:723–33.

War Manpower Commission, Division of Occupational Analysis. 1945. Factor analysis of occupational aptitude tests. *Educ. and Psychol. Measmt.* 5:147–55.

Wechsler, D. 1944. *The measurement of adult intelligence*. Baltimore: The Williams & Wilkins Co.

————. 1949. *Wechsler Intelligence Scale for Children (WISC)*. New York: The Psychological Corporation.

————. 1955. *Wechsler Adult Intelligence Scale (WAIS)*. New York: The Psychological Corporation.

————. 1967. *Wechsler Preschool and Primary Scale of Intelligence (WPPSI)*. New York: The Psychological Corporation.

Wittenborn, J. R. 1945. Mechanical ability, its nature and measurement, I: An analysis of the variables employed in the preliminary Minnesota Experiment. *Educ. and Psychol. Measmt.* 5:241–60.

9

Interests

The counselor preparing for a series of counseling interviews may use the material covered in this chapter in several ways. Data about interests may already be included in the client's record; this necessitates synthesizing these data into a form usable with the client, and requires that the counselor be skilled in the interpretation of such data. This chapter can provide him with a review. The counselor and client may discuss in the initial interview the need for collecting further data about interests in addition to that already available; then the counselor needs to point out the process and instruments by which further data about interests will be collected. A brief discussion with the client of the instruments to be used and vital points in the client's approach to completing them may make the data produced by the instruments more usable, and is apt to produce a more candid response by the client. Again, this chapter should provide a review of pertinent material used by the counselor in this process.

The counselor may wish to discuss with the client the value of data about his interests in broadening an understanding of his behavior and in providing an insight into his motivation. For college-bound clients and clients from upper levels of general intelligence, data concerning interests may provide the only useful differentiation of educational or vocational possibilities. For other clients, such data may provide a clue to specific areas of investigation before they make further life choices.

These are some of the ways in which information about the client's interests can be useful in preparing for counseling interviews.

BRIEF HISTORY OF THE MEASUREMENT OF INTERESTS

The measurement of interests closely parallels that of mental ability in its development. Early in the twentieth century when Binet was making the first scientific attempts to measure intelligence, other psychologists were attempting to do the same for interests. Fryer's *Measurement of Interest in Relation to Human Adjustment* (1931), which covers the history of the subject, is considered the basic landmark in the field because it is a comprehensive summary of the theorizing and experimenting that went on in this area of human personality up until about 1930. Although a considerable part of this early work is of little more than historical value because of the lack of statistical techniques possessed by the early workers for handling data, ignorance of sampling techniques, and poorly designed experiments, the reader of Fryer's volume will be impressed by the fact that all of the problems that confront the appraiser of interests today are mentioned by Fryer.

Fryer considered that there was a dual approach to the appraisal of interests, a subjective and an objective one. The subjective aspect was evaluated by the use of inventories, questionnaires, and rating scales. The objective approach was a measurement of one's observable reaction to stimulation. Some of the objective measures that Fryer considers are information tests, free-association tests, learning tests, and distraction tests. It might be noted that little has been done with this objective approach to the measurement of interests since the time of Fryer's writing except for isolated instances such as the development of the *Michigan Vocabulary Profile Analysis*, which measures interests on the basis of one's knowledge of the vocabularies of the different fields of interests, and some limited attempts at vocational information tests.

Another rather interesting aspect of Fryer's ideas is that he separated motivation from interest. In the course of his writings Fryer (1931, p. 349) derives a theory of interest that states:

Objective interests are acceptance reactions and objective aversions are rejection reactions. It may be that the acceptance, or turning toward stimulation, and the rejection, or turning away from the stimulation, are correlated with pleasant and unpleasant experiences. Subjective interests, or likes, would appear to be acceptances of stimulation and subjective aversions, or dislikes, would appear to be rejections of stimulation. At any rate, they may be regarded as acceptance-rejection experiences.

In spite of this, it is only recently that users of interest inventories have begun to interpret them in terms of patterns of acceptance and rejection.

The second landmark in the history of the measuring of interests is Strong's *Vocational Interests of Men and Women* (1943). In this large volume Strong summarized the vast amount of data that had been collected over the years through the use of the *Strong Vocational Interest Blank (SVIB)*. Much of this work will be discussed later when the *SVIB* is taken up in detail. In the 1930's, Kuder began developing the *Kuder Preference Record: Vocational*. After World War II, it came into common use in the appraisal of vocational interests. Kuder's original approach differed from Strong's in that, instead of developing keys for different occupations on the basis of the inventoried interests of successful individuals in various occupations, he developed an inventory, on the basis of statistical analysis, which resulted in an individual's interests being reported in fields or areas of interests such as mechanical, artistic, clerical, and the like. Forms *A, B, C,* and *E* were of this type. Forms *D* and *DD*, Kuder's latest contributions, are similar to Strong's in that keys are available for specific occupations.

In 1931, Allport and Vernon published their *Study of Values*. This high-level inventory was revised in 1951 and is now known as the Allport–Vernon–Lindzey *Study of Values*. Over the years it has been widely used both in carrying on research with and in counseling university students. In the 1940's, Lee and Thorpe published their *Occupational Interest Inventory*. A novel approach appeared in Weingarten's *Picture Interest Inventory* (1958).

In 1965, a new inventory designed to measure vocational interests of persons in occupations below the professional and managerial level was published by Clark and Campbell. This instrument, *The Minnesota Vocational Interest Inventory* (The Psychological Corporation), resulted from Clark's studies of vocational interests of men in various Navy ratings.

Currently it is based on an additional sample of 7,000 men in civilian jobs, such as carpenters, electricians, routemen, and bakers.

A new edition of the *SVIB:Men* (T399) was published in 1966, and a research edition of the revised *SVIB:Women* also appeared in that year. These were the first substantial revisions of the *SVIB* since 1938; they involved modernizing the items, adding several more scales, and changing the item weights and scoring, and they included a new reference group of professional men in general for the men's blank. In 1969 a series of *Basic Interest scales* was included in scoring for T399 and a new profile was provided.

Changes similar to the *SVIB:T399* were made in the SVIB:W (TW398) and published in 1969 also. New profiles are shown in Forms 9.3 and 9.4.

All these interest inventories mentioned will be discussed in detail later in the chapter.

THEORIES OF INTERESTS

As psychologists measured interests they also began to speculate and hypothesize on the nature of interests. Fryer developed his theory of acceptance-rejection. Early in his major book, Strong (1943, p. 6) reverses Fryer's stand and says that interests are aspects of motivation. A few pages on (p. 10), he states that since interests involve reactions to specific things, they must all be learned. This is his major theory, but as he considers his research data throughout the book, various amendments are made to this theory. Presently (p. 333) he shows that there are significant relationships between mental ability and vocational interests. Most of these correlation coefficients fall between plus and minus .40. He continues (pp. 682–83):

Are interests inherited as are physical traits? The first answer to this question is "No." Interests are related to objects and activities in the environment in quite a different sense from height or color of eyes. Interests are learned. Liking to be an aviator and disliking gardening are reflections of experience. The second answer to this question is that interests are inherited to a certain degree. An interest is an expression of one's reaction to his environment. The reaction of liking-disliking is a resultant of satisfactory or unsatisfactory dealing with the object. Different people react differently to the same object. The different reactions, we suspect, arise because the individuals are different to start with. We suspect that people who have the kind of brain that handles mathematics easily will like such activities and vice versa. In other words, interests are related to abilities and abilities, it is easy to see, are inherited. There is, however, a pathetic lack of data to substantiate all of this.

Strong seems to be saying here that interests are partly a function of innate potential and partly a function of learning through encounters with the environment.

Other researchers have considered interests as arising from the development of personality. Carter (1940) considers the choice of a vocation to be the practical adjustment to the environment. Solutions possible for any individual are limited by his own capacities, needs, motives, and by his and his family's socioeconomic status. If there are no major discrepancies between these factors and the requirements of a vocation, an individual will tend to continue in an occupation. If there are discrepancies, he will seek another vocation. In this way, as time goes on, a pattern of vocational interests forms that is closely identified with the individual.

On the basis of Strong and Carter's work, Darley (1941) suggested cautiously that the data supported the hypothesis that occupational interests emerged from the development of one's personality. Darley's theory was based upon studies made with the three "non-occupational scales" of the *SVIB:* Occupational Level, Interest–Maturity, and Masculinity–Femininity. Later research with these scales and other developments led Darley himself to see defects in his own ideas (Darley and Hagenah 1955, p. 147). Super (1949) criticized both Carter and Darley for unwarranted interpretations of the data, fragmentary evidence, and even for making assertions that are in no way related to the basic research data.

In another approach, Kitson (1942) wrote that vocational interests develop through experiences. It follows that an important task of the counselor is to aid the client in obtaining experiences that will help him in making a vocational decision.

Bordin (1943) stated that the vocational goals and aspirations of an individual form one of the mainsprings of his actions. He notes that the older an individual is, the more likely he is to be vocationally situated and the less likelihood that he will need a change of vocation. Finally, he stated (p. 53): "In answering a *Strong Vocational Interest Test* an individual is expressing his acceptance of a particular view or concept of himself in terms of occupational stereotypes."

Super, a critic of the ideas of Strong, Carter, and Darley, proposed his own theory of multiple causation (1949, p. 46):

Interests are the product of interaction between inherited aptitudes and endocrine factors, on the one hand, and opportunity and social evaluation on the other. Some of the things a person does will bring him the satisfaction of mastery or the approval of his companions, and result in interests. Some of the things his associates do appeal to him and, through identification, he patterns his actions and his interests after them: if he fits the pattern reasonably well, he remains in it, but if not, he must seek another identification and develop another self-concept and interest pattern. His mode of adjustment may cause him to seek certain satisfactions, but the means of achieving these satisfactions vary so much from one person, with one set of aptitudes and in one set of circumstances, to another person with other abilities and in another situation, that the prediction of interest patterns from modes of adjustment is hardly possible. Because of the stability of the hereditary endowment and the relative stability of the social environment in which any given person is reared, interest patterns are generally rather stable; their stability is further increased by the multiplicity of opportunities for try-outs, identification and social approval in the years before adolescence. By adolescence most young people have had opportunities to explore social, linguistic, mathematical, technical, and business activities to some extent; they have sought to identify with parents, other adults, and schoolmates, and have rejected some and accepted others of these identifications; self-concepts have begun to take definite form. For these reasons interest patterns begin to crystallize by early adolescence, and the exploratory experiences of the adolescent years in most cases merely clarify and elaborate upon what has already begun to take shape. Some persons experience significant changes during adolescence and early adulthood, but these are most often related to endocrine changes and less often to changes in self-concept resulting from having attempted to live up to a misidentification and to fit into a inappropriate pattern. Vocational interest patterns generally have a substantial degree of permanence at this stage: for most persons, adolescent exploration is an awakening to something that is already there.

At this point it seems wise also to call attention to two possible dangers in interpretation of patterns on the *SVIB*. There is danger of interpreting a pattern of maladjustment as a stable occupational pattern. A person who is withdrawing because of emotional upset may reject the Group V (Social Welfare) and Group IX (Business Contact) scales on the *SVIB*. After successful therapy, such a person may reverse this pattern and show high scores on scales for these occupations dealing with people. Conversely, a person who cannot solve his emotional problems will sometimes compensate to such an extent that it results in a Social Welfare pattern which is not a valid occupational one.

The other danger is in the interpretation of a pattern of interests developed in a very restricted environment as a stable occupational pattern. A boy brought up in a prominent family with a traditional history as business leaders in a community may show a pronounced pattern on the *SVIB* scales for Business Detail and Business Contact occupations as a freshman entering college. If after he has been in college for some time he retakes the *SVIB*, he may then show a moderate pattern on the Group V scales (Social Welfare) and lowered scores on the business scales. At this point his pattern is really beginning to represent his own interests, rather than those to which he was exposed in the restricted family environment. The original scores might be considered a reflection of family interests, not his. The counselor should interpret these successive testings very cautiously over a period of time, until retests appear stable enough that no further changes occur. Another example of such change in interests is the gifted student from the small community who can do most things well, yet shows no pronounced pattern of interests as he enters a university. Here again, the counselor must wait and see what develops on periodic retests before any sound interpretation can be made.

Ginzberg *et al.* (1951), as a result of studying the interests of boys from the upper socioeconomic level and in the top bracket of mental ability, stated that vocational interests pass through three developmental periods: ages 6–11, fantasy; 12–17, tentative; and 18 and beyond, realistic. In the first period the typical child sees himself doing all sorts of things as an adult. In the second stage he starts selecting a vocation. As he matures, he passes to the final stage. With advancing age, his vocational choices become more realistic and are made on sounder bases. According to the authors of this theory, vocational choice, since it is based upon all that one has undergone before, is essentially irreversible; but there has to be compromise, as vocational choice consists of a balancing of subjective aspects of an individual with the opportunities and restrictions of daily living.

This theory has been taken to task by counseling psychologists (see Darley and Hagenah 1955, Super 1953) for disregarding all past research, statistical naïveté, and a lack of validation.

Briefly, then, these are the ideas the psychologists have set down when they speculated upon the nature of interests. A comprehensive summary of these theories and the research basic thereto is found in Chapter 5 of Darley and Hagenah (1955). Hahn and MacLean (1955, pp. 201–2) summarized the bulk of the research and theorizing on vocational interests up to 1955 succinctly when they wrote:

1. Interests are an aspect of personality shaped by both hereditary and environmental factors.

2. Long-range, stable, occupational interests emerge during the early teens, but mature interest patterns are not fixed for most individuals until an age of approximately twenty-five years.

3. Interests are not necessarily closely related to aptitudes or abilities.

4. Interests probably cannot be created *de novo* and in a short time merely by the classroom presentation of varied and vicarious experiences to youth. Such exposures may possibly, however, start the development of a new zone of interest, help fix existing interests, or uncover latent ones.

5. A strong motivation toward certain types of occupational or avocational

behavior is expressed by a wide number of responses to an extremely wide range of stimuli.

6. Interests, as aspects of personality and as employed by the general clinical counselor, involve both acceptance and rejection of possible lines of activity. For example the typical worker with processes and things (mechanical interests) obtains interest scores which are negatively related to scores which measure a liking for persons and social situations.

7. The estimated, judged, or measured interests of secondary school and college students in an occupation seem to them to be and in fact often are quite unrelated to the training program they must take to prepare them for employment in the occupational family in which they have an identified dominant interest.

8. A legitimate interest in an occupational outlet often has little effect on grades earned in the curriculum leading to that outlet. Much of the training in a medical school may be largely quite unrelated to the particular aspects of medical practice toward which the interest is expressed.

9. Vocational and avocational interests appear to run in similar directions for a large proportion of individuals.

10. The interests of individuals tend to be less varied with increasing age.

Super and Crites (1962) considered the various inventories used to measure vocational interests, with particular emphasis on the *SVIB* and the *Kuder*. They present (p. 382) the results of seven factor analyses of interest measures, but omit two important ones, by Cottle (1950) and D'Arcy (1954), dealing with both the *SVIB* and the *Kuder*. Super and Crites use their own names for the factors emerging from these various studies: "scientific, social welfare, literary, material, systematic, and contact interests." Cottle and D'Arcy both found similar factors in both the *SVIB* and the *Kuder*, which they described as "liking for numerical-spatial activities vs. linguistic activities; routine or business detail activities vs. activities involving qualitative judgments; a masculinity–vs.–femininity factor; contact with people vs. scientific activities; aspiration for material evidence (money)." The designations of Super and Crites, unlike those of Cottle and D'Arcy, are unrealistic in that they are unipolar descriptions of interest factors. Since interest factors are based on negative *and* positive intercorrelations of data, they must result in some bipolar factors. (Note the similarity to Fryer's acceptance-rejection theory.) This point will be discussed again later.

The chapter by Tyler in Borow's *Man In A World At Work* (1964, pp. 184–86) has one of the most recent summaries of current work using vocational interest inventories. Tyler says:

It has become possible to answer with increasing clarity theoretical questions about the structure of vocational interests. As we have already seen, Kuder found that there were clusters of interest items. Persons who preferred one of the activities in such a cluster were likely to prefer many of the others. Strong encountered evidence for relatedness when he correlated scores on the various occupational scales. Several factor-analytic studies using other items or tests have demonstrated that there are some main dimensions along which interests tend to arrange themselves. Persons who have worked on this research problem have come upon what seem to be many of the same major dimensions, regardless of the test or sample used. They differ somewhat, however, in the labels they attach to these dimensions. . . .

For the practicing counselor, one of the most important generalizations to be drawn from several decades of research is that interest tests measure the *direction* rather than the *strength* of a person's interests. Because of the general meaning and connotation of the word "interest," a counselor who loses sight of this fact is likely to be puzzled by what looks like large discrepancies between interest and achievement. For instance, a college student gets an A on the *Strong* [*SVIB*] Author scale but fails his freshman composition course because he cannot bring himself to write themes. The A does not point to a compelling drive to get words on paper. It means only that he likes and dislikes the same sorts of things that writers like and dislike. Interpreting scores as answers to the question "How much?" rather than "What kind?" is probably the most common error in the use of interest tests. At present we have no technique except behavior observation for assessing how strong a person's drive is in the direction in which he wishes to go.

Holland (1966, pp. 9–10) has also proposed theories of interest development as they relate to vocational choice. His propositions are as follows:

Briefly, the theory consists of several simple ideas and their more complex elaborations. First, we assume that we can characterize people by their resemblance to one or more personality types. The closer a person's resemblance to a particular type, the more likely it is he will exhibit the personal traits and behavior associated with that type. Second, we assume that the environments in which people live can be characterized by their resemblance to one or more model environments. Finally, we assume that the pairing of persons and environments leads to several outcomes that we can predict and understand from our knowledge of the personality types and the environmental models. These outcomes include vocational choice, vocational stability and achievement, personal stability, creative performance, and susceptibility to influence. . . .

In our culture, most persons can be categorized as one of six types—Realistic, Intellectual, Social, Conventional, Enterprising, and Artistic. . . . A "type" is a model against which we can measure the real person. Each type is the product of a characteristic interaction between a particular heredity and a variety of cultural and personal forces, including peers, parents, other significant adults, social class, culture, and the physical environment. Out of his experience, a person develops habitual ways of coping with the tasks presented by his psychological, social and physical environment, including vocational situations.

His biological and social heredity, coupled with his personal history, creates a characteristic set of abilities, perceptual skills and outlook, life goals, values, self-concepts (his image and evaluation of himself), and coping behavior (his typical methods of dealing with the problems of living). A type is then a complex cluster of personal attributes.

Holland (1968) summarized his studies and reported a sixth theory that supported the usefulness of the theory just described.

Considerable thought, observation, and research have been devoted to the subject of vocational interest inventories over the last half-century. Much of this has become a matter of record, but there is still a considerable body of knowledge resulting from observations in counseling that does not appear in the literature and therefore is unknown to the counselor unless he happens to meet persons who can tell it to him.

In reading the literature about vocational interests, the student is apt to become concerned with the loose use of terms. Super (1949) brought a semblance of order to the classification of interests when he proposed the following four types:

1. *Expressed or stated interests*. These are the verbal professions of an individual in an activity. Research has shown these to be quite unreliable.
2. *Manifest interests*. Super feels that these are synonymous with participation in an activity or an occupation. As measures of interest they may or may not be valid. Probably most high-school students who participate in the school's dramatic offerings do so because of an interest in dramatics. It is possible, though, that one of the boys is involved merely because of a girl who is there.
3. *Tested interests*. These are the same as Fryer's objective interests. The assumption is that high scores on an achievement test in a specific subject, or one related to a particular job, are related to an interest in that subject matter or job. Again, this may or may not be so. Some people do well in academic situations because of past behavior and conditioning. A high grade results sometimes with no interest, even aversion, simply because a person sees himself as a good student.
4. *Inventoried interests*. These are the ones most frequently encountered by the counselor and the type obtained from an inventory like the *Kuder* or the *SVIB*.

In the counseling situation, the counselor should as far as possible try to obtain information on all of these different types of interests, for the more different types of information collected about the client, the more valid the insights into his behavior and problems.

Kuder, Strong, and others who have developed interest inventories have used names for areas of interests or occupations through which they expressed the results of their inventories. For example, they used "scientific," "artistic," "outdoor," "chemist," and the like. Cottle (1951), as the result of an extensive factor analysis of data including scores on the *Kuder* and *SVIB*, showed that these factors were bipolar in nature. By this is meant that a preference for a type of work is associated with the rejection of another type of work. The bipolar factors used by Cottle are:

1. Preference for activities concerned with people and the communication of ideas.   vs.   1. Preference for activities dealing with things and objects.

2. Preference for activities involving business contact with people.   vs.   2. Preference for activities of a scientific and technical nature.

3. Preference for activities of an abstract and creative nature.   vs.   3. Preference for activities of a routine, concrete, organized business detail nature.

4. Preference for working for people for their presumed good as in social welfare, or for dealing with people and language in social situations.   vs.   4. Preference for activities that are nonsocial in nature, and are carried on in relation to processes, machines, and techniques.

5. Preference for activities resulting in prestige or the esteem of others.   vs.   5. Preference for activities resulting in tangible, productive satisfaction.

Extensive use of this classification has been made in a publication of the U.S. Department of Labor, *Estimates of Worker Trait Requirements for 4,000 Jobs* (1956) and its *Dictionary of Occupational Titles* (1965). It will readily be seen that one pole of each of these factors is related to activities of a linguistic nature which revolve around working with people, those on the left side of the page. The other pole of each factor, on the right side of the page, is related to activities of a nonlinguistic nature revolving around working with processes, related machines, and routine, repetitive activities. Thus over-all descriptions of occupations and clients in terms of linguistic vs. nonlinguistic activities appear more meaningful in counseling than the fragmentary and confusing terms of masculinity vs. femininity of interests. A further implication is involved in the linguistic-nonlinguistic concept. It seems increasingly possible to show, by statistical processes, that previous attempts to describe individuals and vocations in terms of patterns of field and level of interest and ability were basically sound.

At present, the consideration of this classification in the light of techniques of factorial analysis has three limitations. First, the problem to be solved is limited by the method used. That is, the chief purpose of a factor-analytic method like Thurstone's "centroid analysis" is to account for the primary interest factors in a given number of tests or variables. On the other hand, a Spearman analysis is designed to produce a general factor and one or more specific factors. Thus the nature of the interest factors is determined in part by the factorial method chosen. A second limiting element is that the nature and number of tests used in a factor analysis also partially determine the factors operating and therefore the relationship that can be found. In other words, the more different combinations of related interest tests or other variables that can be used in research, the more interest factors are apt to appear in the study. A third limiting factor would be the population sample chosen. Some interest factors have seemed to transcend populations, while others appear unique to a given sample or population. Thus it can be seen that the factor-analytic method chosen, the variables combined for purposes of investigation, and the population sample will be limitations on the nature and number of interest factors that emerge from a given study.

The factorial studies performed on the *SVIB* and *Kuder* must be considered in light of these statements. The factors which have emerged in studies of the *SVIB* and *Kuder* are a result of the method, the peculiar combination of variables, and the samples used in any given study. They are not necessarily the only factors present, nor are the variables without high "factor loadings" invalid. The interest variables with low or zero factor loadings in one study may have high loadings on new factors when combined with new variables in another study.

An illustration of this would be the factorial analysis of the *Minnesota Multiphasic Personality Inventory (MMPI)*, the *SVIB*, the *Kuder Preference Record: Vocational*, and the *Bell Adjustment Inventory* performed by Cottle (1951). In this study of 400 male veterans, high relationships between the two personality inventories were found, as were high relationships between the two interest inventories. However, little relationship between the personality inventories and interest inventories was found. This would seem to be indicating little overlap between personality and interest inventories. Yet when a sub-sample from this group was selected on a criterion of high vs. low scores on the masculinity-femininity scale of the *MMPI*, significant relationships between certain scales of the interest and personality inventories were found; moreover, these could logically be expected to be related. Thus it would seem that the heterogeneity of the sample of 400 veterans was masking relationships, which were found when a sub-sample was selected on the basis of a criterion that reduced the wide differences by emphasizing a given difference in the sub-sample. Thus, the development of a theory about interests and the evaluation of research into the measurement of interests must be interpreted in view of the limitations of the data and of the methods being used. Failure to substantiate the counselor's hypotheses, developed from empirical evidence, may be a function of the experimental design of the research rather than evidence that such hypotheses cannot be substantiated.

THE EVALUATION OF INTERESTS

The appraisal of an individual's interests provides some of the most important and valuable information for the counseling situation. It should be no surprise, then, to find out that over the past half-century certain psychologists have devoted considerable time and effort to the study of this aspect of personality. Interests are important to achievement. This fact alone makes them almost invaluable to the counselor. In addition, results obtained from interest inventories may motivate students in getting concerned about their educational and vocational future; they may serve as guideposts for the counselor in the counseling interview; and they may provide information that to a great extent explains the social and emotional adjustment of an individual.

In the evaluation of interests, it is most convenient to divide them into two types, general and vocational, and consider the determination of each separately. By *general interests* are meant those related to success in the classroom, the avocational use of spare time, and the individual's over-all development. This separation is purely arbitrary and somewhat artificial, but needed to clarify the discussion.

THE EVALUATION OF GENERAL INTERESTS

General interests are most conveniently evaluated by the use of questionnaires, checklists, the writings of students, and measures of achievement.

The Questionnaire

The interest questionnaire is one of the most useful tools of the counselor. Basically it consists of a series of questions covering such items as the subject or subjects liked most in school and those liked least. Sometimes these questions are followed by others asking the client to give a reason for each answer. Related questions ask the client in which subjects best and poorest grades are or were achieved. If the client is a college student, similar questions are constructed about high-school educational experiences. Other questions may be related to the difficulty that the various subjects offer. Also the client may be asked to indicate which subjects seem most practical and which seem to have no significance in respect to personal educational goals. After the questions on subject matter are exhausted, they can be followed by items related to extracurricular activities. Further information is obtained by questions concerning type of activities, degree, awards, and the like. Following this part of the questionnaire, there are usually items covering such questions as the types of magazines and books that the client reads. Perhaps a client is asked to note the names of a half-dozen books recently read or to list articles read in the magazines. The same sort of questions are asked about newspapers. The reading interest may then be followed by items related to television and radio programs and to the movies.

Interest questionnaires also contain items about the individual's hobbies, spare-time activities, and perhaps study habits. Questions related to the client's future, covering the type of work to be undertaken, responsibilities, and possible future salary, are frequently encountered on these instruments. Actually, what they measure depends upon what the user of the instrument feels is significant in the counseling situation.

The counselor should be aware that an interest questionnaire is an important time saver. There is no reason why the client should be asked all the questions in an interview when they can be obtained from him outside the interview. Questionnaires like these can be completed by the client simultaneously with forms that contain biographical data.

Checklists

Checklists are made up of groups or series of items that cover various types of activities. Topics such as "books," "magazines," "radio and television programs," "extracurricular activities," and the like are included. The constructor of the checklist makes as comprehensive as possible a listing under each of the categories. The client then completes the list by checking the activities in which he engages. It must be emphasized that these responses made by clients may not necessarily be valid. They may be a result of the person's concept of the social desirability of the response. The client knows that it is socially respectable to read magazines or books, to attend concerts, to listen to symphonies, and to read certain of the better magazines, and he may distort his responses accordingly. It is also possible that in some subcultures it is considered socially undesirable or sissified to do certain things or carry on various activities. Rather than depart from the group values and attitudes, certain individuals will not mark various activities in which they engage. These effects can be controlled to a certain extent by not only asking individuals to tell which books or magazine articles are read but also asking them to write a sentence or two describing or summarizing what was read. Sometimes establishing rapport and having the clients understand the use of responses to these items helps.

Another type of checklist was developed for use in the Eight-Year Study (see Smith and Tyler 1942). These items cover the usual academic subjects of the curriculum. In making one of these, the teacher or teachers in the various academic areas may be asked to construct items related to activities in their area. Typically this would result in groupings such as biological sciences, physical sciences and mathematics, literature, music, art, social sciences, and the like. If 15 or 20 items are written in each of these areas, arranged in random order, and assembled into an inventory, a comprehensive checklist of activities related to the academic areas results. Typical of these items are the following: "to write stories," "to make chemical compounds," "to make an insect collection," "to sing in a glee club or choir," and "to take part in a class discussion of literature."

There is no hard-and-fast line which separates checklists from questionnaires. As a matter of fact, many questionnaires are made up in part of checklists, especially in the coverage of reading, listening, and leisure-time activities.

Students' Writings

A very useful technique in obtaining information about interests is by the use of a student's writings, especially those of an autobiographical nature. The general use of this tool was discussed in Chapter 2. When the client is asked to write an autobiography, and an outline is furnished indicating the various points that the counselor wishes covered, such a piece of writing is referred to as "structured." Usually the client is asked to write about hobbies, interests, past employment, and future vocational plans. The last gives not only an indication of the area in which he wants to work, but also an indication of the level of aspiration or motivation.

Achievement

Interests are related to achievement. They are an important aspect of the learning situation. In general, one might conclude that one learns best those activities in which he has an interest.

Downie, in an unpublished study, collected inventoried interest data on the freshman class of a large engineering school. Four years later the members of the class were studied and divided into three groups. One large group, "the successful group," consisted of those who were obtaining their bachelor's degrees in engineering in normal time. The second group consisted of those who were also graduating, but in another school of the same university in which the engineering school was located. The third group was made up of those who had withdrawn voluntarily from school for various reasons other than academic deficiencies. They had not been dropped. The first and third groups consisted of about 300 individuals each, and the second group of about 90 men. It was shown that those who were obtaining degrees in engineering scored significantly higher on the scientific and computational scores of an interest inventory administered to them as freshmen than the others. The students in the second group, most of whom were obtaining degrees in a liberal arts curriculum, scored significantly higher on the literary key of the same inventory. The third group, being much more heterogeneous in composition, had no clear-cut pattern, but there was a trend for them to be high in the mechanical area of the inventory, which has less to do with total requirements of an engineering curriculum. Counselors have noted empirically that engineering students with a high pattern on Group IV of the *SVIB* also tend to drop out of an engineering curriculum.

Unfortunately, the relationship between interests and achievement is complicated (as are all human variables) by the fact that some individuals succeed in a given area in spite of their measured or stated interests. For example, take two college students of equal academic ability, both of whom are taking a required course in freshman chemistry and both of whom are known to have no interest in chemistry. As a matter of fact, their degree of interest may be described as rejection. One obtains an A in both semesters of the course; the other receives an F and three years later may still not have passed the course. Any counselor soon runs into behavior of this type and begins to wonder. Some students are so conditioned as a result of educative and other life processes that, given any academic or learning situation, they tend to perform as they have in other similar situations in the past. If a student sees himself as an A student, he will earn A's in new courses regardless of his interest in them. Other students of equal ability learn or study more selectively. Interests are important to them. Then it follows that personality factors, particularly self-concept, are related to the integrating of interests and achievement. It might be noted that even the A student described here will probably take no more chemistry courses once the required ones are out of the way.

Strong, in his book on the vocational interests of men and women (1943), summarizes a large amount of research on this relationship between academic success and scores on interest inventories. None of this will be repeated here, other than to note that such correlation coefficients are usually low, practically all between −.40 and +.40. The highest positive correlation coefficients were obtained between achievement and scientific and linguistic interests, the negative ones were found in the areas of business and sales interests and in the area referred to as Social Welfare. Strong (1943, p. 528) summarizes as follows:

All this suggests the following hypothesis: If a student has sufficient interest to elect a course, his grade will depend far more on his intelligence, industry, and previous preparation than on his interest. Interests affect the situation, however, in causing the student to elect what he is interested in and not to elect courses in which he is not interested. When a student discovers that he has mistakenly selected a course in which he finds little interest, he will finish it about as well as other courses, but he will not elect further courses of a similar nature. Because of this situation it is difficult to obtain a real measure of the relationship between interest and scholarship, since those with less than a fair amount of interest in the subject seldom take the course at all.

One test, the *Michigan Vocabulary Profile Test* (published by Harcourt, Brace & World, Inc.), has been constructed to measure interests by the method of measuring achievement. This test consists of eight subtests, each made up of 30 items covering human relations, commerce, government, physical sciences, biological sciences, mathematics, fine arts, and sports. The rationale of the test is that a high score on any one of the subtests indicates an interest in that area. Not many studies have been published using this test and those that have, as might be expected in the light of the previous discussion, have not demonstrated too well the validity of such a concept.

THE EVALUATION OF VOCATIONAL INTERESTS

By far the largest amount of research and publication in the area of interests has been done in relation to vocational interests, and most of this has been related to the *Strong Vocational Interest Blank*. Other major inventories in use today are the various forms of the *Kuder* inventories (published by Science Research Associates), the *Minnesota Vocational Interest Inventory* (The Psychological Corporation), the *Occupational Interest Inventory* (California Test Bureau), and the *Allport-Vernon-Lindzey Study of Values* (Houghton Mifflin Company).

The Strong Vocational Interest Blanks

The *Strong Vocational Interest Inventories* consist of 400, 399, or 398 items which the client marks like *L*, dislike *D*, or indifferent *I*. The scale consists of eight parts: (I) Occupations; (II) School subjects (from algebra to zoology); (III) Amusements; (IV) Activities (such as repairing a clock, writing reports, and methodical work); (V) Peculiarities of people (progressive people, pessimists, foreigners); (VI) Order of preference of activities (selecting from sets of ten activities the three that would be enjoyed most and the three that would be enjoyed least); (VII) Comparison of interests between two items (outside work vs. inside work); and (VIII) Rating of present abilities and characteristics ("Am quite sure of myself," "Am approachable," and "Win friends easily"). There is a form for men and a form for women. Most of the research has been carried out using the men's form, and all that follows will pertain to that form unless otherwise stated. The women's blank will be discussed later.

The *Manuals* (Strong 1945, 1959, 1966; Campbell 1969) note that, since changes in interests are considerable between the ages of 15 and 20 as shown by research experience, the inventory should not be used with individuals who are less than 17 unless they are especially mature. Because of their youth, the interest scores of males under 20 are apt to be lower than they will be 5 or 10 years later. Darley and Hagenah (1955) state that the inventory can be used with ninth and tenth grade students with I.Q.'s of 105 or more. Forbes and Cottle (1953) showed that the average reading difficulty level of the *Strong*, based upon five techniques of measuring reading difficulty, was 11.4, and that on the Forbes' formula devised specifically for standardized tests, the readability level was college sophomore. This indicates that the vocabulary of the inventory is too difficult for a large part of the high-school population. For responses to be valid, the individual has to know terms like "psychology," "physiology," and "physics." The same is true for the various occupations such as social worker, labor arbitrator, and civil engineer. There are many in high school who do not know what these occupations are. The writers feel that this instrument is best used with sophisticated, bright upperclassmen in high school and with university students and adults.

At the present time, the 1938 *SVIB* is scored for more than 40 different occupational keys and for 3 non-occupational scales (see Form 9.1).

In the 1966 revision, the Interest maturity scale has been dropped "because it has consistently failed to hold up in validity studies (Strong 1966, p. 52)," and a Specialization scale and Academic achievement scale have been added. Optional scoring may also be secured on a Social introversion-extroversion scale. What scales and what editions are used depend somewhat upon the counseling needs in a given setting. Hand scoring of the older forms is difficult and laborious, because a separate key has to be used for each of these scales and because the responses to each item are weighted from +4 to −4 in the light of which of the 3 possible responses the client made. At the present time, to avoid scoring these tests by hand, or locally with scoring machines, the completed blanks are sent to centers that have an electronic scorer capable of scoring and printing the results very rapidly. Hankes' Testscor and National

Computer Systems in Minneapolis and the Measurement Research Center in Iowa City are examples of such centers.

Results are recorded in letter grades, A through C. Strong (1943, 1959) states that a letter grade of A means that the individual has the interests of individuals successfully engaged in that occupation. The rating of C means that individuals do not have such interests. The other ratings, B+, B and B−, mean that the person probably has those interests but that one cannot be certain. Scores of A include just under 70% of the norm group, the B ratings about 26% of the norm group, and the C scores, the remainder (Strong 1943, p. 66). A *T*-score of 40, which is the beginning of the B+ range, is achieved by 82% of the criterion group in each occupation, 97% in the occupation score above the middle of the shaded or chance area. (See Figure 9.1 on the 1938 form. Other forms used in reporting results observed with the SVIB are shown in Figures 9.2, 9.3, and 9.4.)

In setting up the keys for the various occupations, Strong placed those items in a key for a specific occupation that significantly separated successful men in that occupation from "professional men-in-general." Success was defined as earning a certain salary per year, length of experience in the occupation, level of training, and the like. "Men-in-general" has meant several things to Strong. At first it meant all the other successful professional men who completed the blank but who were not considered in the group for whom the key was being made. The 1938 form was revised to include a fair representation of business and professional men earning $2,500 and above per year in the later 1930's. (Today's equivalent would be considerably higher.) A client, then, who receives an A rating for a specific occupation such as physician has responded to the items as successful physicians did in Strong's sample.

In the 1966 revision, "men-in-general" really means professional and businessmen tested on the SVIB between 1925 to 1965, whose responses have been applied to the 291 common items and used as the point of reference for differentiating the responses of each criterion group. The criterion groups for the 1966 revision are described in Strong (1966, pp. 56–64).

The counselor should become familiar as rapidly as possible with the SVIB profile sheets that will be used in his agency—such as that shown in Figures 9.1, 9.2, 9.3, and 9.4. Occupations are arranged in groups based upon the correlations among interest scores of the different occupations (Strong 1945). In daily usage these different groups are referred to by special names, such as I, Scientific; II, Technical; V, Social Welfare; VIII, Business Detail; IX, Business Contact; and X, Linguistic.

At the bottom of Figure 9.1 are the three non-occupational scales. The first of these is known as the Interest-Maturity or *IM* scale. Strong (1943) defined this as the quantitative measurement of the differences in inter-

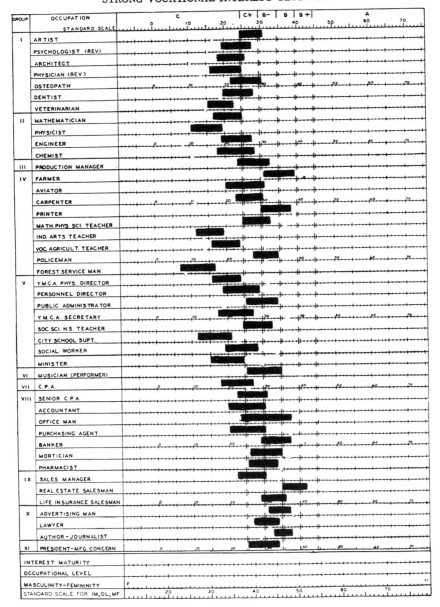

Used by permission of Testscor, Inc.

Figure 9.1

PROFILE SHEET FOR THE *STRONG VOCATIONAL INTEREST BLANK: MEN,* 1938 EDITION

Name .... Age .... Date .... Agency or school .... Case no. ....

Group	Occupation	Raw Score	Standard Score	C					B—	B	B+		A			
				0	5	10	15	20	25	30	35	40	45	50	55	60	65
I	Artist															
	Psychologist (rev.)															
	Architect															
	Physician (rev.)															
	Psychiatrist															
	Osteopath															
	Dentist															
	Veterinarian															
II	Physicist															
	Chemist															
	Mathematician															
	Engineer															
III	Production Manager															
IV	Farmer															
	Carpenter															
	Printer															
	Math. Sci. Teacher															
	Policeman															
	Forest Service															
	Army Officer															
	Aviator															
V	Y.M.C.A. Phys. Dir.															
	Personnel Manager															
	Public Administrator															
	Vocational Counselor															
	Y.M.C.A. Secretary															
	Soc. Sci. Teacher															
	City School Supt.															
	Minister															
VI	Musician															
VII	C.P.A. Partner															
VIII	Senior C.P.A.															
	Junior Accountant															
	Office Worker															
	Purchasing Agent															
	Banker															
	Mortician															
	Pharmacist															
IX	Sales Manager															
	Real Estate Slsmn.															
	Life Insurance Slsmn.															
X	Advertising Man															
	Lawyer															
	Author-Journalist															
XI	President															
	Occupational Level															
	Masculinity-Femininity															
	Specialization Level															
	Interest Maturity															

Reprinted with permission.

Figure 9.2

EXAMPLE OF THE MEASUREMENT RESEARCH CENTER TAB CARD REPORT: 1938. *STRONG VOCATIONAL INTEREST BLANK: MEN*

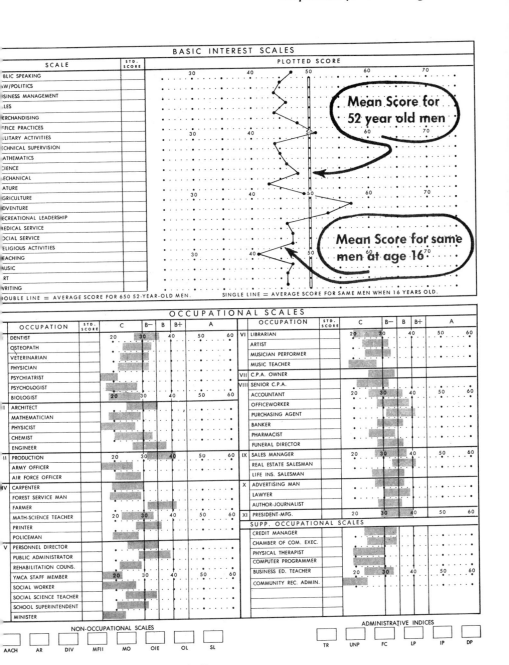

Used by permission of Stanford University Press.

Figure 9.3

PROFILE OF *STRONG VOCATIONAL INTEREST BLANK: MEN* (T399), 1969 REVISION

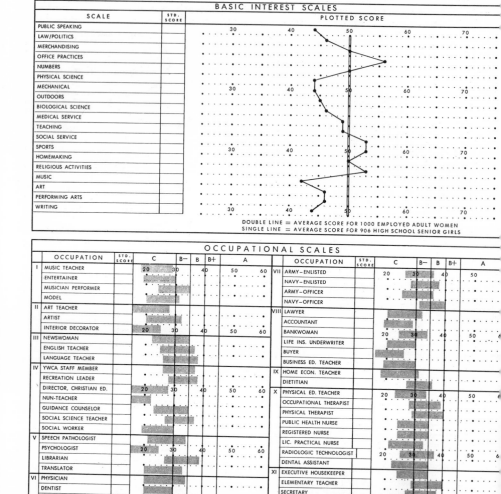

Used by permission of Stanford University Press.

Figure 9.4

PROFILE OF *STRONG VOCATIONAL INTEREST BLANK:*
WOMEN (TW398), 1969

ests of 15-year-old boys in contrast to men between the ages of 23 and 27. Darley and Hagenah (1955, p. 45) concluded that the *IM* scale is "not a clear index of growth or change of interest patterns; it is, however, a possible index of general maturity of outlook." Research by Rhodes (1956) on effect of response set indicates that high *IM* scores are a function of the preponderance of like responses over dislikes. Counseling experience has shown that a high score is most closely associated with Group V and an interest in the social sciences. As noted previously the *IM* scale has been dropped in the 1966 revision.

The second non-occupational scale is the Occupational Level or *OL* scale. Strong originally described this as a scale that contrasted the interests of unskilled men with those of business and professional men earning $2,500 per year and up. Darley (1941) indicated that this scale gave a measure of a man's level of aspiration, "the degree to which the individual's total background has prepared him to seek the prestige and discharge the responsibilities growing out of high income, professional status, recognition, or leadership in the community." Kendall (1947), Gustad (1952), and Ostrom (1949*a*, *b*) have shown the relationship of the *OL* scale to achievement in the university, to staying power in school, and to interest patterns in certain areas. Gustad (1954) showed that primary interests (see below) in the verbal-linguistic fields were associated with high *OL* scores, whereas low *OL* scores went along with primary interest patterns in the technical fields. Rhodes has shown that these occupational differences are at least partially a function of tendency to respond with "like" or "dislike," respectively (1956). Darley and Hagenah (1955) report that the highest *OL* scores were associated with primary interest patterns in the business contact and linguistic areas, next in size those in the biological and physical sciences. Primary patterns in the social service and business detail areas had *OL* scales at the mean (50). Primary interest patterns in the technical area had a mean *OL* score of 43, considerably below the mean on the scale itself. Barnett *et al.* (1952) and Barnett, Stewart, and Super (1953) reported studies which tended to cloud the picture somewhat. However, the evidence seems to point out that this index is a useful and meaningful one, showing a client's level of aspiration when the score is either high or low and when interpreted in the light of differences among the various occupational groups.

Carkhuff and Drasgow (1963), in a summary of research on the *OL* scale, indicated that the most logical interpretation was that it represented the socioeconomic level of the respondent's interests. Actually, observation in a counseling situation indicates that high scores on Occupational Level are achieved by marking few items in the Indifferent category and are associated with high scores in managerial, sales, and promotional occupations.

The third special key is referred to as the Masculinity-Femininity or *MF* scale. As originally determined by Strong, its purpose was to separate the interests of men and women. Darley (1941) described masculinity-femininity as "a continuum based upon the extent to which an individual's attention is held by technical, depersonalized, manipulative, concrete activities or objects in his environment (masculinity) or by cultural, aesthetic, personalized, symbolic, appreciative activities or objects, in his environment (femininity)." Darley and Hagenah (1955) showed that high *MF* scores on the men's blank were obtained by individuals whose primary interest pattern was in either Technical or Physical Science areas; those whose primary interest patterns were in Business Detail and Business Contact had *MF* scores just below the mean; and those with primary patterns in the Biological Sciences were below the mean. Individuals with patterns in either the Social Service or Linguistic areas were considerably below the mean on the *MF* scale.

The criterion group for the *MF* scale in the 1966 revision has a mean of 50 ± 10. In the *Manual* (1966, p. 19), Strong states, "A random sample of 100 women from the original female group had a mean of 30.7 and a standard deviation of 7.6; overlap with the men was 27%."

In summary, masculine interests, which might better be called non-linguistic interests, reflect an interest in things and processes. Most typically the interests of the engineer or mechanic are of this type. On the other hand, feminine or linguistic interests are associated with an interest in people and attempts at communication, such as written or spoken verbal activities. Clergymen, counselors, clinical psychologists, and poets have typically "feminine" interests. The counselor should note that this continuum of interest, as now defined, has nothing to do with the *physical* dichotomy of sex. Males may have feminine interests and females may have masculine interests. Sexual deviation or abnormality is *not* the personality aspect measured by this scale. Graphically, the dimension has two overlapping distributions, one for each sex, ranging from masculinity to femininity, the most feminine males overlapping in score the distribution of the most masculine females (Figure 9.5).

Two new non-occupational scales have been included in the 1966 *SVIB:Men*. One is a Specialization scale *(SL)* developed from the work of Strong and Tucker (1952), differentiating specialties in medicine from a reference group of "physicians-in-general." It is interpreted as a tendency to narrow one's interests through advanced study in a specialized area (usually graduate work). Stewart (1964) has discussed it in detail.

The other new non-occupational scale, Academic Achievement *(AACH)*, attempts to predict grades and success in school (Strong 1966, p. 19).

Darley (1941) described the patterns used in evaluating interests on the Strong inventory. A primary pattern is one in which a preponderance

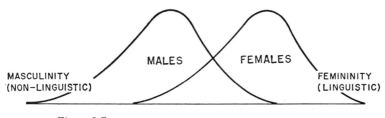

Figure 9.5

OVERLAP OF INTERESTS BETWEEN THE TWO SEXES

of A and B+ scores occur within an interest group. For example, an A in both Social worker and Social science high school teacher and a B+ in Personnel director would constitute a primary pattern as all three are Group V, the Social Welfare area. Secondary patterns are made up of a preponderance of B+ and B scores in a group, and tertiary patterns are composed of primarily B and B— scores. Rejection patterns exist when the preponderance of scores for a given grouping of interests fall to the left of the chance area on the profile sheet. On Form 9.1, the chance area for each occupation is blackened. Any score falling in this blackened area could have been this high by chance alone. A score to the left of the area is known as a rejection. For an individual to obtain a score in this part of the sheet he has to reject definitely the activities related to the given occupation. Only 3% of the men in a given occupational criterion group score below the middle of the shaded area. Thus, a score below the shaded area is quite unlike that of most persons in the given occupation. The alert counselor regards scores on this side of the profile sheet as of equal importance with significant scores to the right of the darkened area. Too often, rejection scores are overlooked.

Hagenah reports (Darley and Hagenah 1955) the result of analyzing the *SVIB* profiles of 1,000 freshmen at the University of Minnesota. She found that 193, or 19.3% of these students, had no primary interest pattern, 410 had a single primary interest pattern, 303 had two or a double primary pattern, 88 had three or a triple pattern, and 3 individuals had four primary patterns. In a similar analysis of secondary patterns, 260 were found to have no secondary pattern, 429 a single, 234 a double, and 42 a triple secondary pattern. In terms of patterns of rejection, 64 individuals had no rejection pattern, 399 had two, 251 had three, and 47 had four rejection patterns. In a further analysis of the same data, Hagenah reports the simultaneous occurrence of primary and secondary patterns, primary and rejection patterns, different types of primary patterns, different secondary patterns, and different rejection patterns. The counselor will find that this use of patterns is most helpful in explaining the results of the inventory to the client. Hagenah's work also points up the fact that there are many students who have no primary interests and that some are also without any secondary ones. Some beginning counselors are startled the first time that this situation appears in a real case. A similar study dealing with superior students is reported by Stewart (1959).

Methods are needed for handling patterns or profiles of individuals and of groups in research with interest and personality inventories. Cronbach and Gleser (1953) discuss the problems involved in such an approach. They stress the point that one method will provide one part of the answer and that another method will provide another part. So far there is no simple way to substantiate clinical subliminal cues about this area of pattern analysis. The present systems for handling profiles on the *SVIB* do not include ways of showing both similarity in profiles and differences in height between the profiles at the same time.

In the case of the *SVIB*, it is the pattern of high and low occupational and non-occupational scores together which helps differentiate curricular or occupational choices. A high score on the Production manager scale, along with high scores on other managerial scales and a moderate masculine pattern on the non-occupational scales, may be pointing toward the technical aspects of factory management, while a low score on the Production manager scale, high scores on other managerial scales, and a feminine pattern on the non-occupational scales may point toward the personal contact aspects of business management. High occupational scores on scales for Engineer, Chemist, and Sales manager may be pointing toward technical sales in chemical engineering, while high scores on the scales for Engineer and Chemist, and low scores on the Business contact and Business detail scales may be pointing toward research aspects of chemical engineering. (It should be noted that many other data are considered with a given client and that his choices are not made on *SVIB* scores alone.) This illustrates why the combination of acceptance *and* rejection, or like *and* dislike, is important in interpreting the total pattern.

As noted earlier, much research has been carried on using this interest inventory. Strong and his students have been instrumental in doing a large amount of this work. Strong (1953, 1955) reported on a study that began in 1930 when a group of Stanford University freshmen were administered his inventory. In 1949, a follow-up study was made of these same freshmen, the inventory readministered, and their occupations at that time studied. Strong reported that half of these students continued in the occupation of their early choice, 30% changed to an occupation correlating .71 to .00 with their original choice, and 20% changed to an occupation quite unrelated to their original choice (correlation of −.01 to −.71). This can be transformed into a validity coefficient of .69. He further notes that at the age of 18.7 years, half of these freshmen had selected an occupation that they finally entered—or one very close to it. From this he infers that many must have made their vocational choice while in high school; thus, it follows that vocational counseling is a necessity in any high school. Those who changed their occupations did not select an occupation with as high prestige value as those who did not change. Also, individuals who changed their occupation to occupations correlating from .71 to −.71 with their original choices scored lower both in 1930 and in 1949 on their average interest score than those students who either did not change or who changed to a very closely related occupation.

In another study, Stordahl (1954) considered the results obtained from testing and retesting a group of metropolitan and nonmetropolitan boys with a time gap of 2 to 2.5 years between the administrations. He found a high relationship between their scores on the two testings, the over-all average for both groups being in the low .70's. On examining the letter ratings, he found that the C's were the most stable, 68% of the C's on the first testing being C's on the second. The A's were next, 60% being the same from test to test. The intermediate letter ratings were less stable. In the same research he studied the permanence of the different interest patterns. Again he found that the extremes were the most permanent, 58% of the primary patterns and 81% of the "no patterns" being identical on the retest. Counselors should note, then, that clients should be informed that intermediate scores on the *SVIB* can move in either direction on a retest, but that the extreme scores are apt to change very little. It would be highly unusual for a rejection to become a score like those of successful persons in a given occupation and vice versa.

In another study conducted with students at Yale, Trinkaus (1954) studied a group first tested in 1935–1936 and then retested in 1950, approximately 15 years later. His results were very similar to those obtained by Strong with Stanford students. Specifically, he found that A and C scores were more stable than B scores, and that, of the first two, the more stable were the C's. From this he concluded that the counselor should pay more attention to extreme scores and that he should place more confidence in the stability of the low ones than in the high ones. He also noted that the B scores are more safely interpreted as an indication of future weakening rather than strengthening of an interest in a specific occupation.

In another study, Powers (1954) reported an average correlation of .69 on the vocational scale for a group of 109 individuals tested in 1931 and again in 1941. McArthur (1954, 1955) studied 63 Harvard men who were tested first in 1939 and again in 1953, after a 14-year interval. In general his results confirm those of other studies, with the exception that the *SVIB* was of considerably less value in prediction when used with boys from private schools than with graduates of public schools. He suggests that his study and many others, mostly unreported, offer evidence that private-school graduates have values and needs that differ considerably from those of public-school graduates. Campbell (1966) has presented evidence of the stability of interests within an occupation over a 30-year period.

Cottle (1968, pp. 33–35) has discussed the possible results of response set in interpreting the *SVIB:M:*

> Recent research has focused attention on the amount of response set involved in the score on scales of various inventories. Fredericksen (1965, p. 240) says, "Interpretations of the correlations of set scores with inventory scores are thus confused not only by possible confounding of set and content in inventory scores but also by different possible cause and effect relationships and by different possible perceptions of what is desirable." One way to explore response set on the *SVIB* is to mark three separate answer sheets: one all *Like,* one all *Indifferent,* and one all *Dislike.* If this is done for the *SVIB:M,* it produces the scores shown below. Only the significantly high (T = 40 or more) and low (T = 10 or less) scores are shown for the *SVIB:M* marked all *Like:*

High		Low
Osteopath	Mortician	Artist
Production manager	Pharmacist	Mathematician
Math. phys. sci. tchr.	Life ins. salesman	Physicist
Printer	Int. maturity	
Policeman	Occup. level	
YMCA phys. director	Specialization level	
Personnel director	Masculinity-femininity	
Public administrator	(Sales manager and Real	
YMCA secretary	estate salesman are	
H.S. soc. sci. tchr.	just below the sig.	
Social worker	level)	
Minister		
Senior CPA		
Accountant		
Office manager		

It is difficult to perceive whether this result of marking all items *Like* is just a function of the construction of the *SVIB:M* or an actual part of a series of patterns for those occupations marked "High." Perhaps an occupational characteristic of men in these occupations is to like more things than they dislike. The concern of the counselor at this point is to know what proportion of responses on the answer sheet were marked *L.* From this he can see how much effect this response set had in helping to produce any of the acceptable interest scores listed "High" above. Not enough research has been done to know whether it is possible to get high scores on those occupational scales without a preponderance of *Like* responses.

When an *SVIB:M* answer sheet is marked all *Indifferent,* the following results occur:

High		Low
Farmer	Forest service	Pres. mfg. concern
Aviator	YMCA secretary	
Carpenter	H.S. soc. sci. tchr.	
Printer	Musician performer	
Math. phys. sci. tchr.	Senior CPA	
Voc. ag. tchr.	Office manager	
Policeman	Interest maturity	
	Masculinity-femininity	

Again, it is important for the counselor to know the proportion of *Indifferent* responses in order to estimate the effect of this response set on scores in the occupational groups listed above.

When an *SVIB:M* answer sheet is marked all *Dislike*, the following results appear:

High	Low	
Real estate salesman	Psychologist	Forest service
Advertising man	Veterinarian	All Group V occupations
Lawyer	Aviator	Senior CPA
Author-journalist	Carpenter	Accountant
Pres. mfg. concern	Printer	Office manager
Occupational level	Policeman	
(Just below sig. level are	Math. phys. sci. tchr.	
Architect, Life ins. sales-	Industrial arts tchr.	
man, Specialization level,	Voc. ag. tchr.	
Interest maturity, and	Policeman	
Masculinity-femininity.)		

It can be seen from the results above that marking *SVIB:M* items all *Dislike*, in converse to the other two responses, produces more low scores than high scores, particularly in Groups IV and V. The high scores occur in Groups IX, X, XI, and Occupational level.

Counselors have wondered why so many *SVIB:M* profiles show high scores for Printer, Policeman, H.S. math. sci. tchr., H.S. soc. sci. tchr., Senior CPA, Office man, Interest maturity, and Masculinity-femininity. The results reported indicate this probably occurs because of a preponderance of *Like* and *Indifferent* responses over *Dislike* responses. The occupational scales listed as having high scores from either *L* or *I* responses are also the ones with the highest chance-score possibility (shaded area on the profile). While Farmer and Real estate salesman are not in this list, they do have high chance-score possibilities, real estate salesman probably because any preponderance of *L* and *D* responses produces a high score. It appears then that this response set result explains the majority of high "chance scores" on the *SVIB:M*. In like manner, few *Indifferent* responses may produce high scores on Real estate salesman, Life ins. salesman, and Occupational level. Almost any combination of *L*, *I*, and *D* responses seems to produce a high score on Specialization level and may account for the limited use this scale has had.

The *SVIB:M* scales where a high score is *not* produced by response set in any one direction and therefore are probably true occupational scores are: Psychologist, Physician, Dentist, Veterinarian, Mathematician, Physicist, Engineer, Chemist, City school superintendent, and Purchasing agent.

It is not known yet how these data on response sets apply to the 1966 and 1969 revisions.

In addition to the material presented previously about the 1966 revision of the *SVIB:Men,* the following points should be noted:

1. The scoring weights have been changed from +4 to −4, to +1 to −1. This makes it easier to hand-score the blank if an error is suspected.
2. The shaded or chance area on the profile has been changed so that it now represents the middle third of the professional men-in-general score distribution.
3. The scales are a mixture of the old criterion groups and new groups, and the counselor using the blank needs to study these carefully to know which are which.
4. About 20 items appear to produce different responses today than they did 30 years ago (Strong 1966, p. 52). This produces somewhat different criterion group scores and higher scores on the more recently added scales.
5. Although the percentage of overlap is somewhat higher between criterion groups and the professional men-in-general group, the separation between criterion groups is claimed to be better.
6. Campbell *et al.* (1967) have explored the possibility of area scales like those of the *MVII* (basic interest scales) and have added them to the T399 and TW398 profiles.

All of this research conducted with the *SVIB* suggests that it is a valid instrument when used with the groups for which it was developed. When compared to other psychometric devices such as intelligence tests, it holds up excellently, and from the viewpoint of stability and prediction it fares even better. There is no question that the *Strong Vocational Interest Blank* is one of the best and most useful instruments the counselor uses. However, considerably more empirical evidence is needed before research on the 1938 form can be applied to the 1966 and 1969 revisions.

The Strong Vocational Interest Blank for Women

The *SVIB:Women* is very similar in both its make-up and scoring to the men's form. It differs in that there are keys for a smaller number of occupations and in that, of the non-occupational keys, only the F–M scale is present in the 1938 form. A high score on this scale means femininity for women and a low score is a masculine score. This is the reverse of the M–F scale for men. In the 1969 revision of the women's blank, the F–MII scale is reversed (a high score is masculinity), and Academic Achievement (*AACH*), Diversity of Interests (*DIV*), and Occupational Introversion-Extroversion (*OIE*) scales have been added. The use of this inventory has varied considerably from place to place. Strong recommends that women be tested only with the women's blank.

Since there is some evidence (Seder 1940, Stewart 1959) that the vocational interests of successful professional women do not differ greatly from those of successful men, women are administered the men's blank in some counseling centers. In others women are administered both blanks, the men's blank with its additional scoring keys acting as a supplement to the women's blank. Most of the earlier research done with the *SVIB* has been done with the men's blank. In the eyes of some counselors this is a very important reason for using it in preference to the women's. There is a complicating factor in the women's blank in that the housewife scale correlates high with nurse, elementary school teacher, office worker, and stenographer, the coefficients ranging from .59 to .80. Factor analyses of this form has led Super (1949) to conclude that there is a home-vs.-career factor present, most strongly related to the housewife scale, negatively related to various careers for women, and not found in similar factor analyses of the men's blank. The old problem of the woman's being a housewife or a career woman is involved with the use of this form of the *SVIB*, and this tends to lower the usefulness of the women's blank in appraising the vocational interests of women as compared to the effectiveness of the men's blank with males.

Related to this is the evidence on response set patterns discussed by Cottle (1968, pp. 35–37) in material on the *SVIB:W* similar to that discussed above for the *SVIB:M*. He says that:

Similar results occur when the *SVIB:W* answer sheet is marked all *L, I,* or *D*. For example, marking all items *Like* has the following results:

High		Low
Social worker	Home econ. tchr.	Librarian
Lawyer	Dietician	
Housewife	Nurse	
Elem. tchr.	Lab. technician	
Office worker	Physical therapist	
Stenog.-sec.	Femininity-masculinity	
Bus. ed. tchr.		

When all items are marked *Indifferent,* the following results appear:

High		Low
Housewife	Math.-sci. tchr.	Author
Office worker	Lab. technician	
Stenog.-sec.	Physical therapist	
Bus. ed. tchr.	Engineer	
Phys. ed. tchr.	Femininity-masculinity	
Occupational therapist		

When all items are marked *Dislike*, it produces the following:

High	Low
Artist	Social worker
Author	Soc. sci. tchr.
Librarian	YWCA secretary
Physician	Home econ. tchr.
Femininity-masculinity	Phys. ed. tchr. (coll.)
	Occupational therapist
	Nurse
	Musician, tchr.
	Physical therapist
	Engineer

The *SVIB:W* scales which show high scores *not* affected by a preponderance of any one response are:

English teacher	Buyer
Psychologist	Dentist
Soc. sci. tchr.	Musician, tchr.
YWCA sec.	Musician, performer
Life ins. saleswoman	

Counselors have wondered why most women get high scores on Housewife, Office worker, Stenographer-secretary, and Business education teacher. The terms "prior-to-marriage occupations," "general feminine interests," and "non-career occupations" [Super] have been used to explain that these are temporary occupations for many women. The real explanation of these frequent high scores for most women is the preponderance of any combination of *Like* and *Indifferent* responses over *Dislike* responses. The same condition produces high scores on Laboratory technician and Physical therapist, while a preponderance of *Dislike* and *Indifferent* responses over *Like* responses produces a high score on the femininity pole of the Femininity-masculinity Scale.

Obviously no one answers these inventories all *L*, all *I*, or all *D*, but if the counselor is to make any interpretation of the scores on scales affected by such a response set tendency he must know the proportion of *L*, *I*, and *D* responses among the total number of items. *This count of each kind of possible response should be made a standard part of the scoring of all personality and interest inventories.* [It has been made part of the scoring of T399 and TW398 and is shown on 1969 profiles for those inventories.]

Limited attempts at pattern analysis have been made with the women's *SVIB*. In general there is a tendency for counselors to expect women to score high on the scales in the middle of the profile (Housewife, Elementary school teacher, Office worker, Stenographer-secretary, and Business education teacher). More important vocationally are clusters of scores in the linguistic occupations toward the top of the profile, or clusters of scores in the nonlinguistic occupations toward the bottom of the profile. Usually the women's *SVIB* is used with some other measure of interests in order to get further clarification and a sort of cross-validation. *The Kuder Preference Record: Vocational* is one of these other measures.

The Kuder Preference Record: Vocational, Form C, and The Kuder General Interest Survey, Form E

The Kuder interest inventories published by Science Research Associates are made up of approximately 500 items representing all types of interests arranged in a set of three or triad like the following:

1. A. Design bird houses .... ( )
   B. Sell bird houses .... ( )
   C. Live in bird houses .... ( )

The client goes through the inventory, selecting from each three the one liked most and the one liked least. This provides six possible scoring combinations for each triad. Since some of the activities require special training, the respondent is to assume ability to do any of the listed activities. In every case a choice must be made, even when all are liked or disliked equally. Males and females use the same inventory, but different norms and profiles are available for each sex. There are two forms of the inventory, *CM* or *EM*, in which the responses are placed on an answer sheet for scoring with the IBM scoring machine, and *CH* or *EH* which uses the pin-punch method of scoring. In an attempt to enhance the validity of the instrument, a list of words and phrases is printed on the back of the direction page defining words and phrases that might be unfamiliar to the client. Appearing here are such words as "data," "psychologists," "erosion," "linoleum block," and the like.

Scores are reported for ten areas of human activities: Outdoor, Mechanical, Computational, Scientific, Persuasive, Artistic, Literary, Musical, Social Service, and Clerical. In addition to these there is a Verification or *V* score which is acceptable when it is within the range of 38 to 44. If it is higher than 44, it means that the client has marked or punched too many answers, since the highest possible score is 44. When the *V* score falls between 33 and 37, this is considered to be within the doubtful range, and questions should be asked to determine whether the respondent understood the directions, has difficulty in reading, answered the items carelessly, or actually has interests that are different from others. A score of 32 or less, according to Kuder (1956, 1964), reflects a number of omissions or otherwise indicates reason to doubt the value of the answers given. It is recommended that the inventory be readministered, emphasizing the importance of following directions carefully.

The counselor will find the *Kuder* useful in describing *areas* or *fields* of general activity with two types of clients—the young individual who has made little or no decision about his vocational choice, and the individual who has made a choice and wishes some means of verifying it. In the latter case, cross-validation against the *SVIB* is often done in terms of scores on the *SVIB* group keys. Scoring of the inventory is very easy, so easy that often the subject is allowed to score the answer sheet and to plot the profile on the blanks provided. In scoring the *Kuder*, the answer pad is opened and the number of pinholes appearing in small circles are counted for each key. These raw scores are then entered on the profile sheet. Of course, this method of scoring can be used only when the pin-punch answer sheet is used. Very conveniently, the filling out of the *Kuder* takes about one class period. The next period that the client has free can be spent in scoring and profiling the results.

Any score at the 75th centile or higher is taken as evidence of a significant interest in a particular area. The *Manual* contains a list of suggested occupations for each of the areas of interest. These lists are arranged from the professional occupations down to the unskilled ones. Suppose that a boy has a high score on the Outdoor key. In the *Manual* he will find a list of suggested occupations, which he might learn more about from a library of occupational information or some other source. Frequently a client has two or more significant high scores; there are suggested occupations for combinations of interests also. But these are limited and rather naïve suggestions which deal only with the meaning of high scores.

To take into account Fryer's suggestion of acceptance-rejection patterns, the counselor should also pay special attention to scores that are below the 25th centile. These are the so-called rejection scores, and for an individual to obtain such a score it is necessary to mark items related to a particular area of vocational interest "dislike" every time that one of these items appears. A knowledge of what an individual dislikes is just as important as those things that are liked. These are interpreted in terms of patterns of high *and* low scores. An example is the tendency of engineers to score high on computational and scientific scales and low on the literary scale. Another example is the tendency for people in business contact work to score high on persuasive and low on scientific scales. The counselor will also find that there are individuals who have no significant high or low points. When the profile is made up of scores all of which are near the middle, probably the best conclusion is that the interests of the client are not yet developed. The counselor should suggest a retest in a year or so. Kuder (1956) also suggests that one may encounter a rare individual whose interests are equally balanced in all ten fields. He also notes that a profile of no peaks may be that of an individual whose interests are in the field of personal service or manual labor. Figure 9.6 shows a *Kuder* Form *C* profile.

The development of this instrument was quite different from that of the *SVIB*. It may be recalled that Strong used criterion groups of successful individuals in different occupations. Items which separated these individuals in one occupation from professional men-in-general went to make up the key for that specific occupation. In the various forms of the *Kuder*, the author built items and then constructed keys on the basis of item-analysis results. The first key that Kuder developed was a literary key. This was named from the content of the items. After scoring a group of papers with this key, an item analysis was made. Those items which correlated significantly with the literary scores were kept for the literary key; those that did not were further treated and analyzed until a series of almost pure scales was developed. As a result of the procedure described there are ten scales which, by construction, are internally similar and not highly related to each other.

Research carried on with the *Kuder* since World War II has been considerable. The current edition of the *Manual* lists well over 200 articles reporting such research. Any attempt to summarize these here would be pointless. That this inventory has both reliability and validity cannot be doubted in the light of many of these studies and of counseling experience with it. Studies have shown that the *Kuder* and *SVIB*, administered to the same individuals, frequently produce similar results. However, it might be noted that the *Kuder* has a reading level much lower than the *SVIB*—8.7 vs. 11.4 (Forbes and Cottle 1953). It also, unlike the *SVIB*, is not geared to professional workers or the groups just below. That is, it covers a much wider range of occupational activities.

Form *E*, the *Kuder General Interest Survey,* published in 1964, is intended for use in the junior high-school. It has the same scales as Form *C*, the *Kuder Preference Record: Vocational (KPR:V)*, but there are more items in each scale and thus more reliability. The level of reading difficulty of the items is about sixth-grade. Like Form *C*, Form *E* has a validation scale called the Verification scale. The Verification scale is constructed on the assumption that the respondent's answers will resemble random answers if he is careless, fails to understand the test, or attempts to mark what he considers ideal or socially desirable responses. Kuder (1964, p. 16) says the scale consists of activities that "people in general, responding sincerely, tend *not* to select," even though these activities tend to be socially desirable. The Verification score for Form *E* is a score lower than 14. The mean of the chance scores is reported as 24.67, and the standard deviation is 4.06. Reliabilities for Form *E* are reported separately for males and females. They range from .70 to .94, with the median for boys reported as .81 in grade 6 and .86 in grade 7, while that

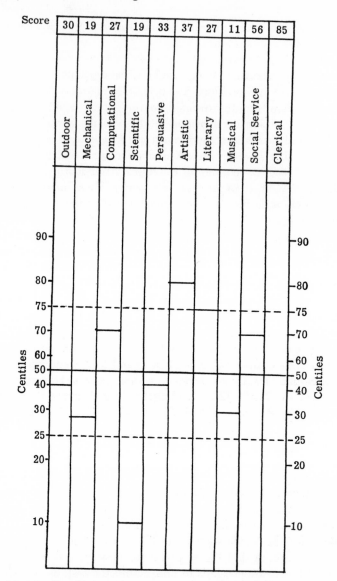

Adapted and used by permission of G. F. Kuder, Copyright, 1951.

Figure 9.6

KUDER PREFERENCE RECORD: VOCATIONAL;
PROFILE FOR A FEMALE

for girls is .87 in grade 6 and .86 in grade 7. The reliabilities reported for senior high-school students are somewhat higher.

The *Kuder*, then, is quite useful in dealing with junior and senior high-school students, particularly those planning to go to work upon completion of high school or earlier. It can be used just when these young people are beginning to pay attention to work and their future. Over the high-school years, the instrument may be used several times to measure growth and development in vocational interests. It is also useful with adults, such as hard-core unemployed who would have no use for the information covered by the *SVIB*. Forms *C* and *E* of the *Kuder* are among the counselor's most basic tools.

Form *D*, the *Kuder Occupational Interest Survey* (*KOIS*), was published in 1956 (Kuder 1966). The original Form *D* is only used now when the answer sheets are to be hand-scored; otherwise, Form *DD* is used. Form *D* or *DD*, unlike other forms of the *Kuder* which are based on interest in fields of *activities*, deals with comparisons of vocational activities or preferences among *occupational groups* with an approach similar to that of the *SVIB*. That is, separate scores for specific occupations are provided instead of the general area keys. Here any similarity to the *SVIB* ends. Construction, scoring, and interpretation of scores in terms of occupational criterion groups and groups in various college curricula (majors) are quite different. The *KOIS:DD* uses 100 triadic items dealing with 17 areas of activity or interest. These were derived by Kuder from the 10 areas of Form *C* and groups of items representing interest in: being active in groups, familiar and stable situations, working with ideas, avoiding conflict, directing or influencing others, working independently, and acting spontaneously in a carefree manner. The alert and informed reader will recognize these latter areas as those largely represented in the *Kuder Preference Record, Personal: Form A*.

Form *DD* yields 79 occupational scores and scores in 20 college curricular majors for males and 56 occupational scores and scores in 25 college majors for females. There are 32 scores for women taken from scales developed for men. These scores are reported as *lambda* correlation coefficients derived by Cleman's method (1958), which is somewhat similar to a biserial correlation coefficient. This inventory also has a Verification scale and other experimental scales which may ultimately become scales like the Validation scales of the *MMPI* and the Non-occupational scales of the *SVIB*. Verification scores between 45 and 60 represent valid answers.

The reading level for Form *DD* is about sixth-grade, and it uses the same reporting form for both sexes. The *Manual* (Kuder 1964) gives a description of the occupational groups.

The Minnesota Vocational Interest Inventory

A new inventory which combines selected features of the *SVIB* and the *Kuder* is the *Minnesota Vocational Interest Inventory (MVII)* (Clark and Campbell 1965). It is based on the differentiation of interest patterns of men in certain skilled and semiskilled occupations from those of a reference group of Tradesmen-in-general (*TIG*). The responses made by the specific occupational group are scored plus, and those made by the *TIG* group are scored minus.

The inventory has 158 triads, from each of which the respondent chooses the response liked most *and* the one liked least. Each triad contains three types of activities carried on by skilled tradesmen. The respondent chooses 316 responses, and the process requires less than 45 minutes. There is no time limit, however. It is intended for ninth-grade through adult levels and for students in college and technical schools intending to work at one of the occupations covered by the inventory.

Clark (1961) originally developed the *MVII* in 1946 to differentiate the interests of men in various Navy ratings. More than 7,000 civilian workers have been used in the development of the scales for 21 occupations. These occupations are listed below, showing their percentage of overlap with the *TIG* group.

Baker, 45%
Carpenter, 52%
Electrician, 31%
Food service manager, 39%
Hospital attendant, 38%
Industrial arts teacher, 27%
Machinist, 41%
Milk wagon driver (routeman), 43%
Printer, 42%
Plasterer, 37%

Plumber, 43%
Pressman, 32%
Printer, 37%
Radio-TV repairman, 27%
Retail salesclerk, 33%
Sheet metal worker, 49%
Stock clerk, 63%
Tabulating machine operator, 30%
Truck driver, 40%
Truck mechanic, 57%

Warehouseman, 49%

The process used to present the validity of responses of these criterion groups as distinct from the *TIG* group involves Tilton's percentage of overlap. This is approximately twice the percentage of classification errors. The percentage of overlap for each Occupational Scale, indicated following each occupation in the list above, ranges from 27% for the Industrial arts teacher and Radio-TV repairman to 63% for the Stock clerk, the median percentage of overlap being 40. This means that an overlap of 40% would misclassify 20% of the criterion group and the *TIG* group, with equal numbers in each group, if the variances were approximately equal. The reliabilities of the Occupational Scales range from .64 to .88, the median reliability being .82; those for the Area Scales (discussed below) range from .62 to .87 and have a median of .83.

The *MVII* has two forms. One is a separate booklet and answer sheet which can be hand- or machine-scored. Scoring stencils are available for this form. The other form has a combined item booklet and answer sheet, and can only be scored at a specified scoring service.

There are nine Homogeneous or Area Scales on the *MVII*, created from clusters of items found to be highly correlated with each other. The research conducted on these areas is described by Norman (1960). An inspection of the content of the items in each cluster and of the patterns of scores on the Area Scales made by the various Occupational Groups produced the following names for each "Area":

H-1, Mechanical	*H*-6, Carpentry
H-2, Health service	*H*-7, Sales-office
H-3, Office work	*H*-8, Clean hands
H-4, Electronics	*H*-9, Outdoors
H-5, Food service	

The Occupation Scales of the *MVII* show which group or groups the respondent's answers resemble most or least. The Area Scales give the pattern of the respondent's answers and describe the client's interests in terms of the correlation between an Occupational Scale and a given Area Scale.

Occupational Scales on the profile sheet were arranged in groups by means of cluster analysis of correlations among the scales. There are two major clusters. The first, 3 to 7, includes Milk wagon driver, Retail sales clerk, Stock clerk, Printer, and Tabulating machine operator. The second, 15 to 19, contains Truck mechanic, Industrial arts teacher, Sheet metal worker, Plumber, and Machinist. These two clusters represent opposite poles of what appears to be the same factor. Three other clusters are composed of Baker (1) and Food manager (2); Carpenter (11), Painter (12), and Plasterer (13); and Electrician (20) and Radio-TV repairman (21).

Scores are reported as standard scores arranged so that two-thirds of any Occupational Group score above T = 45 on their own scale. The *Manual* describes the critical scores used by indicating that scores between 35 and 45 on an Occupational Scale are indicating persons with fewer likes and dislikes similar to those of men in that occupation, persons with scores above 45 definitely share interests in common with men in that occupation, persons with scores below 35 on an Occupational Scale definitely have different interests from the criterion group of men for that occupation. The shaded area in each scale of the profile reflects scores like those made by the middle third of the *TIG* group. The shaded area is similar to that on the *SVIB* in that it reflects, through the amount of overlap, how easy it is to secure high scores on a given scale. Scales with the highest shaded area are Stock clerk, Carpenter, and Truck mechanic, and their percentage of overlap is the highest of all 21 Occupational Scales. It is easiest to score high on these. There is no evidence at present that response set is reflected in such scores.

The highest and lowest Area Scale scores describe, for the client and the counselor, the nature of the responses chosen. The pattern of high and low scores can be discussed in terms of interests characteristic of a given client. Each Area Scale is described by Clark and Campbell (1965).

Among the recent attempts to create new interest inventories, the *MVII* offers the most promise, in terms of the manner in which it was developed and in terms of clients it can help. The *MVII* helps the client find phases of motivation related to vocational interest by helping him to see himself in relation to skilled and semiskilled occupations. In addition it represents the possibility of investigating the nature of these interests, so that a counselor can assist that part of the school population which does not continue beyond high school to make vocational choices.

The Occupational Interest Inventory (Lee-Thorpe)

The *Occupational Interest Inventory* (California Test Bureau) is produced in two forms, *Intermediate*, for junior high school, and *Advanced*, for high-school students and adults. Part I of the inventory is made up of 240 paired items, each describing a vocational activity. The examinee selects the one of each pair that he prefers. From this part of the inventory, six field-of-interest scores are obtained: Personal-social, Natural, Mechanical, Business, the Arts, and the Sciences. In addition to these, a score for each of three types of interest is also obtained: Verbal, Manipulative, and Computational. Part II is made up of 30 items in sets of 3's, each set containing an activity that can be classified as being high, medium, or low in the hierarchy of vocational interests. This section produces a level-of-interest score. The inventory can be administered in less than a school period and is easy to score. Forbes and Cottle (1953) found the advanced form to have a reading-difficulty level of 9.5.

This instrument has in the past been strongly criticized for being put on the market with almost no validation. Some studies have since appeared, and the instrument now merits some consideration by the counselor. One study (Lindgren and Gilberg 1955) consisted of a correlation of all keys on the *Lee-Thorpe* with the conventionally scored occupational and non-occupational keys of the *SVIB*. In general, for the occupational keys these correlations were what might be expected. Level of Interests on the *Lee-Thorpe* did not correlate significantly with Strong's *OL* key, but did with his *IM* key at the 1% level. In another study, Roeber (1949) correlated scores on the *Lee-Thorpe* scales with those of the *Kuder*, Form *B*. This form differs from Form *C* in having no Outdoor key. Here again, there were the significant relationships one would expect to find among keys measuring similar vocational interests. Downie observed this high similarity between the *Kuder* and the *Lee-Thorpe* when both are administered to clients at the university level.

The *Manual* (Lee and Thorpe 1956) contains other validation data. MacPhail (1954) showed very significant profiles for university students in three curricula—B.A., B.S. in chemistry, and B.S. in engineering. Congdon and Jervis (1958) analyzed the profiles of graduates in agriculture, liberal arts (verbal), liberal arts (scientific), and technology based upon scores obtained as freshmen 4 years earlier. The profiles of individuals in the four areas all differed significantly. The counselor may find this instrument a valuable adjunct to either the *Kuder* or the *SVIB*.

Another interest inventory released by the California Test Bureau is the *Picture Interest Inventory*. It differs from all the others previously discussed in that the client reacts to pictures instead of words. Part I consists of 53 triads of pictures, each depicting an individual performing a type of work. The client, on the answer sheet, marks the one that he likes most and the one that he likes least. Part II is made up of 30 similar pictures to which the respondent reacts individually on a Like–Dislike basis. The fields of interest measured are very similar to those measured by the *Lee-Thorpe*. In the *Manual*, the author (Weingarten 1958) reports significant correlations with the scores of the different fields on his manual with corresponding scores on similar or related fields of the *SVIB*, *Kuder*, and *Lee-Thorpe*. It seems that such an inventory as this should remove the effect of a poor reading vocabulary on the evaluation of interests and become increasingly useful with the growing numbers of nonlinguistic clients or those with severe reading problems. The author suggests that this inventory also removes the halo effect that is associated with words used to identify the professional vocations.

The Study of Values

The *Study of Values* (or "interests," as they might be called) consists of 45 items. The first 30 of these are pairs which are to be evaluated in terms of preference or no preference for one over the other. The last 15 items are each completed by 4 statements which are to be ranked on the basis of appeal to the respondent. This instrument was constructed for college students and is usually so used. Forbes and Cottle (1953) showed that it had a reading difficulty level of 12.7, which makes it more difficult to read than all of the others discussed in this section, except possibly the *SVIB*.

This inventory is based upon the writings of Spranger (1928), in which he discusses types of men. His classification is based upon personality, this being to him a reflection of interests and vocational activities. His types of men are: the *Theoretical,* whose dominant interest is the discovery of truth (scientific); the *Economic,* who is characteristically interested in that which is useful; the *Aesthetic,* who sees the highest value in form and harmony (artistic); the *Social,* who loves people (social service or welfare); the *Political,* who is interested primarily in power; and the *Religious,* whose highest value is unity, seeking to comprehend the cosmos as a whole. Naturally, many men are mixtures of these types.

The counselor may find this inventory useful with university students when it is used with one of the other inventories. Research shows that it separates students in different curricula from each other. It can be used, then, in exploring the different fields of interests, and also in educational counseling in selecting a curriculum in line with the individual's interests. Much research has been carried out both with this revision (see Allport, Vernon, and Lindzey 1951) and the original, attesting to the instrument's validity. This research has been summarized by Dukes (1955).

SUMMARY

The counselor considering evidence of a client's interests is often so engrossed with the results obtained from vocational interest inventories that the more diversified evidence of the client's total interests may be overlooked. Admittedly, the evidence secured from vocational interest inventories can be derived in no other fashion, especially the comparison with the interests of professional persons furnished by the *SVIB*. At the same time, this information must be synthesized with the general picture of linguistic or nonlinguistic behavior developed from the client's stated interests, information about hobbies and other leisure activities, school classwork and extra-class activities, work experience, and family background. The non-test information comes from autobiographies, personal data forms, themes, school records, observation, and the initial interview —which were discussed in previous chapters. The synthesis of these data with those about general interests, secured from checklists, questionnaires, and some measures of achievement such as the *Michigan Vocabulary Profile Test,* will provide a much more valid and stable pattern of the general interests of a given client.

When vocational interest inventories are used, they should be carefully chosen in terms of the client's needs, such as his stated vocational plans and the norms appropriate for the age and group in which the client will be functioning. It is absurd to use the *SVIB* with high-school freshmen, particularly those who will never seek professional occupations. The choice of an inventory should also entail the consideration involved in selecting any test. Unless data on validity and reliability are available, the test should only be used experimentally. Research published on a given test should be studied and evaluated to seek further evidence of the usefulness of that inventory.

There are unique characteristics of a given test which may affect its desirability, e.g., the high cost of scoring the *SVIB*, about $1.00 per individual. Different inventories may be chosen according to the specific needs of groups or individuals. A class exploring the world of work and their own vocational interests might best take and score the *Kuder* to see what it shows them.

Keep in mind that vocational interest inventories, although considered among the best constructed and most useful of psychometric instruments, are still paper-and-pencil tests and do have limitations. That they can be falsified or distorted, there is no doubt. Many studies have been made in which students have been asked to complete an inventory from the viewpoint of a certain vocation or interest (see, e.g., Longstaff 1948). Vocational interest inventories may thus be of highly questionable value in selection and employment programs. Since the alert individual can produce the interest profile that is desired, probably these inventories should be used only as instruments in vocational counseling, and not for selection. There does not seem to be any really valid reason why a counseling client would desire to fake the results of these inventories, when he understands and accepts the purposes and goals of the voluntary counseling situation. When counseling is required, scores on interest inventories can take on a different meaning.

REFERENCES

Allport, G. W., Vernon, P. E., and Lindzey, G. 1951. *Study of Values.* rev. ed. Boston: Houghton Mifflin Company.

Barnett, G. J., *et al.* 1952. The occupational level scale as a measure of drive. *Psychol. Monogr.* no. 10 (whole no. 342) 66:1–37.

————, Stewart, L. H., and Super, D. E. 1953. Level of occupational interest: Deadweight or dynamism? *Educ. and Psychol. Measmt.* 13:193–208.

Bordin, E. S. 1943. A theory of vocational interest as dynamic phenomena. *Educ. and Psychol. Measmt.* 3:49–65.

Campbell, D. P. 1966. Stability of interests within an occupation over 30 years. *J. Appl. Psychol.* 50:51–56.

———, et al. 1967. A set of basic interest scales for the Strong Vocational Interest Blank for Men. Minneapolis: University of Minnesota, Center for Interest Measurement Research.

———. 1969. *SVIB manual: 1969 supplement.* Palo Alto, Calif.: Stanford University Press.

———. 1970. *Handbook for the Strong Interest Blank.* Palo Alto, Calif.; Stanford University Press.

Carkhuff, R. R., and Drasgow, J. 1963. The confusing literature on the O-L scale of the SVIB. *J. Couns. Psychol.* 10:283–88.

Carter, H. D. 1940. The development of vocational attitudes. *J. Consult. Psychol.* 4:185–91.

Clark, K. E. 1961. *Vocational interests of nonprofessional men.* Minneapolis: University of Minnesota Press.

———, and Campbell, D. P. 1965. *The Minnesota Vocational Interest Inventory Manual.* New York: The Psychological Corporation.

Clemans, W. V. 1958. An index of item-criterion relationship. *Educ. and Psychol. Measmt.* 18:167–72.

Congdon, R. G., and Jervis, F. M. 1958. A different approach to interest profiles. *J. Couns. Psychol.* 5:50–55.

Cottle, W. C. 1950. A factorial study of the *Multiphasic, Strong, Kuder* and *Bell* inventories using a population of adult males. *Psychometrika.* 15:25–47.

———. 1968. *Interest and personality inventories.* Boston: Houghton Mifflin Company.

Cronbach, L. J., and Gleser, G. C. 1953. Assessing similarity between profiles. *Psychol. Bull.* 50:456–73.

D'Arcy, P. F. 1954. *Constancy of interest factor patterns within the specific vocation of a foreign missionary.* Washington, D.C.: Catholic University of America Studies in Psychology and Psychiatry, vol. 9.

Darley, J. G. 1941. *Clinical aspects and interpretation of the Strong Vocational Interest Blank.* New York: The Psychological Corporation.

———, and Hagenah, T. 1955. *Vocational interest measurement.* Minneapolis: University of Minnesota Press.

Dukes, W. F. 1955. Psychological study of values. *Psychol. Bull.* 52:24–50.

Forbes, F. W., and Cottle, W. C. 1953. A new method of determining readability of standardized tests. *J. Appl. Psychol.* 37:185–90.

Fredericksen, N. 1965. Response set scores as predictors of performance. *Personnel Psychol.* 18:225–44.

Fryer, D. 1931. *The measurement of interests in relation to human adjustment.* New York: Holt, Rinehart & Winston, Inc.

Ginzberg, E., et al. 1951. *Occupational choice: An approach to a general theory.* New York: Columbia University Press.

Gustad, J. W. 1952. Academic achievement and Strong Occupational Level scores. *J. Appl. Psychol.* 36:75–78.

———. 1954. Vocational interests and socioeconomic status. *J. Appl. Psychol.* 38:336–38.

Hahn, M. E., and MacLean, M. S. 1955. *Counseling psychology.* New York: McGraw-Hill Book Company.

Holland, J. L. 1966. *Psychology of vocational choice.* Boston: Blaisdell Press.

———. 1968. Explorations of a theory of vocational choice: Of a longitudinal study using a sample of typical college students. *J. Appl. Psychol.* 52: Monogr. Suppl. no. 1, Part 2.

Kendall, W. E. 1947. The Occupational Level scale of the *Strong Vocational Interest Blank. J. Appl. Psychol.* 31:283–88.

King, L. A. 1958. Factors associated with vocational interests profile stability. *J. Appl. Psychol.* 42:261–64.

Kitson, H. D. 1942. Creating vocational interests. *Occupations.* 20:567–71.

Kuder, G. F. 1956a. *Kuder Preference Record: Occupational, Form D.* Chicago: Science Research Associates.

———. 1956b. *Kuder Preference Record: Vocational, Form C.* Chicago: Science Research Associates.

———. 1957. A comparative study of some methods of developing occupational keys. *Educ. and Psychol. Measmt.* 17:105–14.

———. 1964. *General interest survey manual.* Chicago: Science Research Associates.

———. 1966. *Occupational interest survey: General manual.* Chicago: Science Research Associates.

Lee, E. A., and Thorpe, L. P. 1956. *Occupational Interest Inventory.* Los Angeles: California Test Bureau.

Longstaff, H. P. 1948. Fakability on the *Strong Interest Blank* and the *Kuder Preference Record. J. Appl. Psychol.* 32:360–69.

Lindgren, H. C., and Gilberg, R. L. 1955. Interpreting occupational interest: The relationship between the *Lee-Thorpe Occupational Interest Inventory* and the *Strong Vocational Blank for Men. Calif. J. Educ. Res.* 6:15–21.

MacPhail, A. H. 1954. Interest patterns for certain degree groups on the *Lee-Thorpe Occupational Interest Inventory. J. Appl. Psychol.* 38:164–66.

McArthur, C. 1954. Long-term validity of the *Strong Interest Test* in two subcultures. *J. Appl. Psychol.* 38:346–53.

———, and Stevens, L. B. 1955. Validation of expressed interests as compared with inventoried interests: A 14-year follow-up. *J. Appl. Psychol.* 39:184–89.

Norman, W. T. 1960. A spatial analysis of an interest domain. *Educ. and Psychol. Measmt.* 20:347–61.

Ostrom, S. R. 1949a. The *OL Key* of the *Strong* test and drive at the twelfth grade level. *J. Appl. Psychol.* 33:240–48.

————. 1949*b*. The *OL Key* of the *Strong Vocational Interest Blank for Men* and scholastic success at the freshman level. *J. Appl. Psychol.* 33:51–54.

Powers, M. K. 1956. Permanence of measured vocational interests of adult males. *J. Appl. Psychol.* 40:69–72.

Rhodes, G. S. 1956. An investigation of response sets in the *Strong Vocational Interest Blank for Men* and response set effects on scores of selected *SVIB* scales. Ed.D. Dissertation, University of Kansas.

Roeber, E. C. 1949. The relationship between parts of the *Kuder Preference Record* and parts of the *Lee-Thorpe Occupational Interest Inventory. J. Educ. Res.* 42:598–608.

Seder, M. A. 1940. The vocational interests of professional women. *J. Appl. Psychol.* 24:130–43, 265–72.

Smith, E. R., and Tyler, R. W. 1942. *Appraising and recording student progress.* New York: Harper & Row, Publishers.

Stewart, L. H. 1959. Interest patterns of a group of high-ability, high-achieving students. *J. Couns. Psychol.* 6:132–39.

————. 1964. Selected correlates of the Specialization Level Scale of the *Strong Vocational Interest Blank. Personnel and Guidance J.* 42:867–73.

Stordahl, K. E. 1954*a*. Permanence of interests and interest maturity. *J. Appl. Psychol.* 38:339–40.

————. 1954*b*. Permanence of *Strong Vocational Interest Blank* scores. *J. Appl. Psychol.* 38:423–27.

Stranger, E. 1928. *Types of men.* New York: Stechert.

Strong, E. K. 1943. *Vocational interests of men and women.* Palo Alto, Calif.: Stanford University Press.

————. 1945. *Vocational Interest Blank for Men.* Palo Alto, Calif.: Stanford University Press.

————. 1953. Validity of occupational choice. *Educ. and Psychol. Measmt.* 13:110–21.

————. 1955. *Vocational interests 18 years after college.* Minneapolis: University of Minnesota Press.

————. 1959. *Strong Vocational Blank: Manual.* Palo Alto, Calif.: Counseling Psychologists Press.

————. 1966. *Strong Vocational Interest Blanks Manual.* rev. by D. P. Campbell. Palo Alto, Calif.: Stanford University Press.

————, and Tucker, A. C. 1952. The use of vocational interest scales in planning a medical career. *Psychol. Monogr.* 66.

Super, D. E. 1949. *Appraising vocational fitness.* New York: Harper & Row, Publishers.

————. 1953. A theory of vocational development. *Amer. Psychol.* 8:185–90.

————, and Crites, J. O. 1962. *Appraising vocational fitness.* New York: Harper & Row, Publishers.

Trinkhaus, W. K. 1954. The permanence of vocational interests of college freshmen. *Educ. and Psychol. Measmt.* 14:641–46.

Tyler, L. E. 1964. Work and individual differences. In *Man in a world at work,* ed. H. Borow. Boston: Houghton Mifflin Company.

U.S. Department of Labor, Bureau of Employment Security (USES). 1956. *Estimates of Worker Trait Requirements for 4,000 Jobs.* Washington, D.C.: Government Printing Office.

――――. 1965. *Dictionary of occupational titles.* 3rd ed. Washington, D.C.: Government Printing Office.

Weingarten, K. P. 1958. *Picture Interest Inventory.* Los Angeles: California Test Bureau.

10

___

Evaluation of Other Personal Data

One part of the process of counseling is helping a client get to know how he feels about himself and various aspects of his environment. This is the affective or emotional part of the psychological triumvirate of cognition, motivation, and affect. The previous two chapters have reviewed the various ways of helping a client collect and evaluate data about aptitudes and abilities, and about interests. This present chapter will review the various remaining tools and techniques the counselor will use to evaluate aspects of the client's personality prior to and during the counseling interviews.

Several of these techniques for the evaluation of social and emotional adjustment have already been described. Chapter 2 contained a discussion of personal documents and their use in counseling. There, we also discussed the use of sociometric techniques as methods of identifying the individual who has emotional or adjustment problems. In Chapter 3 there was a discussion of observational techniques, including the use of anecdotal records and rating scales.

In this chapter, attention will be paid to two other aspects of the appraisal of client personality—adjustment and attitudes. The review for the counselor here will cover, first, the structured personality or adjustment inventories. The use of these instruments results in scores for various named components of personality. They usually are used to describe what kind of behavior occurs, but do not tell *why* it occurs. The last part of this chapter contains checklists, or problem checklists, followed by the so-called "projective techniques" or the unstructured and semistructured instruments used in studying adjustment. The chapter will conclude with a discussion of attitudes, as another way of finding out why a client behaves in a certain fashion.

THE NATURE OF ADJUSTMENT

In general it may be said that personality inventories measure that which is very conveniently referred to as "adjustment." What is meant by this term? What problems arise from the consideration and use of the term? Psychologically, *adjustment* is the process that an individual goes through when giving varied response patterns to changes in the environment. All active, living organisms are constantly making adjustments to various aspects of their physical, social, and mental environment. As a result of the adjustment processes, tension is reduced and the so-called "normal" condition results.

There seems to be little disagreement as to what adjustment is. Values become associated with the adjustment process, and descriptions of the well-adjusted individual result. This well-adjusted individual receives various descriptions, depending on who is doing the describing. He may be the relatively consistent individual behaviorally, one who controls emotional behavior, conforms to the mores of the group, becomes increasingly more mature, adapts to reality situations, and the like (see Tindall 1955). All of this is fine in describing some sort of ideal or imaginary man but, actually, adjustment is relative to the society in which an individual resides and to the time when the individual lives in that culture. What is considered a desirable form of adjustment in one culture or cultural subgroup may be considered an illegal practice in another. See examples of the social practices of the primitive societies described in any book on cultural anthropology. Even within one culture, practices and mores are in a constant state of change. A consideration of attitudes toward the use of tobacco, drugs and alcohol, the role of women, and the role of religion in daily living will bear out the point. It is difficult to state exactly what normal behavior is, if indeed it exists at all. *Normal* may be defined here as within the range of socially acceptable behavior at a given time for a given group.

Another aspect of adjustment is that it is quite an individual matter. What is considered to be good adjustment for one individual may be the worst sort of adjustment for another. It is important that the counselor know how the client feels about problems of adjustment. If certain aspects of behavior seem unimportant to the individual, even if they are atypical as measured by a personality inventory or by other group norms, then it follows that the counselor should not make issues of them. It is only when these aspects of behavior become important to the individual that there are problems. Since desirable adjustment is relative and individual, it is questionable whether the norms that accompany many of the adjustment inventories are of any value. This is particularly true when the inventory was administered six months or more previous to the interview.

While much has been written about "desirable adjustment" by teachers and psychologists in the past several decades, it does not follow that all such workers feel that an attempt should be made to force all into a common mold in respect to adjustment. There is a growing feeling that much of this is so much nonsense; the point is made by Lindner (1952) that real progress in human affairs often comes about from the actions of those individuals who differ in their behavior from the group and its mores. Many famous scientists of the past are excellent examples of this. The inference from Lindner's statements would be that emphasis on *good adjustment for all* would lead to a nation of mediocrity and ensuing dullness.

THE HISTORY OF PERSONALITY APPRAISAL

Personality or adjustment has been studied and evaluated since early times, when man first began to reflect upon himself and his world. The ancients in the Near East related the movements and locations of the stars and planets to human personality. The ancient Greeks classified men into types on the bases of the different colored "biles" and "humors." Where the analysis of behavior through palmistry and physiognomy arose is difficult to tell. These also go back to primitive times. Body type has long been associated with personality types, as witness clichés such as "the jolly fat man," "the quick-tempered redhead," or the following from

Shakespeare: "Let me have men about me that are fat; sleek-headed men and such as sleep o'nights; yond' Cassius has a lean and hungry look; . . . such men are dangerous." (*Julius Caesar*, Act I, Sc. II.) Recently there were studies still going on in which body size and shape were related to aspects of adjustment (see Sheldon 1942). In the eighteenth century, phrenology made its appearance. The use of handwriting (graphology) to evaluate personality is most widely used today by nonprofessional individuals. So for over 2,000 years many devices were developed in an attempt to describe man's personality and those factors that affect it. It is interesting to note that practically all of these old and ancient techniques are still in use today and probably will continue to be, because of the difficulty of measuring and defining personality and adjustment in precise terms.

Late in the nineteenth century and at the beginning of the twentieth, attempts were made to measure personality and adjustment "scientifically." Among the first of these techniques to appear were the free-association techniques of Jung. In this method, words are presented to the client and he is told to respond to the stimulus with the first word or phrase that comes into his head. The nature of the response, whether common to a group or unique to the individual, speed of response, and the like were analyzed. During World War I, as was previously noted, psychometric evaluations were made of a very large group of men for the first time. In an attempt to screen out the misfits to prevent their induction into the military service, R. S. Woodworth constructed his *Personal Data Sheet*. This was the first personality inventory, and it differed little in makeup, content, and types of responses from many that are used today. In this inventory, Woodworth attempted to put a psychiatric interview onto a piece of paper, to save the time of having every inductee examined by a psychiatrist. After the war, this and similar inventories were used in educational and business situations. The results obtained with them were disappointing when compared to those for intelligence as measured by the *Army Alpha*, which was developed at the same time. Reliability and validity were difficult to ascertain because of the nature of the instruments and the variables. Since then, the acceptance and use of these adjustment inventories have been rather varied. Periods of rejection have been followed by periods of acceptance when a new "star" appeared on the horizon. Today, as shall be pointed out later, there are many of these available for use by the counselor.

In 1921, another technique appeared that was to create a revolution in the appraisal of personality, this being Rorschach's *Ink-Blot Test*. This date may be considered as the real beginning of the projective or unstructured phase in the measurement of adjustment. The activities of psychologists in World War II and in the decade following it resulted in much research on the *Rorschach* and in the development of other projective techniques that will be discussed later.

STRUCTURED PERSONALITY INVENTORIES

A personality inventory consists of from 100 to 500 or more items like these:

Do you daydream frequently?
Do you often have dizzy spells?
Do you always tell the truth?
Do you like the opposite sex?

Usually the client responds to the items by marking them "Yes" (Y), "No" (N), or "cannot tell" (?). On several there are but two choices, "Yes" or "No." Most of these inventories are of such a length that they can easily be completed in an hour, if the examinee operates at normal speed and responds to the items as they immediately strike him rather than giving thought to each. Typically, scores are presented for a series of traits or characteristics. Profiles are commonly used in reporting the results. In using the inventories, one assumes that personality may be broken down into traits and that these traits have variability, that is, vary in amount possessed from individual to individual. It is further assumed that there is a certain amount of stability of these traits within the individual. Actually, traits may be classified as *character traits*, which are fairly stable, and *mood traits*, which fluctuate from time to time.

The user of a personality inventory should seriously consider the following every time such a document is used:

1. *Are the responses of this individual to the items candid?*
Getting sincere or candid responses is one of the major problems with the use of the inventories. The nature of the items is not disguised, and any but the extremely dull person has no trouble in figuring out what the item is attempting to measure. In any society there are certain standards of behavior. Most individuals know what these are. In responding to the items on the inventory, examinees often offer the responses that they feel are demanded by their society, rather than revealing their own feelings and behavior. Moreover, the examinee may frequently see himself differently from the way others do. Thus, a perfectly candid response may be at variance with societal evaluations. In addition, there is the problem that the examinee does not know who is going to have access to the results and thus marks the inventory in a defensive manner without being really aware of doing so. Many of the items are of a very personal nature or reflect an

indication of antisocial behavior. This may produce a response set in the individual which causes these items to be answered in an erroneous fashion.

Various response sets have been explored by factor analytic methods by Broen and Wirt (1958). They found, in examining 11 kinds of response sets, that three factors accounted for the common variance among these response sets: (1) a tendency to agree with the item vs. denial, evasiveness, or indecision; (2) a tendency to disagree with assertions vs. evading the questions; and (3) a tendency to list or check many adjectives describing behavior. This last factor Broen and Wirt feel may be most characteristic of adolescence. When he has no idea who is going to see his paper, a respondent thinks twice before he answers candidly. Part of these effects can be dissipated if the counselor explains that the chief interest is in part and total scores, and not in specific item responses. It helps also if the counselor has established good rapport prior to testing and the respondent knows that the results are confidential. The explanation that tests are machine-scored also helps.

2. *Does the individual understand the questions, and does he understand himself to the extent that he has insight into his own behavior so that he could mark the inventory candidly if he so desired?*
Research like that of Forbes and Cottle (1953) has shown the relative readability indices for the more widely used personality inventories. In general, the vocabulary level of these, when compared with interest inventories and intelligence tests, tends to be rather low—fifth- and sixth-grade level being typical. Even so, many individuals in any high-school will find the words on some of these inventories unknown to them.

A perusal of the catalogs of the different test publishers will show that one can obtain inventories of this type for use in the primary grades. The writers feel that children at that level of development are in no position to answer these inventories, especially when, as in some cases, each item has to be read to the child individually. The writers further feel that any of these inventories used below grade 13 should only be used in a one-to-one testing situation, and after careful explanation to parents and agency administrators of the purpose to which the scores will be put.

3. *What do the results obtained with personality inventories mean?* It was observed, earlier, that there is no average type of behavior that is considered desirable for all. Actually, the scores obtained with personality inventories are meaningless unless it has been ascertained how the client feels about his behavior. The subject's frame of reference, as he responds to the items, must be understood. For example, as has been pointed out by Anastasi (1961), when a group of 219 students was asked to respond to the question "Do you like to be alone?" they were also asked to indicate exactly why they answered as they did. About one-fourth remarked that they liked to be alone when they had work to do, but not socially. Of these 55, 18 had responded with Yes to the question; 17, with No; and 20, with ?.

Suppose there is a second item, "I stay at home almost every evening." Two individuals both mark it Yes or Agree. Further probing shows that one enjoys being at home nights in order to pursue a hobby that happens to be a more or less solitary one. The other would often like very much to be out evenings with others but, because of his own personal habits and adjustment, he finds that he lacks contacts or the ability to bring this about. It seems clear that it is almost impossible to know how the subject is feeling when he answers any item on an adjustment inventory, and it follows that to a great extent these scores are meaningless unless they are interpreted in terms of the cumulative impact of a series of items in a given area, or in terms of similarity to responses of criterion groups.

4. *What is the reliability of personality inventories?*

In general, the reliability of these instruments tends to be in the .80's, just slightly lower than the reliability coefficients for intelligence and achievement tests. These coefficients, however, may refer to the entire score made with the instrument while, as already pointed out, the total score can be broken down into a dozen or more subscores. In some cases the number of items in one of these subtests may be as small as eight. Reliability, being a function of the length of a scale, is apt to be quite low in such situations.

It follows that, although the entire scale may have acceptable reliability, the subscales do not. This makes the use of many of the so-called "diagnostic profiles" quite questionable. Pauline Pepinsky's discussion of reliability of sociometric devices (1949) applies to these inventories also. She points out that part of the problem is created because each successive measurement is really that of a changed individual, and this tends to reduce reliabilities. Even reliabilities computed from a single administration are not too satisfactory. Most one-test reliabilities assume the items are of the same category and value. In personality inventories this assumption is highly questionable. (See Cottle 1968, pp. 72*ff.*)

5. *What is the validity of the personality inventory?*

As with all instruments of appraisal, it is important that criteria be used in determining the validity of the instrument. One of the major problems with adjustment inventories is that of obtaining adequate criteria against which to validate. Those that are most frequently used are the ratings of teachers, psychologists, psychiatrists, or supervisors in an industrial setting. It so happens that the reliability and validity of many of these ratings may be low, as pointed out in Chapter 3. (Other aspects of validity were discussed in Questions 1 and 2 of this list.) Finally, it may be added that the use or misuse of the inventories has a lot to do with validity.

When these instruments are kept in the clinic or counseling part of the agency, or used as screening devices to pick out those who are emotionally disturbed, or are used with an individual client after rapport has been established and the client understands how the proper completion of the inventory will contribute to helping solve the problems, then the results may be quite valid. However, these inventories are widely used in industry, both in the hiring of personnel and in the promotion of employees within the plant. Since there is no question that the results can be falsified, they are questionable. This is really a misuse of these inventories. Whyte (1956) in *The Organization Man* suggests that, when asked for comments about the world, the respondent give the most conventional, run-of-the-mill, pedestrian answer. He further states that when one is in any doubt about the most desirable answer to any item, the respondent reflect an attitude which includes that he loves both his father and his mother, but his father a little bit more; that he never worries much about anything; that he does not care much about books or music; and that he loves his family but does not let them or their problems interfere with the work of the company.

Falsification is not the only factor that lowers the validity of personality inventories. Another major one is called response set or style (discussed in the previous chapter). *Response set* is defined as the tendency for an individual to respond differently to the concept measured by a test item when it is presented in one format from the way that he would respond when the same idea is presented in another item format. For example, a given subject may respond True to an item on a true-false test, but, if the same idea were presented in a multiple-choice test, he would understand it and respond to it differently. The True response may have been brought about because of his "set" toward test items; that is, if he is not sure of the answers he may mark them True. Another example of response set is some individuals show a tendency to respond in the same way to a majority of the items on an inventory. In a typical personality inventory a client is confronted with three types of possible responses: Yes, No, and Can't Tell or *?*. One individual might mark most of the items Yes. This is the most frequent type of response set, but it is also conceivable that an individual might mark many items No or *?*.

Response sets or styles take many forms other than the one just mentioned, which in its positive aspect is termed *acquiescence*. There are response styles associated with caution, evasiveness, falsification, and denigration; styles associated with the meanings of words such as "agree," "usually," "sometimes," and so forth; styles associated with working for speed instead of accuracy; and others (Cronbach 1946, 1950). Response style has been studied most in relation to personality inventories and some research workers have concluded that what is measured by these inventories is the response set of acquiescence and the tendency to give socially desirable responses (Jackson and Messick 1961; Messick and Jackson 1961).

A related problem is also associated with the *social desirability* of an inventory item. It has been demonstrated that respondents, when they have a choice of two responses of unequal social desirability, tend to select the one that seems more socially desirable. This caused Edwards (1957*b*), in constructing his *Personal Preference Schedule,* to go to great lengths to be sure that the two parts of each of the item couplets on this inventory were of equal social desirability. Thus the client is thwarted in any attempt to select socially desirable responses. The choosing of socially desirable responses is often done unconsciously, and some psychologists feel that it is merely a reflection of the client's own personality. As Crowne and Marlowe (1964) have pointed out, the subject who marks socially desirable responses on personality inventories has a need for self-protection, avoidance of criticism, and an intense desire to maintain a sociably and personally acceptable image of himself. These authors go on to add that such respondents are cautious, conforming, and easily persuaded individuals.

However, not all research shows acquiescence, social desirability, and the like to be the main characteristics tapped by personality inventories. Rorer (1965) and Rorer and Goldberg (1965) have shown that acquiescence is not an important determinant of responses on the *MMPI*. Block (1965) has also discussed effect of response sets on the *MMPI*. So there are two sides to this argument, one that response styles and sets are most important in the determination of an individual's scores on a personality inventory and the other that these response styles or sets are not significant. The issue is still far from settled, a fact which should lead the users of these inventories to be cautious in using results obtained with them. The psychological literature has much research related to the validity of these instruments. Summaries are found in Ellis (1946, 1953), and Ellis and Conrad (1948). It should be noted that some of the studies quoted by Ellis may be of questionable experimental design and may not be reflecting the real validity and reliability of the inventories.

The builders of the newer inventories have attempted to improve the validity of their instruments by the use of different item types, requiring different methods of response, or by establishing so-called validation keys. Certain of these improvements will be mentioned when particular inventories are discussed. In the pages that follow, these inventories will be described under the headings of Old-type inventories; Factorial inventories; and Others, the newer approaches which use item-analysis techniques with criterion groups and which attempt to control response set.

In recent years personality inventories have been under attack because of the invasion-of-privacy issue. It is true that such inventories as the *Minnesota Multiphasic Personality Inventory* (which will be described in some detail shortly) include items about intimate sexual and religious matters, and that it has been used by the State Department, the Peace Corps, and other governmental agencies in screening applicants for positions. Some individuals who were forced to complete the *MMPI* complained about some of the items. The press and various pressure groups made such a stir that both the United States Senate and House of Representatives appointed a special subcommittee to conduct hearings into this invasion of privacy. The content of the hearings and some related activities, especially the defense made by the American Psychological Association, are reported in a special issue of the *American Psychologist* (1965), entitled *Testing and Public Policy*. (See Cottle 1968.) It might be noted that all the commotion settled very little. However, from the viewpoint of the psychologist, the results were generally positive and very instructive. To a certain extent it is true that personality inventories have been misused. It is also true that, when they are used by trained, competent persons and the results combined with data obtained from other sources, meaningful information about a client's behavior is at hand. There are limitations to the use of paper-and-pencil personality inventories, just as there are with all psychological tests. However, the advantages seem to far outnumber the disadvantages.

The invasion-of-privacy issue can be argued from both sides. There are situations where personality inventories are administered as part of a screening battery of tests to select individuals for a particular type of service, such as in the Peace Corps or for confidential work in a military or industrial setting. Here the hiring agency must know if an individual has any traits that would be harmful to the work of the organization to which he is applying. The hiring agency has the right to know all that can possibly be determined about the personalities of all applicants. Thus psychological instruments or methodologies of one type or another must be used. On the other hand, the *routine* administration of such inventories to junior or senior high-school or university students is another matter. The knowing counselor will look over the inventory that he is going to use very carefully, and then select one that he feels will not be offensive to his students or to their parents. Nor will he use them indiscriminately. He will use one when the need arises, and often this will be after he and his client have talked about the inventory and what can be gained by having the client complete it. Then the results obtained are apt to be much more meaningful and valid than those obtained by routine administration of inventories. Very often, when personality inventories are administered in group fashion, some individuals respond at random to the items, as they can see no value in their efforts. Some of these are the ones who make the complaints and criticisms of the inventories. It is more effective counseling when the client has some say in what he is going to do and sees the need and possible results to be obtained from such a plan of action.

In doing research with these instruments, all subjects or their parents should be asked if they wish to participate. If they are not so inclined, they should be excused. No individual should be forced to complete any personality inventory as part of someone's research.

THE OLD-TYPE INVENTORIES

In respect to the types of items included and the types of responses called for, the old-type inventories are very similar to the original Woodworth *Personal Data Sheet.* Two of these are the *Bernreuter Personality Inventory* (Stanford University Press), and the *Bell Adjustment Inventory.* The *Bernreuter* is made up of 125 questions which are responded to on a Yes–No–? scale. Item responses are weighted, increasing both the time and complexity of scoring. Four traits are purportedly measured—neuroticism, self-sufficiency, introversion, and dominance. Flanagan (1935) factor-analyzed the scale and reduced it to two factors—self-confidence and solitariness. It should be noted here that such a factor analysis holds only for the sample on which it was computed and may not hold for other population samples, unless it can be demonstrated they are from a similar population.

The *Bell Adjustment Inventory* (Consulting Psychologists Press 1962) is a more up-to-date version of one of the old-type inventories. This one appeared originally in 1934. The present edition, which can be used with subjects in grades 9 through 16, provides six scores: Home adjustment, Health adjustment, Submissiveness, Emotionality, Hostility, and Masculinity–femininity. The 200 items on this inventory are responded to on a Yes, No, or Can't Say basis. It is self-administering and easily scored. Vance, in Buros (1965), stated that this revised edition has sufficient evidence in the accompanying manual to justify its preliminary use as a screening device. Empirical evidence in counseling indicates that patterns of scores may be more important than single scores. In contrast to the *Bernreuter*, the *Bell* is very easily scored, as the item responses are not weighted. At the present time the *Bell* and *Bernreuter* should be used as no more than screening devices.

A much newer series of inventories is the *California Tests of Personality*, issued by the California Test Bureau. The current revision (1953) consists of two forms that cover five different levels: primary, elementary, intermediate, secondary (grades 9 through college), and adult. Each of these inventories is divided into two parts: one which measures Self-adjustment and another which measures Social adjustment. Scores for both of these parts, a total score, and a score for each of six components making up the two subtests are obtained. There are 180 items on the adult scale, 15 items being allocated to each of the 12 different traits. On the lower forms of the inventory, the number of items on the different subtests decreases. Administering, completing, and scoring the inventory are each easy and simple. There is one characteristic of the items on this inventory that separates them from many other inventories—the items consistently ask the examinee how he *feels* about this or that, as opposed to the other approach, which asks whether one *does* or does not do certain things. Some clinicians consider the responses to individual items valid and meaningful in themselves, even though there may be questionable validity to the total score. The same publishers also issue the *Mental Health Analysis*, of similar format, in four levels including from grade four through adulthood. The two major breakdowns of the scores are into Assets and Liabilities. The writers feel these two inventories are more useful as *individual* tests with persons at the middle level of elementary school, after proper rapport has been established with examinee *and* parents, but of very limited value in the primary grades.

FACTORIAL INVENTORIES

Certain psychologists have developed personality inventories as a result of factor-analyzing existing inventories, using items of their own making, or a combination of both. Guilford has produced a whole series of such inventories, the current edition of which is known as the *Guilford-Zimmerman Temperament Survey* (issued by the Sheridan Supply Co.). Thurstone similarly produced his *Temperament Schedule* (Science Research Associates). R. B. Cattell, on the basis of his factorial investigation, produced several personality inventories, including one of 16 factors.

The *Guilford-Zimmerman Temperament Survey* consists of 300 items that measure 10 traits. These are listed below with several terms under each to give an indication of the nature of the trait:

G: *General activity.* Energy, vitality, and enthusiasm vs. slowness of action and inefficiency.

R: *Restraint.* Serious-mindedness, persistence, and self-control vs. carefree, excitement-loving, and impulsive.

A: *Ascendance.* Self-defense, persuading others, bluffing, and leadership vs. submissiveness, hesitation in speaking, and avoiding conspicuousness.

S: *Sociability.* Many friends and acquaintances and liking social activities and contacts vs. few friends and acquaintances, shyness, and dislike of social activities.

E: *Emotional stability.* Evenness of moods, interest, energy, optimism, and cheerfulness vs. fluctuation of moods, pessimism, and gloominess.

O: *Objectivity.* Being thick-skinned vs. hypersensitiveness, suspiciousness, and self-centeredness.

F: *Friendliness.* Toleration of hostile action, acceptance of dominance, and respect for others vs. belligerence, hostility, resistance to domination, and contempt for others.

T: Thoughtfulness. Reflectiveness, interest in thinking, mental poise, observation of self vs. interest in overt activity and mental disconcertedness.

P: Personal relations. Tolerance of people and faith in social institutions vs. faultfinding habits, suspiciousness of others, and self pity.

M: Masculinity. Interest in masculine activities and vocations, hardboiled vs. interest in feminine activities and vocations, easily disgusted, sympathetic, romantic interests, great interest in clothes and styles.

The items on this inventory are all stated in the affirmative rather than in question form and they all use the second-person pronoun. Guilford feels that the use of the direct statement makes possible more simple and direct ideas. Also, the avoidance of the first-person singular makes the items seem less personal to the examinee and less like a cross-examination. Both, he feels, should increase the validity of the responses. Items are responded to on a Yes–No–? scale. The nature of these items is such that they may be used with high-school students with little fear of repercussions, if proper precautions are taken. In general this is a well-made inventory, useful with both high-school and college youth.

It is easy to administer, score, and profile. The profile has positive traits at the top and negative traits at the bottom. One way of spotting forged or falsified profiles is to note whether most of the scores are a standard deviation or more above the mean. Such a "good boy" or "good girl" profile usually indicates the person who is trying to fake a good score. Jacobs and Schloff (1955) have suggested falsification scales for the *GZTS*, but they do not seem any more effective than the observation of preponderance of high scores just suggested. More than 3 items left unanswered among the 30 in each scale tend to invalidate that scale. However, the counselor can make a tentative interpretation of the scale by indicating the band of raw scores within which the actual score would be. Since items scored on any scale only act to raise the score, the actual score, if all items had been answered, would be between the obtained score and the obtained score plus the omitted items. Such a procedure has the advantage of allowing some interpretation of scores and still indicating that the obtained score represents a band rather than a pinpoint on a scale. This inventory, like those discussed previously, is probably best used as a screening device for the rough identification of traits unique to a given individual as contrasted to others, and to get a preliminary measure of ability to relate to others.

Another group of personality inventories based upon the factor-analytic approach includes those developed by R. B. Cattell, such as the *IPAT Sixteen Personality Factor Questionnaire* (1962) and the *IPAT High School Personality Questionnaire* (1960). Only the first of these will be briefly described here, as they are very similar in general makeup. This

Inventory consists of two forms, *A* and *B*, each made up of 187 items, 10 to 13 of which are used to measure each of the 16 factors. The items are similar to those usually encountered on such instruments, and each is responded to by a choice of Yes, In Between, or No. There is also a simplified edition, Form *C*, made up of 105 items.

It is suggested that Forms *A* and *B* be administered simultaneously. Even when this is done and the results combined, the size of the resulting reliability coefficient suggests that the scales be used only for group prediction. The inventories have been constructed with great pains and skill but even so, they have been found wanting by researchers and users. Some research has shown that the 16 factors may be reduced to less when factor analysis is applied to scores obtained with the inventories. Each individual scale is made up of a relatively small number of items; this in itself is partly responsible for the low reliability coefficients of the various scales. There is also a lack of information about validity, especially of a predictive nature. In the *Manual* are representative sets of occupational profiles on the inventory, one of which is based upon only 13 cases. The idea behind the use of these profiles is that individuals who remain in an occupation for any length of time have become adjusted to it, and that their profile thus becomes an ideal pattern for the selection of entrants to that occupation. Finally, the author uses esoteric terms such as "premsia" and "threctia," in describing his factors. At the present time these inventories should best be considered as being in the research stage.

OTHER TYPES OF INVENTORIES

The Minnesota Multiphasic Personality Inventory

This inventory, the *MMPI* as it is usually called, is published by The Psychological Corporation. It was constructed as a screening instrument to aid physicians in the identification of abnormal emotional states in order that they might make referrals to a psychiatrist. Items on it were obtained from earlier inventories, texts, and forms used in psychiatric examinations. Items are responded to with True, False, or Cannot Say (*?*). For most scales, items were chosen on the basis of their ability to produce differing responses between a psychiatrically diagnosed criterion group and a normal group without history of psychological abnormalities. The items are scored in the direction of abnormal responses. Except for three scales—the Correction scale *K*, Masculinity-femininity *M–f*, and Social introversion *Si*—there was no attempt to attach meaning to low scores. Actually there are two forms of the inventory, an earlier one consisting of 550 cards which the examinee separates into three piles as he responds to the items, and a later form, a booklet made up of 566 items answered on the conventional IBM answer sheet. There are other adaptations such as a shortened form made up of the first 366 items plus any K-scale or Si-scale items beyond item 366, and an edition in Braille. A most comprehensive and descriptive summary of the administration, interpretation, and application of the *MMPI* appears in Dahlstrom and Welsh (1960).

Scores are reported using standard T-scores with a mean of 50 and a standard deviation of 10. Results are plotted on a profile sheet. Interpretation consists of analyses of these profiles or patterns. To assist with this, Hathaway and Meehl (1951) have produced an atlas containing a large number of coded profiles and brief case histories of almost a thousand patients arranged according to similarity of profile. This atlas is used as an aid in the interpretation of the profile of the client.

Scales on this inventory are classified into two types: validity scales and clinical scales (Form 10.1). The validity scales are a response to the concern of psychologists to get valid responses with these instruments and to the numerous studies showing the fakability of such inventories. The four *validity* scales are:

1. *Cannot say, ?*. This is the total number of items placed in the *Cannot say* category. The Manual (Hathaway and McKinley 1943, 1951) states that high *?* scores (100 or more) invalidate the test, and that scores between 70 and 100 indicate that the individual's actual scores would deviate even more if he had not used the question category so freely in completing the inventory. The booklet form produces few unanswered items.

2. *Lie scale, L*. The purpose of this scale is to pick out those individuals who attempt to falsify their score by selecting responses that appear socially or morally desirable. A high Lie score indicates that the true value of the other scales may actually be higher than indicated by the obtained scores. This scale, together with the K-scale, tends to identify various response sets.

3. *Validity scale, F*. This scale is used to determine if the inventory was taken and scored properly. Originally high scores were taken to indicate that the subject was careless, did not understand the items, or that scoring and recording errors were made. Later research showed that a high score on this scale was identified with a psychosis or with deliberate faking.

4. *Correction scale, K*. This scale is referred to as a "suppressor," meaning that it is supposed to increase the effectiveness of the clinical scales in diagnostic work. There is little evidence, outside of the statements of the authors, that it performs this function. (See Cottle 1953, 1968). A score on the K-scale by itself, when high, may indicate the defensive person trying to appear normal, and a low score may indicate a self-critical individual or an individual trying to make himself appear abnormal. The most recent profile for the test only accounts for the effect of high scores (defensiveness) on K, and "corrects" selected scales for the effects of such defensiveness.

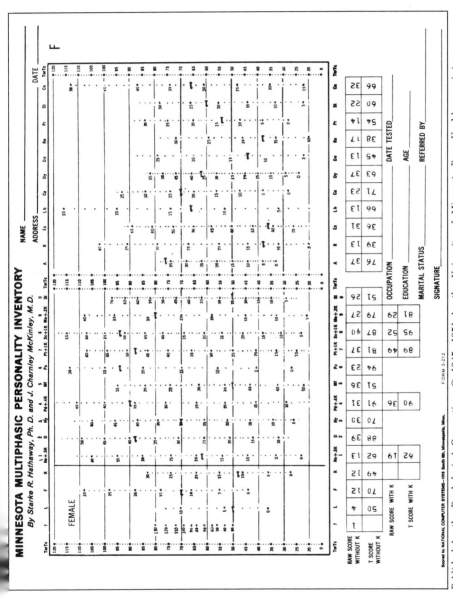

Figure 10.1
N.C.S.-MMPI PROFILE SHEET

Published by the Psychological Corporation; © 1945, 1951 by the University of Minnesota Press. Used by permission.

Below is a brief description of the ten basic *clinical* scales:

1. *Hypochrondriasis, Hs.* A deviant high score indicates abnormal concern about bodily functions. A *T*-score between 60 and 70 indicates the person who is somewhat more concerned about physical symptoms than most people but who may not necessarily be "abnormal" in this respect.

2. *Depression, D.* A high score indicates poor morale and feelings of uselessness and pessimism when it is the single high score. When it appears high along with other variables, the different patterns indicate various psychological states. The most common pattern is a high score on *D* and *Pt*, which identifies the individual under more than usual psychological tension. The height of these two scores is usually an indication of the degree of tension the individual feels.

3. *Hysteria, Hy.* A subject with a high *Hy* score is considered to be like patients with various types of hysteria symptoms. A *T*-score between 60 and 70 may be reflecting the person who tends to "clutch" in pressure situations and who lacks self-confidence.

4. *Psychopathic deviate, Pd.* A high score on this scale, according to the *Manual*, indicates an individual with an absence of deep emotional response, an inability to profit by experience, and a disregard of social customs. A *T*-score between 60 and 70 indicates the individual who dislikes rules and regulations and having to conform. This may be evidenced in behavior, however, by refusal to conform (rebellion) or by conformance accompanied by covert resentment.

5. *Masculinity-femininity, Mf.* Measures the tendency for an individual to have the basic interest pattern of the opposite sex. Cottle (1953, 1968) summarized the research on this scale as follows: college males tend to score higher than the general population; a high score for men means an interest in people, language, and ideas, whereas a high score for women indicates an interest in mechanical, scientific, and computational activities; certain vocational groups, such as seminarians and music-education students, tend to have high scores on this scale; a high score *sometimes* is found with evidence of homosexuality.

6. *Paranoia, Pa.* A high score on this scale, according to the *Manual*, associates the individual with a group of patients characterized by suspiciousness, oversensitivity, and delusions of persecution. Scores between 60 and 70 usually indicate the person who reads more into what others say or do than they intend. This is usually accompanied by difficulties in interpersonal relations.

7. *Psychasthenia, Pt.* This scale is supposed to measure the similarity of individuals to patients having phobias or compulsive behavior. A score between 60 and 70 characterizes the individual who prefers routine or organized activities which follow the same pattern. Such a score may indicate the worker who persists until the work is completed. It acts as a check on the *Hypomania* score.

8. *Schizophrenia, Sc.* This scale, according to the *Manual*, measures responses characterized by bizarre and unusual thoughts or behavior. A score between 60 and 70 seems to be characteristic of the individual who uses solitary recreation to get away from the "present."

9. *Hypomania, Ma.* A high score on this scale is stated to indicate an individual with marked overproductivity of thought and action, most of which is never carried through to completion.

10. *Social introversion, Si.* A high score characterizes the individual who prefers activities carried on alone or with a few people. A low score seems to describe the individual who likes to meet and deal with people in groups.

It might be noted again that there is no general agreement about the meaning of extremely low scores on any scale except *K, Mf,* and *Si.*

Over the years, considerable research has been carried on with this inventory. Cottle (1953) summarized the research done between 1940 and 1950, and in the last chapter indicated some more extensive interpretations when using the inventory with normals. One of the important aspects of the research on this instrument has been the development of new scales. Some of these additional scales are called Socioeconomic status, Dominance, Responsibility, Neuroticism, and Prejudice. As a matter of fact, psychologists have developed scales for all sorts of conditions by analyzing how the responses of members of the group being studied differ from another group. Items to which the responses differ significantly between groups go to make up the new scale, which is scored in the desired direction and cross-validated with a second group supposedly having the same psychological status as the first criterion group. Summaries of these research articles are found in the *Manual* accompanying the inventory or in the later volumes of Buro's *Mental Measurements Yearbooks.*

Cottle (1968, pp. 94–95) has discussed the most commonly used new *MMPI* scales as follows:

Newer *MMPI* Scales, as shown on the National Computer Systems profile [Form 10.1] have had limited use in counseling normal individuals. As can be seen from their descriptions, they have had much more usage in the clinical setting with abnormal patients. However, the counselor in a school setting needs to be aware of their potential, so they are described briefly in the following pages. There are eleven of these scales, beginning with Welsh's (1956) first factor *A* of 39 items and second factor *R* of 40 items, . . . an indicator of anxiety and an indicator of internalization, respectively. Hathaway and Briggs (1957) discuss some of these newer scales and their normative data (*A, R, Es, Dy, Rp,* and *Cn*), but the most useful reference again is Dahlstrom and Welsh (1960).

The third scale added is Barron's (1953) Ego strength (*Es*) of 68 items which are supposed to identify individuals who tend to improve more with therapy (higher score) than those who do not. A fourth is Hanvik's (1949) Low Back Pain Scale (*Lb*) whose 25 items are used to differentiate between veterans with a real physiological problem and those with psychosomatic problems related to pains in the back. A fifth scale is the 36-item Caudality Scale (*Ca*) developed by Williams (1952) and used to identify persons with "focal damage of the parietal lobe from those with frontal lobe lesions" (Hathaway and McKinley, 1951:21). Navran's (1954) 57-item Dependency Scale (*Dy*) is the sixth of the Newer Scales to be included. He used ratings by judges and an item-analysis process to develop a scale purportedly measuring the amount of dependency present in patients who prolonged their response to therapy versus those who responded more rapidly. He also investigated differences between normals and abnormals on this scale.

The next two scales, the 28-item Dominance (*Do*) and the 32-item Responsibility (*Re*) were developed by Gough and others (1951, 1952). The *Do* Scale partials out persons who exhibit social initiative, persistence, and leadership skills. The *Re* Scale is supposed to identify persons who can assume obligations to the groups in which they function and are dependable and trustworthy. The 32-item Prejudice Scale (*Pr*) was also developed by Gough (1951) to measure the psychological insecurities reflected by social prejudice against minority groups. It identifies individuals with high scores who are prudish, rigid, authoritarian, and pseudo-religious. This scale is negatively related to the *K* Scale and the *St* Scale, while being positively related to the *F* Scale and most of the Clinical Scales (except *Hy*). The Social Status Scale (*St*) of 34 items, as developed by Gough (1949), tries to measure an individual's psychological conditions associated with socio-economic class when subjects had been divided into upper and lower groups using the Sims Score Card (1927). It has a moderate correlation with the *K* Scale of .53 (Perlman, 1950).

The last of the Newer Scales is the 50-item Control Scale (*Cn*) developed by Cuadra (1953) on a very carefully done comparison of hospitalized patients and out-patients. He hypothesized they would differ on control of self. Current, but limited, information indicates the items of this scale appear sensitive to the elements in self-control which identify persons who need to be confined versus those who can manage themselves under out-patient treatment.

It can be seen from the brief discussion of the last eleven scales that they are of limited use in the school setting at present. It should also be noted that they need more research to clarify their interpretation.

The item composition of each of these Newer Scales is shown in Dahlstrom and Welsh (1960:448–468).

As mentioned earlier, the usual procedure in studying scores on this inventory is by analyzing profiles. Psychological behavior is not simple and usually can be attributed to multiple causation with multiple effects. Hence, most of the scores to the individual scales have limited meaning by themselves, but become very significant when considered as part of a profile or pattern. The *Atlas for the Clinical Use of the MMPI* serves as a guide for the analysis and interpretation of these profiles, as do Dahl-strom and Welsh (1960). Over the years, certain profiles have appeared so frequently that they have been given common names.

The literature shows that several studies have found a neurotic factor and a psychotic factor in research with the *MMPI*, but it should be borne in mind that other studies may produce additional factors. It is significant for the counselor that general agreement in several studies on the exis-tence of a neurotic and a psychotic factor in the *MMPI* is supported also by empirical observations from counseling itself. The *MMPI* scales with highest factor loadings on the neurotic factor are Hypochondriasis, De-pression, and Hysteria. Experience in counseling has already shown these three scales to be related, and highest among the patterns on the clinical scales in the psychoneurotic and psychosomatic illnesses. They have been named the "neurotic triad." The position of the Depression scale in the pattern of the neurotic triad, highest with psychoneurotics and lowest with psychosomatic symptoms, seems to be a key in the diagnosis and prediction of results of counseling and psychotherapy. Evidence from counseling indicates this neurotic triad may be related to jobs of a cycli-cal nature which are characterized by highs and lows of production.

The psychotic factor has highest loadings on the Paranoia, Psych-asthenia, and Schizophrenia scales of the *MMPI* with abnormals. (For nor-mal subjects, *Pa* often seems to be a part of the neurotic factor.) These three scales have been identified in counseling as the "psychotic triad," and have been found to be most prominent in clients with psychotic tendencies. Here, as in the case of the Depression scale in the neurotic triad, the position of the Psychasthenia scale seems to reflect the amount of tension present and hence gives an estimate of the response to coun-seling or psychotherapy. Counseling observations indicate that some rise on the *Pt* scale (T = 55 to 65) of the normal individual appears character-istic of the worker who performs well in a routine, repetitive situation and who sticks with a job until it is done.

An example of part of the problem involved in interpretation of *MMPI* profiles will illustrate the difficulty of handling profiles. Certain of the clinical scales of the *MMPI* are referred to by Welsh (1952) as "character" scales; namely, Hysteria, Psychopathic deviate, and Hypomania, while others are called "mood" scales, such as Hypochrondriasis, Depression, and Psychasthenia. By this, Welsh means that the character scales remain fairly constant in the repeated measurement of an individual, while the mood scales may fluctuate according to the amount of psychological pres-sure operating on this individual at a given moment. Unless the counselor is aware of the difference between these two kinds of scales in the *MMPI*, it is difficult to see any similarity in an individual's profile from a test taken when he feels more secure or at ease and one from another test taken when he feels under tension. At first glance the profiles will appear widely different. It is only as the character scales are compared for two or more test administrations to the same person that similarities begin to emerge. It is only when the client discusses with the counselor the possible cause of variation in tension, that causes of variation in the mood scales from test to test for that client are at least partially explained.

Problems such as these are involved in the meaning of patterns of scores on the *MMPI*. It is necessary to operate from the hypothesis that people are more alike than they are different, if identification of group patterns for job families is to be made. In this instance, such gross patterns as the over-all masculinity or femininity of interests in personality data are useful in describing jobs of a mechanical-scientific nature vs. those dealing with people. At the same time attention must be devoted to the minor deviations from average in a given individual profile, in order to identify the individual differences among people in a particular job or school curriculum. On the *MMPI*, these minor deviations from average show how a given individual tends to behave and thus what job choices might be most suitable. The counselor should note here that the balance of the total pattern shown by significant high and low scores is the element which usually gives meaning to the pattern and indicates the psychological balance of personality traits within a given individual. Cottle and Powell (1951) have demonstrated that to secure a normal profile it is necessary to have the integrating effect of a human personality. A normal profile is not secured by random methods of answering the *MMPI*.

In the *MMPI* it is this balance of high and low scores which indicates a normal adjustment. An example would be a score on the Psychopathic deviate scale which is high, accompanied by high scores on the neurotic triad. In this type of profile there frequently appears to be sufficient pressure from the neurotic elements to prevent a severe character disorder or sociopathic behavior. Another example would be a rise on Psychopathic deviate and Hypomania, accompanied by a Social extroversion score which is balanced by a slight rise on the Psychasthenia scale.

This inventory has been demonstrated over and over to be an effective tool for the screening of the emotionally disturbed from a group. High scores in almost any combination are an indication of some abnormal behavior. In this way it has been used in universities, industry, and the military services. Research by Forbes and Cottle (1953) showed that the reading level was 5.4 (by an average of five formulas of readability). This would indicate that it could be used with younger clients, except for one fact. Many of the items would be considered highly objectionable by student and parents, especially some which appear related to sexual and religious behavior. Research indicates that this inventory has been used

Table 10.1
RELIABILITY COEFFICIENTS FOR CARD VS. BOOKLET
FORM OF THE *MMPI* WITH 100 COLLEGE STUDENTS

	N	L	K	F	Hs	D	Hy	Pd	Mf	Pa	Pt	Sc	Ma
r_{cb} Males	68	.51	.79	.77	.72	.65	.65	.81	.83	.53	.92	.90	.78
r_{cb} Females	32	.34	.72	.72	.91	.69	.83	.79	.79	.63	.87	.82	.75
r_{cb} (Product moment)	100	.46	.76	.75	.81	.66	.72	.80	.91	.56	.90	.86	.76

with some success in vocational and educational counseling. Certain vocational groups have been shown to have typical profiles. However, the research on this aspect of the *MMPI* is quite limited, and few generalizations can be drawn. It must also be reiterated that the individual scales cannot be used *alone* for differential diagnosis.

The reliabilities of the individual scales, as reported in the *Manual*, tend to be in the .70's. Cottle (1950), using correlations between scores on the individual or card form vs. the group or booklet form, showed coefficients on the clinical scales ranging between .51 and .92 for males, and between .34 and .91 for females with a median between .79 and .80; a week was the maximum time between the two administrations. When this inventory is used by a professionally competent person, there is evidence that it has validity. Results obtained with it agree with other evidence contained in the case history. Ellis (1946, 1953) and Ellis and Conrad (1948), in summaries of the validity of personality inventories, showed that the *MMPI* consistently appears to show the most evidence of validity of all these inventories. It might be noted that Ellis, especially in his 1946 study, set up exceptionally high standards for acceptable validity.

It must be emphasized that the counselor should learn to use this instrument under supervision. The *MMPI* should be considered a highly professional instrument, with a complex interpretation learned only in a training situation. As with the *Binet, Wechsler*, and some of the projective methods, a casual reading of manuals or looking at profiles or case studies is not considered an adequate way for the beginning counselor to achieve competence in the use of the inventory.

The Minnesota Counseling Inventory

The *Minnesota Counseling Inventory* (*MCI*) was constructed using items from both the *MMPI* and the older *Minnesota Personality Scale*. The *MCI* (The Psychological Corporation) consists of 355 items that are responded to on a Yes-No basis. The *MMPI* items that were used were rewritten to make them more suitable and thus more acceptable to high-school personnel and to students and their parents. Nine scores result from the use of the inventory: Social relationships, Family relationships, and Emotional stability from the old *Minnesota Personality Scale;* and Conformity, Adjustment to reality, Mood, and Leadership from the *MMPI* items. There is also a Validity scale derived from the *MMPI* L-scale, and a Question scale based upon the number of items omitted. Odd-even reliability coefficients for these scales show considerable variation, from the .50's to the .90's. Test-retest coefficients cover about the same range, all indicating that there is not enough stability to warrant their use in individual counseling.

Since this inventory is based in part on the *MMPI*, scores obtained with it are probably (as are those from the *MMPI*) strongly affected by acquiescence and the giving of socially desirable answers (Jackson and Messick 1961). The authors of the *MCI* apparently have done very little to control response bias, and probably the ensuing validity is lowered. The inventory was validated by having teachers select individuals considered high on the various traits, to see if the scales actually measured what they were purported to measure. The scales that measured the more overt types of behavior gave more indications of validity than those that measured the more internal or personal aspects of behavior.

The California Psychological Inventory

Another inventory developed from research with the *MMPI* is the *California Psychological Inventory* (*CPI*) published by Gough (1956). The inventory has 480 items contributing to scores for 18 scales. It uses normative groups composed of persons from educational settings who have not been designated as abnormal. Thus it presents some advantages over the *MMPI* for use with high-school and college students.

About 200 of the items are from the *MMPI* and are identified with various scales which Gough constructed in his research with that instrument. Gough (1964) says that for 12 of the scales he has used a system of construction called the "empirical technique," because as his criterion he first defined the dimension of behavior he intended to measure and then collected items pertinent to that dimension in an experimental scale. He then chose contrasting high- and low-scoring groups on that scale, and examined their behavior in terms of adjectival descriptions as the outside criterion. The remaining scales were constructed by item analysis.

The *CPI* is a 12-page booklet which can be hand-scored, machine-scored, or scored with a special National Computer Systems process. The proper answer sheet should be specified at purchase. The instrument usually takes about 50 minutes to administer, but is technically "untimed." It has separate sex norms composed of 6,000 males and 7,000 females. It uses standard *T*-score units. Factor analyses of the *CPI* show that four or five factors seem to account for most of the variance of the 18 scales, with general agreement on the two factors measured in the first two groups of scales. Readability is about ninth-grade level.

There are three validating scales: Well-being *Wb*, Good impression *Gi*, and Communality *Cm*. On the *Wb* scale a low score indicates persons who malinger or "fake bad" on such inventories. Very high scores on the *Gi* scale indicate the person who tries to "fake good" or who is most concerned with manipulating others. The higher the *Cm*-scale score, the more the individual's responses resemble those of the original normative groups. Gough considers that persons with scores *below* 25 of the 28 items did not understand the inventory, answered randomly, or were careless in responding.

The other 15 scales are: Dominance *Do*, Capacity for status *Cs*, Sociability *Sy*, Social presence *Sp*, Self-acceptance *Sa*, Responsibility *Re*, Socialization *So*, Self-control *Sc*, Tolerance *To*, Achievement by conformity *Ac*, Achievement through independence *Ai*, Intellectual efficiency *Ie*, Psychological-mindedness *Py*, Flexibility *Fx*, and Femininity *Fe*. They are interpreted in terms of the meaning of each scale, in terms of the interaction between scales, and in terms of profile analysis. The *Manual* (1964), and also Cottle (1968), discuss the construction and interpretation of the *CPI* in more detail.

FORCED-CHOICE TECHNIQUES

In the 1930's, Kuder began experimenting with the forced-choice technique in the development of his vocational interest inventory. The form and use of forced-choice items were illustrated in the previous chapter when the *Kuder Preference Record* was discussed. During World War II and in the period shortly thereafter, this technique was applied to personality inventories. The general feeling was that the forced-choice technique reduced the ability of the subject to falsify the results. Since this is most important when the inventories are used for employment and promotion, it is not strange that the original research with the use of this technique in adjustment inventories began in an industrial or military setting. For example, Jurgensen (1944) developed a so-called *Classification Inventory* for industrial use. Shipley, Gray, and Newbert (1946) developed the *Personal Inventory* for psychiatric use in the Navy. Each item of this inventory consisted of two parts, and the respondent had to select the one that best described him. The items were paired on the basis of social acceptability but differed on the basis of the frequency with which they were chosen by so-called "normals" and "disturbed." Jurgensen's differed from this in that the items were in triad form like the *Kuder*, the respondent selecting the ones that he most and least preferred. The main objective, as has been pointed out, was to decrease the likelihood of falsifying or fudging the results. Edwards and. Thurstone (1953) applied the psychological scaling methods to the equating of items on the basis of equal social acceptability. In the *Personal Preference Schedule* (*PPS*), Edwards (1954, 1959) describes methods that he used in equating the pairs of items making up the *PPS* on the basis of the degree of social acceptability of each.

The research on this alleged claim of lowering fakability by advocates of forced-choice inventories is far from conclusive. Linden (1958) administered the *Guilford-Zimmerman Temperament Survey* to groups of university students, in its original form and in two forced-choice forms, one made up of three responses per item and the other of two parts to each item. Each form was given under normal administering conditions; then, for each form, the respondents were asked to make themselves appear as they would under certain described circumstances. The forced-choice forms were put together using methods suggested by Edwards for assuring that the different parts of each item had equal social acceptability. In brief, Linden produced results that were inconclusive, although in general, it was more difficult to fake responses on the three-part forced-choice form of the inventory than on the other two. Faking seemed related to the scales, for on some scales it was possible to shape the results to the respondent's desires on all three forms.

The *Edwards Personal Preference Schedule* will be discussed as an example of a forced-choice type of inventory supposedly balanced for response set. According to the *Manual,* the instrument was designed to measure a number of relatively independent variables that were obtained from a list of manifest needs developed by H. A. Murray *et al.* (1953). This inventory measures 15 of these needs:

1. *Ach.* *Achievement:* to do one's best, to be successful, to do a difficult job well.
2. *Def.* *Deference:* to get suggestions from others, to find out what others think, to let others make decisions.
3. *Ord.* *Order:* to have work neat, to plan in advance, to keep files neat and orderly.
4. *Exh.* *Exhibition:* to say witty things, to tell clever jokes, to be the center of attention.
5. *Aut.* *Autonomy:* to be independent of others, to say what one thinks about things, to criticize others, to avoid responsibilities.

6. *Aff.*   *Affiliation:* to be loyal to friends, to participate in friendly groups, to share and to do things with friends.

7. *Int.*   *Intraception:* to analyze one's motives and feelings, to understand how others feel about things, to predict the behavior of others.

8. *Suc.*   *Succorance:* to receive a great deal of affection from others, to be helped by others, to have a fuss made by others when not feeling well.

9. *Dom.*   *Dominance:* to be a leader, to argue for one's point of view, to settle arguments, to supervise, and to tell others how to do things.

10. *Aba.*   *Abasement:* to feel guilty when one does something wrong, to feel timid and inferior, to feel better when giving in.

11. *Nur.*   *Nurturance:* to help friends when they are in trouble, to treat others with kindness and sympathy, to have others confide in one.

12. *Chg.*   *Change:* to do new and different things, to experiment, to try new jobs, to move about the country.

13. *End.*   *Endurance:* to keep at a job until it is finished, to work hard at a task, to avoid being interrupted while working.

14. *Het.*   *Heterosexuality:* to associate with members of the opposite sex, to be in love with one of the opposite sex, to read books about sex.

15. *Agg.*   *Aggression:* to attack contrary points of view, to make fun of others, to become angry, to blame others when things go wrong.

In addition, there is a *Consistency* variable based upon a comparison of the number of identical responses made in two sets of the same 15 items. A Consistency score of 10 or higher is considered by Edwards to indicate that the subject is not responding to the items on the basis of chance alone.

In building the inventory, Edwards compared each of the 15 traits with every other trait two times. The maximum score, then, for any given variable is 28. The respondent goes through the 225 pairs of items making up the inventory, and from each pair of items he selects the one that he believes most characteristic of himself. The inventory is rather long, and university students require about a full period to complete it. Scoring is straightforward, with hand-scored or IBM answer sheets available.

Reliability coefficients reported in the *Manual* show that this type of inventory is neither more nor less reliable than the usual form. A table of intercorrelations among the 15 variables shows that, in general, these intercorrelations are quite low—the highest, .46 between Affiliation and Nurturance—being quite atypical. Validity is demonstrated in the *Manual* by showing correlations between the different scales of the *EPPS* and the *Guilford-Martin Personnel Inventory* and the *Taylor Manifest Anxiety Scale.* Significant correlations in the expected direction were obtained for the scales where they would be expected. The *EPPS* seems to add a lot of information to the counseling situation. Some users of the inventory in counseling situations feel that it gives excellent insights into the makeup of the client.

Allen (1957) administered both the *MMPI* and *EPPS* to 130 university students. Intercorrelations were then computed between the various scores obtained upon the two instruments. Of the 630 correlations, 69 were significant at the 5% level and 21 at the 1% level. All of these significant coefficients, however, were quite low, indicating that these two inventories are in general measuring rather different aspects of personality.

In another study, Merrill and Heathers (1956), as a result of administering the same two inventories to another college group, concluded that since the intercorrelations among the various keys of the two instruments are not high, both are useful in the counseling situation. They state that while the *EPPS* indicates the relative strength that an individual gives to certain needs, the *MMPI* shows degrees of responses similar to well-defined clinical groups. They point out that data from one inventory supplement those from the other, just as information from the *Allport-Vernon-Lindzey Study of Values* supplements data obtained from the *SVIB*. In another study, Dunnette *et al.* (1958) correlated scores on the *EPPS* with 11 group scores from the *SVIB* and with the 18 scores obtained from the *California Psychological Inventory* (an instrument similar to the *MMPI*). A large number of rather low but significant correlations resulted. The authors concluded, "To a great extent then, the correlations shown among scales in this study are reflections of tendencies to be dominant, confident, and sociable on the one hand as opposed to tendencies toward permissiveness, dependency, and individualistic activities on the other."

A review of the research literature of the *EPPS* shows that this inventory is not all that its author had hoped it would be. Many of the studies revealed that the *EPPS* was not a valid measure of the 15 "basic needs," as claimed. A study by Levonian *et al.* (1959) showed that the *EPPS* measured a series of narrow factors based upon common items, rather than any large factors. These writers pointed out that the failure of the inventory to produce the expected results was caused in part by the use of the same item statements in several different item pairs, which resulted in a significant amount of overlap among the scales. Also, scoring the same item on two different scales introduced overlapping variance in the different scales. It was pointed out that some of the trouble might be related to the fact that the two parts of each item being of equal social desirability makes it difficult for the subject to make a choice between them. It is possible that the equality of social desirability of the two parts of each item may make both parts equally inapplicable; thus, the client has a difficult time trying to be accurate and consistent. Another problem with scores obtained with forced-choice scales such as the *EPPS* and the various *Kuder* instruments is that the scores can be used as a type called "ipsative," as opposed to those obtained with an instrument such as the *Guilford-Zimmerman Temperament Scale* or the *Strong Vocational Interest Blank,* which are of the normative type. Ipsative measures result in an individual's being high on some scales and low on others. When the means are computed for all subjects over all scales of an inventory, they are all approximately the same. Differences between the scores of any one subject reflect only relative strengths and weaknesses *of that individual.* Differences among students on a particular scale cannot really be interpreted in a normative fashion. Knapp (1964) using *Gordon's Survey of Interpersonal Values* (Science Research Associates), an ipsative measure, showed that when the scale was used in its usual form and when it was again administered by preceding each item with the statement "It is important to me" and asking the subject to respond Yes or No, thereby making it a normative measure, that quite different results followed. He reported that when a group of naval offenders and nonoffenders took this inventory in both forms, statistically significant results were obtained on the Conformity and Independence scales with the normative form, but not with the ipsative one. The normative data showed that nonoffenders placed a greater value on conformity and that offenders placed a greater value on independence. Today the general opinion among test experts is that it is incorrect to use ipsative measures when one would like to determine intercorrelations among variables. Ipsative data should not be used in factor analysis. The reason for all of this is that individual differences, when ipsative measures are used, have little meaning, because there is not a single scale upon which to measure all individuals (Guilford 1954). When ipsative scores are correlated, the resulting coefficients tend to be slight and negative.

Other ipsative inventories are *Gordon's Personal Inventory* and his *Personal Profile* (both published by Harcourt, Brace & World, Inc.)

Summary

Considerable space has been given to a description and discussion of several personality inventories, but it does not cover all those that have been published. The reader who wishes more information should consult Anastasi (1968), Downie (1967), Kleinmuntz (1967), the last several volumes of Buros, or the catalogs of the various test publishers. Again, it must be emphasized that personality inventories are useful to the counselor when they are used correctly. Much of the evidence of lack of validity that has been produced has come about because of their misuse. This section will be closed with reference to a comment by Meehl (1945), in which he points out that the responses to the items on these inventories are not important as *facts*, but as indicators as to how the client *feels* about the items. It is not important whether the client does or does not have frequent colds when compared to others. What is important here is that such an individual *feels* that he has frequent colds and is thus seen to be concerned about his health. The cumulative effect of the responses to such items as this leads to the identification of individuals with abnormal concern about their health.

PROBLEM CHECKLISTS

Problem checklists differ from structured inventories mostly in the method in which the client responds to the items on them and in the method of scoring. In one of the most widely used of these checklists, the *Mooney Problem Check List* (The Psychological Corporation), the client is confronted with a list of problems covering varying areas of adjustment and is asked to read through the list carefully and to underline those statements he feels are problems. When he has finished the checklist, he is told to go back and draw a circle about the number in front of those problems he feels are bothering him most. Actually, there are no scores for this checklist. Since the problems are arranged in groups representing similar problems, a summary may be made of the number of problems checked in each of the areas. But here the scoring ends. There are no labels to attach to the individual on the basis of his profile, nor are there profiles based upon so few items that they are unreliable.

The Mooney Problem Check Lists

In the current revision of the Mooney checklists, four forms are available: College, *C;* High-school, *H;* Junior high-school, *J;* and Adult, *A.* In the College and High-school forms there are 330 items, 30 in each of the following areas:

I. Health and physical development *HPD*
II. Finances, living conditions, and employment *FLE*
III. Social and recreational activities *SRA*
IV. Social-psychological relations *SPR*
V. Personal-psychological relations *PPR*
VI. Courtship, sex, and marriage *CSM*
VII. Home and family *HF*

VIII. Morals and religion *MR*

IX. Adjustment to college or school work *ACW, ASW*

X. The Future: Vocational and educational *FVE*

XI. Curriculum and teaching procedure *CTP*

The Junior high-school form is made up of 210 items, 30 in each of 7 areas. The items are systematically arranged in groups, in a six-page folder. For example, the items appraising the Health and physical development area occupy the top five positions in each of six columns. The number of items marked in this area is easily summed, and the number checked by the client is inserted into a space at the right. Items making up each of the other areas are arranged in like fashion.

After the client responds to the items, he is asked if he feels that the items that he checked actually present a good picture of his problems. He is then asked to summarize his problems in his own words. There is adequate space on the back of the checklist for this. Finally he is asked if he would like to talk about these problems with some member of the staff and, if so, with whom.

The items for these checklists were obtained from such sources as the analyses of paragraphs written by 4,000 high-school students in which they described their personal problems; a review of 5,000 cards itemizing the personal and educational needs expressed by students in grades 6, 9, and 12; an intensive analysis of expressed problems of 250 students in grades 7 through 12; analyses of case histories and counseling interviews; and the like. The authors used the following criteria in selecting the items for the lists (see Mooney and Gordon 1950): (1) phrased in the language of students; (2) short for rapid reading; (3) self-sufficient as individual phrases; (4) common enough to be checked frequently in a large group of students or serious enough to be important in an individual case; (5) graduated in difficulty from relatively minor to major concerns; (6) vague enough in rather personal or delicate situations to enable the student to be able to check the item and still feel that he can conceal his problem in later conferences if he chooses to do so; and (7) centered within the student's own personal orientation. Such an approach in item construction and selection assures that the instrument has content validity. Research has also demonstrated that these checklists possess both concurrent and predictive validity.

Reliability coefficients reported in the *Manual* are above .90. These were obtained by successive readministrations of the inventory to the same individuals, and hence are coefficients of stability. This is the only type of reliability coefficient that can be correctly obtained for an instrument of this type.

In using this checklist, the counselor should, after frequency counts of the different areas have been entered into the proper spaces, note the areas of greatest and least concentrations of problems. The client's summarizing statement should be read, and similarities and discrepancies looked for. Then the counselor should examine other data about the client, interrelate all the material, and decide the direction that the counseling situation might most profitably take. As Mooney and Gordon (1950) note in the *Manual:*

it is clearly necessary to evaluate the problems marked by the individual in terms of his particular environmental and psychological situation and in terms of the particular circumstances under which the *Problem Check List* was given. Only then can interpretation result in a realistic appreciation of the individual's problem world and, subsequently, in guidance that is appropriate in concrete situations. Merely counting the problems is not enough for these purposes.

These checklists are also very useful in screening out those individuals who are in need of considerable counseling or possibly psychotherapy. The authors suggest that this can be done by using the total number of items checked on the entire list, the number of items marked in a particular area, the responses to particular items, and the client's statement as to whether or not he would like to discuss the results of the inventory with a staff member.

In summary, the *Mooney Problem Check Lists* are both reliable and valid indicators of client problems. They have the additional advantage over personality inventories that the client is not forced to respond to the items. There is a permissive atmosphere about them, and about statements such as, "Here is a group of problems that individuals like yourself have." "Would you care to check over those that are your problems and talk about the results with a counselor?" The client, if he does not wish to do this or feels that his problems are of no importance, then does not make a lot of responses that in the end would be worthless. And since there are no scores, there can be no labels that can be placed upon an individual. It is all too easy for uninformed individuals to take the results from some personality inventories and associate certain terms as "paranoid," "schizophrenic," "psychopath," and the like with an individual. It must be recalled that it is yet to be demonstrated that these inventories are capable of use for differential diagnosis.

The SRA Youth Inventory

The *SRA Youth Inventory: Form A* (Remmers and Shimberg 1949) is a checklist consisting of 298 items covering the following areas: (1) My school; (2) After high school; (3) About myself; (4) Getting along with others; (5) My home and family; (6) Boy meets girl; (7) Health; and (8) Things in general. This checklist resulted from an investigation conducted by the Purdue Opinion Panel on the problems of high-school youth. Teen-agers in both urban and rural schools located all over the United States were asked to write anonymous essays about their problems. These essays were examined and analyzed by the members of the Purdue Opinion Panel, and finally the items making up the *SRA Youth Inventory* emerged from the study.

As with the *Mooney Check Lists*, the client goes through the list marking those problems that he feels are related to him. The inventory differs from the *Mooney* in that centile norms for urban and rural boys and girls are available for each of the areas measured by the checklist. In addition, there is a Basic difficulty score that is based upon 109 items that are felt by psychologists to be most indicative of basic personality problems. When this checklist is used as a screening device, it is suggested that these Basic difficulty scores be obtained for all students, and that those with the highest scores be the first scheduled for counseling.

Form S, the revised edition of the *SRA Youth Inventory* (Remmers and Shimberg 1956), is very similar to the original edition except in the manner of making the responses to the items. The authors have established what they call an intensity dimension. Each item is followed by three squares of decreasing size and a 0. The instructions tell the respondent to mark the largest square if the statement describes one of his most serious problems; the middle-size box, if a moderate problem; the smallest box if a small or occasional problem; and the 0 if the statement does not express the way he feels. An intensity score is obtained by multiplying the number of marks in the largest squares by 3, those in the second size boxes by 2, and the number of checks in the smallest boxes by 1, and summing all three products. Since both of these checklists are used similarly to the *Mooney* in screening and counseling, it is unnecessary to repeat what was previously mentioned about usage.

Adjective Check List

Another type of checklist is exemplified by the *Adjective Check List* developed by Gough (1955). This list consists of 300 adjectives ranging from "absent-minded" to "zany." The client is told to go through the checklist rapidly and to place a mark in front of each one that he feels to be self-descriptive. The list is scored for 14 scales, covering such variables as Originality, Good judgment, Likeability, Rigidity, and Social poise and presence. In scoring the checklist, attention is paid not only to those adjectives that have been checked, but also to those that were not checked. For example, on the Originality scale the directions are to score

1 point for each of 8 adjectives checked and 1 point for each of 34 adjectives not checked. In the *Manual,* data are presented showing reliability coefficients somewhat lower than those usually obtained with the typical adjustment inventories. Studies showing relationships with other techniques used for appraisal of personality are also reported. At the present time, the evidence indicates that this adjective checklist is a useful research instrument. It is simple, short, and, as the author says, "nonthreatening."

PROJECTIVE TECHNIQUES

The various techniques that are grouped under this heading are all similar in that an ambiguous stimulus of one sort or another is presented to the client and he is required to make a free response to this stimulus. These methods are referred to as being "unstructured," "semi-structured," or "free-response" in their makeup and use. The general idea underlying all of them is that it is hoped by the examiner that the client will bring out significant statements and feelings that may offer the examiner insight into the client's behavioral problems.

Included under this general heading of projectives are such devices as the *Rorschach Inkblot Test,* the *Thematic Apperception Test (TAT),* sentence, paragraph, and story completion techniques, word association, analysis of drawings and paintings, play analysis, the autobiography, diary, and essay, and the responses to various test situations such as the *Rosenzweig Picture Frustration Test.* In the pages that follow no attempt will be made to discuss these various techniques in any detail, although a few that the counselor might be able to use will be described. The student who wishes to read about these instruments in detail is referred to Abt and Bellak (1950), Anderson and Anderson (1951), Bell (1948), or Lindzey (1961). The general problems associated with projective techniques and their use in counseling will also be considered.

Most projective tests are individual tests requiring the presence of the examiner to record the responses of the examinee. To collect the data, and especially to analyze them, requires that the examiner be trained in the specific method. To be able to use the *Rorschach,* the psychologist finds that he has to take several graduate-level courses or attend a workshop or seminar conducted by a *Rorschach* specialist. Responses are interpreted under guidance, just as with the *Stanford-Binet.* There is a little difference here, however, in that the various specialists seem to have different ways of interpreting the same responses. Projective tests are more customarily used as basic tools by the clinical psychologist. In his training he takes courses that enable him to use these devices. The

counselor should not attempt to interpret them unless this extensive training has been completed. The counselor should, however, know the function these devices perform and should be able to use the information
provided by the clinician who administered the instrument.

As noted earlier in this chapter, projective tests have been around for
some time, beginning with the word-association techniques that go back
to Jung and the inkblots of the *Rorschach* test in 1921. In clinics many
are used daily, and thousands of articles about them have appeared in
the journals over the years. Probably their popularity is great because
of their general makeup. They are novel, interesting, and diverting from
the viewpoint of the client, and clinicians *feel* that they *work*. They may
divert the client's attention from other immediate problems.

When one applies the usual criteria for an acceptable test to projective
techniques, one is apt to find that these devices fall far short of standards
of acceptance. Very little study of reliability is found except for discussions of the reliability of the scorer, such as have been associated with the
use of the essay examination in the classroom for the past 60 years. The
validation studies are no better. Many of them are statistically naïve,
the experimenter making no attempt to cross-validate his results. Cronbach (1949) summarized the research on the validity of the *Rorschach*
by saying that, of the results or differences reported significant at the 5%
level, the majority were probably due to chance. Kelly (1954) makes one
of the most apt summaries of the use of these techniques when he says:
"The curious state of affairs wherein the most widely (and confidently)
used techniques are those for which there is little or no evidence of predictive validity is indeed a phenomenon appropriate for study by social
psychologists." For many of these instruments, normative data are either
absent or of very poor quality. The builder of a projective device frequently uses, as norm groups, patients in clinics or hospitals. Little attention is paid to individuals whose behavior is within the normal range.
Thus, unless the clinicians are themselves quite well adjusted and have
considerable information about normal behavior, each interpretation by
a different clinician of the same series of responses may vary. In the
space below some of the more frequently encountered projective tests
will be described briefly.

Rorschach

Probably the most popular of all projective instruments is the *Rorschach*. This consists of a series of 10 cards, each of which contains a
large inkblot on a white background, 5 in black and 5 in color. The client
is asked to tell what he sees. The responses are recorded and then
analyzed by one of several methods. In general, uniqueness of response

is what is felt to be of most psychological significance. There are several formal scoring systems, but no general agreement on scoring has been reached.

TAT

The *Thematic Apperception Test* (*TAT*) consists of a series of cards, some for men, some for women, and others that are responded to by both sexes. On each card is an ambiguous picture, such as might be used to illustrate a story in one of the popular magazines. The client is asked to tell a story about the picture as each is handed to him. Specifically, he is asked to tell what he feels has happened and what is going to happen. His stories are then evaluated according to the *Manual* (Murray 1943). The evaluation is usually made on the basis of themes that tend to recur from picture to picture.

Sentence Completion

Typical of sentence completion techniques is the *Rotter Incomplete Sentences Blank* (Rotter and Rafferty 1950). This instrument consists of 40 so-called "stems" like the following:

I need _____
Best friends _____
Women _____

The client filling out the blank is to complete each of the sentences in such a way as to express his real feelings.

The *Manual* contains scoring examples for males and females separately. Responses are scored on a 7-point scale, values ranging from 6 to 0. The most undesirable responses have the highest values. For example, to the stem "At bedtime," the response "I become depressed" receives 6 points; "I am tired" (a neutral response) receives 3 points; and "I go to sleep right away" (an example of the most positive type of response) receives 0 points. Samples such as these are prepared for the evaluation of the student's responses. Scoring is not difficult, and it does not take long for a scorer to become adept at assigning values to various responses. A high score is a reflection of poor adjustment; a low score indicates desirable status. Split-half reliability coefficients in the low .80's are reported for the *Rotter* in the *Manual*. Validity has been demonstrated by differences between mean scores of individuals rated "adjusted" and "maladjusted."

Rotter and Rafferty (1950) summarized the general advantages of their blank in the *Manual* by noting that: (1) there is freedom of response; (2) there is some disguise of the purpose of the test; (3) group administration is efficient; (4) no special training is needed for administration; (5) scoring is quite objective; (6) time of administration is short; and (7) the method is flexible in that new stems may be made for different purposes. As disadvantages, the authors note that: (1) machine scoring is impossible; (2) disguise is not as great as in the other projective tests; and (3) with uncooperative, illiterate, or disturbed subjects, insufficient responses often result. This listing of advantages and limitations adequately covers all similar blanks.

The chief purpose of a blank like this is to serve as a screening device to pick out those individuals in a group who are in need of counseling. Of the different projective tests, this is one that meets standard criteria.

Similar to these sentence completion tests are others referred to as "paragraph" or "story completion." In general, they are the same as those described except that a paragraph or a story is started and the client is asked to finish it.

Other Projective Techniques

The remaining projective techniques, such as methods of diagnosing play, analysis of paintings and drawings, situational tests, and others, have value to the clinical or child psychologist but have little to offer the counselor directly.

Summary

Most of the research that has been done on the use of projective techniques in the counseling situation has been on the *Rorschach*. Patterson (1957) reviewed and summarized this research adequately, and concludes that in the light of the known reliabilities and validities they have little to offer the vocational counseling situation. Studies that claimed success with the *Rorschach* in vocational or educational prediction failed to hold up under cross-validation. In other studies, it was shown that simple paper-and-pencil tests did a much better job and, of course, were much cheaper in time and costs. Patterson concluded that "The widespread use of projective techniques, and their enthusiastic acceptance and extension in all areas of applied psychology, with so little critical analysis of their value is amazing." The counselor should remember that there are much better instruments meriting further research and development. When we know more about the *SVIB*, the *SCAT*, the *DAT*, and the *MMPI*, perhaps then, if the projective tests still exist in that remote time, their value in vocational counseling might be investigated.

ATTITUDES

Attitudes are usually defined as the tendency to react toward or against an object or value. Attitudes arise from daily experiences. They may be likened to a potential which is built up within the individual and which is released as the individual responds in a certain manner when the proper stimulation is presented. Consider politics, for example. Suppose that an individual is a Democrat. When a political stimulus is presented, as in a political discussion, the Democrat responds in a way that reflects his feelings and opinions about the Democratic Party. These are his attitudes. Attitudes are either learned from personal experience or are unconsciously adopted from one's social environment. Children tend to reflect the same religious, political, and racial attitudes as their parents, a result of social inheritance. *Interests* are very similar to attitudes. As a matter of fact, they may be considered a special type of attitude. Attitudes may best be thought of as comprehensive, including, along with those aspects of an individual that are usually considered attitudes, other concepts, such as interests, values, mores, appreciations, and the like.

In the pages that follow, only a brief discussion of the evaluation of attitudes will be presented. Anyone who wishes to pursue the topic in detail should see Remmers (1954) or Edwards (1957a). Summaries of the techniques used in attitude appraisal are found in Downie (1967).

The measurement of attitudes began in a scientific manner with the work of Thurstone (see Thurstone and Chave 1929). Thurstone and his students at that time constructed scales for the measurement of attitudes toward many concepts, especially those of a controversial nature—war, evolution, and Prohibition, for example. While these early scales are dated and mostly useless today, the technique used by Thurstone is frequently encountered. Thurstone's method involves the writing of a large number of items about the attitude under study. These should be variable enough to cover all shades of opinion. The items are next presented to a number of judges (Thurstone said at least 50) who are asked to sort them into 11 piles, the pile at one extreme reflecting the most favorable attitude and that at the other end the most unfavorable, the neutral attitude being represented by the center pile. Since it is assumed that the piles are equally placed along a continuum, the method is known as that of "equal-appearing intervals." Each item is given a scale value on the basis of the median value assigned to it by the judges. When there is much disagreement about an item, it is discarded. Each item ends up with a specific value, and the scale is constructed by selecting a series of 20 or more items that cover a wide range of scale values. For example, below are several items from the scale *Attitude toward the Law*, with their respective scale values:

The law is more than the enactments of Congress; it is a sacred institution. 10.5: highly favorable attitude.
Some laws command our respect while others are mere regulations. 6.1: neutral attitude.
The law is just another name for tyranny. 0.8: highly unfavorable attitude.

In completing a Thurstone-type scale, the respondent goes through the items and places a mark in front of those with which he agrees. The scale values of these are taken, and the median is computed. This average, falling somewhere between 0 and 11, will give an indication of the examinee's attitude toward the object in question. In each of the *Manuals* are norms for translating the medians into qualitative terms.

Likert Scales

The major difficulty with the use of Thurstone's scales is that they are laborious and time-consuming in their construction. This is especially true in reference to obtaining a large number of competent judges for each scale and in the amount of time spent in evaluating the items by the judges. Likert (1932) developed another method that does not have this limitation. After items reflecting various degrees of the attitude toward the object in question have been written, the respondent answers each item on a 5-point scale: Strongly agree, Agree, Undecided or no opinion, Disagree, and Strongly disagree. Favorable items have a value of 5, 4, 3, 2, and 1 ranging from Strongly agree to Strongly disagree. Unfavorable items are scored in reverse fashion, values of 1, 2, 3, 4, and 5 ranging from Strongly agree to Strongly disagree. A high score, then, would reflect a favorable attitude toward the attitudinal object. After administering the items on the experimental form of the scale, an item analysis is made. Those items that correlate highest with the total score are retained and become the next form of the scale. The construction of a scale like this is very simple. Studies have shown that the correlation between scores, when the same attitude is appraised by both the Thurstone and Likert method, is very high. It is not strange then that a good share of modern attitude testing is done with scales of this type. Items on both the *Minnesota Teacher Attitude Inventory* and the *Minnesota Inventories of Social Attitudes* are of this type (both published by The Psychological Corporation).

Other Techniques

Many of the techniques that have been previously discussed may be used for evaluating attitudes. For example, both the autobiography and the essay may be structured to cover attitudes. Sentence and paragraph completion have been used to evaluate social and racial attitudes. Observational techniques, in the form of anecdotal records and rating scales, are very useful methods. There are a few standardized scales available, but these are not too numerous. Checklists of one type or another may offer evidence of attitudes. A method referred to as "error-choice" disguises the purpose of the scale (Kubany 1953). The test, as constructed, is made up in part of a group of items that are very simple and that have a correct answer. Mixed with these is another group of items that have no correct answer, both the alternatives offered as answers are wrong, one erring in one direction and the other in the opposite direction. The score consists of the individual's responses to these items; if he tends to select the responses going in one direction, this is taken as his attitude toward whatever the scale is measuring.

The chief problem with the use of instruments to measure attitudes is validity. The psychological and educational literature is full of studies that reveal validity coefficients of 0 or thereabouts. *In simple language, this usually means that there is no relationship between what individuals say they would do (their attitudes) and their behavior.* The causes of such poor results are varied, depending upon the technique used and the user. Measurement of attitude has to be divorced from other types of measurement; sometimes it has been administered as part of an achievement test. Just the hint of a grade will cause the real attitudes to be concealed, and socially desirable responses (at least from the viewpoint of the teacher) substituted. Then the attitudes of an individual may be classified as private and public attitudes. An individual has no objection to letting others know about his public attitudes, but private attitudes are another matter. These make up one's own very intimate religious, political, sexual, or other attitudes. There are times when many do not wish to reveal them, feeling they are nobody else's business. Another problem is that sometimes the attitudinal object is so general that the respondent can easily agree that it is desirable. However, when specifics that make up the general attitude are responded to, the respondent reacts differently to them. In other words, although favoring "internationalism," the respondent opposes the various things necessary for internationalism. Good rapport with the respondent, more disguised scales, and the evaluation of the more public attitudes may do a lot toward the attainment of acceptable validity and the avoidance of socially acceptable responses and other kinds of response sets. Combining observation and attitude measurement may help, also.

A knowledge of a client's attitudes is important in counseling. Different attitudes are associated with different occupations. Even within an occupation, attitudes differ, depending on what the individual is doing. For example, elementary teachers reflect attitudes different from those of high-school teachers when their attitudes are measured by the *Minnesota Teacher Attitude Inventory* (see Downie 1958) and the *Experimental Attitude Scale* (see Ashlock and Cottle 1958). There is no question that similar attitudinal differences can be found in many vocations. Among the various vocations the differences are even more pronounced. For example, consider the attitudes of contrasting groups such as social workers and policemen, labor organizers and plant managers or supervisors, research physicists and clinical psychologists. It can also be shown that the attitudes of teachers and counselors differ. Attitudes, then, are another important aspect of the counseling situation.

Socioeconomic Status

It has been previously mentioned that scores made by clients should be interpreted in the light of what is known about the client's socioeconomic and cultural background. The effects of environment on intelligence-test scores have been noted. Information about the client's background may be collected in various ways. In some school situations, especially in smaller schools, certain teachers—especially home economics and agriculture teachers—have entrance to the homes of some of the students. In hospitals or other agencies, social workers gather such data. In other groups it is almost impossible to know about background without asking the client. Asking the client the occupation of his parent is one method. However, when the counselor asks the client, he soon becomes frustrated by, first, the problem of the candidness of the client's response and, second, the meaninglessness of it. "Machinist" can cover many occupations of varying degrees of skill and responsibility. "Railroad worker" covers everyone from track walker to president.

In an attempt to obtain valid measures of background, various score cards and scales were developed. For example, the obsolete *Sims Score Card* was made up of a series of items covering the education of the parents, the occupation of the parents, the physical aspects of the home, and the like. Responses were filled in by the student. *The American Home Scale* (Psychometric Affiliates) is similar, measuring four areas: cultural, aesthetic, economic, and miscellaneous. Both of these can be easily distorted by the respondent's giving socially desirable answers. Warner, Meeker, and Eells (1951) have developed an *Index of Status,* based upon occupation, source of income, housing, and dwelling area of the individual being evaluated.

Another approach is the *Sims SCI (Social Class Identification) Occupational Rating Scale,* published by Harcourt, Brace & World, Inc. (Sims 1952). This consists of 42 occupations, ranging from professional worker down to the most unskilled type of laborer. The examinee responds to each of these on the basis of feeling that individuals in each of these occupations are in a higher *H,* lower *L,* or the same *S* social class as people in the examinee's own family. Completion and scoring of this instrument require only a very few minutes. The cost is very low. Not much research is available on this scale, but evidence in the *Manual* points to a possible useful inventory for the evaluation of socioeconomic status.

SUMMARY

In dealing with the results obtained with personality or attitude inventories, the counselor must be extremely cautious. These are very useful instruments, but in using them it is very important to know something about the conditions under which the clients completed the inventories. It is important to know whether or not the client understood the purposes of the inventory and accepted the fact that the results would be most useful to him and the counselor in the ensuing counseling situation if he filled it out properly and carefully. Unless the counselor knows something about the response set or motivation of the client taking the inventory, the results are apt to have little validity. Only some of these inventories have built-in devices aimed at detecting invalid or falsified responses.

The counselor should also use freely some of the other available instruments in collecting data concerning a client's adjustment. Perhaps in this area of human behavior, more than in any other, it is most desirable for the counselor to have as many evaluations as possible, hoping that the data obtained by the inventory, when used along with information collected by other techniques or from other sources, will lead to a better and more valid picture of the client's personality patterns and problems.

REFERENCES

Abt, L. E., and Bellak, L. 1950. *Projective psychology.* New York: Alfred A. Knopf, Inc.

Allen, R. M. 1957. Relationship between the *Edwards Personal Preference Schedule* variables and the *Minnesota Multiphasic Personality Inventory* scales. *J. Appl. Psychol.* 41:307–11.

Allport, G. W. 1942. *The use of personal documents in psychological research.* Soc. Sci. Research Council Bull., no. 49.

American Psychological Association. 1965. Testing and public policy. *Amer. Psychol.* 20:857–993.

Anastasi, A. 1968. *Psychological testing.* 3rd ed. New York: The Macmillan Company.

Anderson, H. H., and Anderson, G. L. 1951. *An introduction to projective techniques.* Englewood Cliffs, N.J.: Prentice-Hall, Inc.

Ashlock, R. A., and Cottle, W. C. 1958. An experimental scale on attitudes. *Univ. of Kansas Bull. of Educ.* 2:106–9.

Bell, J. E. 1948. *Projective techniques.* New York: Longmans, Green & Co., Inc.

Block, J. 1965. *The challenge of response sets.* New York: Appleton-Century-Crofts.

Broen, W. E., Jr., and Wirt, R. D. 1958. Varieties of response sets. *J. Consult. Psychol.* 22:237–40.

Cattell, R. B. 1960. *Manual for the IPAT High School Personal Questionnaire.* Champaign, Ill.: Institute for Personality and Ability Testing.

———. 1962. *Manual for the IPAT 16 Personality Factor Questionnaire.* Champaign, Ill.: Institute for Personality and Ability Testing.

Cottle, W. C. 1950. Card vs. booklet form of the *MMPI. J. Appl. Psychol.* 34:255–59.

———. 1953. *The MMPI, A Review.* Lawrence, Kansas: School of Education, University of Kansas.

———. 1968. *Interest and personality inventories.* Boston: Houghton Mifflin Company.

———, and Powell, J. O. 1951. The effect of random answers to the *MMPI. Educ. and Psychol. Measmt.* 11:224–27.

Cronbach, L. J. 1946. Response sets. *Educ. and Psychol. Measmt.* 6:475–93.

———. 1949. Statistical methods applied to Rorschach scores: A review. *Psychol. Bull.* 46:393–429.

———. 1950. Further evidence of response sets and test design. *Educ. and Psychol. Measmt.* 10:3–31.

Crowne, D. P., and Marlowe, D. 1946. *The approval motive: Studies in evaluative dependence.* New York: John Wiley & Sons, Inc.

Dahlstrom, W. G., and Welsh, G. S. 1960. *An MMPI handbook: A guide to use in clinical practice and research.* Minneapolis: University of Minnesota Press.

Downie, N. M. 1967. *Fundamentals of measurement.* 2nd ed. New York: Oxford University Press, Inc.

Dunnette, M. D., *et al.* 1958. Relation among scores on the *Edwards Personal Preference Schedule,* the *California Psychological Inventory,* and the *Strong Vocational Interest Blank* for an industrial sample. *J. Appl. Psychol.* 42:178–81.

Edwards, A. L. 1953. The relationship between the judged desirability of a trait and the probability that the trait will be endorsed. *J. Appl. Psychol.* 37:90–93.

————. 1954. *Personal Preference Schedule: Manual.* New York: The Psychological Corporation.

————. 1957a. *Techniques of attitude scale construction.* New York: Appleton-Century-Crofts.

————. 1957b. *The social desirability variable in personality assessment.* New York: The Dryden Press, Inc.

————. 1959. *Personal Preference Schedule: Manual.* New York: The Psychological Corporation.

————, and Thurstone, L. L. 1953. An internal consistency check for scale values determined by the method of successive intervals. *Psychometrika.* 17:169–80.

Ellis, A. 1953. Recent research with personality inventories. *J. Consult. Psychol.* 17:45–49.

————. 1946. The validity of personality questionnaires. *Psychol. Bull.* 43: 385–440.

————, and Conrad, H. S. 1948. The validity of personality inventories in the military service. *Psychol. Bull.* 45:385–426.

Flanagan, J. C. 1935. *Factor analysis in the study of personality.* Stanford, Calif.: Stanford University Press.

Forbes, F. W., and Cottle, W. C. 1953. A new method for determining readability of standardized tests. *J. Appl. Psychol.* 37:185–90.

Gough, H. G. 1955. *Reference handbook for the Gough Adjective Check List.* Berkeley, Calif.: University of California Institute of Personality Assessment and Research.

————. 1956. *Manual for the California Psychological Inventory.* Palo Alto, Calif.: Consulting Psychologists Press.

————. 1964. *Manual for the California Psychological Inventory: Revised.* Palo Alto, Calif.: Consulting Psychologists Press.

Guilford, J. P. 1954. *Psychometric methods.* 2nd ed. New York: McGraw-Hill Book Company.

Hahn, M. E., and MacLean, M. S. 1955. *Counseling psychology.* New York: McGraw-Hill Book Company.

Hathaway, S. R., and McKinley, J. C. 1943. *Minnesota Multiphasic Personality Inventory: Manual.* New York: The Psychological Corporation.

————. 1951. *Minnesota Multiphasic Personality Inventory: Manual.* New York: The Psychological Corporation.

————, and Meehl, P. E. 1951. *An atlas for the clinical use of the MMPI.* Minneapolis: University of Minnesota Press.

Jacobs, A., and Schloff, A. 1955. Falsification scales for the *Guilford-Zimmerman Temperament Survey.* Los Angeles, Calif.: Sheridan Supply Co.

Jackson, D. W., and Messick, S. 1961. Acquiescence and desirability as response determinants on the *MMPI. Educ. and Psychol. Measmt.* 21:771–90.

Jurgensen, C. E. 1944. Report on the *Classification Inventory*, a personality test for industrial use. *J. Appl. Psychol.* 28:445–60.

Kelly, E. L. Theory and technique of assessment. 1954. *Ann. Rev. Psychol.* 5:281–310.

Kleinmuntz, B. 1967. *Personality measurement: An introduction.* Homewood, Ill.: The Dorsey Press, 1967.

Knapp, R. R. 1964. An empirical investigation of the concurrent and observational validity of an ipsative measure versus a normal measure of 6 interpersonal values. *Educ. and Psychol. Measmt.* 24:65–73.

Kubany, A. J. 1953. A validation study of the error-choice technique using attitudes on national health insurance. *Educ. and Psychol. Measmt.* 13: 157–63.

Levonian, E., *et al.* 1959. A statistical evaluation of Edward's *Personal Preference Schedule. J. Appl. Psychol.* 43:355–59.

Likert, R. 1932. A technique for the measurement of attitudes. New York: *Arch. Psychol.* no. 140.

Linden, J. D. 1958. The development and comparative analysis of two forced-choice forms of the *Guilford-Zimmerman Temperament Survey.* Ph.D. dissertation, Purdue University.

Lindner, R. L. 1952. *Prescription for rebellion.* New York: Holt, Rinehart & Winston, Inc.

Lindzey, G. 1961. *Projective techniques and cross-cultural research.* New York: Appleton-Century-Crofts.

Meehl, P. E. 1945. The dynamics of structured personality tests. *J. Clin. Psychol.* 1:296–303.

Merrill, R. M., and Heathers, L. B. 1956. Relations of the *MMPI* to the *Edwards Personal Preference Schedule* on a college counseling center sample. *J. Consult. Psychol.* 20:310–14.

Messick, S., and Jackson, D. W. 1961. Acquiescence and the factorial interpretation of the *MMPI. Psychol. Bull.* 58:299–304.

Mooney, R. L., and Gordon, L. V. 1950. *The Mooney Problem Check Lists: Manual.* New York: The Psychological Corporation.

Murray, H. A. 1943. *Thematic Apperception Test: Manual.* Cambridge, Mass.: Harvard University Press, 1943.

———, *et al.* 1953. *Explorations in personality.* New York: Oxford University Press, Inc.

Patterson, C. H. 1957. Use of projective tests in vocational counseling. *Educ. and Psychol. Measmt.* 17:533–55.

Pepinsky, P. 1949. The meaning of "validity" and "reliability" as applied to sociometric tests. *Educ. and Psychol. Measmt.* 9:39–49.

Remmers, H. H. 1954. *Introduction to opinion and attitude measurement*. New York: Harper & Row, Publishers.

————, and Shimberg, B. 1949. *SRA Youth Inventory, Form A: Manual*. Chicago: Science Research Associates.

————. 1956. *SRA Youth Inventory, Form S: Manual*. Chicago: Science Research Associates.

Rorer, L. G. 1965. The great response-style myth. *Psychol. Bull.* 63:129–56.

————, and Goldberg, L. R. 1965. Acquiescence on the *MMPI*. *Educ. and Psychol. Measmt*. 25:801–17.

Rotter, J. B., and Rafferty, J. E. 1950. *The Rotter Incomplete Sentences Blank: Manual*. New York: The Psychological Corporation.

Sheldon, W. H. 1942. *The varieties of temperament: A psychology of constitutional differences*. New York: Harper & Row, Publishers.

Shipley, W. C., Gray, F. E., and Newbert, N. 1946. The personal inventory. *J. Clin. Psychol.* 2:318–22.

Sims, V. M. 1952. *Sims SCI Occupational Rating Scale*. New York: Harcourt, Brace & World, Inc.

————. 1948. The essay examination as a projective technique. *Educ. and Psychol. Measmt*. 8:15–31.

Strang, R. A. 1949. *Counseling technics in college and secondary school*. New York: Harper & Row, Publishers.

Thurstone, L. L., and Chave, E. J. 1929. *Measurement of attitudes*. Chicago: University of Chicago Press.

Tindall, R. 1955. Relationships among indices of adjustment status. *Educ. and Psychol. Measmt*. 15:152–63.

Warner, W. L., Meeker, M., and Eells, K. 1949. *Social class in America*. Chicago: Science Research Associates.

Welsh, G. S. 1952. An anxiety index and an internalization ratio for the *MMPI*. *J. Consult. Psychol.* 16:65–72.

Whyte, W. H. 1956. *The organization man*. New York: Simon and Schuster, Inc.

11

The Counselor's Research

In the previous chapters, discussion centered about the use
by the counselor of established tools and procedures for gathering
information about the clients that he meets. In this chapter
consideration will be given to another important tool of the
counselor—research.

The counselor will find, in the course of his active career,
that many problems arise in relation to the materials discussed
in the previous chapters. He may question the value of a test or
of a testing program. He may wonder whether a procedure
that he is using is accomplishing what he had planned or whether
it is the most efficient of several procedures that might be
used to achieve the same ends. He may be interested in the
effectiveness of his program or of a certain part of it. Increasing

enrollments may force him to try out new and different approaches. He may want to know what the students who leave his school do on leaving, and what changes this may signal for counseling or for the curriculum. The answers to these and many other questions are all found by carrying on research. Much of the information the counselor gathers through research becomes part of his daily procedures in preparing for counseling.

In many educational and other agencies, the counselor, because of his training and background, is often asked to be a member of a committee which is evaluating the entire program or some particular phase of the program. A counselor has an important role in this evaluation, and he often can become a leader in such a group when he is familiar with the materials and procedures used in research. He should understand test scores, questionnaires, and evaluative criteria, and he should know how to gather and manipulate such data through statistical processes and computer procedures to make the results meaningful. He has been a continuous student of the interaction of individuals with the school environment. It follows, then, that he should be an important and useful member of a group studying the complete outcomes of education.

The pages that follow attempt to give the counselor an understanding of what research actually is and offer a brief introduction to some of the most frequently used research tools and processes. The counselor interested in more than this will find much additional material in several of the texts on research listed in the references at the end of the chapter.

Many counselors develop a concept of research during their student days that is hardly conducive to interest in doing research. In the words of Rummel (1958, p. 3): "Research, as the typical college student understands the term, is a relatively long investigation carried out primarily in libraries with the results presented in a highly documented paper of some length." The counselor gradually learns that research is much more than this. In the same work, Rummel notes that research includes all specialized and thoroughgoing investigations in which educated people engage. The chief purpose of research should be to answer questions that arise as the counselor carries on his daily activities. Very simply, research is an attempt to find out new things, to study new uses of those tools and procedures already possessed, and to investigate the worth or validity of the existing procedures.

Research is a way of thinking. John Dewey (1933) set forth five steps through which one goes in solving a problem: (1) a felt need; (2) the statement of the problem; (3) a statement of the hypothesis; (4) the collection of data; and (5) the testing of the hypothesis in the light of the collected data, and the drawing of a conclusion. These are the same steps that the counselor goes through when carrying on research. It should follow that there is nothing esoteric about research. It is basically another use to which the counselor can apply the tools and procedures previously discussed in this book, to enhance his skill as a counselor and, in the long run, to provide improvement of the counseling process.

It is not the purpose of this chapter to present detailed information on research techniques in education and psychology. Hillway (1956), Rummel (1958), and Selltiz *et al.* (1959) each contain much important information on research methodology in the social sciences. In this chapter, types of research problems associated with counseling and some illustrations of research methods will be presented. Focus in this chapter is on the types of research most useful in modifying and expanding counseling procedures.

Many counselors avoid research activities, perhaps overcome with the awesome connotations of the term in this scientific age. Such fears are groundless, although research does take time. If any research is to get done, the counselor should see that a certain part of his time is budgeted for it, and he should be determined to see that time so allotted is actually spent in carrying on research. It is very easy to give up this time to other, seemingly more important, activities.

The veteran counselor has no trouble finding topics for research, but for the student counselor and the beginner this may not be the case. Working in an area of specialization and thus becoming an expert is bound to lead to many of the unanswered questions in that area. This, then, is a primary source of research ideas. A reading of the research of others, as reported in journal articles, monographs, theses, or books, should lead the thoughtful counselor to problems for research. New ideas presented in the literature may lead the counselor to see if they would actually work in his own agency. Another source for research ideas is the dissatisfactions arising within the counselor's work. Certainly, days come when he feels that a given technique or method could be improved to provide more effective results. Then there is the generalized wondering that any intelligent counselor should do: Is the entire counseling or guidance program contributing anything to the welfare of the clients? And, if so, exactly what? In the pages that follow, an attempt will be made to show how research may be carried out by the counselor. Once a piece of research is started, other research problems often seem to stem from it endlessly.

In carrying on any research project, the counselor has first to see if what he wishes to do is feasible, or perhaps practical. There is no point in starting research that cannot be finished because of the time involved, the financing required, or the inaccessibility of the data. Frequently a research worker starts out to collect data and soon finds that his subjects do not answer his questionnaire or complete his tests or scales. Some research plans require that respondents spend several hours filling out the forms. The easiest way for the subject to handle such documents is to throw them into the wastebasket. The counselor should also determine ahead of time if he can manipulate the data after he obtains them. Frequently the amount of data becomes so large that it must be placed on data-processing cards for analysis. Such a procedure is expensive in terms of time and money. Finally, the counselor should see if he really can analyze the data. Most important here is whether or not he has the statistical background necessary for working with his data and interpreting his results correctly or if appropriate statistical consultants are available.

APPROACHES TO RESEARCH

A large part of the research in counseling has been evaluation. Dressel (1953) lists three major approaches to such research: First, the study of the counseling process itself. Here are included studies of the extent of the client's participation in the counseling process, the counselor's activity in the counseling situation, and the like.

Second, he lists studies of the outcomes of counseling. Much research is of this type, perhaps because it is the easiest to do. Such topics as improvement in school work, improvement in social and emotional adjustment, changes in attitudes, and vocational selection and placement are frequent subjects for research studies in this category. Often the client is asked to evaluate the outcomes of counseling, showing how it helped him or failed to do so.

Third, Dressel notes that much research is based upon data derived from the use of tests and other techniques. This research is mostly related to the use of the various instruments and their validity. Related to this is the development of agency norms to replace those supplied by the publisher of the instrument used. Each measurement device used by an agency should be evaluated, and statistics concerning its usefulness to the agency should be compiled.

While it is easy enough to give lip service to the *evaluation* of counseling and guidance services, when one begins to carry on such a study he soon runs into a number of troubles. In any evaluation procedure in education, the first step is to determine the objectives being evaluated. This in itself is a huge and sometimes very difficult task. Usually the major objectives of a course of study or of an entire educational experience are determined by the discussions and debates of experts. When these individuals are finished, the resulting stated objectives, while imposing and impressive, actually cannot be evaluated because of their broad, general nature. For example, an objective of counseling might be stated as "satisfactory vocational or educational adjustment."

A little thought will show the difficulty involved in trying to evaluate this objective of satisfactory vocational adjustment. First, the terms have to be defined and the definitions agreed upon. Then the nature of the kinds of evidences to be used, and their sources, have to be determined. As has been stated many times by evaluation experts (Smith and Tyler 1942), these broad general objectives have to be stated in terms of human behavior. Specifically, then, how does the individual who is well adjusted behave vocationally? After the behavior has been determined, methods have to be devised to evaluate or measure it. This calls for the construction of practical, valid, and reliable tests and other evaluation tools to be used in the appraisal process. And, finally, there has to be an analysis and then a synthesis of these fragmented evaluations into a whole.

As Rushong (1953) has summarized it, counseling is essentially a learning situation. Those techniques that have been developed for the evaluation of the outcomes of other learning must be used when counseling is evaluated. Otherwise, the results of the so-called evaluations are meaningless and useless.

The major obstacle in setting up a functional evaluation program is in obtaining valid evaluative criteria. Many past research studies have used improvement in grades, better adjustment, more social participation, and the like as evaluative criteria. As previously stated, such terms as these are not desirable because of their vagueness. Take the phrase "better adjustment." If in a group of individuals each was asked to tell what "better adjustment" meant to him, it is highly possible that there might be as many different explanations of the term as there were participants.

Travers (1949) separates the types of evaluative criteria used in counseling into two groups: subjective and objective. Included as subjective criteria are the satisfactions an individual obtains from his job, an assessment of his personal adjustment including both his social life and emotional status, and the general satisfactions that the client feels with the counseling process. The subjective criteria Travers dismisses as useless because evaluative instruments have not yet been developed which can produce valid appraisals. Satisfaction, he noted, is of little value as a measure of counseling effectiveness, because people tend to be satisfied by and feel that they have been helped by the most useless types of quackery.

Travers' objective criteria include grades, income, job stability, tenure, completion of educational or vocational plans, life goals, and the like. Even these objective criteria have to be used with caution. One of the most common objectives of educational counseling is to improve a student's grade point average. This is frequently shown to happen: The student's grades do improve. The question is whether this is a result of changes that have been brought about in the counselee, or the result of the counselor's helping the student select easier courses and professors with the more generous grading practices, or to the Hawthorne effect. The second of these is hardly a valid criterion to be used in evaluating counseling. In regard to these objective criteria, Travers notes that many of these goals are long-term ones and hence, to be valid, evaluation activities must be carried on over a long period of time. In other words, the approach should be longitudinal rather than cross-sectional. A much more inclusive listing of evaluative criteria is found in Benson (1949).

A survey of research into the effects of counseling indicates many negative findings, especially when the major goals toward which counselors strive are considered. However, if counseling is not concerned with major personality changes, its results are often positive. Tyler (1960) referred to the fact that a lot of counseling is related to helping a client obtain a certain amount of control over his future—by helping him with his educational plans or helping him to stay in school, helping him with vocational plans or helping him to find part-time work, or helping him to solve some of the minor problems encountered in daily living. Such activities as these she referred to as "minimum change therapy."

Blocher (1966) has expanded upon this concept in what he called developmental counseling. His idea of developmental counseling is that it is an attempt to change human behavior by assisting human development based upon the assumption that individuals are capable of choosing the way in which they wish to develop. The outcome variables of developmental counseling that he would attempt to measure are: (1) commitment to goals by the client, evaluated by his actual behavior; (2) competence, as evaluated by his grades, aptitudes, and study habits; (3) consistency, appraised by observing the client taking courses or entering a training program; and (4) control, evaluated by determining how a client manages frustration or meets his physiological and psychological needs in line with the value system formulated in counseling.

A second type of research that the counselor carries on may be classified as *follow-up*. While this is a type of evaluation study, it is a rather specific and distinct one. Unless the counselor knows what has happened to the clients who have passed through the agency in which he works, it is rather difficult to feel well satisfied about the job the agency is trying to do or to know exactly which kind of procedures to continue and which to curtail or eliminate. An example of this type of research would be the follow-up of graduates and school drop-outs which is carried on by most schools, to learn the kinds of placement in jobs and in further schooling that have been achieved by the people who have left that school. This in turn indicates possible revisions of the curricular or counseling program of the school.

One of the simplest ways to conduct a drop-out study or a follow-up study of this nature is to enlist the help of the current graduating class in a follow-up of those who left school the preceding year. This has the advantage of acquainting most of next year's school-leavers, the present graduating class, with the kinds of information needed, and some of the difficulties involved in follow-up procedures. It acquaints them with the purposes of a follow-up survey to which they may later be asked to respond, and it makes them more aware of the value of such a program to the school. The most useful procedure is to contact, either by telephone or in person, the people who left school the preceding year. If this cannot be done, the kind of information needed might be placed on a return postal card as the next best way of getting the information. A postal-card survey limits the kinds of information to be requested and makes it necessary, also, that statistical procedures be fairly simple in order to handle this limited information. One technique is to have the high-school seniors who are helping with the survey compile a list of students who left school the preceding year, breaking it down into those who went directly into jobs and those who went on to further education. Then different kinds of postal-card questions can be developed for each group. Members of the group who have gone to work can be asked questions like those in Form 11.1, while those in the group who have gone on to higher education could be asked questions like those in Form 11.2. These are short and simple questions adapted to a postal-card survey. Of course, more elaborate follow-up questionnaires might be used.

Any of these methods offers specific advantages. The direct interview produces the information with more certainty than any of the others. Time can be used economically through a structured series of questions which would be the same for each interviewer and each person being interviewed. This produces a standardization highly useful in the statistical handling of the information which is collected. If direct interviews are not possible, the mails—and telephone interviews for those who do not respond by mail—can be used. It should be noted here that a double postal card, signed by someone who is known to the recipient, is more frequently returned than one with an impersonal message or one signed by someone unknown to the recipient. Experience indicates that mailing long questionnaires with return stamped envelopes is the poorest method of conducting a survey of school-leavers.

Such a procedure obviously requires careful planning, not only to get the kinds of information which are useful to the agency, but to insure a way of asking for this information which will give as much freedom of response as possible and at the same time be as easy to handle statistically as the information permits. A careful tryout of preliminary forms of a follow-up survey will indicate many of the places where the survey can be improved to secure a clear, useful response. In addition, a tryout will make it possible to see whether the statistical techniques proposed for handling the data will actually do the job.

A third type of research is related to *the counseling process itself*. In these days of increasing enrollments, counselors may find themselves using more and more group techniques in preference to individual ones. Then it follows that an investigation should be made to see which of the two approaches is more effective. In a similar fashion, the so-called eclectic as opposed to the client-centered approach might be compared.

A fourth important area of research for the counselor is in the development of local school norms, the special norms required for rehabilitation clients, and the job description required for work in a given plant or office. The development of such norms and the statistics for use with them are matters which should be given serious consideration by a counselor in a given agency. For example, it is highly important to begin as soon as possible the development of longitudinal information that will be collected and interpreted over relatively long periods in the history of an agency.

An example is the collection of information on the *General Aptitude Test Battery*. Information collected over a period of time could be highly useful to an agency, but when collected on a given group of people it must be set aside until those people have held various kinds of employment successfully or unsuccessfully. Then the successful workers can be contrasted with the unsuccessful workers in a given occupation to give a pattern of scores which might then be described as characteristic of successful workers and lacking in unsuccessful workers.

One method of obtaining local norms is to follow a given group through an agency or through various kinds of work and educational activities outside the agency in order to see what happens to this group at various stages. Too much of the research available at the present time has been developed on a given group at a given age. The results are generalized to other groups who are older or younger, on the assumption that they will resemble the original group at the same age. This is not necessarily so. The only assumptions which can be made are those which are based upon a knowledge of the behavior of a given group of individuals at various points in their school and work career. Generalizations can be made *only* after the same group has been studied *at* ages 15, 20, 25, and so on. Only then is it possible to see what changes take place over a period of years. Then it is not necessary to generalize about the kind of behavior a given group of 15-year-olds will exhibit at age 25 from the behavior of current 25-year-olds who may have no relationship to the group of 15-year-olds whose future the counselor is trying to predict. The

Form 11.1

POSTAL CARD FOLLOW-UP FOR EMPLOYED GRADUATES

1. What was your first full-time job after leaving school?

2. For what firm?

3. Are you on a different job now? What?

4. From which of the following did you learn about your job(s)?
   _____ Family or friend
   _____ School
   _____ Found it myself
   _____ Private employment agency
   _____ State employment agency
   _____ Other (Explain)

5. Do you plan any other schooling?

6. Can we help you in any way in planning jobs or training?

7. Name:

8. Address:

Form 11.2

POSTAL CARD FOLLOW-UP FOR GRADUATES
CONTINUING SCHOOL

1. What school did you attend after leaving high school?

2. What course did you take there?

3. Are you enrolled there now?   Same course?

4. Where did you learn about the school?

5. Can we help you in planning schooling or locating a job?

6. What activities are you in at school?

7. Name:

8. Address:

problems involved in the development of specific local norms have been described in Chapter 6.

A fifth and very useful area of research is related to the various tools of the counselor. For example, in predicting academic grades, which does the better job, a long battery or a short 20-minute intelligence test? It is an accepted fact that clients can cheat on personality inventories. Can a typical inventory be changed to another form such as the paired-comparison form, and this cheating at least lessened? Should bright senior-high-school girls be given the *Strong Vocational Interest Blank* for women, or does the men's blank provide adequate and valid information? Suppose the *Kuder General Interest Survey* is used with all freshmen. The counselor might be interested in knowing what profiles are associated with successful completion of the various school curricula. These are just a few of the many research problems that an alert counselor might find worth carrying on.

Closely related to the above is the development and compilation of *new information* of use to the agency from the clinical hunches the counselor gets or the subliminal cues he receives as he works with clients. Research to add information in each of these areas does not have to be difficult or involved. It should be an outgrowth of the experiences the counselor undergoes in the agency. It should be a result of the kind of questions which appear normally in the course of the counselor's day. The questions should be such that the answers will add information to the counselor's store of knowledge about counseling and make it possible to do a better job with clients.

A sixth area in which research effort should be expended is in a *survey of placement opportunities available* to the clients of the agency. Whether it is a public school, an employment service, or a rehabilitation agency makes little difference. The sources of placement available to the agency need to be explored periodically and reevaluated, and possible new placement sources discovered. In the public schools this involves an exploration of employers' needs and an exploration of the school resources which will supply those needs.

A seventh area of research would be to make an investigation of the *population* from which an agency's clients came. It has been observed that the clients of a given agency tend to resemble each other very closely. For example, the clients entering a large Veterans Administration Hospital are apt to come from a certain socioeconomic group, have a more or less similar level of educational attainment, and engage in occupations of similar levels and fields. A survey of several hundred entering patients will give the counselor an excellent overview of what his clients are like, what their needs are, and how the counseling program may be adapted to serve them best. A similar survey or study would also be most useful for the high-school and university counselor.

An eighth and final type of investigation (and a necessary one) is a study of the *sources for referral*. No counselor is equipped to handle all types of clients. Neither does he have the time to do so. When cases arise that are outside his domain, he should know exactly where this individual client might best be referred for help. Then it follows that the counselor should be acquainted with all of the community agencies in his city. He should not only know what they do in respect to cases and therapy, he should have established effective relationships with each. The counselor should even go beyond his own city, and include the clinics associated with the public and private universities within his state.

EXAMPLES OF RESEARCH

Probably the main purpose of research is the gathering and evaluating of data with the aim of making each counselor a more effective one. The work of Gelatt (1967), described here in some detail, embodies much that any counselor can do. In this work, he applied information and decision theory to the students' problems of planning for college. As Gelatt has pointed out (1962), the purposes of decision theory are to help the student make good educational and vocational decisions and to assist him, as well, to develop skill in decision making. To achieve these ends the client must have all the pertinent information as well as the know-how to put everything together effectively to make an optimal choice. So, he must be aware of the possible outcomes, know of the alternative actions, understand the probability of the various outcomes, and be able to assess their desirability or value. Getting such information and making it available constitutes a major part of the research of a counselor.

Gelatt illustrated these points with an example from the school system in which he was then working. The purpose of his program was to help ninth- and eleventh-graders make decisions about their post-high-school education. As a start, a group of "experience tables" were constructed. The first of these showed the types of activity engaged in by the graduates of his high school the first year after graduation: 9% were employed full time, 3% entered the military service, 37% were enrolled in junior colleges, 8% entered colleges with the highest admission standards, and so on.

The second table for use with the ninth-graders showed what individuals with different grade averages were doing their first year after graduation: 3 out of 10 of the ninth-graders with A averages were in colleges with the highest admission requirements, 5 out of 10 were in colleges with high requirements, 1 out of 10 was in a college with medium entrance standards, and 1 out of 10 was in a junior college. Of the students with C averages as ninth-graders, none was in a college with the highest entrance requirements, 1 out of 10 was in a college with high entrance requirements, 2 out of 10 were in colleges with medium entrance requirements, 5 out of 10 were in junior colleges, 1 out of 10 was in the military, less than 1 out of 10 was employed, and 1 out of 10 was married and seeking work. Such information was obtained and graphed for the other letter grades.

The third table contained information about courses that go beyond the usual requirements for graduation, such as college mathematics and advanced courses in English, languages, and the sciences. The graphs show how many students out of each 10 with various ninth-grade averages attempted a number of special courses and the grades they received in the special courses. The fourth set of tables showed the possible outcomes for students with different high-school grade averages in certain colleges and universities. For example, it was shown that a student with an A average in high-school had 4 chances in 10 of obtaining first-year grades of B to A, 5 chances in 10 of obtaining C to B, and 1 chance in 10 of obtaining below C at Stanford University. As might be imagined, the collection of data and the making of tables such as these demand much time and effort of the counselor. But such tables are worthwhile because they contain data basic to effective counseling.

Tables like these should impress the student with the fact that in making decisions about his high-school and post-high-school plans many factors have to be considered. The counselor provides each student, when he comes for counseling, with data like this. But it is only part of the picture. Each student has various values or preferences for certain outcomes. The counselor's task is to help him examine any choice that he has made in the light of all the pertinent data as it fits the value system and needs of that student. The counselor helps the student go beyond the data and assists him to comprehend the meaning of the data for him. The whole process has to be highly individualized. It follows that it is the appropriateness of how the final choice is made, as well as the choice itself, that determines how well the client will carry out his decisions.

THE DEVELOPMENT OF A DESIGN FOR NEW RESEARCH

As the counselor gains experience, many of the activities that take place in preparation for counseling and during counseling interviews raise questions which can be answered only by a personal or agency research program. Many beginning counselors are quite concerned about the way in which a research problem develops and the method by which a research design is drawn up. As has been pointed out, research should develop naturally from the questions which arise in a counseling program. Simple, practical research designs can best grow out of such questions. An attempt will be made to illustrate this, using the steps undertaken by a counselor in developing a scale to identify potential drop-outs before they leave school.

A survey of the literature on drop-outs over a period of years indicated that there are many ways of describing people who leave school. This problem is unique, as far as the counselor is concerned, in that these drop-outs can be described only after they have left school. At the time the study was begun there was no way of identifying drop-outs before they left school so that something could be done to help them, either in better placement in activities while they remained in school or in better placement in jobs or other training when they left school. As a consequence, 15 characteristics that seem to describe most drop-outs were used as a basis for developing inventory items that would center about these characteristics. There were about 10 items for each of the characteristics and these items were combined into a 150-item scale called *The Life Adjustment Scale #1*, described in the work reported by Herrman and Cottle (1958).

Since it was possible to leave school in Kansas at the end of eighth grade or at age 16, whichever came first, *The Life Adjustment Scale #1* was administered by Herrman to 1,834 eighth- and ninth-grade pupils in a large Kansas metropolitan area. Later these groups were followed up and the drop-outs were identified. It was found that three semesters and one summer later, 61 boys and 53 girls had dropped out of school. The answer sheets for these individuals were matched with those for an equal number of boys and girls drawn by use of a table of random numbers from the remainder who had stayed in school. (It is easier in comparing proportions and computing statistics if equal numbers of experimental and control groups are contrasted because simpler statistical techniques exist for handling equal numbers.) The drop-out boys ranged in age from 13 to 17 with a mean of 14.7; the girl drop-outs ranged in age from 13 to 16 with a mean of 14.2. The age of the group of boys who stayed in school ranged from 13 to 15 with a mean of 13.8; that of girls, 13 to 17 with a mean of 13.5. The drop-outs thus tended to be older than those who stayed in school, as has been shown by most of the other drop-out studies which have been conducted.

When the two groups had been selected, other statistical techniques were used to compare the responses of the boy drop-outs with those of the boys who stayed in school, and of the girl drop-outs with the responses of girls who stayed in school, on each of the 150 items of the inventory. Using the machine answer sheets of the contrasting groups, a complete item count of the responses of each group to each item was made. The count for boy drop-outs and boy stay-ins, girl drop-outs and girl stay-ins, was made separately. Then the number of drop-outs and stay-ins of each sex answering a specific item *true* was converted into proportions of the total group of drop-outs or stay-ins for each sex. Guilford (1954) has provided a table which allows the reading of phi coefficients from proportions of two *equal* samples responding to test items. (See Guilford 1965, or Downie and Heath 1965.)

The phi coefficient and chi-square for each item were used to evaluate the item's usefulness in discriminating the two groups within each sex. Items that discriminated at the .01, .05, and .10 levels of confidence were selected as characteristic of boy or girl drop-outs, respectively, and used in making a scoring key which was keyed in the direction of drop-out responses. There were 60 items which differentiated between the boy groups at this level of significance, and there were 58 items which differentiated between the girl groups. The choice of the 10% level of significance was made because there were 11 items at this level common to both boys and girls, out of a total of 28 common items. It has also been found, in previous research with this type of scale and item, that an item at the 10% level might be significant at a higher level in succeeding studies, and retaining such items would prevent the dropping of items which might be of use as the research continued.

These statistical procedures identified a total of 89 items out of the basic 150 which differentiated the responses of drop-outs from those of boys or girls who stayed in school. In a preliminary attempt to cross-validate these items, a small group of 20 girls and 20 boys who had dropped out of school in another city of Kansas were matched with a randomly selected equal number of boys or girls who had stayed in the schools of that city. Significant differences were found between the drop-outs and those who stayed in school, using these validation groups of boys or girls. As a result of applying tests of significance (*F* and *t*), it was found that those who stayed in school responded significantly different from those who had dropped out.

Epps and Cottle (1958) reported on a follow-up of the original data collected by Herrman in December, 1954. In the more recent study, the ninth-graders had been graduated from high school and the eighth-graders in the study were beginning seniors. Thus, most of the people in the study had had considerable opportunity to leave school, and relatively few of those remaining would leave if their behavior was similar to those previously studied. The list of school-leavers, other than those reported in the Herrman and Cottle study, was composed of 146 boys and

152 girls who dropped out after Herrman's original drop-out group had been studied. Their responses were matched with an equal number of answer sheets of boys and girls drawn from the remaining stay-in group by use of a table of random numbers. Both groups ranged in age from 13 to 17 years when tested in the eighth and ninth grades. The mean age of the drop-out boys was 13.9 while that of the boys who stayed in school was 13.6. The mean age of the drop-out girls was 13.7; of the girls who stayed in school, 13.5. There was little difference in age between the two groups.

Again, item analysis techniques were used to identify items differentiating between drop-out and stay-in responses for boys and girls. The procedure for doing this is as follows:

1. Collect data.
2. Run item count. Score both true and false items.
3. Tally the count and group the columns as indicated. (Tally drop-out and stay-in groups separately, by sex.)

	111111111111
Question 1	111111111111
	111111111111
Question 2	111111111111

4. Make table of proportions and convert both drop-out and stay-in groups in terms of proportion of true responses.
5. Use Jurgensen (1947) or Downie and Heath (1965) to look up phi coefficients.
6. Test for significance of phi coefficients by using the following formulas:

$$\text{phi}_{.01} = \frac{2.576}{\sqrt{N}} \qquad\qquad \text{phi}_{.10} = \frac{1.645}{\sqrt{N}}$$

$$\text{phi}_{.05} = \frac{1.960}{\sqrt{N}}$$

These are the values of the phi coefficients significant at the three levels, where N equals the total of drop-outs and stay-ins. An optional procedure, when a computer is used, is to compute chi-square directly and omit the phi coefficients. $(X^2 = N\phi^2)$

7. Cut the scoring stencil and score the papers.
8. Make a frequency distribution and find the mean and variance, or use a computer program to do this.
9. Do F and t tests of significance between the experimental drop-out and stay-in groups, as check.
10. Score papers of validation drop-out and stay-in groups. Do F and t tests in the same fashion as in steps 8 and 9.

The scale has proved efficient in identifying potential drop-outs. A comparison of the scores of drop-out groups with those of corresponding stay-in groups showed that the drop-out groups had significantly higher scores. A statistical comparison of the variances indicated that the ranges of scores for each of the paired groups was similar in all but three cases, so that the difference was solely a difference in means.

An interesting point is that the first study, conducted about the time most of these pupils had reached the end of ninth grade, uncovered more significant items than the second study, made when most of the students had reached graduation. Since the groups in the second study were more than twice as large as the first drop-out group, it might have been expected to find *more* significant items, simply because the larger groups might respond to a greater variety of items which would reflect their reasons for leaving school. Also, because the group was larger, the level of significance required for each item would be lower. A comparison of the two studies, however, indicated that the drop-outs in the later studies were not as different from the stay-ins as were the groups in the original studies. The drop-outs in the groups reported by Herrman and Cottle were so different from those who remained in school that they left school as soon as it was legally possible to do so—either at the end of the eighth grade or within a year of that time. In the second sample, reported by Epps and Cottle (1958), those who eventually dropped out had been sufficiently similar to those who had stayed until graduation that many of them remained in school close to 3 of the 4 necessary high school years. The drop-outs in the second study were more like the boys and girls who stayed in school until graduation; it was more difficult to show differences; and there *were* fewer differences.

These two studies offered sufficient evidence that potential drop-outs could be identified; hence *The Life Adjustment Scale #1* was revised into a scale called *The School Interest Inventory*. Forty-two linguistic or nonlinguistic items were added in place of items which appear to be only padding in the early studies. A number of studies were conducted attempting to identify those items that differentiate between the responses of boys and girls to the scale.

It was anticipated that more than the original 42 nonlinguistic–linguistic items (*NL*) would show such differentiation. Ultimately the *NL* scale may become a way in which boys and girls at the ninth-grade level may be helped to make curricular choices during high school. The way in which the nonlinguistic-linguistic item identification was undertaken was as follows:

1. Clean and check the markings on the answer sheets so that only those answered properly will be tallied by the item counter.

2. Sort the papers by grade and sex, equalizing randomly the number in each grade group by sexes. That is, if there are 130 papers for boys in grade 9, there should be 130 papers for girls. If there are more papers for one sex than the other, they should be equalized by pulling at random the necessary number of excessive papers.

3. Do the item analysis by grade and by sex, separately.

4. Check for differences within the same sex, by grade, according to each item. This is done by computing the significance of difference in percentages using a nomograph prepared by Lawshe and Baker (1950). If there are no differences between the boys in each grade, then the boys from each grade can be combined into one group of boys. The same procedure should be followed for the girls. If there *are* differences, the grades will have to be treated separately to see which items differentiate between boys and girls, say, in grade 9 and between those in grades 10, 11, and 12, respectively.

5. Obtain the phi coefficients or chi-squares by items between sexes, making sure that the N of each sex is still equal. These are computed as indicated earlier in this chapter.

6. Pick the items differentiating between the sexes and punch these into a scoring key according to the differentiation in the boys' direction. This key is called a "nonlinguistic scale."

7. Score the papers of both boys and girls. Check to see, by the use of both F and t tests, that there are no differences between groups of boys or between groups of girls in this study, but that there are differences between the boys *and* girls in each of the groups. This is a check on the accuracy of the process thus far, because by construction this scale must differentiate between boys and girls.

8. Select and score an additional set of papers of boys and girls on this NL scale. This makes up the validation group.

The results of these studies led to expanded research with the instrument. In 1963, the current form was administered to 25,000 students in grades 7 to 9 in ten states, and their records were examined two years after testing to ascertain which students had dropped out. Analyses were made with randomly stratified groups, grouped by age and socioeconomic status. Those items that consistently differentiated between drop-outs and stay-ins were selected for the present drop-out scales, which were developed from a study of responses of 1,300 drop-outs and an equal number of a matched group of stay-ins. Further analyses were made of the items by Cottle (1961, 1962).

In selecting original items for the new scales, the inventoried responses of 150 drop-outs of each sex were paired with the inventoried responses of an equal number of stay-ins. The pupils were grouped by grade, sex, age, school, and course of study. Phi coefficients and chi-squares were obtained for each item separately for males and for females. The significance of each phi coefficient was identified by use of a table (Jurgensen 1947). Those items differentiating between drop-outs and stay-ins beyond the .20 level of significance in at least two of the four comparisons were retained for the final scales. The scales are made up of 90 items for boys and 86 items for girls. The items which appeared at a significance level of .20 or less in two or more studies were well beyond the .01 level of significance for the scales in which they appear (Sakoda, Cohen, and Beall 1954).

Studies with several hundred students in grades 7 through 9 show that the inventory is consistent when administered twice to the same person. Reliability coefficients secured by test-retest procedures, over an interval of one to two weeks, are presented in Table 11.1. Figures are given by type of school, grade, and sex, and for grades and schools combined. Most of the reliabilities are in the .80's and seem appropriate for a test used in individual counseling.

The means and standard deviations in Table 11.1 illustrate the differences among groups. The sex differences in means cannot be entirely explained by the differences in the number of items for boys and girls. Boys consistently achieve higher scores than girls at all levels. The means of private-school students are far below those from public schools in the same geographical area. Table 11.1 shows an irregular trend for scores to increase at later grade levels.

Some of the items in the inventory do not appear on either drop-out

Table 11.1

TEST-RETEST RELIABILITIES, MEANS, AND STANDARD DEVIATIONS FOR VARIOUS GROUPS[*]

Type of School	Type of Examinee	Number	Corre-lation	Mean	Standard Devia-tion	$SE_{Meas.}$
Public	7th-grade males	105	.92	21.84	9.03	2.53
Public	8th-grade males	82	.78	24.46	10.70	5.03
Public	9th-grade males	78	.87	22.55	8.69	3.13
Public	7th-grade females	109	.82	15.17	6.98	2.86
Public	8th-grade females	94	.86	17.81	8.17	3.02
Public	9th-grade females	66	.92	19.01	7.80	2.18
Private	8th and 9th-grade males	130	.78	14.68	6.49	3.05
Private	8th and 9th-grade females	78	.92	11.88	6.20	1.74
All males, 7th through 9th grades		395	.85	20.17	9.47	3.69
All females, 7th through 9th grades		347	.88	15.88	7.76	2.72

[*] Data for these studies were gathered with the assistance of Mr. John McGowan, East Junior High School, Brockton, Massachusetts; Sister Anne Marie, S.U.S.C., Rose Hawthorne School, Concord, Massachusetts; and Rev. John R. Vigneau, S.J., of Xavier High School, Concord, Massachusetts.

scale. These items are being studied in an attempt to develop additional scales. Research already completed gives evidence that six such scales may be developed: a Nonlinguistic and a linguistic scale, a boy and girl delinquent scale, and a nonachiever scale for boys and for girls. If the drop-out scale indicates that a given examinee is a potential school drop-out, it would be helpful to know whether his interests lie in linguistic areas such as English, social studies, and foreign language or in nonlinguistic areas such as art, shop, or home economics. If a Nonlinguistic-linguistic scale can be developed, it could provide information for the student to use in choosing courses and majors in senior high school.

In an attempt to predict potential delinquents in junior high-school, responses of Massachusetts groups of 200 male delinquents and 200 female delinquents to the items of *The School Interest Inventory* were contrasted with those of 200 male nondelinquents and 200 female nondelinquents (HEW Grant RD-2842-P68). These were divided into subgroups of 100 each and subjected to chi-square item analysis techniques. The same procedure was followed with groups of 200 male delinquents and 200 female delinquents vs. 200 male nondelinquents and 200 female nondelinquents in Rhode Island. Items which appeared significant at the .20 level in at least one subgroup of 100 delinquents of the same sex in each state were used to construct a Male Delinquent scale and a Female Delinquent scale. The Male Delinquent scale contains 61 items and the Female Delinquent scale contains 85 items.

These two scales were used to compare responses of Connecticut groups of 134 male delinquents with those of 134 male nondelinquents and to compare responses of 95 female delinquents with those of 95 female nondelinquents. Response differences were highly significant (far beyond the .001% level). Kuder-Richardson Formula 20 reliabilities for the Male Delinquent scoring key ranged from .70 to .76 with a median reliability of .71. Reliabilities for the Female Delinquent scoring key ranged from .83 to .87 with a median reliability of .85. This indicates that the items of each scale appear to be quite homogeneous in spite of the fact that they can be divided into seven categories by inspection of their content. Thus it seems possible to use these two scales to identify potential delinquents in upper elementary school grades and to initiate a preventive program to minimize their becoming delinquents.

This is an illustration of how curiosity about things appearing in previous research and in counseling experience may combine with a need for identifying such individuals as potential school drop-outs or a need for differentiating between a linguistic and a nonlinguistic group to give a counselor clues to needed research. It also illustrates how experimental designs of this nature can be constructed without a great deal of difficulty. The main problem involved in any research carried on by the counselor is the amount of time it takes and the effort required to find this time in a busy schedule where there are too many clients for each counselor. However, until research indicates the effectiveness of the counselor's preparation for counseling and of the counseling procedures themselves, the counselor is on very shaky ground.

THE USE OF THE COMPUTER IN RESEARCH

In recent years much of the drudgery associated with the analysis of research data has been alleviated by the computer. The use of the computer in research has to be planned carefully, however. All too often a student collects data and then searches around for methods of analyzing it. He frequently turns to the computer center to see how they can assist him with his problem. This leads to complications, some of which have no solution.

It is just as important that the student decide how he is going to analyze data as it is to plan how he is going to collect data. This needs to occur *before* data are collected. The beginning researcher must become acquainted with the processes involved in programming data for analysis by the computer. The data that are collected have to be punched on a card appropriate to a given machine. Some types of data are easily adapted, others are not. Some data cannot be quantified for punching on such cards. If the student is using a questionnaire in his research, it should be constructed with the coding and punching process in mind. Responses should be so arranged that the key-punch operator can readily transfer the data from the questionnaire to the computer card. In planning the questionnaire it is also important to employ many demographic variables that may be useful in analyzing the results. For example, age, sex, marital status, last grade completed in school, and the like should be included so they may be used later in various methods of analyzing the data. It is much wiser to include too much rather than too little information when data are being collected.

The student should also determine if a program already exists for the type of analysis that he wishes to make. Many times he finds out too late that there is no program available in the local computer center or in any other such center. This leaves him with the task of writing his own program or of having some one else write it for him. For most students who have not had a course in writing programs, this is an almost impossible task, and taking the course, though in itself very helpful, actually delays the work considerably. Searching for someone who has the ability *and* the time to write a new program often is a very difficult and frustrating task.

In planning his research, the student will find that much of the analysis is simplified if he has an equal number of cases in the groups being studied. This has been mentioned before and is again emphasized, even for work that is going to be analyzed on the computer. Many statistical procedures and programs were developed with equal numbers of cases, and when unequal groups are used, adaptations or modifications have to be made. Often these are far more laborious than the effort needed to obtain equal numbers in each sample. Scientific sampling techniques may be used to reduce groups to equal sizes with no visible effect on results. The interested student should consult a table of random numbers found in most statistics books and review their use in sampling procedures.

Once the data have been submitted for analysis and the "print-out" of results obtained, the researcher still has work to do. He has, first, to learn to read and understand the material from the computer. Sometimes this is difficult and assistance is needed. Second, he must learn not to accept the results obtained from the computer as final. Spot-checks must be made to see if the results are correct. One of the writers was once reading a doctoral dissertation written by one of his students in which chi-square was used as a test of significance, and he noticed that the chi-square values were not consistent with the data upon which they were based. Several were recomputed by hand and it was found that those obtained from the computer were all much larger than they should have been. Obviously some of the conclusions derived in the study were wrong and the whole dissertation had to be redone after the statistics were recomputed. *Computer processes are fallible!* Their results always have to be checked, if the researcher wants to be sure of his interpretations.

Still, computers are the most wonderful and useful tools that the researcher has ever had. When used properly and when the data for them are collected and organized properly, they result in a research program becoming a pleasant and enjoyable activity. If the study reported above (Herrman and Cottle 1958) were done today, considerable time and effort would have been saved by adapting the collection of the original data for the computer. In the construction of the first scale, the subjects could have placed their responses directly upon a computer card which would have been immediately punched by machine for analysis by the computer. The item counts and all tests of significance of differences between the criterion groups would have been done directly on the computer, and the results would have been obtained by reading them from the print-out from the computer. Those items that were shown to discriminate between drop-outs and stay-ins would then be reassembled into another scale for use with a cross-validation group.

Similarly, the Epps and Cottle study (1958) could have been adapted for the modern computer. Since the data from the subjects were coded by sex and by drop-out or stay-in status, an item analysis which distinguished the items that differentiated male or female drop-outs from their corresponding stay-ins could have been made on the computer. This is also true of the rest of the research reported in this chapter. The point is that the computer does all the counting for the researcher, makes the tests of significance that are desired, and finally leaves only the interpretation of the results to the one doing the research, after he has satisfied himself that the computer work is correct.

SUMMARY

This chapter has been an attempt to show how various kinds of counseling research can contribute to the information needed prior to counseling and can contribute to counseling itself by making it more effective. The kinds of research which have been considered are those dealing with: a follow-up of agency clients; the placement of agency clients in further education or in jobs; the construction of local norms and the gathering of the statistics necessary to do this, in order to make the work with clients more effective on a local basis. The way in which attempts can be made to evaluate the counseling program itself was discussed, and, lastly, some examples of how new research can contribute information of value to the counselor and the client.

REFERENCES

Benson, A. L. 1949. *Criteria for evaluating guidance programs in secondary schools*. Washington, D.C.: U.S. Office of Education.

Blocher, D. H. 1966. *Developmental counseling*. New York: The Ronald Press Company.

Cottle, W. C. 1961. The *School Interest Inventory*. *Psychol. Reports* 9:66.

————. 1962. Dropout, delinquent, and other scales of the *School Interest Inventory*. *National Council on Measurement in Education: 19th Yearbook*, pp. 94–96. East Lansing, Mich.

————. 1966. *The School Interest Inventory*. Boston: Houghton Mifflin Company.

Dewey, J. 1933. *How we think*. Boston: D. C. Heath & Company.

Downie, N. M. 1967. *Fundamentals of measurement*. 2nd ed. New York: Oxford University Press, Inc.

————, and Heath, R. W. 1965. *Basic statistical methods*. 2nd ed. New York: Harper & Row, Publishers.

Dressel, P. L. 1951. Personnel services in high school and college. *Occupations*. 29:331–40.

————. 1953. Some approaches to evaluation. *Personnel and Guidance J.* 31:285–94.

Epps, M. M., and Cottle, W. C. 1958. Further validation of a dropout scale. *Vocational Guidance Quart.* 7:90–93.

Froehlich, C. P. 1949. *Evaluating guidance procedures: A review of the literature.* Washington, D.C.: U.S. Office of Education.

Gelatt, H. B. 1962. Decision making: A conceptual frame of reference for counseling. *J. Counsel. Psychol.* 9:240–45.

————. 1967. Information and decision theories applied to college choice and planning. In *Preparing school counselors in educational guidance.* New York: College Entrance Examination Board.

Guilford, J. P. 1965. *Fundamental statistics in psychology and education.* 4th ed. New York: McGraw-Hill Book Company.

Herrman, W. L., and Cottle, W. C. 1958. An inventory to identify high school dropouts. *Vocational Guidance Quart.* 6:122–23.

Hillway, T. 1956. *Introduction to research.* Boston: Houghton Mifflin Company.

Jurgensen, C. E. 1947. A table of phi coefficients. *Psychometrika.* 12:23–29.

Lawshe, C. H., and Baker, P. C. 1950. Three aids in the evaluation of the significance of difference between percentages. *Educ. and Psychol. Measmt.* 10:263–70.

Pepinsky, H. B. 1953. Some proposals for research. *Personnel and Guidance J.* 31:291–94.

Rushong, H. D. 1953. Present status and trends in the evaluation of counseling. *Educ. and Psychol. Measmt.* 13:418–30.

Rummel, J. F. 1958. *An introduction to research procedures in education.* New York: Harper & Row, Publishers.

Sakoda, J. M., Cohen, B. H., and Beall, G. 1954. Test of significance for a series of statistical tests. *Psychol. Bull.* 51:172–75.

Selltiz, C., et al. 1959. *Research methods in social relations.* New York: Holt, Rinehart & Winston, Inc.

Shoben, E. J., Jr. 1953. Some problems in establishing criteria of effectiveness. *Personnel and Guidance J.* 31:287–91.

Smith, E. R., and Tyler, R. W. 1942. *Appraising and recording student progress.* New York: Harper & Row, Publishers.

Travers, R. M. W. 1949. A critical review of techniques for evaluating guidance. *Educ. and Psychol. Measmt.* 9:211–25.

Tyler, L. 1960. Minimum change therapy. *Personnel and Guidance J.* 38:475–79.

Williamson, E. G., and Bordin, E. S. 1941. Evaluation of vocational and educational counseling: A critique of the methodology of experiments. *Educ. and Psychol. Measmt.* 1:5–24.

12

Supervision in Counseling

The counselor preparing for counseling has two reasons for understanding the purposes and practices of supervision in counseling. In his collection of data about the client he makes use of the efforts of counseling support personnel who make varying contributions to the pool of available data. Among them are persons responsible for getting clients to counseling, who usually have considerable information about the client if they are taught how to organize and present it. These "outreach" and counseling support personnel need adequate supervision if they are to become maximally effective in the counseling process. Clerks carrying out various psychometric activities, such as the administration, scoring, and profiling of group tests, can make a more effective contribution if they are shown how to add objective observations of the circumstances under which the client approached a given test. The counselor who can teach these people to contribute more fully through his effective supervisory activities has enhanced the counseling experience of his client as well as helping counseling support personnel do a more efficient job.

The second reason for understanding the supervisory process is to help the counselor work more effectively with his own supervisor. When the counselor expands his own knowledge of supervisory practices, he can understand what his supervisor is trying to do to help him become a better counselor. He looks upon this relationship and these activities with his supervisor as a means of acquiring the competencies the supervisor has developed during his counseling experience. By trying out various counseling tools and processes under the expert guidance of the supervisor, the counselor can expand his skill and learn to evaluate their effectiveness with clients. An understanding of the supervisor's purposes produces the teamwork in the learning experience so necessary to the counselor's growth. Counselor and supervisor working as a team produce a more meaningful counseling experience for the client.

THE NATURE OF SUPERVISION

There has been much discussion, and there are varied opinions, of the nature of supervision in counseling. Walz and Roeber (1962) have emphasized the instructional or teaching aspects of the counseling supervisor's role, while Arbuckle (1958) states that a supervisor is probably more of a counselor with trainees than he is a teacher. Kell and Mueller (1966, pp. 99–144) have presented supervision as an extension of counseling impact and change. Their view is a therapeutic, Freudian one which emphasizes discussion of negative aspects to a greater degree than positive phases of supervision. Patterson (1964) takes the sensible middle ground that supervision is neither teaching nor counseling, but contains aspects of both of these professions. Johnston and Gysbers (1966), in presenting a survey of supervisory reaction to various case presentations, emphasize the democratic, minimally structured aspects of supervision. Clark (1965, p. 65) presents the following definition:

Counseling supervision may be conceptualized as a continuum along which trainees are assisted in moving from the low differentiation and integration of a relatively small number of the processes, attitudes, skills and techniques involved in counseling to the high differentiation of all these various elements.

Whether one is being supervised in counseling activities or is supervising some one else engaged in some selected aspect of the counseling process, it is essential to have an understanding of the interactions that occur during supervision. There are certain communalities in the supervision of counselor's aides and support personnel that occur also in the supervision of less experienced counselors in a practicum experience or in the supervision of less experienced counselors in an agency setting. There are also unique aspects of such supervision which will be discussed in appropriate places in this chapter. For purposes of this discussion, the person being supervised will be referred to as the "counselor," but the principles being discussed also apply to the supervision of support personnel by the counselor.

For the supervisor, supervision is a counseling-*teaching* process involving a knowledge of effective procedures in each of these professions. His purposes are to protect the trainee being supervised, the client being counseled, the agency or institution for which he works, and his profession. He protects the trainee by demonstrating to him the most proficient ways to cope with the client's needs (Peters and Hansen 1963). He teaches the trainee in didactic fashion or by counseling him, and also by participation in the counseling process itself (Hansen and Moore 1966; Cottle 1952, 1955). His role varies at different points in the practicum and with the level of the practicum (Gysbers and Johnston 1965), causing him to formulate new theories and to innovate according to the needs of the situation. Perhaps his most important function is to structure the trainee's experience in the instructive, consultative, and counseling functions identified as factors in a factor analysis of supervision by Delaney and Moore (1966). Their fourth factor, "critique of counseling performance," really is a second major function of the counseling supervisor. A third function is to offer sufficient support to trainees that they operate without his dominance or their dependence upon him (Kell and Mueller 1966, pp. 109–10). If he is a university supervisor, he must be able to work with his supervisory counterpart in an agency setting (Boy and Pine 1966).

For the person being supervised, it is intended as a counseling-*learning* process and is a somewhat unusual counseling experience because of this difference. It starts with a one-to-one relationship with a master counselor who exposes the trainee to cognitive materials and requires him to handle his affective growth (self-understanding) as well (Peters and Hansen 1963; Wicas and Mahan 1966). After an orientation to the setting and personnel involved, the trainee moves through observation, procedures, and processes, including a review of tools and techniques covered previously, to a consideration of his professional frame of reference (Aubrey 1967). In this professional frame of reference he not only acquires professional competence and learns what *not* to do, but he begins to fashion his own professional ethics and professional value systems. He is forced through his practice to recognize his own professional limitations and referral needs.

For both supervisor and supervisee it can be a useful, shared, professional growth experience, if they really understand the purposes and the interactions and if they approach it with the focus on a joint enterprise for the client's benefit. This benefit, toward which all three are working, includes self-understanding, acceptance, exploration, choice and, finally, action resulting in a more effective and satisfactory life.

COMMON ELEMENTS IN SUPERVISION

The Relationship in Supervision

Just as in teaching or in the counseling experiences discussed in Chapter 4, supervision of counseling processes cannot be effective until a sound relationship based on confidence and mutual trust is created (Johnston and Gysbers 1966; Kell and Mueller 1966). It must be emphasized over and over that this is a professional relationship with a twofold purpose: to aid the person being supervised to become more proficient in his attempts to help a client, and to aid the client to make useful life choices. Because of its nature and the three-way interaction it involves, the process can become somewhat strained and artificial until the supervisor has established his role with the counselor and with each client of that counselor with whom the supervisor has contact. It has been the experience of the writers that a brief, concise explanation to each client of the supervisor's function in the counseling process seems to be an extension of structuring in counseling and readily establishes the supervisor's role in the eyes of the client. But the establishment of an effective relationship with the *counselor* involves many more unusual forces and takes much more skill on the part of the supervisor.

To achieve this relationship, the supervisor must be able to indicate by his speech, his thought, and his attitudes that his major concern is for the development of the counselor into an effective, professional person. When the supervisor is sufficiently well-adjusted to focus his attention outside himself and *on the process* being conducted, when he is able to convey to the counselor his concern for that counselor's comfort and success in the evaluations he makes, then he builds in that person a readiness to undertake and, when necessary, to share the counseling activity as a learning process. The supervisor must be able to convey his suggestions about modifying professional behavior to the counselor with the appropriate amount of threat to promote maximum growth. He must be able to focus the counselor's attention on changes to improve the process, rather than upon internalizing the comments intended to promote such change. To accomplish this, the supervisor phrases his comments in a fashion that permits a given counselor to use them constructively rather than perceiving them as a personal attack. Achieving this requires considerable knowledge about the person being supervised, but is highly rewarding in the personal-professional relationship it fosters with that person. Much of this relationship is established in the same way as with clients (see Chapter 4).

Once such a relationship begins to develop, the person being supervised can concentrate on *his* relationship with the client and on learning to become as effective as possible with that client. One more distraction has been eliminated from the counseling process, and the activities essential to foster change in the client become the center of attention. The counselor can now give undivided attention to his responsibilities to the client.

Actually, these relationships among supervisor, counselor, and client can be enhanced most effectively when the client becomes the center of attention and his welfare is the primary consideration. Much of the artificial nature of supervision can be overcome if the first thought of each member of the triad is the client's needs and well-being. This satisfies the supervisor's responsibility for protecting the client, and it permits the supervisor to show the counselor how to help the client best. It also reduces pressure on the counselor because he sees the true purpose of critical comments: to promote the growth of the client through more appropriate and skillful counseling procedures.

In this process the counselor often makes mistakes. This is a part of his learning to work with differing clients, and of learning that a process which works with one client is not necessarily appropriate for another. He can do this only if he is permitted the freedom which may even result in errors, if he is helped to evaluate the result, and if he is assisted in modifying his behavior to avoid ineffective procedures in the future. Thus, while he may make occasional errors in learning to counsel, he should not be permitted to continue or to repeat them. The supervisor must develop a tactful way to make the counselor aware that changes are necessary, and he must be ready for more drastic procedures if the mistakes continue. For example, when a test profile is being discussed, a counselor should learn not to use the term "normal" when describing the client's behavior, because many clients infer that those scores which are not called "normal" must be *abnormal*. If the counselor learns to use the terms "average score" or "average group" to convey the meaning of "usual," "normal" or "lacking in differentiation," he conveys less threat to the client and the information he transmits is more usable.

Whatever process he uses, the supervisor must be able to focus on the needs of both the counselor and the client. He should be able to help them to relax and work together. He must work to create a situation where the client can discuss his needs freely and the counselor is sufficiently free from pressure to carry out his functions in the counseling process. To do this, the supervisor should be able to sense what is happening and discuss it candidly with the counselor and, if it seems advisable, with the client. Effective and open communication is vital in creating and fostering the supervisory relationship.

Communication in Supervision

Just as perceiving and transmitting data to clients was a central focus in Chapter 4, a similar but more involved process of perceiving and transmitting information to persons being supervised is added in the supervisory situation. The ability of the supervisor to sense what is happening, to formulate his role in this interaction, and to convey it clearly to the counselor or client, is essential to the counselor's growth in professional competence.

The supervisor must bear in mind that the counselor also senses what is happening, but usually in a more confused or vaguer way. Usually the counselor is hampered by feelings about the novel aspects of the situation. Instead of being selective, he is trying desperately to recall and apply all that he has learned that *appears to him* to be appropriate. He is concerned that he will not do a professional job. He wants to appear competent and congruent to both client and supervisor. He may even see the setting as an obstacle to his effective functioning in the counseling process. Knowledge that he is or will be observed by a presumably more competent professional is also a distraction. All the feelings he builds up as a consequence act as inhibitors to his being proficient in communication with both client and supervisor. He may be quite unaware that he is omitting essential steps, or he may even be unable to sense what his client is telling him, because his attention is distracted by these other pressures.

The supervisor must help the counselor overcome this by communicating to him what is happening, as he discusses it during the evaluation phase of supervision.

Just as with clients, however, the supervisor and counselor interact on a nonverbal as well as verbal level. Bodily posture, physical attitude, gestures, facial expressions, eye movements, distance, and grosser physical movement are all a part of the communication process at a very low level of awareness for most persons. The supervisor has to bring these to a much higher level of awareness within himself and within the communication system of the person he is supervising. Most competent counselors have had some experience with audio and video recording of interviews, but their attention has usually been upon the oral-aural aspects of these encounters. It is often useful to reverse this process in a supervisory situation and listen to a tape recording or watch a video tape to emphasize the *nonverbal* cues they present or fail to show. A process of presenting excerpts from cases has recently been developed. It is referred to as "micro-counseling" and usually emphasizes only a given aspect of counseling or supervision.

In the case of the tape recording it is obviously impossible to watch what happens in the interview, but the supervisor and counselor can listen in an attempt to *infer* what the silent cues mean and what was happening on the nonverbal level. This focuses attention on important gaps in the process that occur when one is not able to *watch* the interaction in the interview. It often indicates how a counselor, by unwarranted inferences, may be adding data that were never present because he was not observing what the person was *doing* to the same extent that he observed what the person was *saying*. Or, conversely, it may show him that he is overlooking information contained in behavior expressed other than in words, or in the strange absence of topics ordinarily discussed in an interview. The omission of any mention of one parent may be perfectly natural, but it could also mean avoidance of a topic highly relevant to the modification of the client's behavior in counseling. The supervisor could call the counselor's attention to these gaps and show how they can be used to the client's advantage in the counseling process. Listening to a tape recording of an interview also has the advantage of permitting the neophyte to perceive the meaning behind what his client is saying when, as counselor, he is no longer faced with the immediate pressure of trying to function in the actual interview. It produces an "Oh, that's what he was really saying" effect.

Many of these points can also be demonstrated in a replay of all or parts of a video-taped interview, and nonverbal cues can be highlighted by turning off the sound. Forcing the counselor to concentrate on watching his behavior and that of his client without the distraction of conversation, and making him recall what was happening, let him see how much he can learn about his client without resorting to words and conversation. Watching a play or other material on television with the sound turned off is another device a counselor can use to sharpen his awareness of nonverbal cues.

Verbal cues, for the supervisor and counselor, begin with the supervisor's observation of the counselor's behavior in interaction with clients. The mechanics vary, depending on whether the supervisor is observing directly through a one-way screen or a video-tape, or participating as a third person in the counseling process. Sometimes his observations are indirect, in the form of a tape-recording, or a trainee log report, or an anecdote about a problem in a situation where tape recording was not possible. They could also take the form of comments on a case study or a statement about a counseling frame of reference he has asked the counselor to prepare.

Some of the supervisory process can be accomplished in direct observation through notes the supervisor makes concerning incidents he feels are important teaching situations. He can call attention to an overlooked cue or to a meaning the counselor has missed by giving a series of notes to the counselor after observing or listening to the session with a client. In these notes he may also include suggestions for alternate procedures or for possible new procedures to be associated with a given topic in future interviews with a given client. If he is participating as a third person in the interview itself (see the Cornwell material later in this chapter), he may wish to break in to demonstrate a particular process or to highlight data the counselor may be overlooking. A major concern in this situation should be that the client understands that it is a teaching situation as well as a counseling process. As much as possible, the supervisor must not divert or interrupt the normal flow of the interaction. It has been the experience of the writers, in more than two decades of such direct participation, that these three-person interviews in beginning practicum can be more productive and more parsimonious of supervisory time than observation by any other methods. Most clients are interested in the process and usually somewhat intrigued by the three-way interaction. Most counselors feel somewhat protected and proceed to carry on more effective counseling. The supervisor tapers off his participation, and even observes through a one-way screen in succeeding interviews, after he is satisfied that the trainee can handle the case alone.

When this direct participation is tape-recorded, a replay enhances the trainee's learning by letting him focus on places where the supervisor participated and try to figure out why. He can see how the supervisor handled a topic and later experiment to see whether this technique is useful to him. He can see how proper phrasing and timing reduce threat and permit candid discussion of topics he was afraid to handle. The supervisor can also make notes calling the counselor's attention to what was occurring at important moments during counseling, or he can request that the trainee note or excerpt selected points in the interview in order to save time in a replay during supervisory sessions or for demonstration and discussion in seminars where practicum interviews are reviewed. Similar procedures can be followed when video tapes are reviewed. Both audio and video tapes can be edited or excerpted for a pre-practicum or practicum tape library.

Role-playing can also be a useful supervisory technique, emphasizing and teaching effective counseling concepts or helping a trainee overcome some personal problem which is detracting from his performance. Whether he plays the part of supervisor, counselor, or client, the counselor has an opportunity to perceive behavior under less stress than in an actual encounter during the counseling process. He can begin to move outside his role as trainee and appreciate the reactions of the other participants. This increases his empathic skills and helps him improve, expand, and diversify his professional behavior.

Structuring in Supervision

In the process of supervision, a certain amount of structuring is necessary. Because a third person is involved and the interactions are more complex, the functions and responsibilities of the counselor and supervisor may become confused by one or both of them. It is well to review such functions periodically and to be sure that neither counselor nor supervisor are usurping the other's responsibilities or those of the client. It is impossible to keep the supervisory process out of the client's awareness, so it is probably best, when necessary, to discuss with him what is happening and the ways it may affect him. If this is done openly, prior to counseling, the entire process seems to be more natural to all three participants. At the same time, the responsibilities of each participant become clearer as each role is differentiated. Frequently, when the client sees the counseling process as a learning experience for the counselor as well as for himself, he identifies more closely and quickly with the process and the counselor, and so participates more fully in counseling. As the role of the supervisor develops, the presence of the client in the process forces the supervisor toward a discreet impact and as little distortion of dynamics as possible. This benefits the counselor, because he is freer to produce and to experiment with varying counseling procedures. At the same time, he knows he is observed and will be called to account, so he is trying to be as proficient as possible. Whether structuring is discussed openly or inferred from what happens in the process, the roles of three persons must evolve.

In general, structuring should make it clear that the role of the client is exploration of possible behavioral choices or "possibility structures," as Tyler (1963, 1969) has called them, and the translating of such choices or decisions into action for his future. The role of the counselor should emerge as that of the person learning to take part in the counseling process by using techniques which control the climate within which the client's exploration takes place and by using processes which open the doors of new understanding and behavior to the client. The role of the supervisor should develop as that of a more experienced person than either the counselor or client, lending that experience to both of them in order to make the counseling process a richer one for both and to assist the counselor to become more versatile, proficient, and effective in his professional activities.

The place of all the procedures described in this chapter is also a part of the structuring that occurs during supervision. Each of the three participants should perceive, or have pointed out to him, the varied tasks he must carry out in counseling. This is why it is so important that the supervisor create a climate within which the counselor and the client can raise questions about any of the three roles and what is happening in the counseling process. Each of them must be able to understand, to accept, and to live with what is happening, if counseling is to be truly useful.

VARIATIONS AMONG SETTINGS

Supervising Counselors' Aides or Support Personnel

Whether counselors' aides or support personnel (Kennedy 1967) are persons with no formal preparation for counseling activities or are counseling students in preparation, their supervision by an experienced counselor presents certain unique elements that need consideration and possibly added preparation by the supervisor before he can supervise effectively.

Support personnel may be individuals who serve as a connecting link between the world represented by the counselor and a highly distinct and different subculture from which his clients come. They are usually persons in transition from their subculture to the general culture who are still acceptable and effective among their former associates. Such a person may be a gang leader, a resident of the Appalachian region, or a representative of Irish, Italian, Cuban, Puerto Rican, Negro, Mexican-American, or American Indian subcultures. The urban and rural areas where these persons live frequently represent a subculture so different that the value systems of the suburban and other rural cultural groups with which the counselor is quite familiar do not apply. Some person who can bridge the cultural gap is needed. Such support personnel interpret the client to the counselor or the agency, or the reverse, and are also needed to promote the initial contacts of the client with the counselor. They perform a function the counselor-supervisor needs to understand, but not undertake. He needs to be able, however, to utilize and facilitate their efforts toward an increased use of his agency's services by clients from their subculture. To do this, the supervisor must help the support personnel grow in understanding of the purpose and function of the agency in a way that makes them more effective in interpreting the agency to potential clients. He has to make them more comfortable in their work while helping them to understand and accept their own problems of transition, so that they, in turn, can anticipate and interpret such processes to clients from that subculture.

If the supervisor approaches the task with the attitude that he can learn just as much or more than he wants to teach someone else, half the battle is won. If he is aware that he needs to learn before he can teach, supervision is more effective. Arrogance, satisfaction, or superiority has no place in this process. The supervisor is a learner, too. Unless he can understand, appreciate, and accept most of the elements of his aide's subculture, he cannot be effective. He cannot work with support personnel with such an inhibiting approach. He must be *with* these people, but not necessarily *of* them; accepted by them, but not as one of them. He empathizes, but does not identify or "buddy" with them. This fosters his professional activities with them.

On the other hand, the support person has to understand and accept his position in this professional interaction. He cannot afford to feel superior to his former associates, even though he may be, if he is to work effectively with them. If he has made his own adjustment well, he has no need to feel superior. He can fit into both cultures, the old and his new working area, appreciating the real values of each as they are a part of him. Until he can reach this point, the supervisor has to help him when his personal feelings may interfere with his performance and work with him to overcome them.

A major element in the success of both parties in this task is an appreciation of the value systems in each other's worlds and an understanding of how these are apt to promote or hinder effective and successful counseling activities. Perhaps a reference by the supervisor to material on the disadvantaged like that in the December 1965 issue of the *Review of Educational Research*, to the Coleman Report (1966), or to Amos and Grambs (1968) can help him to be more effective in this process.

Supervising Counseling Practicum

Supervision in counseling practicum involves unique problems, created at least in part by the somewhat forced and artificial nature of the encounter between beginning counselors who need help in attaining professional competence and volunteer clients who come for help aware that it is not a usual counseling setting. Even the physical conditions under which such a counseling process takes place or the necessity for tape or video recordings of the encounter distort it from an ordinary (if there are any) series of counseling sessions.

The effect of some of these special conditions has been explored by

Cornwell (1959), who highlights some of the problems with which the supervisor and counselor must cope. The problems are illustrated in her evaluation of a practicum for beginning counselors conducted in various forms over a 12-year period. It is one of the very few explorations of the client's and counselor's reaction to the presence of the supervisor as a third person in the interviews as well as to the other conditions which set practicum apart from regular counseling sessions. Her work also illustrates some of the problems in evaluating the kinds of experience offered in practicum.

The problems can be grouped under two headings. First is the problem of the responsibility of the supervisor to the counselor in practicum and to the volunteer client being used to provide the counselor with the necessary experience in interviewing. Second is the problem of evaluating a practicum program, which involves judging the actual procedures carried on in that practicum by the supervisor in evaluating and teaching the counselor in training.

In the beginning counseling practicum at the University of Kansas at the time at which Cornwell did her study, the supervisor sat in on every interview. The counselor-trainee carried 10 cases and received 2 semester hours of graduate credit for his work. The trainee was a person concluding the work required for the Masters degree, or beginning his work toward a Specialist or Doctoral degree. The clients were volunteer high-school seniors who were concerned with appropriate educational or vocational choices after they left high school. The emphasis on educational and vocational choice tended to reduce the number of factors which the beginning counselor must handle in his first experience at interviewing and counseling. In order to find cases, volunteers were solicited either in local high schools or in schools in which the counselor worked as a teacher. The volunteer clients received the same services as ordinary clients. At least two interviews were held with each. The first interview was directed toward the validation and expansion of information from a biographical data form, school records, and other available sources. At the end of this initial interview, the client and the counselor decided what other information was necessary for more adequate educational or vocational choices. This usually required the use of interest inventories and selected aptitude tests. Following the initial interview, other interviews were held as deemed necessary to help the client secure information and make adequate educational and vocational choices.

The supervisor conducted the initial interview with the first client as a demonstration for the counselor, and also conducted the first interview in the second series (following the initial interviews) to demonstrate interpretation and synthesis of case data. All these interviews were recorded with the client's permission. The recordings were also used by the neophyte counselor to identify points in the interview when the supervisor felt it was necessary to participate or to point out any idiosyncrasies of the counselor which had to be changed. The recordings tended to give a fairly clear picture of the areas the supervisor felt it important to explore, and the reasons why the supervisor felt it necessary to speak during the interview. The counselor also used the recordings to avoid taking notes. This permitted more concentration during the interview on the client and less on the mechanics of note-taking or summarizing.

The presence of the supervisor in each interview did not seem to have an adverse effect upon the progress of the interview. However, since this was only an impression gathered over a period of time by the supervisor, it was necessary to check it through a program of evaluation. Periodic oral checks with the counselor and the client tended to support this observation, but actual results of research, conducted apart from the practicum, were needed to find out what the client and counselor felt was really happening. This was the first aspect of the practicum covered in Cornwell's investigation (1959).

Another aspect of the situation which needed investigating was that dealing with the effect upon the client and the counselor of recording the interviews. A third area was that dealing with the effect of the surroundings in which the interviews were being held. Some of the interviews were held in school classrooms, others in any unused corner that the school could provide, still others in regular counseling rooms in a local school or university counseling center. The answers to these and other questions needed to be based on a research project, rather than on subjective judgments made by the people supervising counseling practicum or the people who had observed what was happening in the counseling practicum program. For this reason, questionnaires were developed which would try to get at these questions about the counseling practicum.

The questionnaires used were the combined product of pilot studies and discussions in counseling seminars and in the class meetings held in connection with this practicum. The actual questions asked of the practicum counselor are shown in Table 12.1, together with the responses of 43 counselors. As far as possible, a negative, positive, and neutral form of response were included for each item, so that there were always three degrees of possible response. In the construction of the questionnaire itself, these options were randomized so that the effect of marking at one extreme or another of the groupings would be minimized.

In the same way, items were constructed for a questionnaire to be sent out to clients who had completed counseling in the practicum program between 1953 and 1959. The questions in the final form of the questionnaire sent out to these former clients are shown in Table 12.2 together with the responses for: (1) the total group of 130 clients responding; (2)

Table 12.1

RESULTS OF QUESTIONNAIRE COMPLETED BY 43
COUNSELORS WHO HAD COMPLETED THE HIGH-SCHOOL
COUNSELING PRACTICUM AT THE UNIVERSITY OF
KANSAS GUIDANCE BUREAU

Question	Total answers	Percentage of response
1. Has the course proved helpful to you?	43	
a. It was as helpful as any of the other courses I took.	11	26
b. It helped me apply the knowledge I gained in other courses.	31	72
c. In actual work situations it has not been helpful.	1	2
2. Was it helpful to you to have the counseling supervisor participate in each interview (present at all times) in the first Practicum?	43	
a. I felt it cut down on my effectiveness as a counselor.	10	23
b. The presence of the supervisor gave me the security I needed for my first interview.	23	53
c. The presence of the supervisor made no difference.	10	23
3. Was the method of participation by the supervisor helpful in improving your counseling?	39	
a. It was helpful for the supervisor to do the first interview, so I would have a broad pattern to follow.	32	82
b. It would have been more helpful for the supervisor to have done the second interview following the discussion of my first interview.	4	10
c. Some other method of suggestions and supervision would prove more helpful.	3	8
4. Did you gain enough additional help in the Practicum class meetings to warrant continuing them?	41	
a. I got some help; they could be held once or twice during the course.	14	34
b. They were helpful and should be continued as they were scheduled.	27	66
c. I could have spent my time to better advantage.	0	0
5. How did the class of trainees affect you?	40	
a. I resented or felt threatened by their comments.	2	5
b. I felt that what they said was of minor importance.	8	20
c. I found their comments quite helpful.	30	75
6. Did it disturb you to have the recordings of your interviews played in class?	34	
a. I was a little disturbed at first but found the comments helpful.	31	91
b. I do not think this is helpful as it is too disturbing.	0	0
c. All the recordings were about the same. I did not get much out of listening to other people's recordings.	3	9
7. Did you feel that the use of the tape recorder in interviews was helpful?	43	
a. I felt I could remember the important points about the interview.	1	2

b. I found it very helpful not only in picking up
points about the interview, but in helping me correct undesirable verbal habits.   42   98
c. I felt it hindered me in my effectiveness; it made
me too self-conscious.   0   0

8. Were the surroundings in which you did your counseling satisfactory?   43
a. The surroundings were not conducive to good
counselor training.   4   9
b. The surroundings did not affect me.   16   37
c. The surroundings were not perfect, but were as
good as possible.   23   53

9. In terms of semester hours preparation, where in the
training of counselors should Practicum be offered?   42
a. After 16 or 20 hours preparation (Master level)   36   86
b. After 28 or 30 hours preparation (Specialist level)   5   12
c. After 56 or 60 hours preparation (Doctoral level)   1   2

(Check as many opinions as necessary)
10. If the procedure in Practicum were changed, which of
the following should be eliminated?   48
a. Counseling supervisor participating in each interview   14   29
b. Tape recorded   0   0
c. Playing of trainee recordings in class   3   6
d. Practicum class meetings   2   4
e. Having interviews at local schools   4   8
f. No major changes   25   52
g. Others   0   0

From H. Cornwell, Reactions of clients and counselors to a beginning practicum. Unpublished
Specialist project, University of Kansas, 1959.

clients in the 1953-to-1955 group; and (3) the clients in the 1956-to-1958
group. This division was made to see whether any items would be answered differently by earlier groups of clients counseled in more varied
and inconvenient settings than by more recent clients.

The results shown in Table 12.2 indicate relatively little difference between the groups of clients. Most of the differences which do exist appear
to be the result of changes in the practicum program which have tended
to produce a better relationship between the client, the counselor, and
the supervisor participating in the practicum interviews. In general, Table
12.2 seems to indicate that clients felt free to talk about anything they
wished in the series of practicum interviews. Approximately 60% of the
clients felt that the presence of the supervisor as a third person in the
interview made no difference. Another 30% felt that the supervisor made
them feel more comfortable. Only 10% or less of the clients responding
indicated that the supervisor as a third person in the interview made it
more difficult to talk in the interview. (It should be noted that Table 12.2
shows that significantly more of the clients from the early group were
adversely affected by the presence of the supervisor, since 14% of those

Table 12.2

RESULTS OF QUESTIONNAIRE COMPLETED BY 130
CLIENTS IN HIGH-SCHOOL COUNSELING PRACTICUM AT
THE UNIVERSITY OF KANSAS GUIDANCE BUREAU
FROM 1953–1959

Question	Total Response	Per Cent	1953–55 Response	Per Cent 1953–55	1956–58 Response	Per Cent 1956–58
1. Did you feel free to discuss and ask questions in the interview?	130		43		87	
a. I could talk only about things connected with school or a job.	17	13	10	23	7	8
b. I could talk about anything.	108	83	30	70	78	90
c. It was hard to discuss almost everything.	5	4	3	7	2	2
2. How did working with a counselor and a supervisor affect you?	130		43		87	
a. The supervisor (Third) person made it difficult to talk.	10	8	6	14	4	5
b. The supervisor (Third) person made no difference.	80	62	28	65	52	60
c. The supervisor (Third) person made me feel more comfortable.	40	31	9	21	31	36
3. Did you feel that the counselor was genuinely interested in you and the things you talked about?	130		43		87	
a. I felt the counselor was interested in helping me work out the best solution to my problem.	105	81	28	65	77	89
b. The counselor did not seem genuinely interested in me or the things I talked about.	5	4	3	7	2	2
c. I felt like the counselor was just doing the job assigned.	20	15	12	28	8	9
4. Did the presence of the supervisor make you feel that your interview was important?	130		43		87	
a. The presence of the supervisor made me feel that the counselor did not know very much.	5	4	1	2	4	5

b. I felt they were combining their efforts to help me.	80	62	20	47	60	69
c. I had no feeling on the matter.	45	35	22	51	23	26
5. Did you feel at ease in the first interview?	130		43		87	
a. I was nervous during the entire interview.	5	4	4	9	1	1
b. I felt a little nervous at first but soon got over it.	114	88	35	81	79	91
c. The interview was almost over before I felt at ease.	5	4	2	5	3	3
d. I was not nervous at all (added by counselees when answering questionnaire).	6	5	2	5	4	5
6. Did the fact that the interview was recorded affect you in any way?	130		43		87	
a. I forgot all about it once I started talking.	53	41	13	30	40	46
b. I held back information because I knew it would be recorded.	1	1	1	2	0	0
c. I thought at times about the recorder but did not care.	76	58	29	67	47	54
7. Did you feel free to refuse to have the interview recorded?	130		43		87	
a. I thought it was silly but did not care.	2	1	2	5	0	0
b. I was perfectly willing to have the interview recorded.	127	98	40	93	87	100
c. I did not want the recording made but did not feel free to refuse.	1	1	1	2	0	0
8. Were the office surroundings such that you felt free to talk?	130		43		87	
a. The room seemed close and crowded.	8	6	5	12	3	3
b. I did not notice the surroundings enough for them to affect me.	104	80	36	84	68	78
c. The surroundings made me feel free and relaxed.	18	14	2	5	16	18
9. Was the material explained clearly in the interview?	130		43		87	

Table 12.2 (Continued)

Question	Total Response	Per Cent	1953–55 Response	Per Cent 1953–55	1956–58 Response	Per Cent 1956–58
a. The part of the material I did not understand was explained again when I asked questions about it.	101	78	33	77	68	78
b. I did not understand what was said to me.	0	0	0	0	0	0
c. The counseling supervisor used different words to explain the material so I could understand.	29	22	10	23	19	22
10. Did the interview and follow-up letter cover most of the questions you had?	130		43		87	
a. I found out some things I did not know. I guess it was worth the effort.	32	25	14	33	18	21
b. I felt that nothing had been accomplished. It was not worth the effort.	2	2	1	2	1	1
c. I feel I know now what I am capable of doing. All high-school senior boys and girls should have the opportunity to go through this procedure.	96	74	28	65	68	78
11. Did you understand the use of the recorder?	130		43		87	
Yes.	119	92	38	88	81	93
No.	11	8	5	12	6	7

From H. Cornwell, Reactions of clients and counselors to a beginning practicum. Unpublished Specialist project, University of Kansas, 1959.

indicated a negative reaction compared to approximately 5% of the later group.)

About four-fifths of the clients felt that the counselor was genuinely interested in helping them work out the best solution possible. Approximately 60% of all the clients felt that the supervisor and the counselor were combining efforts to help (the number was significantly larger in the later group). Another 35% had no feelings about the relationship between supervisor and counselor. Only 4% had negative feelings about the presence of the supervisor in the interview, according to their responses to Question 4.

In response to Question 5, about whether the clients felt at ease in the first interview, the bulk of respondents (88%) indicated that they were a little nervous at first but soon got over it, and 5% voluntarily added the response that they were not nervous at all. In response to a question dealing with tape-recording the interviews, 41% said they had forgotten all about the recorder once the interview began, and another 58% said they thought at times about the recorder but did not care that it was used. This left only one person who said information was held back because the interview was being recorded. About 98% of the respondents said they were perfectly willing to have their interviews recorded. To the question dealing with the physical surroundings, 80% said they did not notice the surroundings enough to have them affect the interview or their feelings.

About 78% felt that a second explanation by the counselor of material which was not clear eliminated any difficulties the clients had encountered in understanding what was discussed in the interviews. Another 22% said that the presence of the counseling supervisor, who used different words to explain material, made it easier to understand the material. No respondent selected the answer which read, "I did not understand what was said to me." To the other question dealing with the interview and the follow-up letter covering information useful to the client, 75% said they felt now that they knew more about what they should be doing educationally and vocationally. They felt this was a worthwhile experience for all high-school senior boys and girls. Another 25% said they had found out some things they did not know and felt it may have been worth the effort. Only 2 of the 130 clients felt that it was not worth the effort that they had expended.

Table 12.1, which states the questions which were answered by 43 counselors completing the beginning practicum at the University of Kansas, also gives the distributions of their responses. To the first question, 72% responded that the practicum helped them to apply knowledge gained in other courses. Only 1 person felt that the course had not been helpful later in an actual work situation. 33 indicated that the presence of the counselor supervisor in each interview either lent security to the counselor or made no difference, while 10 counselors, or 23%, felt that it cut down their effectiveness as counselors. In a further discussion of the method of participation by the supervisor, 32 felt that it was helpful for the supervisor to do the first interview so that they would have a broad pattern (subject to their own adaptations) to follow in succeeding interviews. Only 3 felt some other method of suggestion and supervision would have been more helpful. Group discussions or classes connected with practicum were felt to be important by the 41 people responding to Question 4, and no one felt that this time could have been spent to better advantage during the practicum. Only 2 of the 40 counselors responding to Question 6 said they resented or felt threatened by the playing of their recordings during the class meetings of practicum counselors. Of the 34 counselors responding to the question dealing with the playing of recordings in class, 31 indicated they were somewhat disturbed by it but later felt that the comments were helpful, while another 3 felt they did not get much out of listening to other counselors' recordings. None indicated that this was too disturbing to be helpful. It should be noted, however, that 9 of the counselors who had completed practicum failed to answer this item. They may have had some negative feeling about the playing of their recordings in a class group of the counselors taking practicum the same semester.

As far as the use of the tape recorder in the interviews was concerned, 42 of the 43 counselors felt that it was very helpful, not only in picking up points about the interview but in helping them understand and correct undesirable verbal habits. None felt that it hindered his effectiveness or made him too self-conscious. About 53% felt that the surroundings for the counseling interviews were as good as possible, and another 16, or 37%, felt that the surroundings had not affected them. Only 9% felt that the surroundings were not conducive to good counselor training. The responses to Question 9, dealing with the number of semester hours of preparation prior to the practicum experience, may have been somewhat biased by the fact that a disproportionate number of counselors taking this practicum had only obtained a Master's degree. 86% of the respondents indicated that a minimum of 16 to 20 hours' preparation was sufficient for the counseling practicum offered to beginning counselors. This fits the practical situation of schools hiring counselors with only a Master's degree, and their judgment is also supported by studies of the use of persons with limited training as counselors (Truax and Carkhuff 1967). Question 10 made it possible for the counselors to make recommendations about practicum procedures. 29% felt that the participation of the counseling supervisor in each interview could be changed or eliminated, and 52% felt that no major changes were needed in the practicum program at that time.

These data, although collected some time ago, are still interesting because they indicate the feelings of a group of counselors and clients concerning interviews conducted in a counselor practicum sequence where the supervisor sat in on *each* interview. Since it was possible for them to respond anonymously to a person other than the one who was conducting the practicum course, they were free to indicate their real response, handicapped only by whatever positive feelings they may have felt toward the person who supervised their practicum program. The results, within the limits indicated, are one series of expressions about questions many counselors have asked. These questions deal with the effect of the circumstances under which counseling takes place, the effect of counseling interviews, and the effect of the actual presence of a supervisor in the interviews. The direction of the preponderance of responses in Tables 12.1 and 12.2 seems to indicate the overshadowing of any effect of the personal relationships between the supervisor and the counselor upon the clients or of the effect that the supervisor himself may have had upon the counselors in the practicum program. This is one illustration of a way in which an evaluation of counseling programs may be conducted.

Table 12.2, modified as in Form 12.2, is used at Boston College to follow up the client's reaction to practicum counseling experiences. Form 12.2 is preceded by Form 12.1, which is given to the client as he completes his counseling sessions. The content of these forms can be modified in terms of practicum objectives for the client.

Table 12.1 has been modified to Form 12.4, also used at Boston College to follow up the counselor's reaction to his practicum counseling experiences. Form 12.4 is preceded by Form 12.3, which is given to the counselor as he completes each interview tape.

Form 12.5, completed by the supervisor after each interview, records his perception of the manner in which the counselor performed in each interview with each client. The items represent the particular objectives of beginning practicum for secondary and college counselors at a given institution and are modified as these objectives change. Such a form also makes it possible for the coordinator of practicum services to maintain a file of practicum evaluations for each counselor and to use them for references to employers as well.

Ivey and others (1968) have discussed the use of counseling incidents presented on video tape as a means of teaching and of supervising counseling.

SUPERVISION IN AN AGENCY

One discussion of appropriate supervision in an agency setting is Stern's (1963) about counseling supervision in the Baltimore schools. In this school system, the counselor is given the first year to orient and establish himself. Supervision begins with the second year. No single technique of counseling is emphasized, because the emphasis is upon purposeful communication between client and counselor. Supervision begins with instruction in using tape recorders and a topical review of the principles of counseling. Group meetings are held to handle these topics and to discuss excerpts from tapes illustrating specific aspects of counseling.

Form 12.1

CLIENT EVALUATION FORM

Instructions: At the end of your counseling sessions we would like you to complete this form by marking the appropriate number for your choice of one of the six answers below as your response to each item.

Client No. _____

Counselor No. _____

1. Yes, definitely
2. Yes, most of the time
3. I am not sure how to answer this
4. No, only occasionally
5. Definitely no
6. This item does not apply

_____ 1. Did you feel you could discuss anything you wished in your interviews?

_____ 2. Did you feel you could ask any question you wished?

_____ 3. Did you like working with a counselor and a supervisor?

_____ 4. Did you feel the counselor was genuinely interested in helping you with your problems?

_____ 5. Did the knowledge of the supervisor's activities have any negative effect on your counseling experience?

_____ 6. Did you feel comfortable in the first interview?

_____ 7. Did you feel comfortable in the following interviews?

_____ 8. Did the interviews cover most of the questions you had?

_____ 9. Did the fact that the interview was recorded keep you from discussing important things?

_____10. Did the conditions covering the use of the recorder suit you?

_____11. Did the office surroundings have any negative effect on your interviews?

Did you feel your material was explained clearly so that you could use it to make decisions?

_____12. Interview topics and discussion

_____13. Information from records

_____14. Test instructions

_____15. Aptitude and ability test scores

_____16. Interest inventory scores

_____17. Personality inventory scores

18. How would you describe your over-all reaction to your counseling experience? (Use back of sheet.)

CLIENT EVALUATION FOLLOW-UP

Client No. _____

1. Did you feel free to discuss topics in the interview?
   a. I could talk only about things connected with school or a job.
   b. I could talk about anything.
   c. It was hard to discuss almost everything.
   d. There were other things I was afraid to talk about.

2. Did you feel free to ask questions in the interview?
   a. I could talk only about things connected with school or a job.
   b. I could talk about anything.
   c. It was hard to discuss almost everything.
   d. There were other things I was afraid to talk about.

3. How did working with a counselor and a supervisor affect you?
   a. The supervisor made it difficult to talk to my counselor.
   b. The supervisor made no difference.
   c. The supervisor made me feel more comfortable.
   d. I would rather have talked just with the counselor.

4. Did you feel that the counselor was genuinely interested in you and the things you talked about?
   a. I felt the counselor was interested in helping me work out the best solution to my problem.
   b. The counselor did not seem genuinely interested in me and the things I talked about.
   c. I felt like the counselor was just doing the job assigned.
   d. I would rather have talked to the supervisor.

5. Did the knowledge of the supervisor's presence make you feel that your interview was important?
   a. The knowledge of the supervisor made me feel that the counselor did not know very much.
   b. I felt they were combining their effort to help me.
   c. I had no feeling on the matter.
   d. I wished the supervisor would not participate.

6. Did you feel comfortable in the first interview?
   a. I was nervous during the entire interview.
   b. I felt a little nervous at first but soon got over it.
   c. The interview was almost over before I felt at ease.
   d. I was not nervous at all.

7. Did you feel comfortable in the following interviews?
    a. I was nervous during the entire interview.
    b. I felt a little nervous at first but soon got over it.
    c. The interview was almost over before I felt at ease.
    d. I was not nervous at all.

8. Did the fact that the interview was recorded affect you in any way?
    a. I forgot all about it once I started talking.
    b. I held back information because I knew it would be recorded.
    c. I thought at times about the recorder but did not care.
    d. I asked that the recorder not be used.

9. Did you feel free to refuse to have the interview recorded?
    a. I thought it was silly but did not care.
    b. I was perfectly willing to have the interview recorded.
    c. I did not want the recording made but did not feel free to refuse.
    d. I was not asked for permission to record the interview.

10. Were the office surroundings such that you felt free to talk?
    a. The room seemed close and crowded.
    b. I did not notice the surroundings enough for them to affect me.
    c. The surroundings made me feel free and relaxed.
    d. The surroundings were so poor they upset me.

11. Was the material explained clearly in the interview?
    a. The part of the material I did not understand was explained again when I asked questions about it.
    b. I did not understand what was said to me.
    c. The counseling supervisor had to use different words to explain the material so I could understand it.
    d. I had no problems understanding the counselor's explanations of the material.

12. Did the interview and summary letter cover most of the questions you had?
    a. I found out some things I did not know. I guess it was worth the effort.
    b. I felt that nothing had been accomplished.
    c. I feel I know what I am capable of doing.
    d. All people should have the opportunity to go through this procedure.

13. Did you understand the use of the recorder?
    a. Yes
    b. No

14. If the supervisor participated in your interview, what was your reaction?
    a. I liked him being there, it made me more comfortable.
    b. I didn't care one way or the other.
    c. He knew more about me than the counselor.
    d. He made me too nervous, I wished he wasn't there.

COUNSELOR EVALUATION FORM

Instructions: The counselor should complete this form after receiving his tape of each interview by selecting one of the responses below for each item and marking the response number in front of that item.

Supervisor No. _____

Client No. _____

Counselor No. _____

1. Yes, definitely
2. Yes, most of the time
3. I am not sure how to answer this
4. No, only occasionally
5. Definitely no
6. This item does not apply

_____ 1. Did you feel you established effective rapport with this client?

_____ 2. Did you feel you controlled interview climate?

_____ 3. Did you sense that you had empathy with your client?

_____ 4. Did you think your phrasing and timing of questions was effective?

_____ 5. Was your phrasing and timing of other responses as useful?

_____ 6. Did your client respond as you expected him to?

_____ 7. Was your supervisor's over-all participation satisfactory?

    _____a. Was this a good learning experience for you?

    _____b. Were his demonstrations useful to you?

    _____c. Did his participation help you?

    _____d. Did his evaluation help you?

    _____e. Was your client's response to supervisory activity satisfactory?

_____ 8. Were you satisfied in your over-all reaction to supervision of your counseling?

_____ 9. Was your client's reaction to use of the recorder satisfactory to you as a counselor?

_____10. Were physical surroundings of the counseling professionally satisfactory for counseling purposes?

Did you think your effort to interpret client data was understood in terms of:

_____11. Interview topics and dialogue?

_____12. Information from records?

_____13. Test instructions?

_____14. Aptitude and ability test scores?

_____15. Interest inventory scores?

_____16. Personality inventory scores?

_____17. Do you feel your client's total reaction to counseling was satisfactory?

Form 12.4

QUESTIONNAIRE TO BE COMPLETED BY COUNSELORS

1. Has the Counseling Practicum proved helpful to you?
   a. It was as helpful as any of the other courses I took.
   b. It helped me apply the knowledge I gained in other courses.
   c. In actual work situations it has not been helpful.
   d. It was a waste of time I could have used in other ways.

2. Would it have been helpful to you to have the counseling supervisor participate in each interview (present at all times) in the first Practicum?
   a. I feel it would cut down on my effectiveness as a counselor.
   b. The presence of the supervisor would have given me the security I needed for my first interview.
   c. The presence of the supervisor would have made no difference.
   d. The supervisor was there and I liked it.

3. Was the method of participation by the supervisor helpful in improving your counseling?
   a. It was helpful for the supervisor to do a first interview, so I would have a broad pattern to follow.
   b. It would have been more helpful for the supervisor to have done an interview following the discussion of my first interview.
   c. The supervisor's suggestions and supervision were helpful.
   d. I learned more from listening to tapes than from the supervisor.

4. Did you gain enough additional help in the Practicum class meetings to warrant continuing them?
   a. I got some help; they could be held once or twice during the course.
   b. They were helpful and should be continued as they were scheduled.
   c. I could have spent my time to better advantage.
   d. Classes embarrassed me, they were a waste of time.

5. How did the class of trainees affect you?
   a. I resented or felt threatened by their comments.
   b. I felt that what they said was of minor importance.
   c. I found their comments quite helpful.
   d. I think every counselor should have such an experience.

6. Did it disturb you to have the recordings of your interviews played in class?
   a. I was a little disturbed at first but found the comments helpful.
   b. I do not think this is helpful as it is too disturbing.
   c. All the recordings were about the same. I did not get much out of listening to other people's recordings.
   d. I was not disturbed because it is a good learning device.

7. Did you feel that the use of the tape recorder in interviews was helpful?
   a. I felt I could remember the important points about the interview.

b. I found it very helpful not only in picking up points about the interview, but in helping me correct undesirable verbal habits.

c. I felt it hindered me in my effectiveness; it made me too self-conscious.

d. The recorder was no help at all.

8. Were the surroundings in which you did your counseling satisfactory?

   a. The surroundings were not conducive to good counselor training.

   b. The surroundings did not affect me.

   c. The surroundings were not perfect, but were as good as possible.

   d. The surroundings were quite adequate.

9. In terms of semester hours preparation, where in the training of counselors should the beginning Practicum be offered?

   a. After 16 or 20 hours preparation (Master level)

   b. After 28 or 30 hours preparation (Specialist level)

   c. After 56 or 60 hours preparation (Doctoral level)

   (Check as many opinions as necessary)

10. If the procedure in Practicum were changed, which of the following should be eliminated?

    a. Counseling supervisor participating in each interview.

    b. Counseling supervisor observing by mirror.

    c. Counseling supervisor using two-way communication.

    d. Tape recordings of each interview.

    e. Use of video tapes.

    f. Use of closed circuit television.

    g. Playing of trainee recordings in class.

    h. Practicum class meetings.

    i. Having interviews at local schools.

    j. Having interviews on college campus.

    k. No major changes.

    l. Others.

Form 12.5

SUPERVISOR EVALUATION OF COUNSELOR

INSTRUCTIONS: Fill out this form for the counselor after each interview. Clients are lettered A to G. Interviews are numbered 1, 2, and 3. If there are more than three interviews, use extra blank. For each of the questions indicate your evaluation ranging from 1 to 6. After all interviews are completed fill out the last column entitled "average for all interviews" and give this evaluation to the director.

RATINGS

1. Yes, definitely
2. Yes, most of the time
3. Average
4. No, only occasionally
5. Definitely, no
6. This item does not apply

Client	A			B			C			D			E			F			G			Average of all
Interview	1	2	3	1	2	3	1	2	3	1	2	3	1	2	3	1	2	3	1	2	3	interviews
1. Did he create a comfortable atmosphere?																						
2. Did he identify client problems?																						
3. Did he empathize effectively?																						
a. Establish an effective relationship with the client?																						
b. Indicate he sensed and understood what the client was communicating about?																						
4. Were his interview questions appropriate?																						
a. Well phrased for his purpose?																						
b. Well timed?																						
c. In logical order?																						
d. Within client's verbal range?																						

5. Were his responses appropriate and effective?

6. Did he interpret tests meaningfully?

   a. Demonstrate a knowledge of each test used?

   b. Demonstrate general knowledge of test scores?

   c. Did the client understand him?

7. Did he structure effectively?

8. Were his syntheses of data useful to the client?

9. Did he develop summaries regularly during interviews?

10. Did he abstract from tapes in a useful way?

11. How did he react to supervisor recommendations?

12. Did he administer tests properly?

13. Did he work well with subordinates?

14. Were his relations with cooperating agency effective?

15. Did he write a concise, clear report of case?

16. Was his over-all conduct ethical and professional?

Stern claims that an emphasis upon the counselor's unique contribution to the school's educational effort and the leaving of responsibility for administrative ratings of counselors to school principals rather than to counseling supervisors are strengths of the program. This supervisory program attempts to integrate theory with practice and to help counselors evaluate their growth and identify future professional goals.

Many other examples could be given, but the purposes and activities differ from other trainee situations discussed previously only in that the trainees are persons who have usually completed one year of formal graduate preparation and are full-time employees. Thus they have had some exposure to a counseling practicum and know the purposes of supervision. If their supervisor was competent, they are now better able to function effectively under supervision in a full-time work setting. Their aim, as well as that of their supervisor, is for them to work as rapidly as possible toward constantly decreasing supervision.

Usually counseling supervision in an agency is aimed toward orientation of new counselors toward the unique needs of that agency and to help each counselor focus on areas in his own work that he and his supervisor feel can be improved.

No matter how long a person has been a professional counselor, however, or how competent he may be, he can profit from periodically recording his interviews on audio or video tape and reviewing them by himself or with others. Supervisors themselves usually accomplish this in their demonstrations for trainees, but all professional counselors should practice it.

SUMMARY

This chapter has endeavored to deal with problems the supervisor, the counselor, and the client encounter during the supervision of counseling. The goals of each and the practices by which these goals are reached have been considered. Every professional person preparing for counseling should be aware of these goals and practices and be willing to work toward them as a part of his growth in the profession. The counselor's role in the supervisory process has been considered from two viewpoints: (1) his supervision of support personnel who are learning to help him with specific phases of preparation for counseling; (2) his being supervised, either in practicum or by a senior person in a counseling agency. A clear understanding and acceptance of the principles of supervision are essential if the counselor is to utilize them in his preparation for counseling.

REFERENCES

Amos, W. E., and Grambs, J. D. 1968. *Counseling the disadvantaged youth.* Englewood Cliffs, N.J.: Prentice-Hall, Inc.

Arbuckle, D. 1958. Five philosophical issues in counseling. *J. Couns. Psychol.* 5:211–16.

Aubrey, R. F. 1967. Elementary school counseling practicum: Some suggestions. *Couns. Educ. and Supervision.* 7:13–19.

Boy, A. V., and Pine, G. J. 1966. Strengthening the off-campus practicum. *Couns. Educ. and Supervision.* 6:40–43.

Clark, C. M. 1965. On the process of counseling supervision. *Couns. Educ. and Supervision.* 4:64–67.

Coleman, J. S., *et al.* 1966. *Equality of educational opportunity.* U.S. Department of Health, Education, and Welfare, OE-38001. Washington, D.C.: Government Printing Office.

Cornwell, H. 1959. Reactions of clients and counselors to a beginning practicum. Unpublished Specialist project, University of Kansas.

Cottle, W. C. 1952. Supervising counseling practicum. *Kansas Academy of Science.* 55:468–71.

———. 1955. The supervisor participates in training interviews. *Voc. Guidance Quart.* 4:18–20.

Delaney, D. J., and Moore, J. C. 1966. Student expectations of the role of practicum supervisor. *Couns. Educ. and Supervision.* 6:11–17.

Gysbers, N. C., and Johnston, J. A. 1965. Expectations of a practicum supervisor's role. *Couns. Educ. and Supervision.* 4:68–74.

Hansen, J. C., and Moore, G. C. 1966. The off-campus practicum. *Couns. Educ. and Supervision.* 6:32–39.

Ivey, A. *et al.* 1968. Micro-counseling and attending behavior. *J. Couns. Psych.* Monog. Suppl. 15.

Johnston, J. A., and Gysbers, N. C. 1966. Practicum supervisory relationships: A majority report. *Couns. Educ. and Supervision.* 6:3–10.

Kell, B., and Mueller, W. J. 1966. *Impact and change: A study of counseling relationships.* New York: Appleton-Century-Crofts.

Kennedy, E. G. 1967. Support personnel for the counselor: Their technical and non-technical roles in preparation. *Personnel and Guidance J.* 45:857–62.

Patterson, C. H. 1964. Supervising students in the counseling practicum. *J. Couns. Psychol.* 11:47–53.

Peters, H. J., and Hansen, J. C. 1963. Counseling practicum: Bases for supervision. *Couns. Educ. and Supervision.* 2:82–85.

Review of Educ. Research. 1965. Education for socially disadvantaged children. 35:5.

Stern, H. J. 1963. A counseling approach to counseling supervision. *Couns. Educ. and Supervision.* 2:69–71.

Truax, C. B., and Carkhuff, R. R. 1967. *Toward effective counseling and psychotherapy.* Chicago: Aldine Press, 1967.

Tyler, L. E. 1964. The methods and processes of appraisal and counseling. In *The professional preparation of counseling psychologists: Report of the 1964 Greyston Conference,* eds. A. S. Thompson and D. E. Super. New York: Bureau of Publications, Teachers College, Columbia University.

———. 1969. *The work of the counselor.* 3rd ed. New York: Appleton-Century-Crofts.

Walz, G., and Roeber, E. C. 1962. Supervisor's reactions to counseling interview. *Couns. Educ. and Supervision.* 2:2–7.

Wicas, E. A., and Mahan, T. W., Jr. 1966. Characteristics of counselors rated effective by supervisors and peers. *Couns. Educ. and Supervision.* 6:50–56.

Index

411